YALE STUDIES IN ECONOMICS : 7

EUROPE AND
THE MONEY MUDDLE

From Bilateralism to

Near-Convertibility, 1947-1956

by ROBERT TRIFFIN

237293

GREENWOOD PRESS, PUBLISHERS
WESTPORT, CONNECTICUT

Library of Congress Cataloging in Publication Data

Triffin, Robert.
    Europe and the money muddle.

    Reprint of the 1957 ed. published by Yale University
Press, New Haven, which was issued as no. 7 of Yale
studies in economics.
    Includes index.
    1. Currency question—Europe. 2. Monetary policy—
Europe. 3. Foreign exchange problem—Europe.
I. Title. II. Series: Yale studies in economics ;
no. 7.
[HG925.T74 1976]   332.4'94   76-26932
ISBN 0-8371-9026-6

Originally published in 1957 by Yale University Press, New Haven

Reprinted with the permission of Yale University Press

Reprinted in 1976 by Greenwood Press,
a division of Williamhouse-Regency Inc.

Library of Congress Catalog Card Number 76-26932

ISBN 0-8371-9026-6

Printed in the United States of America

DEDICATION

THIS BOOK is dedicated, with all due apologies, to the many people who unwittingly shaped the author's views but who should in no way be held responsible for them:

Paul van Zeeland, John H. Williams, and Alvin H. Hansen, who tried to teach him money and banking at Louvain and at Harvard;

Walter R. Gardner and Edward M. Bernstein, who taught him as much or more at the Board of Governors of the Federal Reserve System and at the International Monetary Fund, and were rash enough to launch him upon an advisory career to central bankers in Latin America and in Europe;

Milton Katz and Robert Marjolin, who courageously kept an affectionately loose rein over their ECA and OEEC technicians during the negotiation of the European Payments Union Agreement;

Sir Stafford Cripps, Hugh Gaitskell, Hubert Ansiaux, Guido Carli, Pierre Calvet, Paul Rossy, H. K. Von Mangoldt, S. Hartogsohn, H. Ellis-Rees, S. Posthuma, Gérard Bauer, F. A. G. Keesing, Roy Bridge, Frank Figgures, Alberto Ferrari, F. G. Conolly, Jacques Graeffe, Willy Selleslags, Fernand Aspeslagh, Thomas Schelling, Richard M. Bissell, John Hulley, Alex Lachman, and the countless other financial statesmen and technicians who tirelessly and enthusiastically worked together to beget the European Payments Union and guide its first faltering steps in a turbulent world.

v

By Way of Introduction:
A Book Review by the Author

I. WHAT THIS BOOK IS ABOUT

TRIFFIN'S STUDY deals primarily with policy rather than theory. It attempts to explain and appraise the highlights of Europe's monetary recovery since World War II, and to derive from this experience a number of conclusions for national and international monetary policy.

Chapter 1 on "The World Dollar Shortage" discusses the broader background of Europe's balance of payments problem. The author distinguishes the facts, theories, and policies of the dollar shortage school, finds many contradictions among them, but concludes nevertheless that much may be learned from the controversy if its thesis is broadened into an investigation of the conflicts among independent national policy decisions—by other countries as well as by the United States—in an interdependent world.

The second chapter reviews and compares national monetary developments and policies in postwar Europe. Its main originality lies in the attempt to integrate into a comprehensive structure three methods of approach and sources of data usually compartmentalized and parceled out among balance of payments, national income, and monetary analysts. This integrated treatment puts into sharp relief the crucial role of the monetary and credit system in the financing of any excess of current demand over current production. It relates closely the emergence of external deficits and internal inflationary pressures as alternative, even though complementary, outlets for such excess demand in an open economy. Internal inflationary pressures may in turn become manifest either in price rises—"open inflation"—or in overliquidity—"latent inflation"—or, of course, in both. In contrast to purchasing power parity theorists, Triffin regards *both* of these phenomena—price rises and overliquidity—as of great significance for the analysis of balance of payments fluctuations and exchange rate readjustments.

The nature of the 1947 crisis and of the following recovery is traced for OEEC Europe as a whole and its twelve major member countries through a welter of tables and charts. These data are organized in such a way as to bring out the similarities and contrasts between events and policies in the latent inflation countries (the United Kingdom, the Netherlands, and the Scandinavian countries), the open inflation countries (Greece, Italy, and France), and the countries where both forms of inflation were already brought under control by 1947 (Switzerland and Belgium).

The 1947 monetary crisis, however, was not confined to national imbalance in the various countries of Europe. Nor could it be solved by national policies aiming at the restoration of over-all internal and external balance in their own economic system. The utter collapse of the international framework for trade and payments had made bilateral bargaining power, rather than national balance, the major regulator of each country's external transactions. The restoration of a multilateral trade and payments system was a task which lay far beyond the reach of any country's national policies. The second part of the book (Chaps. 3–5) thus turns from national to international monetary policies and institutions. Chapter 3 outlines the early attempts to restore a world-wide system of multilateral trade and payments through the establishment of the International Monetary Fund and the restoration of sterling as a key currency. The failure of these efforts left a vacuum which in Europe was filled by new methods of regional cooperation, strongly backed from the outset by the United States Economic Cooperation Administration (ECA). European bilateralism was first brought under some sort of collective control in 1947–49, and then deprived of its major underpinning by the creation of the European Payments Union in 1950. The techniques used and the results achieved in this fight against bilateralism are reviewed and appraised in Chapters 4 and 5 of the book.

The last three chapters outline the current position and prospects of the convertibility problem and present the author's own conclusions as to the proper role and integration of world-wide institutions, regional cooperation, and national policies in the reconstruction of a workable system of international trade and payments.

II. WHAT DOES IT SAY?

The hurried reader will save himself much time and effort if he is ready to accept or reject, without further ado, the following conclusions of Triffin. To put it in a nutshell, he believes that:

1. The causes and cures of European countries' domestic inflation and external deficits can best be analyzed in terms of the over-all excess of demand above current production levels and of the methods by which such excess demand was financed.

2. The current evolution and prospects of the international pattern of payments are such as to permit quick progress toward the restoration of convertibility by the European countries, even with respect to their dollar transactions.

3. The maintenance of convertibility, together with high levels of economic activity and low levels of trade restriction, would be highly precarious if it remained based only—as in the nineteenth century—on the spontaneous adoption and unflinching pursuit of such policies by independent, uncoordinated, national decisions on the part of sovereign countries.

4. The minimum harmonization of national policies necessary for the success of the above objective would involve mutual commitments and cooperative measures extending far beyond the traditional scope of world-wide international agreements and institutions. Regional cooperation among closely interdependent and like-minded nations may create new institutional norms, intermediate between the complete merging of national sovereignties into a single national state and the extremely loose relationships which can be established at this stage among all members of the international community. Such arrangements may well be recognized as inferior to more ambitious, but utopian, world-wide models, and yet be justified as the best practicable alternative to international chaos.

5. While far short of ideal, the methods of regional cooperation developed in Europe since the war have proved highly beneficial

to the participating countries and have enabled them to liberalize
their restrictions against third countries as well as among themselves. Regional arrangements of this character, while admittedly
discriminatory in some respects, can accelerate and consolidate
progress toward world-wide currency convertibility and trade liberalization, introduce elements of stability in international economic
relations, and help limit the international spread of recessions and
restrictions.

The reader would be well advised to retain some degree of
healthy skepticism with respect to these various points.

Triffin's analysis of postwar monetary policies in Europe relies
heavily on a highly simplified model of monetary analysis, strangely
reminiscent of the most naïve versions of the quantity theory of
money. This may be traced to a laudable desire to make use only
of operational concepts adjusted to easily available and comparable
statistical and accounting data. On the other hand, many readers
will consider the resulting construction as merely formal rather
than explanatory in character,[1] and as tending to confuse true
theory with purely definitional tautologies. One must certainly
regret the lack of a more explicit discussion of the relationship between theoretical hypotheses and accounting framework in the
rather cursory presentation by Triffin of the general model into
which he pours his balance of payments, production, expenditure,
money, and credit data for a dozen European countries.

This is all the more inexcusable as a few references to the definition of "monetary balance" developed by Dutch economists such
as J. G. Koopmans, C. Goedhart, M. W. Holtrop, J. Tinbergen,
and H. J. Witteveen might have reassured academic readers as to
the differences between his theoretical model and the timeworn
quantity theory of money.[2]

On the empirical side, there is no doubt that the classification
of twelve European countries into three clear-cut groups introduces

1. See Milton Friedman's recent strictures of the Walrasian system as providing
a merely formal framework for organizing our ideas but having little to contribute
to the "substantive hypotheses about economic phenomena" which "are an essential
ingredient of a fruitful and meaningful economic theory." Milton Friedman, "Léon
Walras and his Economic System," *American Economic Review* (Dec. 1955), p. 908.

2. The excellent volume by Don Patinkin on *Money, Interest and Prices: An
Integration of Value Theory* (Evanston, Ill. 1956) came out as the present study was
going to press.

some semblance of order into the chaotic jumble of data and indices which pretend to describe and characterize the comparative evolution of money, credit, prices, liquidity, and balances of payments over a period of eight turbulent years. Even then the over-all picture remains pretty confused. Most of all, however, the various computations underlying the indices of monetization, domestic inflation, liquidity, cost competitiveness, etc. put a heavy load on the pitifully slender "guesstimates" involved in the original data. Anyone who has ever played with national account estimates and watched their bewildering revisions from year to year could not fail to share this reviewer's skepticism before the apparent precision of the quantitative results hatched from these dubious eggs.

The author's optimistic position with respect to the current and prospective balance in the world's dollar transactions will be deemed far more plausible today than when first presented in earlier and gloomier days. There will be more raised eyebrows now than shrugged shoulders even among the devotees of the dollar shortage theories. I very much doubt, however, whether many people will be swayed by the evidence and arguments presented by Triffin. Most of them—including this reviewer for one—will refuse to gaze into the crystal ball and come away with any firm guess about a "typical" or "normal" pattern of postwar payments in a world where unpredictable monetary and trade policies may, at any time, modify and upset the basic forces determining the equilibrium or disequilibrium of a country's international transactions.

For this very same reason, the conclusions of the author as to the indispensable role of international cooperation in the restoration, but particularly in the preservation, of a workable system of multilateral trade and payments will command far more general agreement. The same cannot be said, however, for his transparent bias in favor of regional, rather than world-wide, agreements and institutions. The parallel drawn between the futility of the International Monetary Fund and the achievements of the European Payments Union will strike the reader as particularly unfair. The Union's score is admittedly high if one measures its achievements in relation to its modest objectives. We should not forget, however, that the Fund's ambitions were much greater, and therefore more difficult to implement, but that they remain an essential goal for the orderly development of international monetary relations. Triffin has clearly allowed himself to be swayed far too much by individual prejudices, undoubtedly derived from his personal experiences, successes, and failures as a "money doctor" in Latin America, as a staff member of the IMF, and as one of the earliest proponents, active negotiators, and most ardent defenders of the EPU Agreement.[3]

The glowing account of regional cooperation among the OEEC countries tends to slide over the very real threat pointed out by most classical and neoclassical economists, i.e. the growth of discrimination and the development of autarkic blocs even more dangerous, politically and economically, than national protectionism. That this has not yet happened is no guarantee that it may not happen tomorrow. Triffin's appeal to political considerations to bolster his defense of discriminatory or preferential arrangements among so-called "like-minded" countries may indeed be due to a subconscious realization of the weakness of his economic arguments. He may well be right in preferring the regional half-cake to the nationalistic no-cake, but doesn't he give up too easily the attempt to bake a whole, truly international cake? The job may be hard. It may take a long time to achieve. It is still worth striving for.

Finally, the emphasis on multilateral clearing as the keystone of any international monetary institution will probably be the subject of a hot debate among specialists and technicians. It is by no means clear, to this reviewer at least, that such multilateral clearing cannot be performed more practically and efficiently by the market itself than by any supercentral bank or clearing agency. I would agree with Triffin that his proposals would obviate many of the pitfalls of the interwar gold exchange standard, but the discussion of an international agreement along these lines still seems highly academic at this stage. It is even doubtful whether the present EPU Agreement could be revamped in this direction without driving out of the organization the country whose cooperation is most necessary for its success and particularly for its continued opening toward the outside world. Current trends point much more, as Triffin himself recognizes, in the direction of full convertibility than of regional clearing mechanisms. Many of us would

---

3. This is particularly obvious in the extraneous and totally unnecessary passages devoted to the question of multiple exchange rates in Latin America and to the negotiation of the EPU Agreement.

regard this as a gain rather than a loss, and would have a greater faith in market convertibility than in intergovernmental agreements and organizations as a foundation for world trade and payments.

III. HOW DOES IT SAY IT?

Triffin's study bears all the marks of having been written hurriedly, and of trying to ride two horses at the same time. It would have gained, in my opinion, by being divided into two separate volumes specifically devoted to national monetary policies on the one hand, and to international monetary policies and institutions on the other. The author's only excuse for inflicting upon his readers this half-digested assemblage must lie in the time-consuming work invested in the processing of current data which would lose much of their topical interest during the course of further revision and publication delays.

But who will be these readers?

Large chunks of the book will be deemed light reading by academic standards. Triffin's colleagues and students in the university world will be particularly aghast at the dearth of footnote references to the current literature on the subject and at the prevalence of a plain common-sense approach devoid of theoretical refinements.

Still, most of the book would be heavy going for the layman and, much as I love Triffin, I confidently predict that his book will not be a book-of-the-month selection.

Its main appeal may be to government economists and other self-styled currency or banking experts directly concerned with the intricacies of European monetary and exchange arrangements.

It looks indeed as if the author had been unable to choose his audience in advance and had wavered between a half-hearted attempt to reach a lay audience and the hope of interesting and persuading specialists already familiar with the topics under discussion. The treatment is indeed highly condensed and elliptical in parts, diffuse and repetitious in others.

The best that can be said for Triffin's book is that it is stimulating and provocative throughout. Let us end on a hopeful note, and wish that a large number of readers be "stimulated" enough by its arguments not to feel too "provoked" by its conclusions.

A REJOINDER

I would take the strongest exception to the sly footnote reference to Walras if I thought it were intended at all seriously. Apart from that, I fully agree with the reviewer and plead guilty on all counts. I feel impelled, therefore, to absolve from all blame:

The Merrill Foundation, which generously financed my leave of absence from Yale while at work on this book;

The Organization for European Economic Cooperation, and particularly Messrs. Milton Gilbert, Geer Stuvel, and John Edelman, who generously gave me every possible assistance for the gathering of the data in Chapter 2;

Mrs. Robert L. West, who patiently checked and rechecked calculations and offered many valuable suggestions;

Mrs. Jerome H. Logan, whose typescript improved so miraculously upon my manuscript;

The Yale Press, which has done an outstanding job with the charts and tables as well as with the text;

My many friends and colleagues in academic and government life whose ideas I sponged or spurned as the whim moved me.

By Way of a Table of Contents

OR

What to Read and Not to Read

This should be a very interesting chapter, since it is so breathtaking in its scope and so controversial in its conclusions. If, however, you disagree with the facts as summarized in section I, you will not be able to make any sense of the theories and policies discussed in sections II and III and might as well skip quietly to Chapter 2, after an irritated glance at the Summary and Conclusions in section IV.

This is a chapter full of melodrama and excitement. The first part of each section describes the 1947 crisis and is as gloomy and unnerving as can be. It is always followed, however, by a comforting success story showing how the dragon was slain and the heroine saved after all. At least until the next installment, for there is no guarantee that "they will live happily ever after."

The monetary sections of this chapter (secs. III and IV) were entitled, in an earlier draft, "How Different Roads May Lead to Rome, But Not All of Them Do." Many people, however, told me that this was too flippant and might infuriate the readers thus enticed to penetrate into the morass of chaotic events and policies in a dozen countries during a particularly turbulent period. It is to spare the casual reader such entanglement that I wrote the Summary and Conclusions in sec. V. He may safely skip the rest of the chapter.

This chapter tells a sad story of high hopes bitterly disap-
pointed. Unpleasant as it is, it deserves pondering by international planners, as it holds a very important moral for them:
In heavy weather, a rudimentary shelter will prove more useful
than the most elaborate blueprint of the dream house they may
hope to erect after the storm has subsided.

CHAPTER 4. BILATERALISM AND ITS PALLIATIVES: 1945–50,
or *How a puzzled Europe tried, in a most puzzling way, to make
sense out of nonsense and failed to put Humpty Dumpty together
again.*   143

This chapter is full of long words, such as bilateralism, multilateralism, etc. Let me reassure you. You will find them quite
tame once you get used to them and they to you.

On the other hand, I cannot honestly urge you to read it. Although it is the shortest in the book, it cannot but be as uselessly
complex and messy as the crazy system of payments which it describes. The average reader will be happy to skip it without even
having to bother about any Summary and Conclusions section.

CHAPTER 5. THE EUROPEAN PAYMENTS UNION: 1950–55, or
*How Europe belatedly discovered Columbus' egg and began to
put Humpty Dumpty together again.*   161

With this chapter, our story takes again a turn for the better. The European Payments Union was not a dream house but a shelter hastily erected in the middle of the storm, and soon subjected to the worse headwinds of the Korean War. It withstood these assaults far better than anyone had expected and was gradually bolstered and remodeled when bright weather permitted a resumption of construction activity. It has not yet been converted into fully habitable and comfortable quarters, however, as the expense would be unjustified as long as lingering hopes for the dream house have not entirely dwindled away.

The most faithful of my hurried readers, by the way, must have done so by now and closed this book for good long ago. If any of them are left, let them try to read section II, A and B, and section V of this chapter.

CHAPTER 6. CURRENT APPROACHES TO CONVERTIBILITY, or *How Great Britain briefly dreamed of returning to her nineteenth-century "splendid isolation," but later discovered unsuspected virtues in the preservation of European monetary cooperation.*   209

The first half of this chapter may be hopelessly out of date by the time it appears in print. There is little in it, anyway, that an intelligent reader cannot find in the financial section of the *New York Times*.

The European Monetary Agreement, on the contrary, is as likely as not to be still waiting in limbo for the awakening sound of the convertibility trumpets. If you are interested in the present rather than in the future, you may postpone reading about it for a while.

CHAPTER 7. TOWARD VIABLE CONVERTIBILITY, or *How to pour old wine into new bottles*   234

Economists will find too much politics in this chapter, and politicians too much economics. It certainly belabors the obvious and need not be read by those who don't have to unlearn the mass of untruths or half-truths which becloud the practical meaning of currency convertibility in the twentieth-century world.

This is, of course, the climax of the book and what it all leads up to. It does not shrink from concrete and—I hope—constructive proposals for economic betterment. Two of these are particularly dear to me: the creation of a clearing house for European central banks, and a badly needed agreement aiming at a true internationalization of international monetary reserves.

It is, therefore, the chapter I would most like to see read by Secretary Humphrey—or his successor—Governor Frère of the National Bank of Belgium—or his successor—and all the other ministers of finance and central bankers whose valued opinions shape monetary policy from day to day. In the long run so dear to my academic colleagues, however, the judgment of everybody else will probably prove more important.

My publisher dolefully confirms that he, too, thinks it more important that this book should be read by everybody else. There are more of them.

CHARTS AND TABLES

The reader who glances at the charts and tables in the text may save himself the trouble of reading the rest of the book. My earnest entreaty *not* to look at the supporting tables in the Statistical Appendix is probably superfluous.

xxiii

CHAPTER 6

CHAPTER 1

The World Dollar Shortage

ECONOMISTS are often criticized for their obstinate loyalty to timeworn theories and their disregard for current realities which do not fit their ready-made abstractions. The opposite criticism might be leveled at them with equal plausibility. They are much too prone to seek permanent explanations for passing economic trends and to build them into new, bigger, and better theories of universal and lasting validity.

One of the latest examples of this slavery to facts is the emergence of the chronic dollar shortage theory. The facts seemed awesome indeed and hardly compatible with the economist's faith in the automatism of balance of payments adjustments. In the six years 1934–39, the United States had drained toward Fort Knox more than $10 billion of gold from the rest of the world and had become the proud but puzzled owner of approximately two thirds of the world stock of monetary gold. After the Second World War, its surpluses on merchandise and services account had totaled nearly $30 billion over the four years 1946–49, in spite of all foreign attempts to dam the formidable flood of U.S. exports through recurrent exchange devaluations and growing trade and exchange restrictions and discrimination.

These facts were soon integrated into ingenious theories of a permanent dollar shortage, impervious to any orthodox adjustment mechanism, and calling for new and imaginative policies both in the United States and abroad. The enormous influence of this whole school of thought on the academic thinking and government policies of the postwar years justifies a closer look at the facts, theories, and policies of the dollar shortage.

I. FACTS

The economists of my generation have all been brought up in a period characterized by persistent United States surpluses, financed by the gold avalanche of the late 1930's and by the huge foreign aid programs of the postwar years. We may perhaps be excused, therefore, for having felt that twenty years of dollar imbalance in world payments could hardly be regarded as a short-run disturbance in the mechanism of international adjustments, and for having gone to the other extreme of considering it as a norm rather than an exception.

Yet nobody had ever heard or thought of a chronic dollar shortage until the world depression of the 1930's. During World War I and the reconstruction period that followed, the belligerent countries had certainly spent more in the United States than they currently earned. They did not see in this phenomenon, however, anything so mysterious as to call for a new economic theory.

A. Before 1914 (see Appendix Table 1)

Prior to 1914 the world had been used to regard the United States as a young, underdeveloped, but fast developing economy, with substantial and persistent deficits in its current account transactions with the rest of the world. These deficits were financed in small part by gold exports—the United States was then an important gold producer—and for the most part by a large and continuous inflow of foreign capital. As economic development progressed, trade deficits gradually made room for growing trade surpluses, but these were more than offset by rising deficits on services, interest, and dividend account. The inflow of foreign capital continued almost unabated until the eve of the First World War.

B. The Interwar Period

The slow evolution of the United States from an underdeveloped, capital-importing economy to a developed, capital-exporting country was accelerated into an abrupt and revolutionary jump as the result of the First World War. Our exports trebled, invisible receipts—principally from shipping—decupled, while foreign disinvestment and U.S. loans, both public and private, reversed the direction of our balance on capital account.

The economic changes brought about by the war had a lasting effect on the international trade and payments pattern. The former capital-exporting countries of Europe emerged with large needs for reconstruction at the very same time that the United States had become the strongest economic power in the world. The United States replaced Europe as the world's banker.

1. The Dollar Gap (see Chart I and Appendix Table 2)

In the twenty-one years that followed, the United States accumulated current account surpluses of nearly $18 billion, financed about one third by capital exports and two thirds by gold receipts from abroad. The world had entered the era of the so-called "dollar shortage."

A closer examination of the data reveals, however, some striking facts which do not fit into any simple explanation of this phenomenon.

First of all, 90% of the total gold inflow of the period ($10.7 billion out of $11.9 billion) took place in the immediate prewar years 1934–39, following a drastic and totally unwarranted devaluation of the U.S. dollar and arising for the most part ($8.4 billion) from an unprecedented capital flight from war-threatened Europe. The remaining 10% of the interwar gold inflow ($1.2 billion) came to the United States during the reconstruction years 1919–25, but created no pressure on foreign reserves since such an amount (less than $200 million a year) represented no more than the normal U.S. share of current gold production abroad. In the intervening eight years 1926–33, gold imports and exports balanced each other almost exactly, both in prosperity and in depression, and new gold production flew almost entirely to foreign countries' monetary reserves rather than to Fort Knox.

It remains true that we accumulated over these twenty-one years surpluses of about $17.5 billion in our current account transactions with the rest of the world. Nearly one half of this, however ($8.3 billion), took place in the first three years following the First World War. By 1922 our surpluses had fallen to about $650 million a year and remained close to that level throughout the prosperous 1920's. They dropped further to an average of $300 to $400

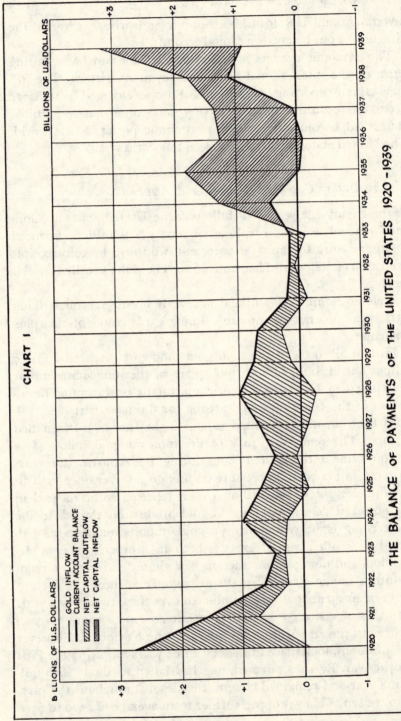

CHART I

THE BALANCE OF PAYMENTS OF THE UNITED STATES 1920-1939

BILLIONS OF U.S. DOLLARS

BILLIONS OF U.S. DOLLARS

GOLD INFLOW
CURRENT ACCOUNT BALANCE
NET CAPITAL OUTFLOW
NET CAPITAL INFLOW

4

million a year during the big depression and until the end of the interwar period.

In view of the changed position of the United States in the world economy, annual surpluses of this magnitude could hardly be regarded as abnormal. They were far smaller—especially in purchasing power—than the average surpluses ($900 million a year) of the United Kingdom in the last prewar years (1906–13). These had attracted hardly any attention at the time, as they had been financed without apparent difficulty by British capital exports.[1] The capital-exporting capacity of the United States in the 1920's was certainly as great or greater than that of prewar Britain, and our capital exports remained indeed in excess of our current account surpluses—thus allowing for a simultaneous increase of foreign investments in the United States—until the financial crisis of 1929.

The gold avalanche of the late 1930's did not reflect a worsening in the world's current account transactions with the United States. On the contrary, the United States current account surplus was then, on the average, little more than half that of the 1920's. The over-all imbalance resulted entirely from a radical shift in the direction of international capital movements. A net outflow of about $640 million a year in the 1920's, and of $280 million a year in the early 1930's, suddenly made room for a net inflow averaging $1,400 million a year. This shift coincided in time with the unwarranted devaluation of the U.S. dollar, the seizure of power by the Nazis in Germany, and the drift of Europe toward the Second World War. There is little doubt that the sudden repatriation of American capital and the inrush of foreign capital into the U.S. were primarily the product of these events, rather than of a fundamental economic disequilibrium between the United States and the rest of the world.

2. *The Dollar Shortage (see Chart II and Appendix Table 3)*

The absence of chronic and persistent balance of payments deficits of the world toward the United States would not, however, disprove in any way the more subtle versions of the dollar shortage theory. These versions, indeed, would readily concede that such

1. See Albert H. Imlah, "British Balance of Payments and Export of Capital, 1816–1913," *The Economic History Review*, 5 (1952), No. 2, 208–39.

deficits are necessarily limited in size and duration by the amount of resources available to finance them. The over-all deficits of the world with the United States could not possibly exceed the relatively modest contribution derived from the sale to the United States of gold currently produced or previously accumulated by the other countries. Foreign expenditures in the United States could not, therefore, permanently and substantially exceed our own expenditures abroad for goods, services, and investment.

The evidence of a world dollar shortage is not to be found in the size or persistence of an actual dollar gap, but in the drastic contraction of dollar expenditures imposed upon foreign countries by our inability to sustain an adequate and expanding flow of U.S. imports and other expenditures abroad. Any large decline in these expenditures must necessarily be followed, sooner or later, by a parallel decline in foreign imports from the United States, and by a closing of the dollar "gap." In the absence of direct measures abroad to restrict such imports—devaluation, tariff increases, quantitative import restrictions or import controls —this readjustment will involve, however, a deflationary spiral in terms of prices, production, national income, and employment.

It is these deflationary pressures which are accented by the dollar shortage—as opposed to the "dollar gap"—theories, and which characterized the depression of the 1930's. American expenditures abroad fell abruptly by 25% to 50% in each one of the three years 1930-32. At the bottom of the depression, they had dropped to a bare fourth of their 1928 level, and remained well below 50% of that level—with the single exception of 1937—until the outbreak of the Second World War.

The impact of this catastrophic fall in foreign dollar receipts was further aggravated after 1933 by the flight of war-scared capital to the United States, but was cushioned somewhat by withdrawals of foreign funds in the period 1931–33 and by gold sales, on an unprecedented and unmaintainable scale (rising from $1.3 billion to $3.2 billion a year), in the following period. Current expenditures by foreigners in the United States market fell nevertheless to 35% of their 1928 level at the bottom of the depression, and recovered only to about 56%, on the average, during the years 1934–39.

This sudden and violent contraction dealt a death blow to the international gold standard shakily restored in the late 1920's. In spite of a rearguard fight by the gold-bloc countries, currency de-

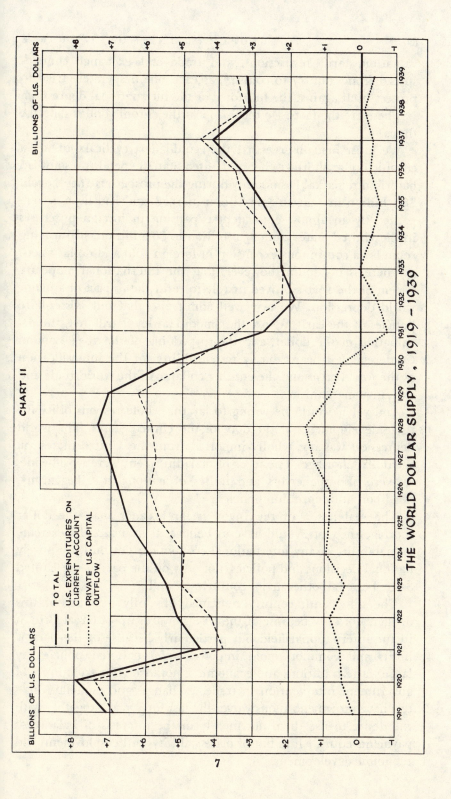

CHART II

THE WORLD DOLLAR SUPPLY, 1919 – 1939

BILLIONS OF U.S. DOLLARS

TOTAL

U.S. EXPENDITURES ON
CURRENT ACCOUNT

PRIVATE U.S. CAPITAL
OUTFLOW

valuation, tariff restrictions, and trade and exchange controls spread from country to country, as each one desperately tried to protect itself against the full force of the international depression.

These are the facts. Do they support the chronic dollar shortage thesis?

We must first observe that they could fit a cyclical but not a chronic dollar shortage theory. United States expenditures abroad had risen remarkably smoothly during the prosperous 1920's, from $5.1 billion in 1922 to $7.3 billion in 1928, and had been accompanied by an almost equivalent expansion in foreign purchases in the United States from $5.0 billion to $6.8 billion, still leaving room for a continuous expansion in foreign gold and dollar assets.

There is no doubt, however, that the international monetary system of the 1920's proved unable to resist the impact of a major world depression. We may well admit also that our laissez-faire policies of the early 1930's, the Smoot-Hawley Tariff Act, the devaluation of the dollar, and the torpedoing of the 1933 London Conference all bear a heavy responsibility for the intensification of the world crisis and the ensuing collapse of the world trade and exchange mechanism.

And yet it would be wrong to lay the whole responsibility for these developments at the door of the United States. The world depression was not wholly imported from the United States via the dollar shortage. The seeds of maladjustment were world-wide, as were also the errors and follies of nationalistic, beggar-my-neighbor, antidepression policies.

The real lesson of the 1930's is far broader than the dollar shortage theorists would have us believe. It indicates the extreme vulnerability of any international economic order built on purely national decisions and policies, not only on the part of the United States but of all other major countries as well.

The nineteenth century remained blissfully unaware of this danger, not only because of the wise stewardship of Great Britain in the international field but particularly because of the narrow limits and common mold imposed upon national policies by laissez-faire traditions and economic ignorance. The techniques of government intervention in trade, exchange, and monetary matters have grown enormously over the last forty years, together with the desire to use them not merely in the interests of balance of payments equilibrium but of price stability, full employment, and economic development.

The world-wide shift from laissez-faire to interventionism thus brought into the open the basic conflict, previously dormant, between the international scope of economic realities and the national framework of economic sovereignty. The dollar shortage theory gives us only a dim and partial view of this fundamental fact. In order to use it constructively, we must first reinterpret it into a broader theory of international economic relations, encompassing far more than the bilateral relations between the United States alone and the rest of the world taken as a single unit.

C. After the Second World War

The French people accuse their generals of always planning for the last war rather than for the next one. Future historians of the economic theories and policies of these postwar years will blame us in the same way for forecasting, interpreting, and fighting our postwar inflation with the tools and weapons inherited from our analysis of the deflation of the 1930's.

1. The Dollar Gap (see Chart III and Appendix Table 4)

The temptation to extrapolate to the postwar era the dollar shortage theory developed in the 1930's was indeed well-nigh irresistible. In the ten years 1946–55, the current account deficit of the world with the United States reached the astronomical sum of $38 billion, i.e. an amount larger than the world's total stock of monetary gold and about three times greater than that of the world outside the United States.[2]

A small part of this deficit was covered by the monetization of newly produced gold and by private capital transactions. The residual deficit to be financed by the monetary authorities approximated $30 billion.

These ten years fall, however, into two very distinct periods. Ninety-six per cent of the deficits was incurred in the first four years of postwar reconstruction (1946–49), and in spite of the enormous

2. These figures, and all other data presented below, leave out of account another $15.7 billion of military aid in kind contributed abroad on a grant basis, mostly after the outbreak of the Korean war. There are two reasons for this exclusion. First of all, there is little likelihood that such goods would have been imported by the recipient countries if they had had to pay for them out of their own resources. Secondly, their physical transfer abroad by the United States is dominated by military considerations of joint defense, rather than by considerations of either economic needs or national defense in the foreign countries concerned.

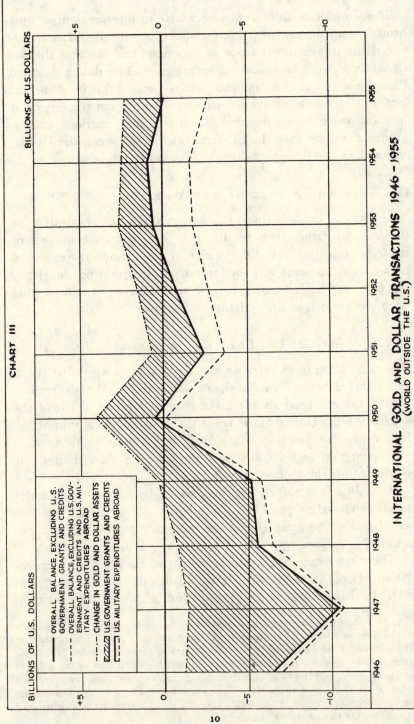

CHART III

INTERNATIONAL GOLD AND DOLLAR TRANSACTIONS 1946–1955
(WORLD OUTSIDE THE U.S.)

BILLIONS OF U.S. DOLLARS

OVERALL BALANCE, EXCLUDING U.S.
GOVERNMENT GRANTS AND CREDITS

OVERALL BALANCE, EXCLUDING U.S. GOV-
ERNMENT AND CREDITS AND U.S. MIL-
ITARY EXPENDITURES ABROAD

CHANGE IN GOLD AND DOLLAR ASSETS

U.S. GOVERNMENT GRANTS AND CREDITS

U.S. MILITARY EXPENDITURES ABROAD

BILLIONS OF U.S. DOLLARS

scale of U.S. foreign aid were accompanied by substantial losses in foreign countries' gold and dollar assets. The drastic reduction of foreign deficits in the following six years (1950–55) permitted on the contrary an unprecedented accretion of foreign gold and dollar assets (by more than $13 billion), in spite of the slashing of foreign aid from $25 billion to $15 billion.

And yet this second period was itself marked by a new and violent payments crisis, arising from the outbreak of hostilities in Korea, the widespread fears of a third world war, and the initial impact of a heavy rearmament program. The extent of the basic economic recovery from the initial postwar difficulties is better revealed by a comparison between the 1947 deficit of $10 billion and the moderate surpluses or deficits (ranging from +$0.8 billion to −$0.3 billion) of the years 1953–56.

Once more, this evidence can hardly be reconciled with the thesis of a persistent and intractable dollar shortage. The early postwar deficits have a far more plausible explanation in the extent of the needs for reconstruction and development bequeathed by the war, and in the willingness of the United States to encourage and finance larger deficits than those which these countries could have met out of their own resources. Data on the net balance of payments, taken by themselves, can indeed prove little either as to the existence of a dollar shortage in 1946–49 or to its rapid correction in 1950–56. It may be observed, however, that the willingness and ability of foreign countries to add to their reserves more than 90% of their foreign aid receipts—rather than spend them currently—after 1949 suggests at least the absence of any stringent pressure on their dollar balance.

Many economists continue to argue, however, that the 1953–56 equilibrium is entirely deceptive, being due to abnormal and transient factors such as an exceptionally high rate of economic activity in the United States, drastic discrimination against dollar imports, and huge U.S. military expenditures abroad. Yet, and contrary to all predictions, the U.S. recession of 1953–54 hardly slowed down the rate of gold and dollar accumulation abroad, and the spectacular improvement observed after 1951 has taken place simultaneously with substantial and growing reductions in dollar discrimination. The real quantitative impact of such discrimination appears to be far smaller today than is commonly imagined. Finally, U.S. military expenditures abroad now provide a safe dollar market for the use of foreign resources, but do not add to these resources. Their eventual tapering off will be gradual at best, and will probably be accompanied by simultaneous reductions in the large internal and external military expenditures which currently absorb a substantial share of foreign countries' production, thus slowing down not only their living standards but also their rate of economic development and their exportable capacity. A reduction in military expenditures throughout the world would test primarily our ability to avoid a world depression, rather than result automatically in any dollar shortage. The feasibility of such adjustments as may prove necessary in the long run may be gauged from the fact that our commercial imports of goods and services increased in the single year 1956 by an amount equal to more than 60% of our total military expenditures abroad in that year.

2. *The Dollar Shortage*

The elimination of the dollar gap would still be compatible, however, with the persistence of a dollar shortage arising from deflationary pressures and restrictive trade policies in the United States and imposing upon other countries internal deflationary policies, or exchange depreciation, or growing trade and exchange restrictions on their dollar expenditure. This corresponds, indeed, to the pattern of "adjustment" through which the dollar gap was eliminated but the dollar shortage perpetuated in the 1930's.

The history of the postwar years, however, presents the sharpest possible contrast with that of the 1930's. First of all, our foreign aid programs greatly increased the supply of dollars available to other countries to meet their expenditures in the United States market. Foreign countries' gold and dollar holdings have risen uninterruptedly since the end of 1948 and were by the end of 1956 $14 billion larger than in 1948 and more than double their 1938 level. Their net distribution as among countries and monetary areas was, moreover, far more adequate with relation to payments needs than at any previous period in world history (see Chart IV and Appendix Table 5).[3]

3. The United Kingdom gold and dollar holdings were still very low, particularly in relation to that country's short-term external liabilities, but reasonably adequate with relation to annual imports if account is taken of the vast proportion of British trade normally settled in sterling rather than in dollars, even under conditions of currency convertibility.

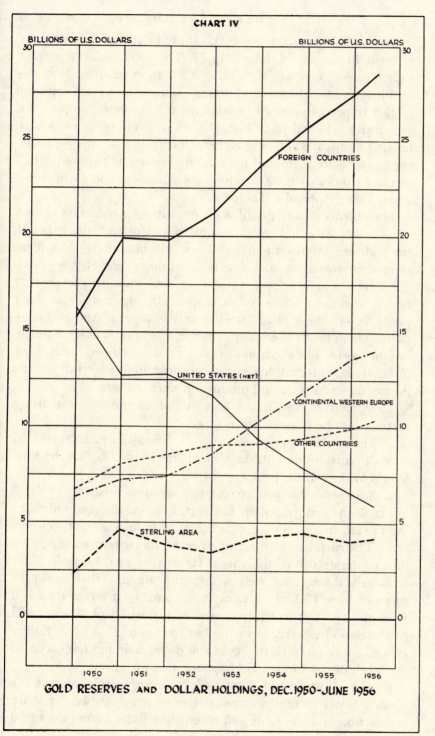

CHART IV

BILLIONS OF U.S. DOLLARS

BILLIONS OF U.S. DOLLARS

FOREIGN COUNTRIES

UNITED STATES (NET)

CONTINENTAL WESTERN EUROPE

OTHER COUNTRIES

STERLING AREA

GOLD RESERVES AND DOLLAR HOLDINGS, DEC. 1950-JUNE 1956

Foreign aid programs, however, cannot be regarded as a normal element in the world dollar supply. The level of United States expenditures for goods, services, and private investment abroad—exclusive of official loans and grants—is a more relevant criterion in this respect. Expressed in constant prices, these "normal" expenditures rejoined their highest prewar level (1928) in the latter part of 1949. They were already in excess of the 1935–39 average by 60% in 1946, and have been running at two and a half to three times that level, or more, ever since the end of 1952 (see Chart V and Appendix Table 6).

The absence of any deflationary pressure of a monetary character is better indicated by the evolution of United States expenditures abroad at current prices. These are now more than three times their 1928 level, and close to seven times their 1935–39 level. They have nearly tripled since 1947, and most of the postwar period has been characterized indeed by upward inflationary pressures—in the United States as well as abroad—and by exceptionally high levels of employment and economic activity throughout the world. The expansionist policies of the United States, both internal and external, have indeed contributed powerfully to the growth of world trade and production since the war.

To conclude, the factual background of the dollar shortage theories may be summarized as follows:

1. The world experienced no great difficulties in balancing its over-all transactions with the United States either before the First World War or in the prosperous 1920's.

2. A large dollar gap on current account, financed by large official loans and grants by the United States, emerged only during the reconstruction years immediately following the two world wars. The surpluses of the United States on current account were of a moderate size in the 1920's, far smaller in the 1930's. They remained throughout well within the amount that could be financed from United States capital exports on a minor scale and from the sale to the United States of a fraction of current gold production elsewhere. Over the last four years (1953–56), the increase in foreign countries' gold and dollar holdings has exceeded the levels of our foreign aid by more than $1 billion.

3. The adjustment of current expenditures by foreigners in the United States to their current dollar earnings involved a sharp contraction of world trade and economic activity during the world

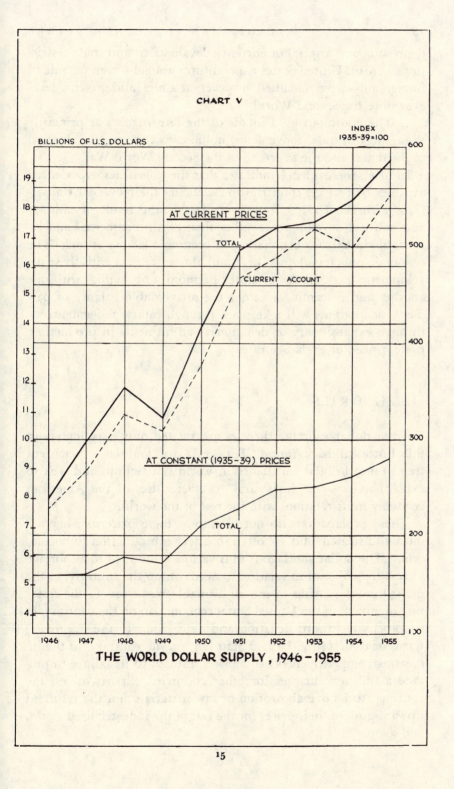

CHART V

INDEX
1935-39=100

BILLIONS OF U.S. DOLLARS

AT CURRENT PRICES

TOTAL

CURRENT ACCOUNT

AT CONSTANT (1935-39) PRICES

TOTAL

1946 1947 1948 1949 1950 1951 1952 1953 1954 1955

THE WORLD DOLLAR SUPPLY, 1946-1955

depression and a spiral of currency devaluations and trade restrictions abroad. United States expenditures abroad—even outside of foreign aid—have remained, however, at a high and growing level ever since the Second World War.

4. The enormous gold inflow of the late 1930's was primarily the result of capital movements, induced by the 1934 devaluation of the dollar and the approach of the Second World War.

In brief, the evidence indicates that the difficulties experienced at times by foreign countries in balancing their over-all transactions with the United States were largely the result of military and political developments rather than of a fundamental and intractable imbalance originating in economic factors as such. The economic policies adopted here and abroad to deal with these developments may, however, either harmonize or conflict with one another and determine whether the unavoidable balance of payments adaptations will take place through capital movements, or through expansionary or deflationary adjustments in production, trade, prices, or exchange rates.

II. THEORIES

Current dollar shortage theories are related only very loosely to this historical background. They take for granted a persistent trend toward dollar imbalance in world transactions and seek to explain it by some "structural" characteristics of the American economy in its relations with the rest of the world.

These explanations do not fit into a single pattern. They are mostly unrelated, and are often in direct contradiction to one another. The dollar shortage is thus variously ascribed to a shortage of resources abroad in relation to needs or, on the contrary, to the difficulties of putting to use all available resources; to the faster rate of growth of the United States economy or, on the contrary, to its proclivity toward deflation and depression; to the improving terms of trade of the United States or, on the contrary, to the increasing competitiveness of its prices abroad; to its failure to provide a sufficient market for other countries' exports or, on the contrary, to its overabsorption of raw materials and the resultant upward push of their prices for the rest of the industrialized world, and so on.

Rather than attempt the wearying task of reviewing each of these various explanations in turn, I shall try and discuss the broader generalizations from which they are usually derived. These may be grouped under three headings:

1. The inadequacy of foreign resources with relation to needs;
2. The faster rate of growth of U.S. productivity;
3. The tendency of the United States economy toward deflation, and of United States policies toward trade restrictions and protectionism.

A. INADEQUACY OF RESOURCES

This is at the same time the most naïve and, to my mind, the most correct of all dollar shortage theories.

The inadequacy of resources in relation to human needs—or at least in relation to human wants—is, of course, a universal phenomenon, whose very existence is at the basis of the economic problem itself. There is no doubt that this inadequacy is far less acute in the United States than in the rest of the world, particularly the more underdeveloped countries in Latin America, Africa, or Asia. There is also very little doubt that wise American investments abroad, far in excess of their current levels, could help accelerate the rate of economic development in many countries, reducing inequalities which spell starvation for millions of human beings and endanger political stability and the survival of free institutions over a large part of the world.[1]

This is probably one of the most fundamental and obvious truths in economics today, but it is also one of the most irrelevant to the explanation of actual balance of payments developments. Deficits are not particularly associated with poverty, nor surpluses with abundance, for nations any more than for individuals. Relatively poor countries like Honduras or Ethiopia traditionally "enjoy" a strong balance of payments position, while the largest postwar deficits have been experienced by far richer countries such as France, the United Kingdom, and Australia.

To make any sense of this type of dollar shortage explanation, we must certainly look beyond the physical ratio of resources

1. In the vast literature on this subject, I would especially like to refer the reader to the most moving, and least technical, pages devoted to it by François Perroux, in *L'Europe sans rivages* (Paris, Presses Universitaires de France, 1954), especially pp. 385–415.

to needs and consider the monetary policies by which rich as well as poor countries may try to raise their productivity or living standards. This, however, is an entirely different matter which will be discussed in section III of this chapter.[2]

B. THE FASTER GROWTH OF AMERICAN PRODUCTIVITY

This second explanation has been most ingeniously and challengingly developed by one of the most boldly questioning minds in this country, Professor John H. Williams of Harvard University.[3]

American productivity, it is argued, is not only much higher than foreign productivity; it is also increasing at a much faster pace, thus creating an ever widening gap which makes it harder and harder for foreign producers to compete with dollar goods, either in the United States, or in third markets, or even within their own markets. Other countries are therefore pushed into an increasingly unfavorable position in their trade with us. Classical remedies to such a situation have become politically unpalatable and would, in any case, involve a constant deterioration in other countries' terms of trade and living standards. This is the basic root and explanation of the chronic dollar shortage, which prevents any return to traditional convertibility mechanisms.

The facts on which this reasoning is based are at least questionable. The conclusions derived from them are even more debatable. There exist no comprehensive data on comparative productivity for the various countries of the world, but the United Nations indices of industrial production consistently show a substantially faster rate of production increase in the rest of the world—even excluding the U.S.S.R.—than in the United States, except in wartime. Industrial production also increased faster—or declined less —in Western Europe than in the United States throughout the prosperous 1920's, the depressed 1930's, and the reconstruction years following World War II, and this in spite of a much faster growth of population in the United States than in Europe.[4] The

2. See below, pp. 22-29.

3. See particularly his *Economic Stability in the Modern World*, Stamp Memorial Lecture, Blackwell, Oxford, 1952.

4. For a more searching discussion of comparative productivity in the United States and abroad, see G. D. A. MacDougall, "Does Productivity Rise Faster in the United States?," *Review of Economics and Statistics* (May 1956), pp. 155-76.

enormous advance gained by the United States over Europe during the last forty years is essentially the product of two world wars, rather than of peacetime developments (see Table I).

Table I. INDICES OF INDUSTRIAL PRODUCTION, 1913–55

(changes in %)

	1913–23	1923–29	1929–37	1937–48	1948–55
World, excluding the U.S.	+4	+82	+47	−1	+74
United States	+50	+25	+3	+72	+33
Western Europe	−24	+46	+19	−1	+76

Note: For exact coverage of each index, see *Sources* below.

Sources:
1. *World, excluding the U.S.:*
    1913–37 (excluding U.S.S.R.): Woytinsky, W. S., and Woytinsky, E. S., *World Population and Production* (New York, Twentieth Century Fund, 1953), p. 1002.
    1937–55 (excluding U.S.S.R., China, and Eastern Europe): United Nations *Monthly Bulletin of Statistics.*
2. *U.S. and Western Europe:* OEEC, *Industrial Statistics, 1900–1955, Addendum,* Paris, 1956, p. 3.

It is also striking to note that the periods of dollar scarcity coincide with those in which U.S. production tended to lag behind, rather than overtake, the rate of progress in foreign countries. We would be tempted, therefore, to reverse Professor Williams' thesis and to associate international dollar pressures with the relative slowdown of U.S. economic activity with respect to that of other countries. This view would also accord with the view of those who fear the international impact of U.S. depressions rather than of U.S. prosperity, and would appear far more plausible from the point of view of economic theory and analysis.

Differential advances in productivity should be expected, first of all, to be accompanied by a faster growth of real income and of consumption and investment expenditures in the more progressive country than in the others. These income effects, taken by themselves, should stimulate larger increases in import demand by the former country than by the latter ones. There is indeed a close correlation between the volume of imports into the United States and the index of total industrial production, and this correlation is closer still in the European countries.

Secondly, productivity increases in a country should be expected to improve the commodity terms of trade of other countries insofar as they are importers of the goods whose production costs have decreased under the impact of technological advances.

Both these effects tend to improve the balance of payments of the more laggard countries. On the other hand, advances in productivity may unfavorably affect the balance of payments of other countries if they lower domestic costs for home goods competing with imports, or of export goods competing with other countries' production in foreign markets. On balance, therefore, differential advances of productivity should be expected to improve the balance of payments of the more laggard countries through their impact on real incomes and terms of trade, but to worsen it through their impact on price competitiveness at home and in world markets. There is no conclusive evidence—theoretical or empirical—demonstrating that the third of these three impacts should, or actually tends to, outweigh the first two. The evidence discussed in section I of this chapter fails to give any such indication in the case of the United States. The rapid growth of industrial advance in the United Kingdom in the nineteenth century was, on the contrary, accompanied by a much faster growth of merchandise imports than exports, British surpluses on current account being due primarily to interest and dividend receipts on the growing volume of foreign investment.

Wage and monetary policies will also play an important part in facilitating or impeding international adjustments to differential rates of technological progress. The maintenance of a competitive cost pattern will be an easier task for all if the increases in real income resulting from technological progress are taken up in the form of higher wages rather than of lower prices.

This leads us into a third version of the dollar shortage theory, relating it to a supposed deflationary bias, rather than to an excessive rate of expansion, in the United States' economy and policies.

C. Monetary Pressures on the Balance of Payments

This third version of the dollar shortage theory is essentially derived from the experience of the years following the 1929 crisis. There can be little doubt that the intensity and duration of the depression of the 1930's were greatly influenced—although not exclusively determined—by sharp and prolonged unemployment in the United States, aggravated for the rest of the world by the Smoot-Hawley tariff increases, the devaluation of the dollar, and the spread of internal deflation and external restrictions from country to country. What happened then undoubtedly might happen again. Yet it seems totally unwarranted to generalize this limited experience into a general theory of a chronic, permanent dollar shortage.

The real lesson of the depression is that the simultaneous maintenance of high levels of economic activity and low levels of restrictions in an interdependent world is inconceivable in the absence of some harmonization of policies among the major trading nations. This obvious truth has a much broader field of application than the dollar shortage theory would suggest. After all, the United States absorbs less than 15% of world imports, as against 35% for continental Western Europe and its dependencies, 26% for the sterling area, and 12% for the United Kingdom alone. The course of economic activity throughout the world can thus be vitally affected by events and policies in other countries as well as in the United States.

Secondly, there is little or no reason to assume that the United States economy is permanently endowed with a deflationary bias, or that our foreign economic policies will bend persistently toward trade restrictions and protectionism. Our postwar record contrasts sharply in this respect with that of the 1930's. The last ten years have been characterized throughout by high and growing levels of economic activity and employment, continued wage increases—by an average of 12% yearly in 1946–48 and 5% yearly in 1948–56—and either stable or rising prices. The strength of organized labor and the ghost of the "Hoover depression" would undoubtedly prompt any administration, whether Democratic or Republican, to take strong action against the development of a major depression, even at the risk of building up potential inflationary forces difficult to control at a later stage. Finally, even though our foreign economic policy has not yet succeeded in fully subordinating sectional interests to the national interest, tariffs at least have been slashed continually and substantially over a long period of years, and the Republican party is no longer a bulwark of protectionism in the United States Congress.

Finally, it must also be recognized that no reasonable rate of growth in the United States can preclude a resurgence of future periods of dollar stringency as a result of a faster rate of monetary expansion, or inflation, abroad than in the United States. Such a tendency was certainly, and almost inevitably, at work in Europe during the early postwar years, but has long ceased to be characteristic of Europe as a whole.[5] Inflationary pressures are more likely to persist in the long run in the younger economies, bent on quickening the pace of their industrialization and economic development. International convertibility plans will have to take into account these differences and introduce sufficient realism and flexibility into their techniques to meet such diverse situations. Large-scale international migration, capital movements, and exchange rate adaptations provided such escape valves to gold standard rigidity for many countries in the nineteenth century. The reconstruction of an effective framework for international trade and payments will necessarily involve similar compromises between domestic and international objectives and commitments.

It is to these policy aspects of the dollar shortage theories that we must now address ourselves.

III. POLICIES

The dollar shortage theories were no idle exercise in pure economics. They led to and inspired—or, one may suspect, were often inspired by—extremely pointed policy advice both to the United States and to foreign countries: The United States should help solve the dollar gap through large-scale grants, credits, and investments, complementing liberal import policies; other countries should help solve it through trade and exchange discrimination against all transactions involving the expenditure of U.S. dollars.

A. UNITED STATES POLICIES

It is difficult to quarrel with the first half of this prescription, i.e. the one addressed to U.S. policy. Its validity does not depend in any way on the questionable balance of payments analyses and forecasts criticized above. Large capital exports by the richer countries are desirable to supplement the inadequate level of domestic savings of poor or war-devastated countries, to accelerate their economic reconstruction and development, and to raise their productivity and living standards. They may often contribute also

5. See below, Chap. 2, sec. III, pp. 48–70.

to the maintenance of economic activity and employment in the richer, capital-exporting countries. Finally, they appear increasingly necessary today to strengthen the free world against internal political instability and disintegration as well as against external aggression.

For a variety of reasons—political as well as economic—private initiative, left to itself, is hardly likely to meet these needs on an adequate scale. Our net capital exports, on private account, have averaged in recent years less than 0.5% of our national income as against more than 1% in the 1920's and five to ten times that proportion in pre-World War I Britain. In the political and economic climate which has prevailed since the end of the Second World War, governmental action was certainly indispensable to ensure an adequate flow of American capital toward the rest of the world, especially outside the Western Hemisphere. Net private U.S. investments outside Canada and Latin America have averaged less than $400 million a year in the period 1951–55.

The Marshall Plan was highly successful in speeding up European reconstruction. Investments in the underdeveloped countries, whether by the International Bank or under the Point IV program, raise much greater difficulties for successful implementation, and have remained rather modest so far.

The gradual relaxation of war fears throughout the world and the progress of economic and financial stability abroad are daily improving the opportunities for private capital to play a more important part in helping foreign economic development. Foreign countries can probably do far more to stimulate U.S. private investments than can U.S. policy itself. There exists, in many countries, a long list of legal and administrative measures which seem designed to repel rather than attract foreign capital. This is particularly true of exchange restrictions on dividend transfers and capital repatriation but extends far afield into all kinds of nationalistic measures, going much beyond what is reasonable and necessary to protect a country's interests against foreign exploitation and economic imperialism.

Further liberalization of United States trade policies is also very clearly in the national interest of the United States itself. There is no need to rehash here all the familiar arguments for freer trade. Counterarguments related to the need to foster infant industries and combat unemployment are certainly highly irrelevant today when applied to the United States economy. As the leading industrial power in the world, we have now the same strategic interest in freer trade that Britain had in the nineteenth century.

B. POLICY ADVICE TO THE DEFICIT COUNTRIES

It is in their advice to foreign countries that the dollar shortage theorists expose themselves to the most serious doubts and objections. In brief, they tend to condemn both deflation and devaluation as means to correct balance of payments deficits, they bypass tariff measures or multiple exchange rates as an alternative method of adjustment, and they fall back on direct trade and exchange restrictions and discrimination as the only escape from the evils of the dollar shortage.

If deflation is equated with a lowering of economic activity and employment, it must indeed be considered as the worst possible method of adjustment. On the other hand, the deflation bogey has often been raised against any and all types of monetary and fiscal restraints, even when designed merely to limit a country's spending to the level corresponding to the maximum resources available to it from its own production, supplemented by foreign loans, grants, and disinvestment. Such a limitation, however, is inescapable anyway. If it is not implemented by monetary and fiscal policy, it will have to be enforced by direct controls or will flow in a more roundabout fashion from internal price increases and external currency depreciation. The maintenance of full employment does not constitute a valid argument against policies directed at the avoidance of overemployment, inflationary pressures, and unsustainable deficits in the balance of payments.

The major objection of the dollar shortage theorists to exchange rate adjustments is that currency devaluation tends to deteriorate the devaluing country's terms of trade, i.e. to force down its export prices more than its import prices. This argument would carry the least weight when applied to a small country with diversified exports, which is therefore unable to exercise any strong influence on international price levels. It applied, on the other hand, with particular force to the simultaneous devaluation of many currencies with respect to the dollar in September 1949. Even in the latter case, however, the statistical evidence is of a mixed character. It is true that the terms of trade of most devaluing countries deteriorated to some extent between the first half of 1949 and the year 1950. It is also true that they improved in the same period for most of the countries which did not devalue in September 1949. On the other hand, the relationship between the rate of devaluation and the extent of the terms of trade deterioration is an extremely loose one. The Swedish terms of trade deteriorated by more than 19% at the one extreme while the Australian ones, at the other, improved by as much as 33%. The major non-devaluing country, the United States, saw its terms of trade deteriorate by 12% in the same period, i.e. by more than any devaluing country with the exception of Sweden, Austria, and Finland. If anything, the September 1949 devaluations probably tended to accentuate the underlying forces which were then favoring raw materials at the expense of manufactured goods.

The terms of trade argument against devaluation usually fails to give proper weight to the consequences of alternative policies. Let us observe, first of all, that the maintenance of an overvalued exchange rate will not, by and of itself, protect a country against a deterioration of its terms of trade. If the resulting balance of payments deficits are allowed to exercise their normal deflationary impact on domestic income and money levels, competitive adjustments may take place through a decline in internal prices and costs as well as through a decline in exchange rates. What commands the deterioration in the terms of trade, in a free market economy, is the elimination of the foreign deficit rather than the choice between the exchange rate technique and the price technique of restoring an equilibrated pattern of international prices and payments.

There is, however, a way to minimize the deterioration of the terms of trade while still improving the country's balance of payments. This is to place the whole burden of readjustment on imports, without seeking any increase in export levels. The welfare implications of such a policy are far too complex to be discussed here.[1] They are, of course, unfavorable insofar as producers and consumers are thereby forced to divert their purchases from

1. See Sidney S. Alexander, "Devaluation versus Import Restrictions as an Instrument for Improving Foreign Trade Balance," IMF *Staff Papers* (April 1951), pp. 379-96.

more to less efficient supply sources, or from more to less desired commodities, thus raising production costs and lowering real living standards. These disadvantages must be weighed against the benefits to be derived from the possible lowering of the prices paid to foreigners for the country's imports and of the possibility of exacting from them higher prices for its exports.

The first problem, therefore, is to determine to what extent a country is actually in a position to influence in this way international prices for its imports or exports by artificially decreasing its demand for the first or its supplies of the latter. Among the many factors which bear on this question, one of the most important will be the share of the country's demand and supply in relation to the world demand and supply of the commodities involved. From this point of view, a small country will usually have a lesser influence on world prices than a large country. Even a large country's imports, however, rarely absorb more than a small fraction of the world's production of any particular commodity. The ability of a country to improve its terms of trade—without provoking too heavy a deterioration in the volume of its exports and in its balance of payments—is therefore more likely to be significant in connection with its export prices than its import prices, and even then only in those relatively rare cases where a single country enjoys a monopolistic or quasi-monopolistic position in the world market for its major export goods.

Wherever such a situation exists, a country may benefit, just as a monopolist does, by reducing the volume of those exports in order to increase their unit prices. The maintenance of an overvalued rate, combined as it must then be with import restrictions, still remains, however, one of the most cumbersome techniques to achieve the desired end. The overvalued rate tends to discourage *all* exports, and not only those enjoying a monopolistic position in world markets. It also stimulates import demand and therefore places an additional burden on the administrative machinery required to reduce imports to the extent necessary to balance the country's external payments.

These difficulties can be obviated through a more direct attack on the problem. An exchange rate adjustment can be used as a general stimulant to exports and deterrent to imports, and specific export restrictions or export taxes can be used to bring about the desired reduction in the volume of only those exports in which world prices can be significantly affected by the country's supply. This should have been more obvious to all if economists had not confused the issue by discussing it in terms of abstract averages of import and export elasticities in general rather than in terms of concrete demand and supply conditions for individual commodities.[2]

The second problem is to weigh the advantages of an improvement in the terms of trade against the costs of restrictive trade policies. These costs will become larger as restrictions become tighter and tighter, have to be applied to more essential and less easily substitutable goods, and increase further and further the differential between foreign import prices and the cost of domestic substitutes. The higher the already existing level of restrictions, the greater, therefore, are the disadvantages of a further tightening of restrictions.[3]

The bias of the dollar shortage theorists in favor of direct controls and discrimination is all the more surprising, therefore, when based on the assumption of an ever increasing gap between productivity in the United States and abroad. In such a case, indeed, the closing of the gap would require ever increasing discrimination against dollar goods. The controls would have to be tightened progressively and indefinitely. The greater the cost advantages offered by American production, the less foreigners would be allowed to buy in the American market. Such a system

2. The reference to "world" demand or supply conditions may involve a similar oversimplification. Even when a country's imports of a given commodity constitute a minor share of the world production of that commodity, they may still constitute the lion's share of any particular country's production and exports. This fact may be used, through bilateral discriminatory or preferential techniques, as a powerful bargaining weapon of trade negotiation. This, rather than the economist's terms of trade argument, lies at the root of many postwar exchange control and trade restriction policies, and will require an extensive discussion in later chapters.

3. It might also be observed that the whole terms of trade argument has very little relevance to the choice of the best policy to correct a balance of payments deficit. If a country can in fact improve its terms of trade without paying an excessive price for this improvement in terms of higher costs and a reduction in consumers' choice, why should it wait to be in deficit before doing so? The same question is equally relevant to many other arguments in favor of trade or exchange controls designed to force a shift in demand from consumption to investment or from less essential to more essential categories of imports. Moreover, these objectives can generally be attained by techniques which make use of, rather than thwart, market forces and the price mechanism. Fiscal and credit policies, tariffs, multiple exchange rates, etc. can often attain the same results as quantitative controls while avoiding at least some of the major disadvantages of the latter.

could only end either in totalitarianism or, more probably, in the ultimate breakdown of the controls themselves. Exchange controls share in this respect with fluctuating exchange rates and so-called policies of "monetary sterilization" or "neutralization" a limitation common to all "compensatory" policies designed to cushion the domestic impact of balance of payments fluctuations. These policies necessarily lose their efficacy if they become one-way streets, insulating the economy against the impact of external deficits only. Neutralization policies will necessarily lead to the exhaustion of a country's monetary reserves if they prevent all downward but no upward adjustments of domestic prices and incomes. Fluctuating exchange rates will similarly end in a total monetary collapse if the national currency fluctuates only downward, but never upward. Finally, exchange controls or discrimination will rapidly become unbearable if they can never be relaxed, but need be screwed tighter and tighter to offset an ever increasing deterioration in the country's competitive position in the world economy.

The chronic exchange control policies derived from the chronic dollar shortage theories are therefore even less defensible than those theories themselves. It remains true, however, that the classical prescription of currency convertibility, exchange rate stability, and free trade tends to limit the pace of expansion of any country to that of the slowest of its major trading partners, and to spread to the world at large any depressive tendencies originating in a major trading country. The temptation to insulate their own economies from such external deflationary pressures became irresistible for most countries during the world depression of the 1930's. Tariff increases, currency depreciation, trade and exchange controls, discrimination, and bilateralism also showed, however, a similar tendency to spread from country to country, defeating the efforts of each to gain at the expense of its trade partners. Yet no country can make itself secure against such behavior on the part of others merely by maintaining the free convertibility of its own currency and a liberal import policy. An international trade and monetary system can no longer be preserved today without some collective efforts at encouraging cooperative, and discouraging disruptive, uses of national economic sovereignty.

The dollar shortage theories were right in emphasizing the special responsibility of the United States in this respect because of its enormous weight in world economic affairs. They were wrong in ascribing to this country an exclusive responsibility in the matter and, most of all, in advocating for its solution abroad policies of maximum economic insulation rather than maximum economic cooperation.

IV. SUMMARY AND CONCLUSIONS

1. The factual evidence demonstrates the close link between so-called dollar shortage phenomena and differential rates of monetary expansion in the United States and abroad arising from acute deflationary pressures in this country in the 1930's, or from abnormal inflationary pressures elsewhere during periods of wartime reconstruction. This accords fully with classical economic theory, and does not lay sufficient ground for generalizing past experience into a new theory of a chronic, structural dollar shortage.

2. In view of its higher ratio of production to needs and of potential savings to profitable investment, the United States is in a position to speed up through appropriate capital exports—public or private—desirable economic development abroad and the raising of living standards from present starvation levels in a number of countries.

3. It is not true, however, that richer countries automatically tend to develop surpluses in their balance of payments, nor that poor countries automatically tend to run into balance of payments difficulties. Balance of payments problems do not arise from the insufficiency of resources with respect to needs, but from the way in which a country's policy—or absence of policy—influences the inevitable adjustment between the first and the latter.

4. Growing concern, throughout the world, with the maintenance of economic stability and satisfactory levels of employment, economic activity, and development undoubtedly results in the adoption of national policies which interfere with the traditional mechanism by which balances of payment were kept in or brought back to equilibrium in the nineteenth century. In many cases, these interferences could easily be avoided without any substantial sacrifice of, and even with substantial benefits to, the attainment of these economic objectives, which are inseparable from modern

thought and political processes. The wastefulness of a permanent system of direct trade and exchange restrictions, in particular, is far more demonstrable and patent than its beneficial effects on a country's terms of trade, economic activity, productivity, and living standards.

5. Finally, the more valid aspects of the dollar shortage theory provide useful glimpses of a far broader problem which is in no way limited to the relationship between the United States on the one hand, and the rest of the world or some individual countries on the other. This is the problem of providing an institutional framework for international trade and payments which will cushion, rather than aggravate, the spread of recessions from one country to the others, and limit the further instability resulting from the clash of national sovereignties, particularly with respect to the adoption of tariff, trade, or exchange restrictions, the manipulation of exchange rates, and the abuse of bilateral bargaining power in trade or exchange negotiations. Countries whose peace, progress, and welfare are intimately interdependent must, in their own interest, learn to use or limit their national sovereignty in the light of their interdependence.

In brief, there is much to be forgotten but also something to be learned from the dollar shortage controversy.

CHAPTER 2

Europe's Economic Collapse
and Recovery: 1947-55

THE END OF the war had been hailed in 1945 as the dawn of a new era of economic and social progress. Bold plans had been drawn up for rapid reconstruction, expansion, and modernization of Europe's productive apparatus, and for structural reforms designed to ensure full employment, distributive justice, and social security for all.

The awakening was grim, as the early postwar years soon showed that the peace would be as hard to win as the war itself. Two full years after hostilities had ceased, Europe found itself on the verge of a financial bankruptcy whose economic consequences threatened to topple over a political and social structure already weakened by ten years of depression followed by the most destructive war in history.

I. THE BALANCE OF PAYMENTS

A. THE 1947 CRISIS

To the outside world, the most spectacular manifestation of this bankruptcy lay in the staggering $9 billion of foreign disinvestment, borrowings, and grants absorbed by Europe in 1947 in a desperate effort to maintain minimum levels of imports, consumption, and investment. In the absence of foreign aid, such a deficit would have just about wiped out the total gold and dollar holdings of Europe. As it was, gold and dollar holdings declined by about one third ($2.5 billion) over the year, the largest portion of the deficit being covered by American and Canadian aid ($5.3 billion) and by various forms of international assistance ($1 billion) from UNRRA, the International Bank for Reconstruction and Development, and the International Monetary Fund.[1]

This enormous deficit could not be attributed in any way to excessive import levels. In spite of urgent needs for consumption, restocking, re-equipment and reconstruction of war-depleted and war-devastated economies, the volume of imports was held down well below the 1938 semidepression levels. Rough estimates of the quantitative impact of these various factors are summarized in Appendix Table 7. The $9 billion gross deficit of 1947 appears to be made up of:

1. An exceptionally high level of capital exports and capital repayments (about $2 billion) arising from gold subscriptions to the capital of the newly formed International Monetary Fund and International Bank ($0.4 billion), from war settlements and capital repayments to the United States ($0.4 billion), from the liquidation of foreign-held sterling balances ($0.6 billion), and from private capital exports or capital flight;

2. An increase from $0.4 to $7.2 billion in the current account deficit between 1938 and 1947 owing to:

a) A volume decline of $5.7 billion in merchandise exports and in services and investment earnings,[2] offset only to a minor extent by a $0.3 billion reduction in the volume of imports and other current payments abroad;

b) A further deterioration of $1.3 billion in the current account balance, due to the unequal impact of price changes on merchandise and services earnings ($7.4 billion) and outpayments ($8.7 billion). This deterioration, let it be noted, was not due to a worsening of Europe's over-all terms of trade (see Appendix Table 10) but to the fact that imports of goods and services far exceeded exports, whether measured at 1938 or at 1947 prices. The over-all terms of trade—for goods and services together—appear to have been slightly better in fact in 1947 than in 1938, owing to the overvaluation of European currencies in the early postwar years.

---

1. See Appendix: Table 7, and IMF, *Balance of Payments Yearbook, 1948 and Preliminary 1949* (Washington, D.C., 1950), p. 36. The figures quoted in the text and in Appendix Table 7 refer to the OEEC countries only.

2. It may be noted in passing that in prewar years the trade deficit was as large, or larger, with other countries as with the United States. Contrary to a widespread misconception, Europe did not offset its trade deficit with the United States through trade surpluses elsewhere. It financed world-wide trade deficits through world-wide surpluses on services and investment account.

B. The 1948–55 Recovery

The recovery achieved in the following eight years is fully as spectacular as the 1947 collapse. The gross deficit of more than $9 billion registered in that year was cut sharply in each of the following years—except 1951—and replaced after 1952 by gold and dollar surpluses far in excess of the tapering-off amounts of economic aid still received from the United States (see Chart VI and Appendix Table 8).

A substantial improvement could, of course, be expected, and did in fact result from the elimination of the abnormal and temporary factors which contributed to the 1947 crisis. This was particularly the case with respect to capital movements other than aid receipts. The 1947 war settlements and gold subscriptions to the Fund and Bank were once-and-for-all transactions which had added about $800 million to the financing requirements of that year. The flight of private capital from war-devastated and war-threatened Europe continued longer, at the pace of about $1 billion a year, but was also reversed after 1951. On the other hand, official financing of development in Europe's dependencies and associated monetary areas, together with rising amortization payments on earlier postwar loans, averaged about $1 billion in recent years, while economic aid receipts fell from $5.8 billion in 1947 to less than $1 billion at the end of the period under review. Excluding economic aid, Europe remained throughout a net exporter of capital at an average rate of more than $1 billion a year. These transactions greatly affected year-to-year fluctuations and added particularly to Europe's balance of payments difficulties in 1949 and 1951, when devaluation and war fears spurred renewed flights from the currency. They play only a minor part, however, in the broad contrast between the enormous over-all deficits of the early postwar period and the large surpluses, before aid, accumulated in later years.

The most impressive and most solid sign of Europe's recovery lies indeed in the shift from the $7 billion deficit on goods and services of 1947 to the sizable and rising surpluses (from $0.7 billion to $1.8 billion) of the years 1952–56.

In volume terms, most of the gains toward a new balance were made in the early part of this period. Exports of goods and services rose by 80% in three years, regaining their prewar level as

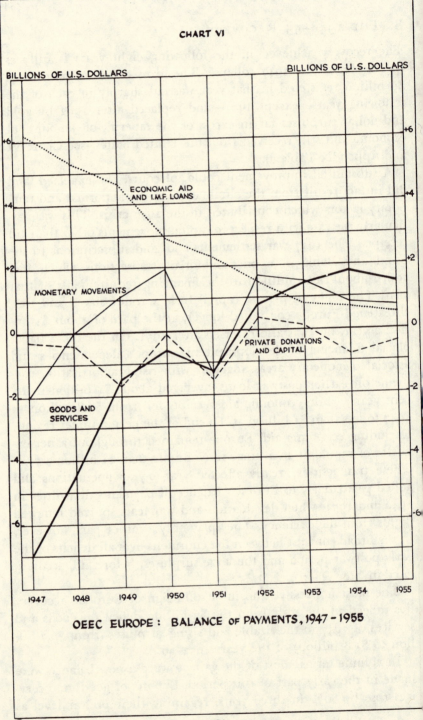

CHART VI

BILLIONS OF U.S. DOLLARS

BILLIONS OF U.S. DOLLARS

ECONOMIC AID
AND I.M.F. LOANS

MONETARY MOVEMENTS

PRIVATE DONATIONS
AND CAPITAL

GOODS AND
SERVICES

+6
+4
+2
0
-2
-4
-6

1947 1948 1949 1950 1951 1952 1953 1954 1955

OEEC EUROPE: BALANCE of PAYMENTS, 1947-1955

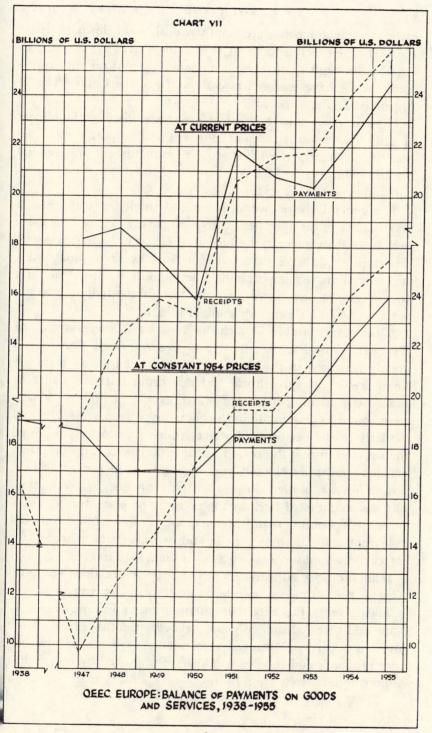

CHART VII

BILLIONS OF U.S. DOLLARS

BILLIONS OF U.S. DOLLARS

AT CURRENT PRICES

PAYMENTS

RECEIPTS

AT CONSTANT 1954 PRICES

RECEIPTS

PAYMENTS

QEEC EUROPE: BALANCE OF PAYMENTS ON GOODS
AND SERVICES, 1938-1955

35

early as 1950. Imports were simultaneously held down by trade and exchange controls to about 10% below their 1938 volume. In the absence of price changes, a moderate surplus on current account would have emerged as early as 1950 (see Chart VII and Appendix Tables 9 and 10).

These volume gains, however, were partly offset by the impact of price changes upon export proceeds and import costs. Two opposite influences need here to be distinguished: the general rise in world prices on the one hand, and the unequal rise in import and export prices on the other.

The general rise in world prices was singled out above as a major factor in the 1947 deficit. Exports having declined far more in volume than imports, the beneficial effects of higher prices on export proceeds were then overshadowed by their unfavorable effects on Europe's import bill. The opposite became true after 1949, when, at 1938 prices, exports rose substantially above imports (see Chart VIII and Appendix Table 10).

A far more durable obstacle to Europe's recovery lay in the divergent evolution of import and export prices. Europe had greatly benefited in the depression years of the 1930's from the low prices of its agricultural and raw material imports in relation to the prices of its manufactured exports. Its terms of trade were bound to deteriorate in the booming postwar years, and particularly in the period of shortages which immediately followed the war and during the period of panic purchases and stockpiling which accompanied the outbreak of hostilities in Korea. This deterioration was slowed down at first by currency overvaluation, but was accentuated later by the excessive or premature devaluations of September 1949.[3] Merchandise terms of trade thus fell catastrophically in 1951 to 73%, and over-all terms of trade—for merchandise and services—to 81% of their 1938 level.

Domestic price adjustments to the 1949 devaluations and post-Korean readjustments in international prices corrected, in the following years, this excessive deterioration of Europe's terms of trade and revealed suddenly and belatedly the full extent of the previous recovery. Measured at constant (1954) prices, the balance on goods and services would have improved by only half a billion dollars from 1951 to 1955—as against $10 billion from

3. See below, pp. 74–80.

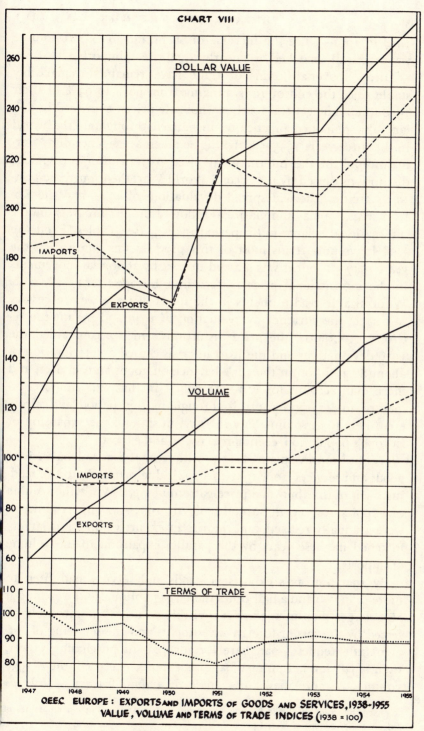

CHART VIII

DOLLAR VALUE

IMPORTS

EXPORTS

VOLUME

IMPORTS

EXPORTS

TERMS OF TRADE

QEEC EUROPE : EXPORTS AND IMPORTS OF GOODS AND SERVICES, 1938-1955
VALUE, VOLUME AND TERMS OF TRADE INDICES (1938 = 100)

1947 to 1951—since the increase of $6 billion in export volume was practically matched by a nearly equal rise of imports.

Europe's over-all terms of trade have remained remarkably stable since the end of 1951, ranging from 90% to 93% of their 1938 level. The general level of wholesale prices, expressed in dollars, also remained practically unchanged throughout the world in the three years 1953–55.[4] If this be taken as evidence of a "normalization" of the international price pattern after the violent disruptions caused by the Second World War, the immediate postwar scarcities, the widespread devaluations of 1949, and the Korean crisis, we may summarize as follows Europe's progress toward international balance in the period 1947–55 (see Tables II and 10).

1. In volume terms most of this progress was attained in the years 1947–51, but it was masked in part by abnormal movements in the international price pattern and Europe's terms of trade. While sizable readjustments in the terms of trade were necessary to correct the currency overvaluation of 1947 and permit the recovery of exports, the price distortions which accompanied the 1949 devaluations and the Korean crisis caused a deterioration of about $2.3 billion in the 1951 balance on goods and services, and more than account for Europe's deficit in that year. Imports remained under rigid controls throughout this period and recovered their 1938 volume only in 1953, in spite of the expansion of Europe's population, economic activity, and exports.

2. The improvement of $2.7 billion in the actual balance of goods and services from 1951 to 1955 is due primarily to the readjustment of the abnormal price pattern of 1951. While the volume of exports rose again substantially in 1952–55, import controls were gradually relaxed, and the rise in export volume was largely matched in these years by the parallel expansion in the volume of imports.

By 1955 Europe's exports of goods and services had risen to more than two and a half times their 1947 volume, and were about 56% larger than in 1938. Net invisible earnings—unfavorably affected by the loss of foreign investments and the servicing of foreign indebtedness—had barely recovered, in purchasing power, their 1938 level, but merchandise exports exceeded their 1938 volume by more than 70%. In its *Economic Survey of Europe*

4. See the table on "Price Indexes Expressed in U.S. Dollars" in current issues of *International Financial Statistics*.

Table II. OEEC EUROPE: IMPACT OF VOLUME AND PRICE CHANGES UPON BALANCE ON GOODS AND SERVICES

(in billions of U.S. dollars)

	Receipts (1)	Payments (2)	Balance (3 = 1 − 2)
I. *Value Changes*			
A. 1938–47	+1.7	+8.4	−6.8
B. 1948–55	+14.8	+6.2	+8.6
1. 1948–51	+9.5	+3.6	+5.9
2. 1952–55	+5.3	+2.6	+2.7
II. *Impact of Volume Changes* [a]			
A. 1938–47	−6.7	−0.4	−6.2
B. 1948–55	+15.8	+5.4	+10.3
1. 1948–51	+9.8	−0.1	+9.9
2. 1952–55	+6.0	+5.5	+0.4
III. *Impact of Price Changes* [a]			
A. 1938–47	+8.4	+8.8	−0.5
B. 1948–55	−1.0	+0.8	−1.7
1. 1948–51	−0.3	+3.7	−4.0
2. 1952–55	−0.7	−2.9	+2.3

Note:
a. Calculated at 1954 prices from Appendix Table 9.

Since the War (Geneva, 1953), the Economic Commission for Europe (ECE) had estimated at 80% the rise of merchandise exports needed to offset the postwar burdens resulting from the worsening of the terms of trade (44% of 1938 export volume), the decline in investment income (23%), normal amortization of the dollar and sterling indebtedness incurred during the war and the early postwar years (6% to 7%), and the increase in governmental expenditures abroad arising from political and military developments (6%).

This clearly reflected the same pessimistic bias which has often marked the otherwise invaluable reports of the Commission. The terms of trade impact was certainly exaggerated,[5] and the improvement of the invisible balance [6] underestimated by the Commission. In actual fact, a rise in merchandise exports of about 70%—

5. Post-Korean price readjustments were still in process at the time the report was being prepared. Even on the basis of the *Survey*'s data, however, the fact that import prices had risen by 25% more than export prices should have required an expansion of export volume by 34% rather than 44% (25% of 1938 export volume, increased by 35% to compensate for the other balance of payments burdens listed in the text).

6. Wartime overseas disinvestment was partly made up by substantial postwar investments and by higher percentage returns resulting from a shift from public utilities to oil production and refining and other industrial investments. The rising level of receipts from U.S. military expenditures in Europe was noted in the *Survey*, but the extent of later increases could hardly have been foreseen at the time.

instead of 80%—was sufficient to finance in 1955 an import level larger than, rather than equal to, that of 1938, and to provide for a surplus of $1.4 billion on goods and services. Together with a fairly stable inflow of $200 to $300 million of private remittances, this left an over-all surplus double or triple the normal rate of debt amortization envisaged in the *Survey*.

The pace and amplitude of Europe's recovery has constantly belied the excessive caution and pessimism which has colored, throughout the postwar years, most expert appraisals of Europe's future prospects and viability. An impressive array of arguments is aligned in support of this pessimism. It is pointed out, in particular, that the recent strength of Europe's balance of payments is dependent on continued high levels of prosperity in the United States, on large military expenditures in Europe by the United States, and on heavy restrictions by Europe on imports from other areas, particularly from the United States.

These arguments cannot be brushed aside lightly. Yet they should not obscure the basic difference between the present situation and that of the early postwar years. None of the three factors mentioned above adds to Europe's resources, although all three are certainly contributing to the ease with which Europe has met in recent years *from its own production* relatively high and growing levels of domestic consumption and capital formation, while improving its net asset position abroad through debt repayment, the accumulation of monetary reserves, and large overseas investments. There is, moreover, little reason to anticipate any sudden and drastic change in the situation, and every reason to hope that gradual changes can be absorbed without undue difficulty.

Thus Europe weathered with relative ease the shock of the United States recession of 1953–54 and of a considerable relaxation of dollar trade and exchange restrictions in 1954–56. A further expansion of imports should certainly be anticipated. The volume of goods and services imports in 1955 was only 27% larger than in 1938, as compared with a 44% growth in national income and a 40% growth in over-all consumption and investment expenditures. Imports have indeed been increasing at a substantial pace during the last three years, and more rapidly than exports in 1955 and 1956.

Europe should probably aim at averaging an annual surplus of about $1 billion on current account in order to finance debt repayments and a satisfactory volume of investment in its overseas territories. This leaves only a slender margin for any further expansion of imports unmatched by corresponding increases in exports. There is, however, no reason to believe that further trade liberalization would curtail savings and increase lastingly the overall level of consumption and investment expenditures. In the absence of inflationary financing by the monetary and banking system,[7] it should merely lead to a shift of demand from home-produced goods to foreign goods, and therefore release productive resources for exports. Difficulties would arise, however, if exports failed to rise owing to the uncompetitiveness of Europe's prices[8] or to the obstacles placed by foreign restrictions on the expansion of its exports. In this case, the shift of demand from home goods to imported goods would initially result in balance of payments deficits and deflationary pressures on production, employment, and incomes. Under modern political conditions, this could hardly fail to stimulate a relapse into trade restrictions, or inflationary monetary and fiscal policies, or both.

The tapering off of United States military expenditures in Europe would raise similar problems of finding new employment for the domestic resources released in the process, and of maintaining balance between Europe's dollar earnings and dollar expenditures. An over-all balance on goods and services would have been maintained in 1954 even if Europe had received no payments whatsoever from this source, but this over-all balance would have been made up of a large deficit toward the United States, offset by an equal surplus on other countries. This latter surplus, however, was financed in large part from European credits and would not have provided the dollars needed to cover Europe's deficit with the United States and other dollar area countries.

Further progress toward currency convertibility and trade liberalization on a nondiscriminatory basis will thus depend on Europe's ability to offset through larger dollar earnings a substantial portion of any additional dollar imports and of any contingent declines in its dollar receipts from United States military expenditures. This need not, of course, involve a corresponding expansion in direct exports by Europe to the United States, but it requires

7. See below, pp. 49–51.
8. Trade liberalization should, by itself, contribute to the lowering of production costs and the improvement of Europe's competitiveness in world markets.

an over-all expansion in Europe's exports to the world, and in United States imports from the world.

The maintenance of international payments equilibrium at high levels of production and low levels of trade barriers requires, first of all, the adoption by the major surplus countries of trade policies compatible with the effectiveness of price and exchange rate adjustments by the deficit countries. It equally requires of the latter the preservation—or restoration—of a competitive pattern of prices and exchange rates and of internal monetary and fiscal policies which maintain over-all demand for consumption and investment within the limits of these countries' productive capacity, augmented by the capital imports they are able to elicit in order to accelerate their economic development or reconstruction.

These problems cannot be fruitfully explored on the basis of balance of payments statistics alone. These record but do not explain the improvement of Europe's external position from the enormous deficit of 1947 to the moderate surpluses of recent years. In order to understand and appraise the broader economic forces underlying these changes, we must now turn to other economic data, particularly to the over-all pattern of Europe's production and expenditures (sec. II), to the domestic monetary policies which financed or held down the external deficits (sec. III), and to the double impact of domestic monetary liquidity and international cost competitiveness on Europe's export and import levels (sec. IV).

II. OVER-ALL PRODUCTION AND EXPENDITURE

Balance of payments statistics record a country's deficit in terms of its external transactions alone. A current account deficit thus represents the excess of a country's imports of goods and services over its exports.

In national accounts statistics, the same deficit is alternatively recorded as an excess of over-all expenditure above over-all production. This necessary identity is, of course, obvious: If a country buys more abroad than it sells abroad, its citizens taken as a group must spend more money currently than they currently earn.

Its merit is to draw attention to another commonplace truth, sometimes obscured in learned balance of payments discussions: In down-to-earth terms, a country's deficit—like an individual's deficit—can always be brought back to its failure to live within its income.

A. THE 1947 CRISIS (*see Chart IX, Table III, and Appendix Table 11*)

Such was clearly the case in 1947 Europe. Consumption and investment expenditures of $148 billion exceeded production by about $7 billion, this excess being necessarily made up by an equal excess of imports—of goods and services—over exports.

Measured in constant (1954) prices, the volume of production had declined by about $13 billion since 1938. This decline was matched about equally by the contraction of consumption expenditure and by the increase in the foreign deficit.

Over-all expenditures exceeded over-all production by only 5%, but this seemingly modest imbalance was enough to create an enormous deficit in Europe's external transactions, since it was met by an excess of about 65% in imports over exports of goods and services. This disproportionate impact is, of course, easily explained by the fact that foreign transactions, for any large country or area, are normally dwarfed by domestic transactions internal to the country or area itself. Yet it is striking to reflect that a curtailment of expenditure of roughly 5% would have been sufficient to wipe out the enormous deficit of 1947 Europe.

Any substantial cut in expenditures, however, would have to bear on consumption rather than on investment if it were not to entail, sooner or later, further declines in production. Private consumption per capita was already 12% below the semidepression level of 1938 and would have had to fall to less than 80% of the 1938 level in order to adjust expenditures to current production. Far more drastic cuts would have been required in countries such as Germany, Austria, Greece, Italy, or France, where production had declined much below the average for Europe as a whole,[1] while it was already well beyond prewar levels in Switzerland, the United Kingdom, and the Scandinavian countries.

1. Unpublished estimates of OEEC show production declines of 32% to 43% in the first three countries.

Nor is this all. The contraction of expenditures would result in a decline of economic activity and employment rather than in an improvement of the foreign balance, unless the resources thus released could be channeled into increased exports or could be used locally in substitution of imports. If exports did not increase, a 39% contraction of imports—of goods and services—to less than 60% of their 1938 volume would have been necessary to wipe out the 1947 deficit. Alternatively, a 65% expansion of exports would have been required to achieve equilibrium at the 1947 level of imports. Either solution would undoubtedly have involved greater cuts in consumption than those indicated above. The substitution of home production for imports would have been well-nigh impossible in many cases and would have been accompanied in others by sharp increases in costs and lowering of productivity. On the other hand, an expansion of exports of the magnitude required to balance Europe's external transactions would—and in fact did—involve a considerable deterioration in the terms of trade and, therefore, a further curtailment of consumption in real terms.

The adjustment of expenditure to 1947 production income could hardly have been effected, in practice, through monetary and fiscal measures alone. Europe would inevitably have undergone even sharper rates of inflation, or tighter rationing controls, or both, than those actually experienced during that period. The resulting burdens on the monetary system and on the administrative machinery of enforcement would almost certainly have strained to the breaking point in several countries the functioning of free economic institutions and the maintenance of social order within the framework of political democracy.

B. THE 1948–55 RECOVERY (see Chart IX,
Table III, and Appendix Table 11)

These dangers were averted through the continuation of large-scale deficits in the balance of payments, financed partly from a decline of monetary reserves in 1947 and 1951, but primarily from American aid, which totaled more than $4 billion a year in 1947–49 and $26 billion for the period 1946–55 as a whole (see Appendix Table 12).[2]

2. These figures include long-term government loans together with grants-in-aid, since both of these techniques were primarily motivated by similar political con-

These American aid programs were often presented by their defenders as indispensable to cover "incompressible" balance of payments deficits in Western Europe. Their opponents, on the other hand, were quick to point out that this was sheer nonsense and that European deficits were largely the *result* of our aid, and would perforce have been corrected much earlier in the absence of such aid. This is indeed perfectly true.

The real significance of U.S. aid was, first of all, to permit a much faster rate of restocking, reconstruction, and new investment, and thus a much faster recovery of production than would have been possible otherwise. It did not contribute so much to the re-equilibration of Europe's balance of payments as to the fact that this equilibrium could be reached at much higher levels of production, consumption, imports, and exports, involving a much fuller use of the benefits of international trade.

Secondly, American aid helped preserve during the worst of the postwar years a level of consumption which, although considerably lower than before the war, succeeded in averting the threatening breakdown of Europe's economic, social, and political order. The large deficits, financed by foreign aid, reduced correspondingly the internal inflationary pressures bequeathed by the war and further augmented by the excess of investment over voluntary savings during the reconstruction period. They probably averted a total monetary collapse in a number of countries, and facilitated everywhere the restoration of the monetary system and the functioning of free economic institutions.

The elimination of the foreign deficits was not achieved through a curtailment of consumption, investment, and imports, but through the persistent growth of production and exports. In volume terms,[3] production increased by $78 billion (or 57%) and exports by $16 billion (more than 160%) between 1947 and 1955.

In spite of the terms of trade deterioration which accompanied the recovery of exports, a mere 13% of the production increase sufficed to turn into a moderate surplus the huge foreign deficit

---

siderations. They exclude, however, military transfers in kind under mutual aid programs (Appendix Table 12, col. 1), since such transfers result essentially from joint defense plans and would be most unlikely to take place under political circumstances permitting the cessation of such financing and programs.

3. Dollar figures are calculated at constant, 1954 prices and exchange rates. See Table III and Appendix Table 11.

Table III. OEEC EUROPE: VOLUME CHANGES IN PRODUCTION AND EXPENDITURE, 1938–55

	In Billions of U.S. Dollars		In % of Production Changes		In % of Previous Levels			In % of Previous Levels Per Capita		
	1938-47	1947-55	1938-47	1947-55	1938-47	1947-55	1938-55	1938-47	1947-55	1938-55
I. Production	−12.9	+77.9	−100	+100	−9	+57	+44	−15	+45	+25
II. Expenditure	−6.7	+67.5	−52	+87	−4	+47	+40	−10	+36	+22
A. Consumption	−7.2	+50.0	−56	+64	−6	+42	+34	−12	+31	+16
1. Private	−7.5	+42.1	−58	+54	−7	+43	+33	−13	+32	+15
2. Public	+0.3	+7.9	+2	+10	+1	+35	+37	−5	+25	+19
B. Investment	+0.6	+17.5	+5	+23	+2	+69	+74	−5	+56	+51
III. Balance (I − II = IIIA − IIIB)	−6.2	+10.3	−48	+13						
A. Exports	−6.7	+15.8	−52	+20	−41	+163	+55	−45	+143	+35
B. Imports	−0.4	+5.4	−3	+7	−2	+29	+26	−8	+19	+10

Source:
Derived from corresponding entries, at constant (1954) prices and exchange rates, in Appendix Table 11.

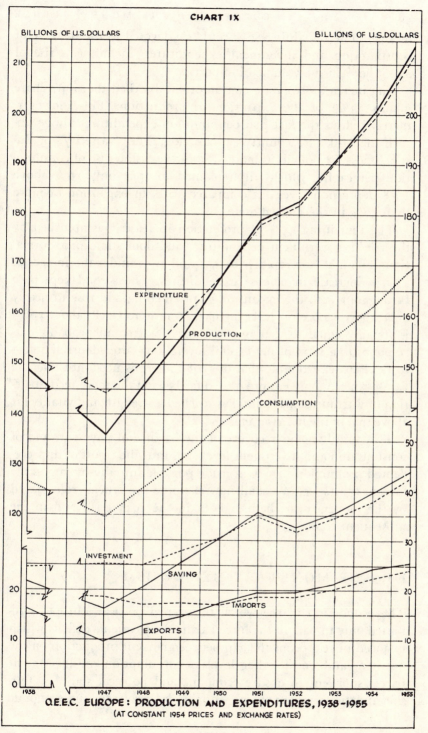

CHART IX

BILLIONS OF U.S.DOLLARS

BILLIONS OF U.S.DOLLARS

EXPENDITURE

PRODUCTION

CONSUMPTION

INVESTMENT

SAVING

IMPORTS

EXPORTS

1938 1947 1948 1949 1950 1951 1952 1953 1954 1955

O.E.E.C. EUROPE: PRODUCTION AND EXPENDITURES, 1938-1955
(AT CONSTANT 1954 PRICES AND EXCHANGE RATES)

47

of 1947. The remaining 87% could be devoted to the increase of consumption and investment expenditures, including a rise of about 30% in the volume of imports.

The increase of private consumption absorbed the lion's share (about 54%) of the expansion of production. This, however, merely reflects the fact that consumption expenditures always absorb the bulk of a country's production. The "austerity" of Europe's postwar policies is marked in the very slow rise of consumption per capita, which still remained in 1955 only 15% above 1938 depression levels, as compared with an expansion of more than 50% in the United States.

The remaining 33% of production increases was absorbed by the rise in government expenditures and domestic capital formation. The first rose rapidly in 1951 and 1952 under the impact of a 60% increase in defense expenditures. The second kept pace throughout with the expansion of production, and rose to nearly 75% above its prewar level in 1955. Its ratio to GNP (about 20%) is roughly equal to that in the United States and probably corresponds to a ratio of net capital formation—after depreciation— to GNP at least double that of 1938. There is no doubt that the European economy has progressed far beyond the mere reconstruction of wartime damage and has reached a strength and vitality far above that of the interwar era.

This simultaneous recovery of the balance of payments and of consumption and investment levels was thus the result of unprecedented production increases, made possible initially by large-scale foreign assistance. We shall now examine the crucial role played by the monetary mechanism both in the 1947 crisis and in the subsequent recovery.

III. THE MONETARY MECHANISM

The economic collapse which threatened postwar Europe is reflected only in part in the huge balance of payments deficits which financed in real terms the gap between current production on the one hand and, on the other, levels of consumption and investment barely sufficient to ensure economic and political stability. Further inflationary phenomena, equally dangerous for the economic and political order, were apparent in the violent price rises and exchange depreciation experienced in many countries, and in the comprehensive techniques of external trade and exchange restrictions and domestic price controls and rationing used everywhere in an effort to combat or conceal the internal and external depreciation of the national currency.

These inflationary pressures varied greatly, in both form and extent, from country to country in 1947, and a similar diversity characterizes the manner and timing of the subsequent readjustments. A thorough analysis would require a detailed examination, country by country, of these contrasting developments and policies. This would far exceed the scope of this chapter, but some highly suggestive comparisons may be derived from a simple analysis built upon comparable data on national income, foreign deficit, internal prices, and money supply, readily available from standard international sources.[1]

The role of monetary policy in an open economy cannot be properly understood unless external deficits and internal inflationary pressures are analyzed jointly as complementary—and in part alternative—manifestations of an *ex ante* excess of over-all *demand* for consumption and investment above the over-all production of goods and services. *Expenditure* can exceed production only to the extent that the excess demand is actually satisfied by an equivalent excess of imports over exports, i.e. by a foreign deficit on goods and services account. The portion of the excess demand that is not satisfied in this manner, however, continues to exert upward pressures within the economy itself, and may either be met by production increases or give rise to inflationary readjustments in the form of price rises (open inflation) or rationing (latent inflation). As long as excess demand persists, therefore, policies designed to control external deficits can only aggravate domestic inflationary pressures, and policies designed to combat the latter can only aggravate the former. Only the removal of the excess demand itself can meet both problems simultaneously.

It is here that the crucial role of internal monetary mechanisms and policies emerges most clearly. The root causes of the excess

1. I hope to edit in the near future a series of national studies, by central bank experts, on postwar monetary policies in the major European countries.

demand may, of course, be extremely varied, and may originate outside as well as within the sphere of monetary decisions as such. Yet the financing of a level of effective demand in excess of production income is necessarily and intimately related to the current and past performance of the monetary and banking sector of the economy.

Insofar as excess demand actually results in an *ex post* excess of expenditure over production, it will be matched by an equivalent deficit on goods and services account. Such a deficit must necessarily have been financed by a corresponding amount of net foreign disinvestment—depletion of foreign assets, capital imports, or gifts received from abroad—by the community itself, or by its banking system. In the latter case, however, the net sales of foreign exchange by the banks have been paid for to them in national currency by the banking public, and the money supply should therefore have declined by an amount equal to the banks' loss of international reserves, unless the banking system has reconstituted it simultaneously through net bank lending or "internal credit monetization." (This term will be used here to designate an expansion of bank loans matched by additions to money supply rather than by an expansion in other liabilities of the banking system.) [2] Let us also define as "total monetization" the sum of internal credit monetization by the banks and of the other resources procured abroad by the nonbanking sectors of the economy through net foreign disinvestment. Data on total monetization would be difficult to assemble directly, but the above definitions permit us to estimate it indirectly as the sum of the foreign deficit, on goods and services account, plus the increase—or minus the decrease—in the money supply. Conversely, we also see that the foreign deficit, financed externally by net foreign disinvestment, must also be financed internally either from total monetization or

2. This definition of domestic credit monetization in terms of money supply only is dictated by the nature of readily available and broadly comparable data. A wider definition of liquid assets would be more illuminating for a detailed analysis of monetary developments in a single country. Let us note, in passing, the exclusion of government deposits from the IMF statistics of money supply used in this study. Domestic credit monetization reflects, therefore, the difference between the evolution of all domestic assets of the banks on the one hand and, on the other, the changes in their domestic liabilities other than currency and demand deposits in the hands of the public. It can be measured, alternatively, by the excess increase of money supply over and above the increase—or plus the decrease—in the net international assets of the banking system.

from the dishoarding of previously accumulated cash balances.[3]

This analysis of the foreign deficit can now be broadened into an analysis of the inflationary process as a whole, showing that foreign deficits and domestic expansionary—or inflationary—pressures constitute alternative forms of economic adaptation to current or past monetization. The above relationships indicate, indeed, that current monetization, insofar as it is not absorbed by foreign deficits, results in an increase of the money supply. To that extent, monetization does not finance an actual excess of expenditures over production income, but it may still stimulate an excess of current demand for consumption and investment over the total goods and services, valued at current prices, available from current production and from the excess of imports over exports. This excess demand may then:

1. Induce—and be satisfied by—an increase in the volume of production;
2. Stimulate—and be thwarted by—rising prices;
3. Be restrained by rationing controls.

Finally, it is also possible that the increase in money supply will be absorbed by a rise in the public's demand for cash balances, and that the additional money created will not, at least for the time being, feed any increase in demand.

Production and price increases can be measured statistically from readily available data or estimates. The comparative tables presented below [4] will boldly label as "domestic inflation index" the index of money supply deflated by the index of GNP volume. Changes in this inflation index are necessarily accompanied and absorbed by the combined impact of changes in prices and changes in liquidity, the latter being defined by changes in

---

3. We can equate the foreign deficit (F) to net foreign disinvestment by the public (D_p) and by the banking system (D_b). But D_b is equal to the contraction in money supply $(-\triangle M)$ *plus* internal credit monetization by the banks (C_b). Total monetization (C) has been defined, on the other hand, as the sum of C_b and D_p. We thus have, in succession:

$$F = D_p + D_b \tag{1}$$
$$D_b = C_b - \triangle M \tag{2}$$
$$C = C_b + D_p = D_b + \triangle M + D_p \tag{3}$$
$$C = F + \triangle M \tag{4}$$

We can also write:

$$F = C - \triangle M, \text{ or } \triangle M = C - F \tag{5}$$

4. Pp. 56, 65 and 321.

the ratio of cash holdings to the value of GNP at current prices.[5]

The main drawback of this schema lies in the ambiguous nature of the liquidity index, which fails to distinguish between "spontaneous" and "enforced" absorption of cash by the economy and to reveal the relative permanence or volatility of liquidity adjustments. Spontaneous changes in liquidity may occur for a variety of reasons, such as shifts of confidence in the national currency, expectations as to the future course of prices, variations in income distribution and payments habits, etc. On the other hand, exchange controls and domestic rationing may limit the individuals' ability to spend their cash as they would wish and induce them to retain—at least temporarily—larger cash balances than they would willingly accumulate otherwise. There is, of course, no reason to expect that in the absence of such measures the ratio of cash to GNP would automatically return to any fixed and unchanging prewar level, and least of all to that of 1938.

Yet large changes in the liquidity index do deserve attention since they often reflect a peculiarly precarious and unstable form of adaptation to monetary inflation. If a large increase in liquidity coincides, for instance, with the maintenance of comprehensive price controls and rationing, and if the subsequent relaxation of these controls is accompanied by a decline in the liquidity index, we cannot go far wrong in diagnosing the initial situation as one of overliquidity. This may lead us in turn to investigate whether existing controls will be adequate to repress effectively and permanently the price impact of overliquidity, whether overliquidity may not have other consequences escaping the influence of such controls, and what may be the probable results of their later relaxation. More generally speaking, whenever substantial rises of liquidity are associated with parallel increases in internal moneti-

5. The various relationships described in the text can be simply expressed as follows:

$$C - F = \triangle M,$$

$$\frac{m}{q} = i = p \cdot l \text{ and, therefore,}$$

$$l = \frac{m}{g} = \frac{m}{pq},$$

where m represents the index of money supply, q the index of GNP at constant prices, i the inflation index, p the index of GNP prices, l the index of liquidity, and g the index of GNP at current prices.

zation of bank credit rather than with declines in prices or production, we should have little reason to trust that spontaneous
cash hoarding will permanently absorb the increase in money
supply, and we should be prepared to face the impact of later cash
dishoarding upon domestic prices or the balance of payments.

The absence, relaxation, or breakdown of price and rationing
controls has, indeed, been accompanied uniformly by price rises
which did, in a number of cases, exceed the rises in the inflation
index, and which therefore brought down the index of liquidity
well below its previous levels. An extremely low index of liquidity
may often reflect a flight from the currency, typical of so-called
"hyperinflation." This adds further fuel to domestic price rises
and external deficits and makes it far more difficult to control
them. On the other hand, if currency confidence can be restored,
the subsequent rebuilding of cash balances to normal levels will
ease the task of monetary rehabilitation and facilitate particularly
the reconstitution of international reserves.[6]

Let us now review, in the light of these concepts, the monetary
evolution of European countries in the postwar period.

A. THE 1947 CRISIS (see Chart X and Table IV)

The war years and the early postwar years led almost inevitably to
a considerable amount of credit monetization in Europe. The
prosecution of the war and the financing of urgent needs for restocking, re-equipment, and reconstruction had involved a continuous recourse to bank credit and large additions to the money
supply and other liquid assets in the hands of the public.

The scope of this credit monetization varied enormously, of
course, from country to country. Switzerland and Sweden, for instance, had been untouched by the hostilities while, at the other
extreme, Germany, Greece, and Italy had suffered most from war
destruction and civil strife.

A number of countries put into operation in 1944 and 1945
so-called "monetary purges" designed to mop up a portion of the
excess liquidities inherited from wartime credit monetization.
These purges were particularly extensive in Austria, Belgium, the
Netherlands, and Norway. While they fell short of their pro-

6. These theoretical deductions will find empirical confirmation in the analysis
which follows. They also fit admirably the analysis of inflationary phenomena in the
1920's and illuminate particularly the so-called "Poincaré miracle" of France.

claimed goals and were partially offset by renewed monetary expansion at a rapid pace immediately afterward, they succeeded in keeping inflationary pressures within more manageable proportions.

Foreign deficits—financed by the depletion of monetary reserves, other foreign disinvestments, borrowings, and gifts—also reduced somewhat the scope of internal monetary expansion associated with over-all credit monetization.

The net result of these various experiences and policies still left, in 1947, a considerable residue of monetary expansion in all European countries. Money supply had risen to twice its prewar level in Switzerland, two and a half to four and a half times in the United Kingdom, Belgium, the Netherlands, and the Scandinavian countries, eight times in France, thirty-two times in Italy, and sixty times in Greece.

This expansion was necessarily and inevitably offset by corresponding changes in production, prices, and liquidity, but the relative role of these alternative types of adaptation varied greatly with the strength of the initial inflationary pressures in each country and with the choice and effectiveness of the anti-inflationary policies adopted to combat them.

Increases in production moderated, but only very slightly, the inflationary pressures in Switzerland and the northern countries. On the other hand, production was still below prewar levels in Germany and the southern countries—particularly Greece—aggravating the inflationary problem of these countries.[7] Our inflation index (money supply divided by GNP at constant prices) thus stood in 1947 at from nearly seven times to ninety times its prewar level in Austria, France, Italy, and Greece, as against approximately twice to three and a half times prewar in the other countries listed in Table IV.

The inflationary pressures which thus confronted the southern countries were clearly more than price controls and rationing could handle, particularly in a highly individualistic environment, where the political cohesion and the administrative machinery necessary for enforcement were traditionally weak and had been weakened further by military war, German occupation,

7. The term "northern countries" will be used throughout to designate the United Kingdom, the Netherlands, Denmark, Norway, and Sweden, and the term "southern countries" for France, Italy, and Greece.

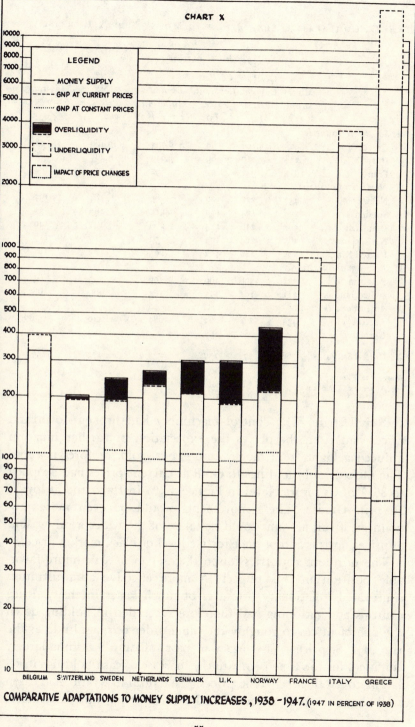

CHART X

LEGEND
— MONEY SUPPLY
----- GNP AT CURRENT PRICES
········· GNP AT CONSTANT PRICES
■ OVERLIQUIDITY
▢ UNDERLIQUIDITY
▢ IMPACT OF PRICE CHANGES

BELGIUM SWITZERLAND SWEDEN NETHERLANDS DENMARK U.K. NORWAY FRANCE ITALY GREECE

COMPARATIVE ADAPTATIONS TO MONEY SUPPLY INCREASES, 1938 – 1947. (1947 IN PERCENT OF 1938)

Table IV. COMPARATIVE ADAPTATIONS TO MONEY SUPPLY INCREASES, 1938–47

(*1947 in % of 1938*)

	Money Supply (1)	GNP at Current Prices (2)	GNP at Constant Prices (3)	Domestic Inflation (4 = 1 ÷ 3)	GNP Prices (5 = 2 ÷ 3)	Liquidity (6 = 1 ÷ 2 = 4 ÷ 5)
I. Southern Countries						
Greece	5,995	13,106	68	8,764	19,160	46
Italy	3,258	3,810	89	3,649	4,267	85
France	811	941	91	892	1,034	86
II. Northern Countries						
Norway	437	222	120	363	184	197
Sweden	255	194	119	214	163	131
Denmark	302	216	113	266	191	140
Netherlands	263	225	103	256	219	117
United Kingdom	302	186	102	295	182	162
III. Belgium and Switzerland						
Belgium	332	396	109	306	365	84
Switzerland	211	194	115	183	169	108
IV. Austria and Germany						
Austria	433	278	63	687	440	156
Germany		68	57		120	
V. United States	366	271	157	233	173	135

Sources and notes:
See Appendix Table 14.

and civil strife. The control machinery had broken down and prices had risen sharply as the expectation of further inflation induced a flight from money into goods, gold, or foreign assets. The ratio of cash holdings to GNP at current prices had dropped to 86% of its prewar level in France, 85% in Italy, and as low as 46% in Greece. These movements would be even more pronounced if full account could be taken of the widespread evasion of price controls and of the effective level of black market prices.

The northern countries found themselves in a far more favorable position in this respect. A more effective administration confronted inflationary pressures of much lesser intensity. Price controls and rationing had therefore succeeded in holding down the rise of prices to roughly the same order of magnitude as the rise in U.S. prices. The legacy of past inflation was thus largely confined, for the time being, to the increase of cash holdings in relation to GNP at current prices. The liquidity ratio had risen well above the prewar level in all five countries, but particularly in the United Kingdom (by 62%) and in Norway (by 97%).[8] Even these increases did not reflect the full extent of a monetary overliquidity which also found outlets in expanded holdings of government securities to which pegging policies leant all the characteristics of "near-money."

The rate of monetary expansion in Belgium and Switzerland— reduced in the first country by the stiff monetary purge of 1944— was roughly comparable to that of the northern countries. The difference lay in the fact that these increases had here been almost exactly offset by price adaptations, leaving little or no residue of the excess monetary liquidity which characterized the northern group of countries and which constituted a continuing threat both to price stability and to balance of payments equilibrium in these countries.[9]

Comparable calculations for Austria and Germany are made highly speculative or downright impossible by territorial changes, and by the unavailability or incompleteness of monetary statistics for the early postwar years. It is clear, however, that the rate of monetary expansion and the decline in production had created in both countries inflationary problems of formidable magnitude. Two successive monetary purges—in November 1945 and December 1947—had canceled about four fifths of the Austrian currency circulation, but still left it at more than four times its prewar level at the end of 1947. Prices had risen roughly in the same proportion, but production declines of nearly 40% had raised the ratio of currency holdings to national income to more than one and a half times its prewar level. As for Germany, it presented in 1947 the most extreme example of an overliquidity crisis. Official prices and wages had risen by only 20% since prewar days, while the volume of money had soared to astronomical figures, and production dropped to less than 60% of its 1938 volume. The monetary system approached ultimate collapse, money being practically superseded by ration coupons on the one hand and black market barter on the other.

The varying nature of the 1938–47 adaptations to credit monetization in the European countries may thus be briefly summarized as follows:

8. Comparable calculations for the United States show an increase of about one third in the liquidity ratio from 1938 to 1947.
9. See below, sec. IV.

1. In the southern countries, monetary expansion had resulted in sharp price increases, outdistancing the rise in money supply in relation to production, and creating a situation of monetary underliquidity verging on hyperinflation.

2. In the northern countries, price increases had been held in check by comprehensive price controls and rationing, at the cost of growing overliquidity (or latent inflation).

3. In Switzerland and Belgium, monetary expansion had been offset almost exactly by the increases of prices and production, and monetary liquidity had approximately returned to the 1938 levels.

The significance of this classification emerges with particular force when one examines the comparative evolution of credit monetization, money supply, prices, and liquidity in the same countries during the following years.

B. The 1948–55 Readjustments

The restoration of monetary balance posed a triple problem to the monetary authorities. First of all, current inflation had to be arrested, i.e. the current generation of purchasing power through internal and external credit and disinvestment had to be brought down to a rate compatible with equilibrium in the balance of payments and a normal growth of money supply. Secondly, the overliquidity inherited from past inflation had to be reabsorbed by production or price increases or by a contraction of existing levels of money supply. Thirdly, exchange rate adjustments would be necessary to counter the resulting distortions in the international cost pattern of the various countries, and to offset the other structural changes affecting the balance of international payments.

1. The Cessation of Current Inflation (see Charts XI, XII, and XIII, and Appendix Table 13)

Current inflation was arrested at a very early stage in Switzerland, Belgium, and the northern countries. In only one country—Norway—did the rate of monetization ever exceed 10% in any year after 1948. In all other countries, it averaged only from −2% to +4% a year over the whole period 1949–55.

In Denmark and Norway, the largest part by far of the purchasing power created by such monetization was offset by continuing balance of payments deficits amply financed by foreign aid

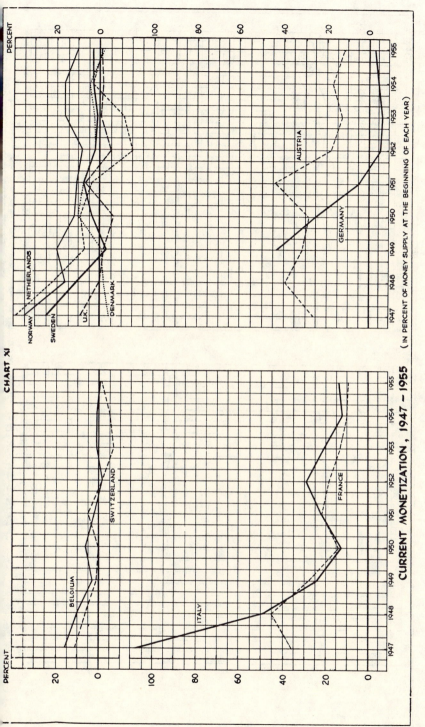

CHART XI

CURRENT MONETIZATION, 1947 – 1955

(IN PERCENT OF MONEY SUPPLY AT THE BEGINNING OF EACH YEAR)

59

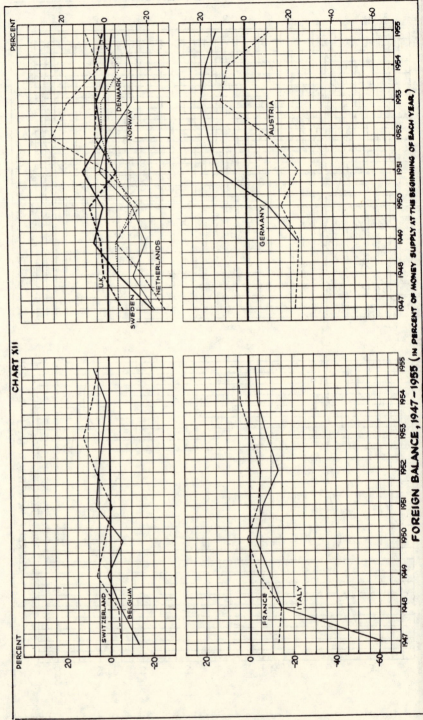

CHART XII

FOREIGN BALANCE, 1947-1955 (IN PERCENT OF MONEY SUPPLY AT THE BEGINNING OF EACH YEAR.)

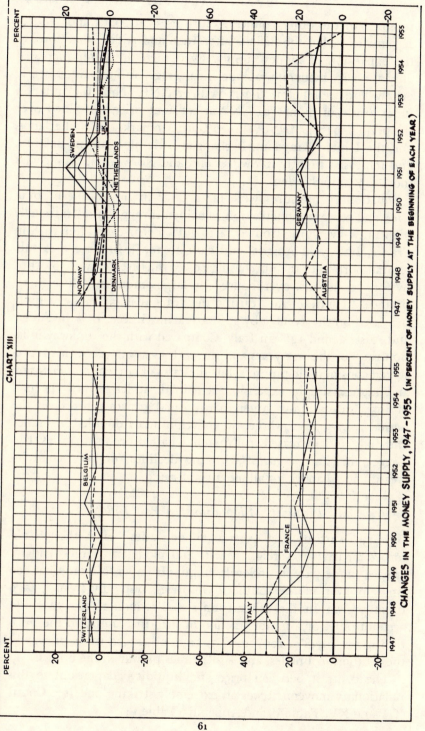

CHART XIII

CHANGES IN THE MONEY SUPPLY, 1947-1955 (IN PERCENT OF MONEY SUPPLY AT THE BEGINNING OF EACH YEAR)

61

receipts. In the other countries, surpluses on goods and services account exceeded the deficits after 1948 and added, therefore, to the expansion of money supply. Even then the latter increased only at a very moderate rate, on the average, and remained nearly everywhere well below the growth of GNP. Thus the inflation index (ratio of money to GNP at constant prices) declined over the period 1947–55 by 10% to 20% in Denmark, the Netherlands, and the United Kingdom. It changed little, if at all, in Belgium and increased slightly in Switzerland and Norway, and somewhat more (15%) in Sweden.

Inflationary pressures were far greater in the southern countries, and current monetization remained throughout at extremely high rates, averaging from 15% to 20% a year even after 1948 in France, Italy, and Austria, and close to 100% in Greece. A substantial portion of the purchasing power thus created was absorbed by foreign deficits, overfinanced by large amounts of foreign assistance. In spite of this, during the years 1949–55 money supply increased on the average by 20% a year in Greece, 15% in France and Austria, and 12% in Italy. Compared with the runaway inflation rates of the war years and the early postwar years, this represented considerable progress, but the rates of current monetization and money supply expansion remained, at least until the end of 1955, substantially larger than normal growth rates. Over the period 1947–55 as a whole, the inflation index doubled in France and Italy and increased to five and a half times its 1947 level in Greece, in sharp contrast with the declines (or very small increases) noted above for all other countries.

2. Price and Liquidity Adaptations to Past Inflation

By 1955 wartime and postwar monetization, even though absorbed in part by foreign deficits and monetary purges, had increased money supply to levels ranging from 30 to more than 500 times prewar in the southern countries, but only from 3 to 6 times prewar in the other countries. Production growth could account only for a minor fraction of such increases, and the inflation index (1938 = 100) stood at from 20 to 500 times prewar in the southern countries, and 2 to 4 times prewar in the others.

The contrast between price and liquidity adaptations to this inflationary movement was an extremely striking one (see Charts XIV and XV, Table V, and Appendix Table 14).

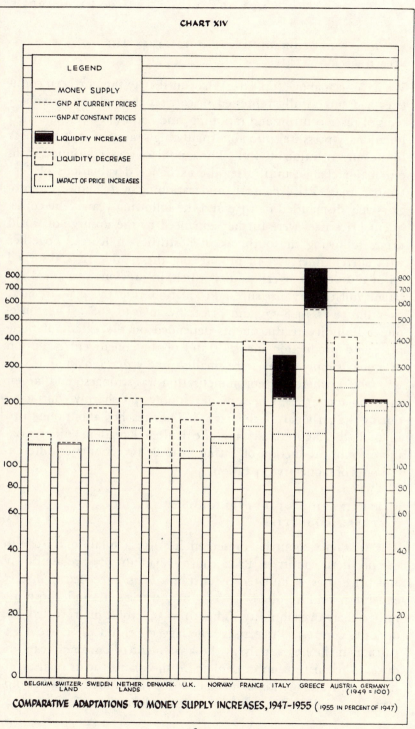

CHART XIV

LEGEND

— MONEY SUPPLY
----- GNP AT CURRENT PRICES
········· GNP AT CONSTANT PRICES
■ LIQUIDITY INCREASE
☐ LIQUIDITY DECREASE
☐ IMPACT OF PRICE INCREASES

BELGIUM SWITZER- SWEDEN NETHER- DENMARK U.K. NORWAY FRANCE ITALY GREECE AUSTRIA GERMANY
         LAND   LANDS   (1949 = 100)

COMPARATIVE ADAPTATIONS TO MONEY SUPPLY INCREASES, 1947-1955 (1955 IN PERCENT OF 1947)

A) THE ABSORPTION OF OVERLIQUIDITY IN THE
NORTHERN COUNTRIES

We have seen above (pp. 56–7) that until 1947 the northern countries had successfully repressed price rises through extensive systems of price controls and rationing, and had therefore channeled
inflationary pressures into abnormally high ratios of cash balances
to the current value of GNP. These policies were continued without major change until after the exchange devaluations of September 1949. Price controls and rationing were, however, progressively dismantled in 1950 and the following years. The consequent price rises were further enhanced by the upsurge of world
prices following the outbreak of hostilities in Korea. Together
with current increases in production, these price rises absorbed
all or most of the overliquidity which, in previous years, had fed
latent inflationary pressures. Production rose by 25% to 60%
over the years 1948–55, and prices by 40% to 50%. The consequent liquidity readjustments depended on the extent of these
price and production increases and of the concurrent evolution
of money supply. They were smallest in Sweden (20%) and Norway (30%), where current monetization was strongest, and largest
in Denmark (45%), where money supply was sharply contracted
during the early part of this period. They reached about one third
in both the Netherlands and the United Kingdom, differential
increases in production offsetting in these two countries differential rates of monetary expansion.

B) ELIMINATION OF UNDERLIQUIDITY IN THE
SOUTHERN COUNTRIES

The southern countries presented in 1947 a total contrast with
the northern countries. Price controls had already broken down,
and price rises, stimulated by currency fears, exceeded monetary
expansion and resulted—except in Austria—in underliquidity
rather than overliquidity. The 1947–55 evolution revealed the
opposite contrast: Price rises now lagged behind the current expansion in money supply as the abatement of currency fears induced a reconstitution of depleted cash balances with relation to
production and national income. Prices continued to move upward, but under the pressure of continued current inflation rather

Table V. COMPARATIVE ADAPTATIONS TO MONEY SUPPLY INCREASES, 1947–55

(1955 in % of 1947)

	Money Supply (1)	GNP at Current Prices (2)	GNP at Constant Prices (3)	Domestic Inflation (4 = 1 ÷ 3)	GNP Prices (5 = 2 ÷ 3)	Liquidity (6 = 1 ÷ 2 = 4 ÷ 5)
I. *Southern Countries*						
Greece	890	574	157	568	366	155
Italy	352	216	156	226	139	163
France	372	404	163	228	248	92
II. *Northern Countries*						
Norway	147	205	136	108	150	72
Sweden	156	196	136	115	144	79
Denmark	98	179	126	78	142	55
Netherlands	145	217	158	92	138	67
United Kingdom	114	178	128	90	140	64
III. *Belgium and Switzerland*						
Belgium	134	149	133	101	112	90
Switzerland	136	137	123	111	112	99
IV. *Austria and Germany*						
Austria:						
1947 = 100	291	422	259	112	163	69
1949 = 100	235	249	153	154	163	95
Germany:						
1947 = 100		407	263		155	
1949 = 100	219	207	191	115	108	106
V. *United States*	121	168	138	88	122	72

Sources and notes:
See Appendix Table 14.

than of overliquidity inherited from past, repressed inflation. Liquidity rose at the same time by 55% in Greece and 63% in Italy, slowing down the impact of current inflation upon prices.

In France, however, currency fears continued to mount until 1949. After a marked improvement in 1949 and 1950, they were rekindled by the Korean crisis. The liquidity index (1938 = 100) then fell to a low of 66 in 1952 and began to recover only in 1953. Price rises have been practically negligible in France in recent years, but over the period 1947–55 as a whole they were far larger than in Italy, although current advances in the inflation index were about the same in both countries.

This contrast reflects in part the different timing of French and Italian price and exchange rate adjustments. The Einaudi reforms of 1947 were accompanied not only by sharp advances in official prices and foreign exchange rates, but also by a collapse of black

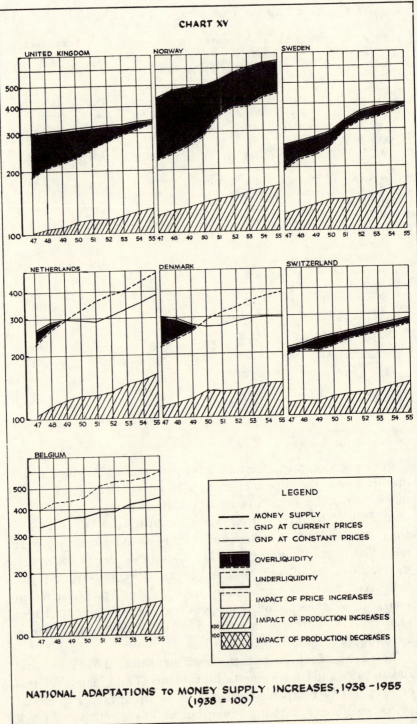

CHART XV

NATIONAL ADAPTATIONS TO MONEY SUPPLY INCREASES, 1938-1955
(1938 = 100)

66

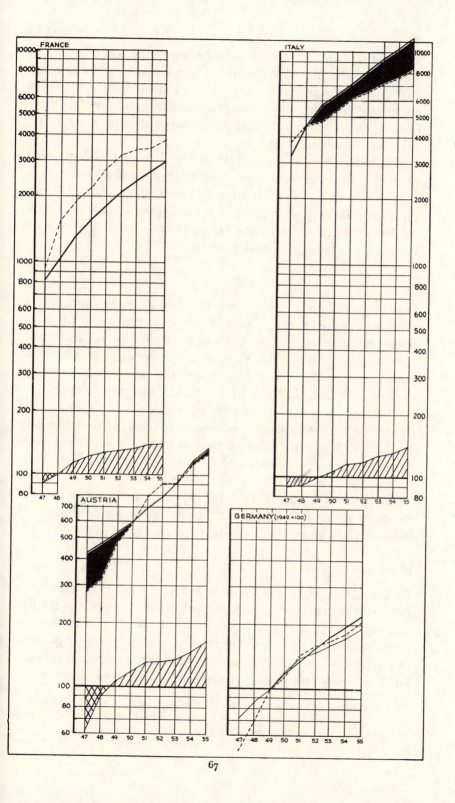

67

market prices and exchange rates during the course of that year. The corresponding adjustments were less drastic in France, and took place only in 1948 and 1949. National income data thus understate the extent by which prices had actually risen in France from 1938 to 1947, and exaggerate correspondingly the actual price increases in the following period.

Real differences also result from the fact that Italian prices were held down by continued large-scale unemployment and by an almost complete liberalization of restrictions on imports from Europe, while they were propped up in France by high and growing levels of external restrictions and internal subsidies, isolating French prices from competitive pressures.

c) SWITZERLAND AND BELGIUM

Wartime overliquidity had been mopped up in Belgium by the monetary purge of 1944, but was largely reconstituted by subsequent monetary expansion. Both in Switzerland and in Belgium, however, prices had been allowed to rise by 1947 by about the same extent as the money supply, and the ratio of cash holdings to national income had returned practically to prewar levels.

The evolution of Belgian and Swiss prices and liquidity over the period 1947–55 reflects this monetary balance. Prices rose only by about 10% over the whole period, as against 20% in the United States, 40% to 50% in Italy and the northern countries, and more than 100% in France and 200% in Greece.

Fluctuations in liquidity were also extremely small in both countries after 1948, the liquidity index showing a decline of 1% in Switzerland and 7% in Belgium from 1948 to 1955.[10]

d) GERMANY AND AUSTRIA

In Germany money supply increased very rapidly in every year following the currency reform, by 10% to 20% a year. In the first two years (1950 and 1951) this reflected a high rate of internal monetization and foreign deficits, but after 1951 the expansion of money was less than the enormous external surpluses accumulated on goods and services account. All in all, the monetary ex-

10. In the Belgian case, however, this near stability followed at 10% decline from 1947 to 1948, suggesting that the 1947 return to prewar levels still left a certain amount of overliquidity in the system. See following page.

pansion (119%) was nearly matched by production increases (91%), prices and liquidity moving only within a very narrow range from 1949 to 1955.

In Austria the rate of monetization remained very high throughout the period, but the large deficits of the early postwar years made room for alternating, and moderate, surpluses and deficits after 1951. Production increases (53%) lagged well behind the expansion of money supply (135%) between 1949 and 1955, and the index of inflation rose by 54%. Price increases (63%) were far larger, however, and the liquidity index (1949 = 100) declined to a low of 76 in 1952 but recovered to 95 in 1955. This probably suggests a considerable residue of overliquidity in 1948, a trend toward underliquidity in 1951 and 1952, and a movement toward balance in 1953 and 1954. Estimates for the liquidity index on a prewar basis would indicate a rise to 156 in 1947, a gradual decline to 87 in 1952, and a subsequent rise to 108 in 1955.

E) LIQUIDITY IN 1955 (see Table VII and
Appendix Table 14, Item VI)

For reasons already indicated,[11] changes in the liquidity index are particularly difficult to interpret. The year 1938 was a year of low economic activity, and therefore of relatively high cash balances with relation to that year's GNP. A lower ratio should probably be regarded as more "normal" for the years of high and expanding economic activity which have characterized the postwar era. A ratio of 70% to 80% of 1938 might possibly be regarded as closer to normal under these conditions. This is the range within which the liquidity index has fluctuated in recent years in Denmark, the Netherlands, France, Greece, and Belgium.

Much higher ratios were still found in 1955 in Norway (142), Italy (140), Sweden and the United Kingdom (104), and Switzerland (107). Changes in income distribution and in bank and payment habits probably account for part of this phenomenon. Swiss currency notes and deposits are also probably inflated by foreign holdings of refugee capital, which explain the high liquidity index in that country.

The maintenance of direct techniques of administrative restrictions—as opposed to monetary restrictions—in Norway, Sweden,

11. See above, pp. 52–3.

and the United Kingdom, particularly on construction and investment, confirms the impression that overliquidity had not as yet
been fully reabsorbed by the end of 1955. While changes in income distribution and bank habits probably account for the considerable increase of the liquidity index in Norway and Italy, it
would appear that past overliquidity had not been fully eliminated in Norway either, and that the recent pace of monetary expansion in Italy may possibly have been building up some overliquidity pressures in that country.

Liquidity indices for Germany and Austria are highly conjectural in view of the complex territorial and monetary readjustments of the last twenty years. The two countries were merged
in 1937, and the reichsmark replaced the Austrian schilling. They
were separated after the war, reichsmarks exchanged again for
schillings in Austria and for Deutsche marks in Germany. Germany was further divided between East and West.

Based on 1937 monetary circulation, the liquidity index for
Austria would seem to be somewhat above 100, while liquidity in
Western Germany is less than 60% of liquidity in the 1938 Reich.
This latter figure appears very low, but is not totally implausible
if one takes into account the contrast between the conservatism
of current monetary policy in Germany and the repressed inflation techniques characteristic of the Hitler era. The liquidity
index has been rising steadily over the last four years, but at a
moderate pace if one considers the stiffness of the 1948 monetary
purge and the expansionary impact of Germany's enormous balance of payments surpluses during this period.

3. Exchange Rate Adaptations

The evolution of postwar exchange rates was overwhelmingly
determined by the differences, noted above, among national policies. The national currency depreciated most in the southern
countries, where domestic prices and costs were unrelentingly
pushed upward under the combined impact of persistent monetization and underliquidity. It depreciated least in the northern
countries, where current inflation had been arrested and price
increases slowed down by price controls and rationing.

The complex interrelationships of exchange rate adjustments,
price and liquidity adaptations, and balance of payments improvements will be discussed further in the next section of this chapter

IV. COST COMPETITIVENESS AND INTERNATIONAL ADJUSTMENTS

A. The 1947 Crisis (see Table VI)

The differences reviewed above in the monetary evolution and policies of the European countries were inevitably matched by corresponding differences in the mechanism and policies of balance of payments adjustment.

Superficially, the size of the external deficits was controlled everywhere by direct trade and exchange restrictions rather than by free market adaptations. In fact, however, the efficacy of such restrictions was far less, and that of market forces remained far greater, than is commonly imagined.

Price inflation in the southern countries had progressed to a point which would have choked off exports entirely in the absence of exchange rate adjustments. On a GNP basis,[1] prices in national currency had risen by 1947 to six times U.S. prices in France, about 25 times in Italy, and 110 times in Greece, in comparison with 1938. With stable exchange rates, such fantastic discrepancies between the internal and external purchasing power of these currencies would have stifled exports entirely and put an unbearable strain upon the machinery of administrative controls over trade and exchange transactions. The preservation of even a trickle of exports and of a minimum degree of effectiveness of import and exchange controls presupposed, therefore, considerable adjustments in these countries' exchange rates.

We find, indeed, that all these currencies had already depreciated considerably by 1947. The official dollar rate had more than tripled in Paris since 1938 and had risen about twenty-five times in Rome and fifty times in Athens. Converted into dollars at these new exchange rates, Italian prices had declined slightly more than U.S. prices, but French and Greek prices still remained about twice as high as U.S. prices in comparison with 1938. Ex-

---

1. Implicit GNP prices are used throughout in the calculation of competitiveness (or purchasing power parity) indices. I have discussed elsewhere the obvious reasons why wholesale price indices, often used in such calculations, are totally irrelevant and misleading. See Robert Triffin, "La Théorie de la surévaluation monétaire et la dévaluation belge," *Bulletin de l'Institut de Recherches Economiques* (Louvain, Nov. 1937), pp. 19–52.

Table VI. EXCHANGE DEPRECIATION, COMPETITIVENESS, LIQUIDITY, AND FOREIGN BALANCE, 1938–47

(1947 in % of 1938)

	Exchange Rate a	Cost Competitiveness b Before Exchange Rate Adjustment	After Exchange Rate Adjustment	Liquidity c	Foreign Balance in 1947 d
I. *Southern Countries*					
Greece	4,952	11,080	224	46	293
Italy	2,523	2,468	98	85	257
France	340	598	176	86	144
II. *Northern Countries*					
Norway	121	107	88	197	136
Sweden	90	94	104	131	138
Denmark	104	110	106	140	114
Netherlands	146	126	87	117	150
United Kingdom	121	105	87	162	120
III. *Belgium and Switzerland*					
Belgium	148	211	143	84	126
Switzerland	98	98	100	108	109
IV. *Austria and Germany*					
Austria	186	255	137	156	291
Germany	134	69	52		163
V. *OEEC Europe*			96		165

Notes:
a. Exchange rate: Index of average price for the U.S. dollar in terms of national currency.
b. Cost competitiveness: (1) Before exchange rate adjustment: Index of ratio of national GNP price level to U.S. GNP price level, both in national currency. (2) After exchange rate adjustment: Index of ratio of national GNP price level, converted into U.S. dollars, to U.S. GNP price level.
c. Liquidity: Index of ratio of money supply to GNP at current prices.
d. Foreign balance in 1947: Ratio of the current value of goods and services imports to goods and services exports in 1947, multiplied by 100 (not converted into % of 1938).

Source and other notes:
See Appendix Tables 15–18.

change rates remained admittedly "unrealistic" in the latter two countries and were sharply devalued again during the following year. Thus currency devaluation wiped out everywhere the largest portion by far of the wide disparities which had marked the evolution of national price levels with respect to U.S. prices.

The problem was entirely different in the northern countries, where price controls and rationing had diverted inflationary pressures from price increases to overliquidity. Prices had risen only very moderately in relation to the United States, and these increases had been largely compensated, or even overcompensated, by exchange rate readjustments of very modest proportions in comparison with those experienced in Greece, Italy, and France.

National price levels in these countries could not be regarded as choking off foreign demand for exports nor as shifting domestic demand from home-produced goods to imported goods. The difficulties lay, not with international price disequilibria, but with the excess liquidity which raised internal demand for goods *in general* above the current levels of production, siphoning imports into the gap and absorbing internally goods and resources which would otherwise have been available for exports.

Contrary to a widespread illusion, import and exchange controls alone could not provide a satisfactory answer to this kind of problem. As long as they were regarded as temporary, they might induce a postponement of demand which would indeed relieve the situation. Long-enduring controls, however, could hardly be expected to induce people to retain willingly in national currency the funds which they were prevented from spending on imports. The demand for imports, choked off by the controls, would merely turn toward other goods, absorbing resources previously used for exports or adding further fuel to internal inflationary forces. Trade and exchange controls could reduce the volume of imports, but would have to be complemented by extensive internal controls and rationing in order to prevent a parallel decline in exports. The impact of overliquidity upon the balance of payments could only be kept in check, therefore, through an all-pervasive system of restrictions, extending over domestic as well as foreign transactions.

In spite of these, and in spite of all special administrative incentives and "export drives," the supply of exports tended to lag behind foreign demand. Distant delivery dates and a sharp deterioration in terms of trade were associated almost everywhere with overliquidity policies. The comparative price pattern stimulated foreign demand for these countries' exports, but domestic overliquidity also stimulated internal demand for goods and services and tended to choke off domestic supply to the export markets.

The third group of countries—Switzerland and Belgium—was closer to external as well as internal balance than any of the others. This was particularly the case for Switzerland, which had suffered least from the war and had succeeded remarkably well in preserving a maximum of internal stability without, however, attempting to isolate itself entirely from the broad fluctuations in world prices.[2]

The external deficit of Belgium in 1947 remained substantial, but it arose largely from restocking needs and could be financed relatively easily. More disquieting was the fact that Belgian prices, expressed in dollars, had risen by about 45% above U.S. prices since 1938. This, however, coincided with an exceptionally strong demand for Belgian exports—of steel particularly—during a period of active reconstruction in Belgium's main export markets, and of low supplying capacity by its major competitors. This situation allowed Belgium to charge "what the traffic would bear" and to support a less competitive cost level than in prewar days. Belgium's international problems arose not so much from over-all balance of payments deficits as from the combination of large surpluses in Europe with large deficits in the dollar area. In an inconvertible world this posed difficult payment problems, which explain the dogged fight of Belgium for the restoration of a multilateral system of payments and the elimination of the bilateral agreements under which most of Europe's trade was conducted and settled in the early postwar years.[3]

B. THE 1948–55 RECOVERY (see Chart XVI, Table VII, and Appendix Tables 15–18)

Fluctuations in European GNP prices after 1947 ran closely parallel to those in the United States, except in Austria, France, and Greece. Price rises were much larger in these three countries and again had to be offset by drastic exchange devaluation. From 1947 to 1955, the Greek drachma, the French franc, and the Austrian schilling were devalued respectively by about 82%, 66%, and 62%.

In the other countries of Western Europe exchange readjustments were confined to the September 1949 wave of devaluations, which cut down the dollar value of the Italian lira by 8% only, of the Belgian franc by 12%, of the Deutsche mark by 21%, and of the British, Scandinavian, and Dutch currencies by 30%.

In the last group of countries, price controls had been effectively maintained until then. A 30% devaluation far exceeded, therefore, the adjustment necessary to restore cost parity with

2. Sweden pursued a more ambitious policy when it revalued the krona by 17% in July 1946.

3. See below, Chaps. 4 and 5.

the United States at the prewar level. It should be kept in mind, however, that these countries—particularly the United Kingdom and the Netherlands—had lost during the war important sources of investment earnings from overseas.[4] These losses had to be made up by a corresponding improvement in the balance of merchandise trade in order to restore balance of payments equilibrium. If this objective were to be achieved, these countries' prices had to become more competitive than they needed to be in prewar days and than purchasing power parity calculations would suggest.

Yet it is difficult to escape the impression that the Dutch, British, and Norwegian devaluations of September 1949 deteriorated these countries' terms of trade far more than was necessary to allow them to compete on the international markets for a level of exports adequate to restore equilibrium in their balance of payments.[5] This impression is confirmed by the huge foreign surpluses accumulated by the Netherlands in recent years. It is superficially contradicted, however, by the persistent external deficits of Norway and the extremely modest size of the United Kingdom's surpluses on current account.[6]

This contradiction may be resolved if one takes account of the impact of monetary liquidity, as well as of cost competitiveness,[7] upon the balance of payments. Foreign demand for these countries' production was stimulated by the overcompetitiveness of

4. Investment earnings from overseas were equal in 1938 to 23% of the Netherlands' export proceeds and transformed a trade deficit of 160 million guilders into a current account surplus of nearly 100 million guilders. They rarely exceeded 5% of exports in postwar years and were much more than offset in 1948 and 1949 by capital expenditures largely connected with military and political disturbances in Indonesia. In the United Kingdom, net invisible receipts fell from 43% of exports in 1938 to less than 20% in the best postwar year (1950) and considerably less in all the other years.

5. The ratio of their GNP dollar prices to U.S. prices in 1950 ranged from 60% to 65% of the prewar ratio.

6. Surpluses on current account were necessary to equilibrate the over-all balance of payments, burdened as the latter was, especially for the United Kingdom and France, with amortization payments on war and postwar debts and with the need to contribute to the financing of economic development in overseas territories and associated monetary areas.

7. Cost competitiveness is measured throughout exclusively with reference to U.S. prices. The relative values of the competitiveness index for the various countries, however, gives an indication of each country's competitiveness vis-à-vis the others. It may be worth noting that the index for Switzerland, which experienced the least dislocation from wartime and postwar events, remains throughout remarkably stable and close to 100, although improving in relation to the U.S. after the outbreak of the Korean war. See Appendix Table 17.

their prices, but the persistence of overliquidity also stimulated internal demand for goods—both imported and home produced—and reduced the supply of domestic production to the export markets. Overliquidity and overcompetitiveness thus tended to counteract each other through their opposite impact on the domestic supply of, and the external demand for, these countries' exports. The countries where liquidity still appeared excessive in 1955—Norway, Italy, the United Kingdom, and Sweden—saw their balance of payments on current account actually deteriorate in recent years, or fail at least to share fully in the spectacular improvements experienced by the rest of Europe during that period.

The double impact of cost competitiveness and monetary liquidity upon the balance of payments is clearly brought out in Chart XVI. These two factors alone do not, of course, constitute a full explanation of all balance of payments fluctuations. Changes in trade or exchange restrictions (at home and abroad), foreign countries' exchange adjustments, and variations in investment earnings and the terms of trade under the impact of international wars or cyclical fluctuations also influence each country's external balance. Yet the general parallelism of the three curves shown on the chart is unmistakable. Most of the major discrepancies in this parallelism arise in 1950 or 1951 and may be explained by disturbances arising from the September 1949 devaluations and the outbreak of the Korean war, rather than from changes internal to each country's own economy.

In Norway, the United Kingdom, Sweden, Italy, Belgium, and France, the curve measuring the external deficit almost always lies between the two curves indicative of liquidity and cost competitiveness in relation to U.S. prices. In the first four countries, the favorable impact of overcompetitive costs upon the balance of payments appears to be offset by the impact of persistent overliquidity.[8] The opposite is true of Belgium and France, where underliquidity tended to offset the uncompetitiveness of costs. The Belgian and French cases, however, exhibit a significant contrast when the fluctuations, rather than the absolute levels, of the three curves are considered. Liquidity fluctuations were usually accompanied in Belgium by parallel movements in the balance of payments, while in France the deficit increased with each

8. In gradually diminishing degree in the northern countries, but only after 1948 in Italy.

Table VII. EXCHANGE DEPRECIATION, COMPETITIVENESS, LIQUIDITY, AND FOREIGN BALANCE, 1938–55

(1955 in % of 1938)

| | Exchange Rate | Cost Competitiveness | | Liquidity | Foreign Balance in 1955 |
		Before Exchange Rate Adjustment	After Exchange Rate Adjustment		
I. *Southern Countries*					
Greece	26,738	33,373	126	71	123
Italy	3,289	2,812	86	140	108
France	1,000	1,218	122	80	91
II. *Northern Countries*					
Norway	175	132	75	142	107
Sweden	130	112	86	104	103
Denmark	151	129	86	76	98
Netherlands	210	143	68	78	95
United Kingdom	175	121	69	104	99
III. *Belgium and Switzerland*					
Belgium	170	195	115	70	92
Switzerland	98	90	91	107	92
IV. *Austria and Germany*					
Austria	483	340	70	108	114
Germany	169	88	52	55	89
V. *OEEC Europe*			78		95

Sources and notes:
See Table VI.

and every decline in liquidity and was reduced with every increase in liquidity. The explanation clearly lies in the very different significance of liquidity movements in the two countries. Belgian underliquidity was primarily the result of the restrictive policies pursued by the monetary authorities in order to stabilize internal prices in the face of external inflationary pressures, and to offset at the same time the impact of cost uncompetitiveness (or currency overvaluation) upon the country's balance of payments. The 1948 and 1951 declines in French liquidity, on the other hand, were closely allied with rising prices and currency fears in an inflationary environment, while the 1949–50 and 1953–55 increases in liquidity reflected a return of confidence in price and currency stability.

Dutch costs, like British and Norwegian costs, appear to have been highly competitive as early as 1947. The Dutch balance of payments, however, was also unfavorably affected during the early postwar years by excessive liquidity. The deficit declined as over-

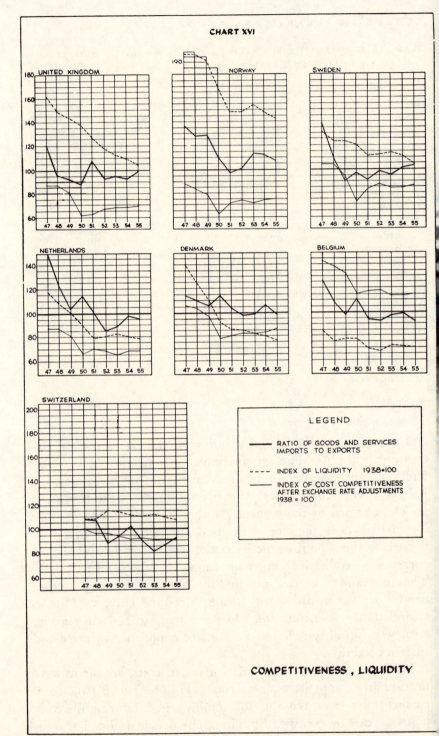

CHART XVI

COMPETITIVENESS , LIQUIDITY

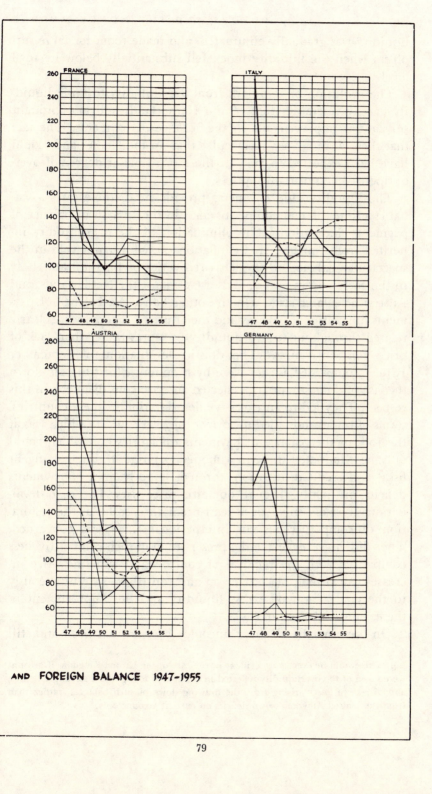

AND FOREIGN BALANCE 1947-1955

79

liquidity was gradually eliminated, and made room for large surpluses when the liquidity index fell substantially below its 1938
level.

The evolution of Denmark from overliquidity to underliquidity closely resembles that of the Netherlands and also brought
substantial improvements in the balance of payments. The fact
that these were far less spectacular than in the Netherlands could
have been expected in view of the much smaller degree of overcompetitiveness of Danish prices.

The liquidity index seems to provide in all these cases a valuable adjunct to cost competitiveness in the analysis of balance of
payments fluctuations. The elimination of the overliquidity inherited from wartime credit inflation played a major role in the
spectacular balance of payments recoveries of Belgium and Italy
in the early postwar years, and of Germany, the Netherlands, and
Austria at a later stage. On the other hand, the balance of payments difficulties of Norway and the United Kingdom were clearly
related throughout to overliquidity pressures rather than lack of
price competitiveness.[9] The drastic devaluations of September
1949, accompanied as they were by strenuous efforts to hold down
the rise of domestic prices, reflected an erroneous diagnosis in this
respect. They led to an excessive deterioration of these countries'
terms of trade, and failed to correct the overliquidity which was at
the root of the balance of payments difficulties and which could
only be eliminated through a monetary purge, through stringent
fiscal and credit disinflation, through large balance of payments
deficits, or, finally, through domestic price rises. The 1949 devaluations were excessive, or at least premature, so far as the restoration of competitiveness in international trade was concerned.
They did, however, make the preservation of such competitiveness
compatible with the removal of controls and with the price increases which took place later on and contributed simultaneously
to the contraction of excess liquidity and the improvement of
these countries' terms of trade.

On the other hand, price uncompetitiveness has been and still

9. This would be even more evident in the case of the United Kingdom if account
were taken of the overliquidity reflected in the rise of foreign-held sterling balances,
and of reserve losses arising from the drawing down of such balances, rather than
from the United Kingdom's own deficits on current account only.

remains one of the obstacles to external balance in the case of France.[10] This uncompetitiveness has been in part the result of price rises associated with currency fears and an excessive contraction of liquid cash holdings. If confidence in the currency can be fully restored, the reconstitution of more normal levels of cash balances will continue to facilitate—as it has done in the last three years—France's progress toward internal and external monetary balance. It still seems likely, however, that the attainment of this final goal will require some exchange rate readjustment if France is to equilibrate its external transactions on the basis of cost competitiveness rather than through increased protectionism and restrictions.

A final word of caution might be added lest some naïve souls interpret this analysis as meaning that the restoration of full monetary balance requires a uniform movement of the indices of liquidity and competitiveness back to the 1938 levels. Generally speaking, lower levels of liquidity than those of a depression year should be regarded as normal under present high levels of activity and employment, and greater price competitiveness than in 1938 would appear necessary to offset the impact of unfavorable changes in investment earnings and the terms of trade upon the European countries' balance of payments.[11] These generalizations, however, do not take into account national variations in liquidity and competitiveness in the base year 1938 and in the impact of wartime and postwar changes on each country's balance of payments and monetary structure. A detailed study, country by country, would

10. Recent deficits on current account have been of a moderate size, and have even made room for small surpluses in 1954 and 1955. This balance, however, is made up of large deficits with foreign areas, compensated in part, or overcompensated, by surpluses within the French franc area. These surpluses, in turn, have been financed by French contributions and capital exports which would have resulted in a large gold and dollar drain if they had not been offset by simultaneous receipts of U.S. aid. Both France and Britain need to be in surplus—and not merely in balance—on current account in order to help finance economic development in their colonies and associated monetary areas. Failing such financing, their current account surplus with these areas would fall sharply, and the maintenance of equilibrium in their current account balance would require a substantial reduction of their deficits with countries outside their own monetary areas.

11. The index of competitiveness with relation to U.S. prices would indicate, for OEEC Europe as a whole, an improvement from 96 in 1947 (1938 = 100) to 71 in 1950 —reflecting an excessive competitiveness and deterioration of the terms of trade— and a stable level of 76 to 78 in the four years 1952–55.

be necessary to take these factors into account, and many of them would in any case be extremely difficult to express in quantitative terms.

What may be retained from this analysis is, first of all, the general trend of Europe toward balance of payments equilibrium and price stability at high and growing levels of production, consumption, and investment. As far as individual countries are concerned, the indices of competitiveness and liquidity should be interpreted within the context of other evidence as to the degree of internal and external balance achieved in recent years, rather than merely with reference to their 1938 levels. Finally, where disequilibria are still manifest in domestic price increases, external deficits, or widespread direct controls, the nature of the problem should be analyzed not in terms of prices alone but also with reference to the impact of past and current credit monetization upon liquidity and the over-all demand for goods. The indices of liquidity and competitiveness may, at this stage, help us choose among different alternative explanations of the disequilibria, even though they cannot be relied upon to indicate any precise level at which equilibrium could be achieved.

V. SUMMARY AND CONCLUSIONS

The analysis presented above may appear exceedingly superficial to economists steeped in the complexities of modern monetary analysis. It rejoins, indeed, conclusions which have long been familiar and trite, and uses only the most commonplace instruments of statistical analysis.

Its only merit, if any, is to integrate the different approaches commonly used in the discussion of these problems, and particularly to throw into relief the convergence of balance of payments data, national accounts data, and monetary and banking data in the analysis of the inflationary process.

If inflation is defined as the excess of current demand for goods and services over national production at current prices,[1] it immediately follows that such excess demand is dependent upon the

---

1. Such excess demand will not, of course, acquire an inflationary character if it brings into employment previously unemployed national resources and is matched, therefore, by increased production at unchanging prices.

financing of the corresponding over-all deficit of the community on current account. This financing, in turn, will depend primarily on the willingness of the monetary and banking authorities to expand their net credits to the community through monetary creation, or on the existence of excess liquidities allowing the community to sustain current expenditures in excess of current income from production.[2]

This excess demand may then be satisfied by an excess of imports over exports or, alternatively, be thwarted by domestic price rises or rationing. Foreign deficits, price rises, or rationing must be regarded as various forms of adjustment to an initial inflationary impulse. Foreign deficits absorb the inflationary purchasing power by mopping up national currency in exchange for the foreign currencies needed to pay for the excess of imports over exports. Price rises also absorb the inflationary impulse by reducing the real value of existing cash balances and monetary liquidities. As distinct from these two forms of adjustment, rationing does not absorb the financial resources which feed the excess of monetary demand over current production. Insofar as it can be effectively enforced, however, it prevents the actual use of these resources and may reconcile the persistence of excess demand with price stability and balance of payments equilibrium.

All three of these alternative adjustments may permit a considerable amount of credit monetization by the banking system. All three are also subject to increasing costs and ultimate limitations, owing to:

1. The limited size of the international reserves and foreign assistance or capital available to finance foreign deficits;

2. The disincentive effects of spiraling price rises or progressively tighter rationing controls on production and savings, and ultimately a generalized flight from money into gold, foreign assets, or merchandise as a measure and store of value and even as a medium for transactions.

American aid financed, in all countries, much larger and more persistent deficits than would have been feasible otherwise. Such deficits reduced domestic inflationary pressures, financed a rapid

2. Direct external financing, bypassing entirely the national monetary and banking system, is generally limited in scope, and allows the excess demand to be met by foreign deficits rather than by domestic inflationary pressures, without any reduction in official reserve levels.

rate of reconstruction, restocking, and investment, and accelerated the recovery of production in all countries.

The residual impact of inflationary financing upon the domestic economy was absorbed by price rises and rationing. Rationing controls broke down earlier in the countries in which the inflationary impulse had been larger. Rapid price rises tended to stimulate a flight from the currency and made it more difficult to control the current generation of new inflationary forces through credit monetization. On the other hand, once inflation was arrested, the reconstitution of normal cash balances could be counted upon to bring about a rapid reversal in the situation, a reduction of speculative inventory levels, a cessation of capital flight, and a gradual flow back into official channels of privately hoarded gold and foreign assets. Such a tendency became manifest in France in 1949–50, was reversed as a result of new inflationary phenomena and price increases associated with the Korean war, but was resumed again in 1952 and the following years.

In the countries where the initial inflationary impulse had been smallest, or had been partially mopped up by monetary purges, price increases could be allowed to complete the necessary adjustment without rekindling new inflationary developments or, alternatively, they could be effectively arrested or slowed down by rationing and the maintenance of a certain degree of monetary overliquidity. The latter policy was initially followed by the United Kingdom, the Scandinavian countries, and the Netherlands, but rationing was gradually dismantled and prices allowed to rise and absorb overliquidity, particularly after the devaluations of 1949 and the outbreak of hostilities in Korea.

Trade and exchange controls were universally resorted to in order to limit balance of payments deficits to available gold and foreign exchange resources, supplemented by foreign loans and grants. Yet such controls alone could not be fully successful, as they would not necessarily have the effect of reducing consumption and investment expenditures to the level of production, but would result in large part in a shift of expenditures from imported to home-produced goods and reduce exportable capacity, particularly after full employment conditions had been reached.

In the absence of fundamental monetary balance, therefore, the external deficits had to be checked in addition either by comprehensive and effective rationing controls, internal as well as external, or by exchange rate readjustments, or both.

Although more moderate in amplitude than those of most other countries, the exchange readjustments of the United Kingdom, the Netherlands, and the Scandinavian countries exceeded what would have been necessary to restore the international competitiveness of these countries' prices. The persistence of balance of payments difficulties after these readjustments must be explained primarily by the impact of overliquidity upon the over-all internal demand for goods in general and therefore upon both import demand and exportable capacity, rather than by price and cost disparities discouraging foreign demand for exports and encouraging domestic demand for imports.

The final abatement of both internal inflationary pressures and balance of payments deficits came only with the restoration of over-all monetary balance. This implied, in turn: (1) the cessation of current credit monetization, (2) the reabsorption of previously created monetary liquidities by production increases, monetary purges, balance of payments deficits, or price increases, and (3) the adaptation of exchange rates to the new pattern of international prices.

By 1953 or 1954, this process of monetary readjustment could be regarded as completed in most European countries. Rationing controls had been abolished almost everywhere, and considerable balance of payments surpluses coincided in 1953, 1954, and 1955 with a rapid relaxation of import and exchange restrictions. Sharp advances in production, exports, and imports also coincided in these years with unprecedented price stability, following a relative stagnation of production and considerable declines in international prices after the collapse of the Korean boom. Upward price pressures became apparent in all countries in 1955–56, but were energetically dealt with everywhere through monetary and fiscal policies, and brought no general resurgence of balance of payments deficits or restrictive trade and exchange controls.

The recovery of the last eight years has achieved far more than a mere reconstruction of wartime destruction and damages. Large-scale investments, combined with monetary readjustments, have brought to European economies a degree of strength and vitality which contrasts sharply not only with the near bankruptcy of 1947 but also with the relative stagnation and recurrent monetary instability of the prewar era (see Table VIII).

The obstacles to the restoration of currency convertibility in Europe no longer lie in the weakness of its economy, in its persistent inflationary proclivities, or in its shortage of dollars, but in fears and uncertainties regarding the future harmonization of nationalistic trade and monetary policies in an interdependent world.

Table VIII. OEEC EUROPE: INDICES OF RECOVERY, 1947-55

	1947	1955	1947-55
I. *GNP Volume* (1938 = 100)	**91**	**144**	**+53**
A. Agricultural Production			
(1934-38 = 100)	83	128	+45
B. Industrial Production			
(1938 = 100)	88	169	+81
II. *Expenditure* (1938 = 100)	**96**	**140**	**+44**
A. Consumption	94	134	+40
B. Domestic Capital Formation	102	174	+72
III. *Ratio of Exports to Imports* (goods and			
services at current prices)	**61**	**106**	**+47**
A. Volume of Exports (1938 = 100)	59	156	+97
B. Volume of Imports (1938 = 100)	98	127	+29
C. Volume Ratio of Exports to Imports			
(1938 = 100)	60	123	+63
D. Terms of Trade (1938 = 100)	106	91	−15
IV. *Balance on Goods and Services*			
(in billions of U.S. dollars)	**−7.2**	**+1.4**	**+8.6**
A. With the United States	−5.4	−0.1	+5.3
B. With Other Countries	−1.8	+1.5	+3.3
V. *Gold and Foreign Exchange*			
(in billions of U.S. dollars)			
A. *Gold and Foreign Exchange Reserves*	**7.9**	**15.1**	**+7.2**
1. Continental Europe	5.7	12.9	+7.2
2. United Kingdom	2.2	2.2	—
B. *Gold and Dollar Holdings*	**9.3**	**17.6**	**+8.3**
1. Continental Europe and			
Dependencies	5.6	13.6	+8.0
2. Sterling Area	3.7	4.0	+0.3
VI. *Exchange Discount on Free Dollar*			
Markets (end of year, in % of par)			
A. *Sterling*			
1. Transferable	−37	−1	+35
2. Security	−57 (1948)	−2	+55
B. *Deutsche Mark* (Sperrmark and			
liberalized capital account)	−47 (1951)	−1	+46
C. *Bank Note Rates in Zurich*			
1. Sterling	−42	−6	+36
2. Deutsche Mark	−27 (1949)	—	+27
3. French Franc	−63	−10	+53
4. Belgian Franc	−13	—	+13
5. Netherlands Guilder	−58	—	+58
6. Austrian Schilling	−16 (1949)	−3	+13
7. Swedish Krona	−37	−2	+35
8. Norwegian Krone	−41	−9	+32

Sources:
I, II, III, and IVB: OEEC *Statistics of National Product and Expenditure* (Paris, 1957).
IVA: *Survey of Current Business.*
VA and VI: *International Financial Statistics* and *Monatbericht* (Schweizerische National-bank).
VB: *Federal Reserve Bulletin.*

CHAPTER 3

The Failure of the International Currency Plans: 1944-47

I. THE NEED FOR COLLECTIVE ACTION

ECONOMISTS and statesmen had long been familiar with the problems and policies of national monetary readjustment outlined in Chapter 2. Neither textbooks nor history, however, offered them much guidance for the other task which confronted them at the end of the Second World War, i.e. for the reconstruction of the international monetary system itself.

They could, of course, look back some twenty years and ponder over the attempt made in the late 1920's to restore, or patch up, the pre-1914 gold standard. This experience, however, was not very encouraging. The new gold standard had functioned fitfully for a few years only and collapsed miserably in 1931. Moreover, this collapse had been followed by an unprecedented growth of nationalistic monetary and trade techniques which radically modified and enormously complicated the problem of international monetary reconstruction.

The task was no longer confined, as it had been after the First World War, to the successful stabilization of fluctuating exchange rates. The breakdown of the traditional gold standard had now proceeded far beyond mere currency instability. Currency inconvertibility had assumed an entirely new meaning with the emergence of new techniques of trade and exchange controls. "Inconvertibility" used to designate an institutional framework under which individual traders remained perfectly free to buy and sell goods, services, and currencies wherever they wished, but were no longer guaranteed a stable rate of exchange for these transactions. It now meant something much more radical: the subordination of all such transactions to administrative permission by the national state.

Tariff duties had always interfered with the classical economist's ideal of a trade pattern determined entirely by competitive forces and the comparative advantages of the various countries in the production of different types of goods and services. Yet tariff duties were inserted into the market mechanism itself and left it free to function and to transmit the impact of competitive price or exchange rate adjustments tending to preserve, or restore, each country's balance in world payments. In contrast, the spread of quantitative trade and exchange restrictions in the 1930's and 1940's aimed to suppress and replace the mechanism of free market adjustments. These restrictions could be changed from day to day in order to offset the impact of price or exchange rate movements, at home or abroad, upon a country's imports from—and partly upon its exports to—other trading countries.

As long as these restrictions were used in a nondiscriminatory manner, they still left intact the interplay of competitive forces in all third countries' markets. Each country's exports would continue to compete on an equal footing with other countries' exports to the rest of the world. This competition would continue to exercise considerable pressures upon national costs and exchange rates, forcing them into some kind of international adjustment as long as each country wished to maintain at least a minimum level of international trade. Even this door was closed, however, during the 1930's and 1940's, with the generalization of discriminatory trade and payments techniques and of bilateral trade and payments agreements. Discriminatory techniques could be used by each country to apply different levels of restrictions to its transactions with its various trade partners. This discriminatory power was then used as a bargaining weapon in trade and payments negotiations. Import preferences by country A in favor of country B could be traded against import preferences or special credit concessions by country B in favor of country A. In the absence of agreement, imports from the partner country might be barred altogether, or at least subjected to severe restrictions, while similar imports from more pliable countries would be admitted in much larger quantities, irrespective of price or quality competition. The extension of these techniques to the bulk of world trade in the early postwar years tended to stifle international competition altogether and to subordinate it to bargaining power as a determinant of each country's import and export pattern.

This vitiated at the very roots any classical prescription of monetary readjustments aiming at the restoration, through competitive market forces, of over-all balance in a country's transactions with the rest of the world taken as a single unit.[1] Such an over-all equilibrium would remain of academic significance to the countries whose export surpluses to, let us say, the sterling area, could no longer be used in multilateral fashion to finance corresponding deficits in other parts of the world. Each country would have to worry about its bilateral trade pattern as well as its over-all equilibrium, and neither of these would be determined by the success of the country's own policies in regaining monetary balance through the cessation of current inflation, the elimination of overliquidity, and the readjustment of its prices or exchange rates to a nonexistent pattern of international competitiveness. Any country might, of course, refuse to enter into any bilateral trade and payments agreements, insist on trading only in convertible currencies, or decline at least to repurchase from its exporters the inconvertible currencies which they might accept in payment. Even then, its own levels of exports and imports would be determined much less by the competitiveness of its prices than by the vagaries of other countries' trade and payments restrictions and bilateral agreements. Any external equilibrium reached on this basis would remain extremely precarious and constantly at the mercy of other countries' decisions and policies. It would, moreover, probably reduce to a mere trickle the international trade of any country which traditionally depended on inconvertible currency markets for the bulk of its exports.

In theory, of course, the convertible country could readjust its own production and trade structure in accordance with these new conditions. It could divert its production into new channels permitting it to shift its exports from the inconvertible markets to

---

1. The whole classical literature on international trade and balance of payments adjustments is built around a "two country" case. The treatment of the "rest of the world" as the second country seems to introduce more realism into the analysis, but implicitly assumes an institutional framework of nondiscrimination in the international trade and payments mechanism. Classical policy conclusions do not in any way come to grips, therefore, with the problems facing an individual country in its trading relations with other countries in an institutional environment of trade bilateralism and currency inconvertibility.

those which remained convertible. There were, however, only a handful of these in 1947, i.e. the United States, Mexico, El Salvador, Guatemala, and Panama, which altogether had never absorbed more than about 10% of European countries' exports. In those circumstances, the restoration of currency convertibility by any individual country was practically unthinkable in the absence of a simultaneous decision by its major trade partners or competitors. To do so alone would expose it to the loss of up to 90% of its normal export outlets, except for essential goods unobtainable from nondollar sources and for which better financing terms —including American credits or grants!—could not be obtained from the dollar countries. To find substitute outlets in convertible countries for the exports thus displaced would be a long and arduous task at best, involving a thorough overhauling of the customary structure of production. In the meantime, large pockets of unemployment would develop among the exporting industries, and the over-all contraction of export levels would force a corresponding reduction in imports. The substitution of home products for imports might then absorb part of the idle resources previously employed in the export industries, but this readjustment would also be a painful and costly one, unlikely to occur overnight.

Even if we could assume that all these adjustments would in fact take place and restore in the end full employment of the country's productive capacity, it is highly doubtful that they would result in a more economic allocation of the country's resources—or of the world's resources in general—than might have obtained under bilateral agreements. In neither case would trade channels correspond to the classical doctrine of comparative advantage. The improvement in the over-all pattern of imports flowing from the elimination of import discrimination by the convertible country would, in all probability, be more than offset by the uneconomic pattern of production and the over-all contraction of foreign trade forced upon it by discriminatory restrictions on its exports to the inconvertible countries. Adam Smith must have shuddered in his grave at the "classical" prescription propounded in his name to meet a situation totally undreamed of in his own time.

Finally, all these upheavals would have to be upheaved themselves at a later stage when other countries, having overcome their initial postwar difficulties, began to dismantle their own bilateral techniques of restrictions and to resume trade on a multilateral, competitive basis. Convertible adjustments to temporary conditions of inconvertibility abroad would then have to be undone in order to revert once more to an adjusted pattern of trade under general conditions of convertibility.

Canadian experts could hardly be suspected of heterodoxy in this matter. Their very lucid statement of the problem as they saw it as early as 1943 rings a prophetic note when we reread it today:

> The facts regarding the distribution of the world's monetary gold reserves and the changes which have taken place in the course of the war in various countries' holdings of foreign securities are too well known to require elaboration. Broadly speaking, and allowing for certain exceptions and time-lags, a cash basis for the settlement of international transactions would mean that any country's capacity to export would be limited to the amount of its own currency it made available to foreign countries through its imports and other current payments abroad—in other words, trade would in effect be reduced to barter. In point of fact, however, there is no possibility that countries would for long allow themselves to be confined in such a strait-jacket. Faced with the problem of an unsalable surplus of export goods and with consequent domestic unemployment, they would refuse to accept the penalty of disorganization of export trade if that penalty could be avoided, even temporarily, by the extension of credit. Countries would embark on bilateral credit arrangements, no doubt linked with deals relating to the purchase and sale of goods; and as soon as certain countries began to adopt this course others would find that they had to follow suit to protect their trade interests. It is difficult to imagine a more fruitful source of international dissension than a competitive trade and credit extension program of this character.[2]

The restoration of an international system of trade and payments after the end of the war was thus recognized at an early stage as a problem whose solution would require international

2. *Tentative Draft Proposals of Canadian Experts for an International Exchange Union* (Ottawa, 1943), pp. 6–7.

negotiation and agreements rather than be left to unilateral, uncoordinated decisions by several scores of sovereign countries. Three broad plans dominated wartime and early postwar discussions in this respect: the Keynes plan for an International Clearing Union, the White plan for a United and Associated Nations Stabilization Fund, and the alternative key currency approach propounded primarily by John H. Williams in this country and embodied in the 1946 Anglo-American Financial Agreement.[3]

II. THE KEYNES PLAN FOR AN INTERNATIONAL CLEARING UNION

The first, and in many ways the most provocative, plan for postwar monetary reconstruction was the Keynes plan for an International Clearing Union. Issued as a White Paper by the British government in the middle of the war, on April 8, 1943, it long vied in the public mind and in learned discussions [1] with its American rival, the Harry Dexter White plan for a United and Associated Nations Stabilization Fund.

A. ECONOMIC PHILOSOPHY OF THE PLAN

The Keynes plan was bold. It was lucidly written. It was intelligent. In view of the dark prospects confronting Britain, it could not avoid also being clever and dominated by British interests and preoccupations. It was, however, frankly offered as a mere basis for discussion, inviting at every turn counterproposals and compromise solutions.

Its theoretical structure rested on an academic diagnosis of the two major monetary threats to postwar prosperity. The first was real enough. It was the danger of an indefinite continuation of

3. Reference should also be made to complementary planning outside the monetary field proper, and particularly to the creation of the International Bank for Reconstruction and Development, to the ill-fated attempt to establish an International Trade Organization, and to the General Agreement on Tariffs and Trade (GATT) which survived from the ITO wreckage.

1. See particularly: John H. Williams, *Postwar Monetary Plans and Other Essays*, New York, 1947; Jacob Viner, "Two Plans for International Monetary Stabilization," in *International Economics*, Glencoe, Ill. 1951; Joan Robinson, "The International Currency Proposals," in *The New Economics*, ed. Seymour E. Harris, New York, Knopf 1950.

a bilateral system of international payments, destructive of triangular trade and preventing each country from using its surpluses with some of its trade partners to settle its deficits with the others.[2] This danger could theoretically be avoided through a full-fledged restoration of the old gold standard. But Keynes was acutely concerned about the so-called "deflationary bias" which had attended the functioning of the gold standard in the last decade before the Second World War. International balance of payments disequilibria manifest themselves in excessive or persistent deficits for some countries, but also in parallel surpluses for others. Under a managed gold standard, the full burden of readjustment tends to fall on the former countries, as a consequence of the depletion of their monetary reserves. The surplus countries, on the other hand, are always able to follow compensatory, or "sterilization," policies which block expansionary adjustments. Balance of payments disequilibria then tend to find their correction exclusively through the deflationary policies of the debtors, unrelieved by monetary expansion on the part of the creditors.[3]

B. MAJOR PROVISIONS [4]

The Keynes plan aimed essentially, therefore, at offering a smooth crossing between the Scylla of world bilateralism and the Charybdis of international deflation. Its two pillars were the provision of unrestricted opportunities for the full clearing of each country's bilateral credit and debit balances and of large and automatic credit financing, through the Clearing Union, of the net surpluses and deficits of the participating countries.

1. Multilateral Clearing

The Clearing Union would not intervene in any way in daily transactions among individual traders or banks. These would con-

---

2. See particularly Arts. 1-a and 1-g, 3, 7, 13, 14, 19, 20, 37, 38, and 40.

3. This point is repeatedly emphasized in Arts. 1-c, 1-d, 1-e, 1-g, and 8, 10, 11, 12, 15, 17, and 18.

4. The emphasis placed in this summary on a number of technical details and drafting ambiguities is designed to underline some points highly relevant to the negotiating process. Their significance will become apparent in the course of the later discussion of the International Monetary Fund, the European Payments Union, the European Monetary Agreement, and the proposals for basic and sorely needed reforms in the present institutional framework of the international gold standard.

tinue to be regulated by the national authorities of the individual member countries. Such regulations might range from complete centralization of foreign exchange supply and demand by central banks or exchange control offices in some countries to complete freedom of foreign exchange holdings and transactions in others (Art. 22).

The Clearing Union would be used only "for the clearing and settlement of the ultimate outstanding balances between Central Banks (and certain other super-national institutions), such as would have been settled under the old gold standard by the ship ment or the earmarking of gold" (Art. 21). Even central banks, however, could continue to deal directly with one another as before. They would be allowed to retain their separate gold reserves and to settle in gold any balances outstanding among them.[5]

The first and basic innovation of the plan would be to provide an alternative, additional means of settlement among central banks in the form of "bancor" accounts on the books of the Clearing Union. Any member country would be entitled to settle a currency balance owed by it to any other member by making a bancor transfer from its own account to the account of the creditor country. All member states would correspondingly agree in advance to accept without limit such bancor transfers in lieu of gold payment, in settlement of currency balances due to them from any other member (Art. 6-6).

The value of bancor in terms of gold would be fixed by the Governing Board of the Clearing Union (Art. 6-4), and the initial value of each national currency in terms of bancor would be similarly determined at the outset by agreement among the member states (Art. 6-3). A country would no longer be free, as it was under the gold standard, to modify unilaterally the par value of its currency. Any such modification would be subject to permission by the Governing Board (Art. 6-3), except that a country whose debit balance to the Union had exceeded a quarter of its quota on the average during at least a two-year period could devalue at its own discretion up to 5%, but could do so only once.[6] On the

5. In his comments on "the position of gold under the plan," Keynes added rather wistfully that they could also "coin gold and put it into circulation, and, generally speaking, do what they liked with it" (Art. 28). "What, in the long run, the world may decide to do with gold is another matter" (Art. 26).

6. This procedure could be repeated later only if the Board was satisfied that it was appropriate (Art. 6-8a). Moreover, during the first five years after the incep-

other hand, the Board itself could take the initiative of requiring a stated reduction in the value of a country's currency, as a condition for bancor drawings in excess of a half of the country's quota.[7]

The practical outcome of these arrangements, therefore, would be to create bancor accounts endowed with international purchasing power in terms of all and any currencies whatsoever, equivalent to gold itself [8] and as freely usable in international settlements among central banks.

2. Financing of Net Settlements

But how could a country acquire such bancor accounts? The problem would not arise for over-all creditor countries, since their very surpluses would automatically feed their bancor accounts with the Clearing Union. Countries in over-all deficit could obtain bancor against deliveries of gold to the Union, but this solution would not preclude the emergence of deflationary tendencies if these countries were short of gold itself. If no pressure were placed on the creditor countries to finance or readjust their own surpluses, the deficit countries might soon find themselves forced to resort to deflationary action to equilibrate their accounts. The maldistribution of monetary reserves and the size of the postwar needs for reconstruction and development would tend to precipitate a world deflation, damaging to creditor and debtor countries alike.

---

tion of the system, the Governing Board would "give special consideration to appeals for an adjustment in the exchange value of a national currency unit on the ground of unforeseen circumstances" (Art. 6-3). These two provisions, designed to introduce more flexibility and realism in exchange rate arrangements, did not really constitute an exception to the principle that exchange readjustments would be fully subordinated to the Board's permission.

7. Art. 6-8b. The extreme creditor countries were treated with kid gloves and would be asked only to *discuss* with the Board what measures—including currency appreciation—would be appropriate to restore equilibrium in their international balance (Art. 6-9b).

8. Art. 31 stated, however, that the power to vary the value of bancor in terms of gold "might have to be exercised if the stocks of gold tendered to the Union were to be excessive. No object would be served by attempting further to peer into the future or to prophesy the ultimate outcome." This suggests the possibility of a devaluation of gold with respect to bancor, but not an appreciation. Bancor might therefore be regarded as superior to gold as a store of value. The Clearing Union might indeed have to concern itself with the inflationary threat resulting from the fact that any country could obtain bancor from it in exchange for gold. It would never have to worry about a shortage of gold, since no country would ever be entitled to demand gold from it against its balance of bancor. See Arts. 6-10, 27, and 29.

In order to parry this danger, the Union would therefore provide substantial bancor credits—or overdrafts—to all its members. The mechanics of the Union would indeed enable it to do this without any limit or hindrance whatsoever, since its creditors could not request payment in gold or any medium other than bancor itself. They could use their bancor accounts only to make payment to other member countries. Such payments could only result either in a shift of bancor balances from one creditor to another, or to a parallel reduction in the bancor balances owed by the Union to a creditor country and owed to the Union by a debtor country. Under such a system, the financial balance of the Clearing Union itself would always be automatically preserved, irrespective of the size of the overdrafts granted by it to the debtor countries (Art. 5).

Yet the Union could not extend unlimited credits to the deficit countries without encouraging total irresponsibility on their part, and without risking the stimulation of a boundless spiral of international inflation. Debtors' quotas or overdrafts would therefore be limited in advance to three fourths of their average trade turnover (exports plus imports) (Art. 6-5). The Board could reduce all quotas uniformly if necessary to correct a general inflationary trend, and could restore them later toward their original level if this seemed desirable to correct a potential deficiency of world purchasing power (Art. 6-13). The level of international liquidities could thus be managed rationally rather than be determined by the accidents of gold discoveries and mining techniques and the vagaries of national policies with respect to gold reserves (Art. 1-c). Taxes of 1% and 2% annually on both creditor and debtor accounts in excess of one fourth or one half a country's quota would also discourage excessive imbalance of either kind.[9] Confronted with an excessive credit expansion, the Board could remit the tax on creditors and raise correspondingly the tax on debtors (Art. 6-7). Finally, strong action could also be taken by

9. These taxes could be escaped by an agreement between a creditor and a debtor, after consultation with the Board, to transform part of their bancor accounts into a bilateral loan by the former country to the latter, since this would decrease correspondingly their imbalance with the Union. We may note, in passing, that this provision might have stimulated a considerable reduction in international interest rates, and would have been particularly favorable to creditworthy debtors such as the United Kingdom. The tax levied by the Union on prospective creditors —such as the U.S.—could easily have climbed otherwise to several hundred million dollars per year.

the Board against debtors wishing to borrow in excess of one half their quota. Such debtors could be required to devalue their currency by any amount that the Board might decide, to control all outward capital movements, and to surrender a suitable proportion of their gold reserves or other liquid assets in reduction of their debit balance. Internal measures adequate to restore balance of payments equilibrium could be recommended, but not imposed, by the Board. Further measures could be requested from debtors whose balances exceeded three fourths of their quota, and persistent indebtedness might be sanctioned by a declaration of default and ineligibility for further drawings on the Union (Art. 6-8).

Beyond one half their quotas, creditors were also required to consult with the Board on the adoption of readjustment measures, but would in the end retain their full freedom of decision. This difference of treatment between excess debtors and excess creditors was clearly designed to gain the acceptance of the latter for a plan whose major advantages were reserved for the former (Art. 9).

3. Other Provisions

Such was the broad outline of the plan. We need not review here Keynes' numerous and imaginative hints regarding other possible functions of the Clearing Union with relation to commodity stabilization schemes, international investment, postwar relief and reconstruction, economic blockades, etc.[10] Most directly relevant to our purposes are the two Articles (37 and 38) on trading policy. Keynes rightly observed that international trade rules—like any other international commitments—had to conform to the national interests of the signatory countries in order to elicit their agreement and cooperation. The existence of the Clearing Union would, however, remove many of the balance of payments obstacles to liberal trading policies. Thus trade restrictions could be ruled out in principle, but with broad exceptions admitted in advance for countries which remained in debt to the Union for a specified proportion of their quota during a specified period. Such exceptions would greatly facilitate the acceptance of the proposed rules by all members of the Union. The worst forms of restrictions and discrimination could be entirely outlawed and, "in any

10. See particularly Arts. 39 and 40.

case, it should be laid down that members of the Union would not allow or suffer among themselves any restrictions on the disposal of receipts arising out of current trade or 'invisible' income" (Art. 38).

C. CRITICISM OF THE PLAN

1. Limitations on Convertibility

This latter provision is particularly interesting as it illustrates the persistency of some British viewpoints in international negotiation. It is indeed identical with the proposed "convertibility for nonresidents" which has loomed so large in the convertibility discussions of the last three or four years, but which would have left the United Kingdom free to impose trade restrictions and discrimination against the countries making use of such conversion rights to convert into dollars an "excessive" portion of their sterling earnings. Article 38 specifically contemplated the possibility of a country in difficulties resorting not only to nondiscriminatory restrictions but also to "barter trade agreements." This was completely illogical in view of the total transferability of currencies established by the Union mechanism, which would have removed any need or justification for bilateral or discriminatory restrictions. The importance of sterling markets in world trade, however, naturally confers on Britain an enormous bargaining strength in bilateral negotiations, and Britain is understandably reluctant to throw away such a weapon when it is experiencing balance of payments difficulties.

The financial provisions of the plan also remained somewhat vague and ambiguous as to the exact mechanism which would assure, in practice, the complete interconvertibility of currencies at stable exchange rates.

First of all, each member state was committed not to alter the value of its currency in terms of bancor, nor to acquire gold at a price in excess of parity. Taken in conjunction with the provision which permitted all members to acquire another currency through bancor transfers, and to obtain a bancor credit against an equivalent payment of gold to the Union, this would seem to imply that actual exchange rates would be effectively stabilized on the market. This, however, is not so evident as might at first appear. Currency appreciation would indeed be ruled out, since any central bank could acquire the currency of another through bancor transfers. But what would happen if an oversupply of a currency on the market tended to depress its actual exchange value? Would the issuing country itself be compelled to intervene on the market and to redeem excess balances of its currency in order to avoid such depreciation? Could any other central bank whose currency was thus appreciating in terms of the depreciating currency repurchase the latter on the market and demand that it be exchanged for gold or bancor either by the issuing central bank or by the Clearing Union? Would this be implied in the provision which "laid down that members of the Union would not allow or suffer among themselves any restrictions on the disposal of receipts arising out of current trade or 'invisible' income" (Art. 38)?

This would seem to be a reasonable interpretation of the intent of the plan, but is not spelled out explicitly in any of its Articles. Countries are specifically allowed to buy foreign currencies from the Union, but not to sell them to it. The only explicit reference to such a type of transaction is in Article 34, where it is suggested that part at least of the "abnormal balances in overseas ownership held in various countries at the end of war"—sterling balances, in practice—be made convertible into bancor by the creditor country without, however, any corresponding debit to the regular bancor account of the debtor country.

The intent of the plan was, most probably, to leave to the issuing country the responsibility of preventing a depreciation of its currency. In the absence of exchange control, this would be achieved by a commitment to redeem, at the par value,[11] balances of its currency offered to it by private traders or foreign central banks. In the case of an exchange control country, this commitment would be limited to currency balances "legally acquired" by the holder, and trade and exchange restrictions could be tightened, if need be, to reduce the outflow of legally convertible balances. It is this possibility which opens the door wide to bilateral pressures and bargaining. Under a system of quantitative trade or

11. Or, more probably, at a slightly lower rate, preserving a certain margin for day-to-day fluctuations, and approximating the old "gold export point." There was, however, no reference to such a margin in the Keynes plan, although it could probably be inferred from the fact that gold settlements might still be effected among central banks and that the Union could "charge a small commission or transfer fee in respect of [bancor] transactions on its books" (Art. 6-6).

exchange restrictions, the licensing authorities may favor imports from some countries and restrict more harshly imports from other countries. Licenses may be granted more freely to imports from countries which give favorable treatment to the country's exports or which refrain from converting into gold or other currencies the currency balances earned from it. Bilateral trade and payments agreements formalize such mutual arrangements and are the very antithesis of multilateralism and convertibility.

Such arrangements were strongly deprecated by Keynes (see Arts. 3, 13, and 40), and one of their major techniques—i.e. bilateral restrictions on the use of currency balances arising from current transactions—was barred by the last sentence of Article 38, already referred to above.[12] Moreover, Keynes proposed that the United States and the United Kingdom "agree together that they would not accept the reserve balances of other countries in excess of normal working balances except in the case of banks definitely belonging to a Sterling Area or Dollar Area group" (Art. 25). This would bar either country from entering into bilateral payments agreements, except with countries in the dollar area in the case of the United States and with countries in the sterling area in the case of Britain. The first of these exceptions was in fact rather academic, in view of the United States' determination to keep the dollar fully convertible. The second, however, was essential for the retention of the preferential currency arrangements which were the keystone of the sterling area system. If the logic of the plan had been followed to its ultimate conclusion, no country should henceforth have been allowed to accumulate foreign currency holdings in excess of normal working balances, except in the form of bancor. Transitional provisions, along the lines suggested in Article 34, would have dealt with outstanding balances through partial funding over a long period, and through partial conversions into bancor accompanied by a similar funding of the resulting claim of the Union on the debtor country.

In brief, the Keynes plan would have outlawed and made operationally impossible the generalization of bilateral trade and payments agreements which in fact characterized the early postwar years. It would, however, have allowed recourse to barter trade agreements by extreme debtors, and kept the door open for the

12. See p. 99.

retention of sterling—rather than gold or bancor—as a means of settlement and an instrument of reserve accumulation for countries in the sterling area.

Curiously enough, these crucial features of the Keynes plan received relatively little attention in the discussions which followed its publication. Criticism centered instead on two other points: the disproportionate voting power of the sterling area in the Clearing Union on the one hand, and the financial laxity and inflationary bias of the plan on the other.

2. Distribution of Voting Power

The first point can be disposed of quickly. It was proposed to base each country's voting power on the size of its quota, and to determine the quotas themselves on the basis of the countries' average trade turnover. Such a criterion would have given the sterling area 30% of the Union's voting power, instead of the 24% which it commands in the International Monetary Fund, and continental Western Europe 36% instead of 22%. On the other hand, the United States would have received only 12% of the voting power instead of 27%. Let us note that the size of the quotas also determined the borrowing rights of the countries but did not limit in any way their lending commitments. This formula was, of course, too obviously ingenious ever to be considered seriously by the United States. Keynes, however, was well aware of the fact and agreed in advance that "a special assessment" could be substituted for his formula "in cases (of which there might be several) when this formula would be, for any reason, inappropriate" (Art. 6-5).

3. Size and Automaticity of Borrowing Rights and Lending Commitments

Far more serious was the proposed size of the borrowing quotas and the fact that all or most of the borrowings might concentrate on one or a few creditor countries, most probably on the United States. The suggested basis of calculation would have created initially about $35 billion of quotas, of which more than $30 billion would have been placed at the disposal of countries other than the United States. The continuous adjustment of the quotas in accordance with the moving average of trade turnover would—on the basis of more recent trade figures—have raised these amounts to the fantastic figures of roughly $115 billion and $95 billion, respectively, by 1955. Keynes' opponents rightly criticized the indefinite inflationary bias of a formula which would automatically increase available borrowings in step with the increased imports which they financed.

Table IX. COMPARATIVE VOTING POWER UNDER THE KEYNES PLAN AND THE IMF ARTICLES OF AGREEMENT

(in % of total)

	OEEC Europe and Sterling Area			Rest of the World				
	Continental						Latin	Other
	£ Area	OEEC	Total	Total	U.S.	Canada	America	Countries
Under the								
Keynes Plan a	30	36	65	35	12	4	8	11
Under the IMF b	24	22	45	55	27	3	10	15

Notes:

a. Based on average trade turnover in 1937–38 for all countries.

b. Actual voting power in 1955. The 1947 voting power was even larger for the U.S., Latin America, and Canada, and lower for the sterling area, but this is primarily due to the fact that a number of countries (including Australia) had not yet joined the Fund at that date.

Once again, however, it should be stressed that the British proposals were designed as an initial bargaining position which was expected to be modified considerably before agreement could be reached. The initial quotas would undoubtedly be scaled down, and the voting power of the United States increased so as to allow it to exercise a greater influence on the decisions of the Board and to ensure the efficacy of the provisions enabling the Board to review the size of quotas in order to combat an excessive expansion of international credit. In any case, the continuous adjustment of quotas envisaged in the plan should have been based on fluctuations in exports alone—rather than in trade turnover—so as to prevent a country from profiting automatically from an inflation-induced expansion of its import levels.

We must also remember that the conditions which the Board could attach to borrowings exceeding half of a country's quota were so stringent as to allow the Board, in practice, to limit borrowing rights to half of the huge totals mentioned above. We may therefore consider that the maximum amount of credits placed at the disposal of the debtors would have been closer to $15 billion than to $30 billion in the initial postwar years, even if *all* other countries had become debtors of the United States to the full extent of their unconditional borrowing rights. Such figures no longer appear absurd when related to the $15 billion of net U.S. aid extended abroad in the fiscal years 1946–48 alone, and the $26 billion of net aid granted between the end of World War II and the beginning of the Korean conflict. Of these $26 billion, more than $19 billion went to Western Europe and its dependent areas, and only $9 billion to the rest of the world. The Keynes plan would have been less generous, particularly with respect to Europe.

Keynes, however, denied repeatedly that the plan's borrowing facilities were intended as long- or medium-term credits for reconstruction or development. He feared indeed the inflationary impact which the plan might have on the world economy during the initial period of postwar shortages, and specifically envisaged a temporary blocking of the Union's credit facilities during this period, and their replacement by *ad hoc* aid, in specified amounts and for specified purposes.[13]

If, however, the Union's credit facilities were really designed for normal, postreconstruction years, their amount was certainly excessive. It would have immediately doubled or tripled foreign countries' gold and dollar reserves, and created international liquidities far in excess of what might reasonably be considered necessary to cover temporary imbalance in world payments. Keynes seems to have wavered between two very different concepts of the needs which the Union's credits would be required to fill. He professed to intend them only for normal, long-run requirements. But he also feared that postwar aid would be niggardly and unequal to the job, and wished in this case to be able to fall back on the Union's credit facilities. "If, on the other hand, relief from outside sources looks like being inadequate from the outset, the overdraft quotas might be even more necessary at the outset than later on" (Art. 42).

Keynes took great pains to justify the automaticity of the Union's credits by analogy with the functioning of a national banking system. The Union's lending would merely put to use the surpluses left idle by the creditor nations. This would remove the

---

13. Arts. 41 and 42. The reader will note the similarity between this temporary freeze and the blocking of IMF credits to countries benefiting from Marshall aid and of the quotas of Greece, Turkey, and Iceland in the early years of EPU.

deflationary impact of such surpluses on the other countries while maintaining the full liquidity of the creditors' balances, which could always be used by them whenever needed to settle deficits in their international transactions. In the same way, the individual depositor in a commercial bank retains the use of his deposits, and is not inconvenienced in any way by the fact that his bank uses his funds in the meantime to finance its other customers. The adoption of such a system in international relations would greatly facilitate international aid or lending programs, as it would be unnecessary to call upon any particular country to commit its own resources for the purpose. Member countries

> have only to agree in general that, if they find themselves with surplus resources which for the time being they do not themselves wish to employ, these resources may go into the general pool and be put to work on approved purposes. This costs the surplus country nothing because it is not asked to part permanently, or even for any specified period, with such resources which it remains free to expend and employ for its own purposes whenever it chooses; in which case the burden of finance is passed on to the next recipient, again for only so long as the recipient has no use for the money.[14]

This "anonymity" or "impersonality" of the creditors would also remove politics from international lending.

The same general argument was used (in Arts. 7, 8, and 9) to dispel the objections of creditor nations to the plan. No burden was placed on them by their bancor holdings, since these remained as liquid and usable as any other accruals of international reserves —gold particularly—in which their surpluses would otherwise be paid. They remained as free as before to reduce their surpluses through increased imports or foreign investments.

> In the absence of the Clearing Union a creditor country can employ the proceeds of its exports to buy goods or to buy investments, or to make temporary advances and to hold temporary overseas balances, or to buy gold in the market. All these facilities will remain at its disposal. The difference is that in the absence of the Clearing Union, more or less auto-

14. See Arts. 12 and 40.

matic factors come into play to restrict the volume of its exports after the above means of receiving payment for them have been exhausted. Certain countries become unable to buy and, in addition to this, there is an automatic tendency towards a general slump in international trade and, as a result, a reduction in the exports of the creditor country. Thus, the effect of the Clearing Union is to give the creditor country a choice between voluntarily curtailing its exports to the same extent that they would have been involuntarily curtailed in the absence of the Clearing Union, or, alternatively, of allowing its exports to continue and accumulating the excess receipts in the form of bancor balances for the time being. Unless the removal of a factor causing the involuntary reduction of exports is reckoned a disadvantage, a creditor country incurs no burden but is, on the contrary, relieved, by being offered the additional option of receiving payment for its exports through the accumulation of a bancor balance.[15]

In appraising these arguments, we must distinguish their international aspects from the national interests of the creditors themselves. The analogy with a national banking system is exaggerated from both points of view. It is right as far as the automaticity of the creditor's bancor lending—and of an individual's deposit account with his bank—is concerned, and there are indeed undoubted advantages to the proposed automaticity of the lending commitments of the creditor countries to the Clearing Union. No depositor, on the other hand, would willingly accumulate deposits in a bank which is itself committed in advance to lend large sums to any Tom, Dick, or Harry on the mere condition that they need the money to finance their deficits. Automatic lending commitments by the creditors are conceivable only if the bank —or Clearing Union—with which they leave their funds keeps an adequate control on its own lending operations and can be trusted to exercise proper judgment in granting or refusing credit to the prospective borrowers. The acceptance of the Keynes plan by the creditor nations would clearly have required, from this point of view, a lesser degree of automaticity for the borrowers

15. Art. 8. See also Art. 40.

and a distribution of voting power very different from that envisaged by Keynes.

This would also have been necessary in any case to retain for the plan its claim to a removal of the "deflationary bias" of the gold standard. Otherwise, the danger would always have been present that a large number of countries would run more or less quickly through the automatic borrowing facilities placed at their disposal, and become unable to finance further deficits. Such a flare of expansion and inflation would then merely lead to the postponement—and not the elimination—of the "deflationary bias," and result in even more violent convulsions in world trade and world prices than would have been possible under the gold standard itself.

Finally, from the national viewpoint of the creditor nations, the "impersonality" of the lenders might well be regarded with a mitigated degree of enthusiasm. National lending can be, and indeed has been for many years, an instrument of national power and a powerful adjunct to diplomacy. Creditor nations would inevitably insist, at the very least, on adequate voting power in international decisions affecting their own lending.

4. Conclusions

These various drawbacks could, however, be corrected in the course of negotiations. Keynes' proposals were only offered, after all, as a "basis for discussion," inviting counterproposals and final compromises. They could, moreover, be corrected without discarding the general structure of a plan which was, and has remained to this day, far superior to any of the practical alternatives offered to it.

Most of the necessary adjustments of quotas, voting power, and so on were indeed incorporated in the final Agreement for an International Monetary Fund. Unfortunately, some of the most valid and fruitful features of the Keynes plan were also lost in the process. The reasons for this are many and varied. One cannot but be struck, however, by the fact that the Keynes plan was practically shelved, with hardly any discussion, from the very start of the negotiations.

The explanation may lie, in part, with Britain herself. It is no

secret that the Bank of England was extremely cool to Keynes'
views and particularly to the creation of a powerful international
monetary institution. At the same time, other influential British
circles preferred discrimination and bilateralism to the multilateral monetary system which the Clearing Union tried to reconstruct.[16] This point of view may well have gained more ad-
herents among the British negotiating team when it became
evident that the United States was not prepared to contribute
to the financing of an international monetary plan the apparently
staggering sums which Britain deemed necessary to underwrite
her own commitment to multilateral policies under the Keynes
plan. Other British experts were inclined to regard as more realistic the alternative proposal of the White plan for a "scarce currency clause" which would force the United States to choose
eventually between a more liberal trading and investment policy
on the one hand, and organized, collective discrimination against
U.S. exports on the other.[17] The fact is that the record of Washington discussions shows little evidence of any serious fight by the
British delegation in favor of the Keynes plan.

On the American side, on the other hand, the whole negotiation
was dominated by the powerful personality of Harry White, his
immense personal conceit, and his ruthlessness both within the
American working group and in the negotiations with other national delegations. Harry White professed to know what Congress
would accept and what Congress would refuse. No plan would

16. Keynes had these circles in mind when, in his speech to the House of Lords
on May 23, 1944, he defended in these terms a return to sterling convertibility:
   To suppose that a system of bilateral and barter agreements, with no one
   who owns sterling knowing just what he can do with it—to suppose that this
   is the best way to encourage the Dominions to center their financial systems
   on London, seems to me pretty near frenzy. As a technique of little England-
   ism, adopted as a last resort when all else has failed us, with this small country
   driven to autarchy, keeping itself to itself in a harsh and unfriendly world,
   it might make more sense. But those who talk this way, in the expectation
   that the rest of the Commonwealth will throw in their lot on these lines and
   cut their free commercial relations with the rest of the world, can have very
   little idea how this Empire has grown or by what means it can be sustained.
Reprinted in *The New Economics*, ed. Harris, p. 371.
   17. See Roy Harrod, *The Life of John Maynard Keynes* (London, 1951), pp.
544–7. Keynes himself did not, at first, take this "half-baked" suggestion very
seriously, and doubted until the end whether Congress would "swallow anything
so extreme." Ibid., pp. 547–8 and 571. The clause was in fact "swallowed" by Congress but never invoked in practice even in the darkest days of the dollar shortage.
See below, p. 127.

have any chance to succeed without American participation, and American participation would clearly have been unobtainable without the full support and untiring efforts of the United States Treasury and of Harry White himself.

III. THE INTERNATIONAL MONETARY FUND

A. THE ARTICLES OF AGREEMENT

The Articles of Agreement of the International Monetary Fund are a legal document, embodying the results of a complicated process of international negotiation and compromise among divergent national viewpoints. Enormous efforts were spent in reaching a maximum degree of precision in order to resolve in advance the many conflicts of interest which might arise later among the participating countries.

The success achieved in this direction has tended to develop the jurisdictional powers and functions of the Fund at the expense of its possible role as a continuous forum for consultation and negotiation. This was soon to prove a handicap as well as an asset in a world environment which differed greatly from that envisaged at Bretton Woods. Many of the Fund's provisions were particularly ill-adapted to dealing constructively with the generalized disequilibria of the early postwar years. Desirable action was often blocked thereby and a great deal of time had to be consumed in trying to modify or supplement, through a very flexible process of interpretation, the obvious intent of the Articles of Agreement

1. Exchange Rates

The problem of exchange stability, treated by Keynes in three or four paragraphs, receives a major emphasis (more than thirty sections, subsections, or subsubsections) in the Fund Agreement. These provisions, however, do not differ substantially from those of the Keynes plan. Each currency will be linked to gold by international agreement, and later changes will require the concurrence of the Executive Board.[1]

1. The discretion left by Keynes to a persistent debtor to depreciate its currency unilaterally by 5% is, however, extended to all members, irrespective of their position in the Fund, and transformed into a right to appreciate—as well as depreciate

2. Trade and Exchange Restrictions

No mention is made of trade restrictions in the Agreement, the whole subject being reserved for the proposed International Trade Organization (ITO). Exchange restrictions, on the other hand, are treated in Articles VI, VII, VIII, and XIV. Essentially each country is left free to regulate international capital movements, but cannot impose, without the approval of the Fund, any restrictions on current payments and transfers. Such restrictions are automatically authorized, however, against a currency declared scarce by the Fund. Finally, during a so-called "postwar transitional period," all Fund members are authorized by the Agreement itself "to maintain and adapt to changing circumstances" any kind of restrictions on current transactions and transfers.

3. Lending Operations

A third series of provisions relates to the lending operations of the Fund. It is here that the most basic differences emerge between the Keynes plan and the Fund plan. First of all, the total size of the quotas is reduced from the huge amounts suggested by Keynes to a more modest $8 billion to $9 billion, and no quota can be adjusted later without a four-fifths majority of the total voting power and the consent of the member concerned.

Secondly, the financial mechanism of the quotas is based on the deposit system of banking familiar in the United States, rather than on the overdraft, or current account, method traditional in the United Kingdom. Each country remains entitled to borrow from the Fund up to an amount limited by the quota assigned to it, but the corresponding Fund loans will be financed from initial contributions—equal in size to the borrowing rights—required from all members. These contributions are paid up to 25% in gold,[2] and for the remainder in the currency of the member itself

---

—their currencies up to 10%. More important is the fact that the Board can no longer recommend an exchange readjustment or impose it as a condition for further drawings. The Board can only reject or concur with the precise readjustment proposed by a member. See Arts. IV and XX, Sec. 4, of the Fund's Articles of Agreement.

2. The gold subscription required, however, may not exceed 10% of the country's net gold and dollar holdings at the date when the Fund signifies its intention of beginning shortly its exchange operations.

or in nonnegotiable, noninterest-bearing securities payable to the Fund on demand. When a member borrows from the Fund, its obligation does not take the form of an overdraft, or debtor balance. The borrowing member instead delivers to the Fund equivalent and additional amounts of its own currency or security obligations.

This technique is responsible for the contorted language of many articles of the Fund Agreement. The word "borrowing," for instance, never appears anywhere in connection with normal Fund operations. All borrowings are dubbed "exchange transactions," meaning that the borrowing country exchanges its own currency (in plain language, its IOU) for the foreign currency which it needs. Repayment or amortization of former borrowings similarly becomes a "repurchase by a member of its currency held by the Fund." The exhaustion of a debtor's quota in the Fund will be reflected in the fact that the Fund's holdings of its currency reach 200% of the quota.[3] The normal obligation to contribute 25% of the quota to the Fund in gold finally results in the fact that a country retains a contingent liability to the Fund—expressed particularly in so-called "repurchase obligations"—as long as the Fund's holdings of its currency exceed 75% of the country's quota.[4]

Thirdly, and of far greater significance to the operation of the system, the lending commitment of the creditor countries is now rigidly limited to the amount of their own quota.[5] The Fund can therefore run short of a given currency and find itself unable to honor drawings in such a currency. The famous "scarce currency" clause (Art. VII) is designed to meet this problem: "If it becomes evident to the Fund that the demand for a particular currency threatens the Fund's ability to supply that currency, the Fund . . . shall formally declare such currency scarce and shall thenceforth apportion its existing and accruing supply of the scarce currency with due regard to the relative needs of members, the general in-

3. The initial 75% subscription in currency, plus withdrawals corresponding to the 25% subscription in gold, plus the 100% of *net* borrowings from the Fund.

4. A precise discussion of these repurchase obligations would require many pages of explanation to be at all understandable. Suffice it to say that they aim at limiting to 50% at most the use of Fund resources in covering balance of payments deficits, and at ensuring that 50% of any later increase in reserves be devoted to the amortization of a country's debt to the Fund. See Art. V, Sec. 7 and Schedule B.

5. Each country's commitment to lend is limited to, and implemented by, its gold and currency subscription to the Fund.

ternational economic situation, and any other pertinent considerations." Such a declaration "shall operate as an authorization to any member, after consultation with the Fund, temporarily to impose limitations on the freedom of exchange operations in the scarce currency."

Before declaring a member's currency scarce, however, the Fund may try to replenish its holdings through borrowings from that member or from any other source. Any such borrowings would require the agreement of the member concerned. The Fund may alternatively "require the member to sell its currency to the Fund for gold."

This latter provision rules out, in practice, the possibility of any currency scarcity for all but the major trading countries.[6] The Fund's supply of national currencies is, of course, the smallest for the countries with the smallest quotas. It holds, for instance, only $370,000 in Panamanian balboas, but its entire gold holdings ($1.8 billion at the end of 1955) could theoretically be used to replenish its supply, in the unlikely event that Fund members began to develop an inordinate thirst for balboas!

The United States alone was expected to develop in the postwar years surpluses sufficient to stimulate dollar borrowings from the Fund substantially in excess of the total Fund holdings of gold and dollars. Gold and dollar subscriptions to the Fund's capital amounted to about $3.7 billion. This was hardly more than a third of the United States surplus in the single year 1947 and half the total borrowing rights of other Fund members ($6 billion of quotas plus their own gold subscriptions, or about $6.9 billion in all).

The scarce currency proposal made a deep impression on some of the British experts.[7] They saw in it a powerful means to bring home to congressional and public opinion in the United States the dilemma of a persistent surplus country. The United States would be forced, by this clause, to face openly the choice between liberal trade and lending policies on the one hand and, on the other, a general discrimination by the rest of the world against American exports.

6. An excellent discussion of this point may be found in E. M. Bernstein, "Scarce Currencies and the International Monetary Fund," *Journal of Political Economy* (March 1945), pp. 1–4.

7. See above, p. 108 and n.17.

4. Convertibility Provisions

Finally, no provision is made in the Articles of Agreement for the multilateral clearing of credit and debit balances. Members can only borrow from the Fund by exchanging their own currency for a specific currency needed to settle deficits in their current transactions. They cannot mobilize through the Fund their earnings with some countries in order to finance their deficits with other countries. Neither can they use automatically such earnings to amortize their indebtedness to the Fund. Such indebtedness can only be repaid in gold or in the currency of convertible countries which are creditors of the Fund.[8]

The absence of a clearing machinery flows, of course, from the limitation of the creditor countries' lending commitments. It constitutes nevertheless a fatal flaw, contradicting the fourth professed purpose of the Fund which is "to assist in the establishment of a multilateral system of payments in respect of current transactions between members" (Art. I-iv). The only reference I have found to the problem in the record of pre-Bretton Woods negotiations was a question by Professor D. H. Robertson, asking how triangular settlements could be effected under the Fund's machinery. Robertson's question was curtly dismissed by Harry White: This was only a technical detail which he would gladly leave to the drafting committee!

As we shall see later, it is precisely this "technical detail" that from the start precluded any real Fund impact on the bilateral system of payments which strangled postwar international transactions. It is the refusal or inability of the Fund to concern itself with this "technical detail" that left a vacuum which Europe and the United States later felt impelled to fill through the creation of a new institution, the European Payments Union.

To say that the Fund Agreement did not concern itself in the least with the twin problems of convertibility and triangular settlements would be excessive. It may not be excessive to state, however, that the Fund provided only a fair-weather solution for these problems.

8. Repurchases cannot be made in any currency the Fund's holdings of which are "above 75 percent of the quota of the member concerned." Art. V, Sec. 7-c-iii and Schedule B-1-c.

If, for example, France needed to make use of her net earnings on the United Kingdom to settle her deficits with some other countries, little difficulty would arise as long as the convertibility of her sterling receipts into other currencies was ensured by the United Kingdom herself. If, however, the United Kingdom refused to assume convertibility commitments, or was excused from them by the Fund,[9] the Fund would wash its hands of the whole affair. France would have to reach with Britain whatever arrangement she could for the settlement of her sterling surpluses. She would even be weakened in such negotiation by Article IV, Section 4-*b* of the Fund Agreement, under which "each member undertakes, through appropriate measures consistent with this Agreement, to permit within its territories exchange transactions between its currency and the currencies of other members only within the limits prescribed under Section 3 of this Article," i.e. within 1% of parity. In order to fulfill this obligation, the French authorities might either have to forbid flatly all sterling transactions within their territories—a decision difficult to enforce and dangerous to adopt toward a strong country commanding vast markets for French exports—or get rid of their sterling surpluses through discriminatory import policies, or buy sterling for official account, thus extending credit to Britain in indefinite amounts. The latter solution, paradoxically enough, would place upon France the burden of financing the convertibility of a currency which its own monetary authorities refused to convert.[10]

It is true that all Fund members undertake in principle, under Article VIII of the Agreement, to maintain the convertibility of their national currency, and may be assisted in this task by their access to the Fund's resources. At first view, therefore, the problem seems to be solved and to require no further Fund action.

The convertibility obligation of Article VIII was, however, totally nullified under Article XIV by the freedom left each member to "maintain and adapt to changing circumstances" their existing

9. The Articles of Agreement contain no overriding provision ensuring non-resident convertibility, such as that suggested in Art. 38 of the Keynes plan.

10. This patent absurdity was indeed at the origin of the conflict which opposed France to the Fund in January 1948, when France refused to guarantee any further the cross-rate of sterling for dollars in Paris. Let us also note that a country which is itself strong enough to buy and sell gold freely for the settlement of international transactions is freed by this same provision of the Fund Agreement of the obligation imposed by the Agreement on weaker countries!

THE INTERNATIONAL CURRENCY PLANS

exchange restrictions. This discretion was to end, but again only in principle, five years after the Fund began operations, i.e. in March 1952. Ten years have gone by, but so far only ten countries have accepted the convertibility obligations of Article VIII.[11]

Moreover, these convertibility obligations are themselves far less comprehensive than one might think, and than would be necessary to ensure the full transferability of all currency balances.

First of all, they do not apply to balances acquired as a result of transactions effected before the removal of the restrictions imposed under Article XIV.

Secondly, they do not apply to balances acquired contrary to the exchange regulations of the country which owes them, and particularly to any balance acquired as a result of prohibited capital movements.

Thirdly, the conversion cannot be requested by a member whose currency has been declared scarce, nor from a member who, for any reason, is not entitled to buy currencies from the Fund.

Fourthly, the Fund may relieve any member of its convertibility obligations.

Last but not least, the country requiring the conversion must "represent" that the balances have been recently acquired *as a result of* "current transactions," or that their conversion is needed for making payments *for* "current transactions." [12]

This list of exceptions is not only formidable. The last of them is also puzzling in the extreme. A central bank which acquires balances in a convertible currency does not do so in connection with any individual transaction, current or otherwise. It buys such balances from the market in order to prevent an appreciation of its own currency, resulting from a *net* excess of its exports of merchandise and services and its capital imports over its imports of merchandise and services and its capital exports. Similarly, if a central bank is called upon to make a payment abroad to another central bank, it is also as a result of a *net* deficit arising from a variety of transactions, in which current and capital movements necessarily lose their individuality. It is difficult to conceive how the "representation" required by Article VIII could ever be made under normal conditions, and therefore how the Article might ever be in-

11. The United States, Canada, Mexico, Cuba, the Dominican Republic, Guatemala, El Salvador, Honduras, Haiti, and Panama.
12. Art. VIII, Sec. 4.

voked to force a reluctant country to convert its balances held by another country.

In practice, therefore, the convertibility of any currency will be assured only as long as the issuing country wishes to maintain it, and the Fund Agreement appears largely ineffective either to impose it in practice or to protect its members against the most damaging consequences of the inconvertibility of any major currency.

B. THE AGREEMENT IN OPERATION

The International Monetary Fund has now been in operation for about ten years. It has been served by many eminent, sincere, and devoted officials, both on its staff [13] and on its Executive Board. Yet the record of these ten years is a grim and dismal one. To deny it would be futile and would be a disservice to the cause of the institution itself. The Fund's failures must be recognized and understood if the Fund is to become one day, in fact as well as in words, "a permanent institution which provides the machinery for consultation and collaboration on international monetary problems." [14]

1. Par Values and Exchange Rates

One of the first tasks assigned to the Fund by its charter was the initial establishment of par values for its members' currencies. Great stress had been placed by the Fund's founding fathers on the need to harmonize postwar decisions on exchange stabilization and to avoid a repetition of the disparate national decisions which, after the First World War, had brought about a chaotic pattern of overvalued and undervalued currencies and largely contributed to the collapse of the new gold standard in 1931. It was therefore with some surprise that on December 18, 1946 the world read in the Fund's *Statement concerning Initial Par Values* that "the initial par values are, in all cases, those which have been proposed by members, and they are based on existing rates of exchange." [15] The

13. If one man is to be singled out from many others, it should certainly be E. M. Bernstein, who served throughout these ten years as the Fund's Director of Research and is, more than any other individual, responsible for the brilliant, imaginative, and objective thinking embodied in innumerable analyses—published and unpublished—of the Fund's problems and policies.

14. *Articles of Agreement*, Art. I: "Purposes," Para. i.

15. See IMF, *Annual Report* (June 30, 1947), p. 70.

Fund was widely accused of trying to consolidate an "unrealistic" pattern of exchange rates, based merely on political expediency and tending to aggravate balance of payments disequilibria and trade and exchange controls.

These criticisms were unjust. The Fund itself proclaimed its readiness to consider, and indeed encourage, members' requests for a revision of their parity as soon as circumstances would make such a course desirable. For the moment, however, currency readjustments would merely lead to an aggravation of internal inflationary pressures and a worsening of the devaluing countries' terms of trade.

> An exchange rate has two functions. The first function . . . is to let the exports flow. The second function . . . is to limit imports. Under present conditions it is not possible for the exchange rate to perform this function in some countries. They cannot count on exchange rates to limit imports to the proper level or to apportion them among those various goods which the economy most urgently needs. . . . For these reasons it appeared to the Fund that for the present the one practical test that could be applied to determine the suitability of an exchange rate was whether it enables a country to export. In testing the initial parities communicated to the Fund, it appeared that the proposed parities would not under prevailing conditions seriously handicap exports.[16]

One of the main considerations invoked was the fact that exports were held down by temporary shortages of productive capacity rather than by excessive costs or prices. Devaluation would neither reconstruct war-destroyed plants nor allow them to sell goods that they were unable to produce. In truth, no single exchange rate could fit both the current situation and that which would develop during the following months and years. The initial exchange rates should not aim at a normal balance in each country's external transactions but at much larger deficits on current account, desirable for the acceleration of economic reconstruction and financed by disin-

16. Camille Gutt, *The Practical Problem of Exchange Rates* (Washington, D.C., IMF 1948), pp. 4–5. The first Chairman of the Executive Board made explicit in this paper the considerations justifying the Fund's decision, which were alluded to more briefly in the *Statement concerning Initial Par Values* and in the first *Annual Report* (1947) of the Fund.

vestment and foreign aid. As time went on, these sources of financing would taper off, but the progress of production would also increase exportable capacity, reduce import needs, and modify radically the data underlying the calculation of an equilibrium exchange rate. Further modifications in these data would result from the uneven success of the various countries in checking current inflation and mopping up overliquidity, and from the policies followed by each country and by its major trading partners with respect of the gradual liberalization of trade and exchange restrictions. Whatever initial par values were set, they would have to be modified considerably, and unpredictably, to fit an extremely fluid and fast-changing environment.[17]

The Fund admitted all this and explicitly disclaimed the intention of freezing par values at their initial level. Yet it can be seen in retrospect that the setting up of initial par values had unfortunate consequences on later developments in the exchange field.

First of all, it could hardly be claimed that the above considerations justified in all cases the maintenance of the exchange rates then in existence. The monetary and economic position and prospects of the various Fund members differed widely with respect to each of the points mentioned above, and would have called for a certain degree of variation in their exchange rate policies. This was particularly true as between the countries undergoing open price inflation and those with effectively controlled prices and latent inflation.

Secondly, the setting up and control of par values by the Fund were aimed at preserving the international community from the threat of competitive devaluations. In fact, however, the postwar period witnessed no threat of this sort, but rather the opposite. Countries were far less inclined to devalue to excess than to maintain overvalued exchange rates behind the protective barrier of comprehensive trade and exchange controls. Even though the Fund was not opposed to desirable readjustments, the procedure involved

17. This reasoning was inspired primarily by the situation of the belligerent countries in Western Europe. Underdeveloped countries in other areas of the world, particularly in Latin America, were also inclined to maintain overvalued exchange rates both in order to take advantage of the seller's markets for foodstuffs and raw materials and to encourage restocking and development expenditures, even at the cost of sacrificing some of the foreign exchange reserves unwillingly accumulated by them during the period of wartime shortages.

in a modification of par values dramatized such changes in a way which encouraged reluctance toward exchange rate adaptations and stimulated instead widespread reliance on the techniques of direct trade and exchange restrictions. Exchange rate stability was achieved, but such stability became meaningless for traders whose access to the exchange market could be blocked or opened from one day to the next by unpredictable decisions of the licensing authorities.

Moreover, this system probably resulted in aggravating, rather than reducing, the amplitude of changes in the official exchange rates themselves. Countries tended to postpone desirable changes in the parity of their currency as long as they felt unsure of the rate at which the new parity could be effectively maintained. Overvalued rates were thus retained for too long and, once the decision to devalue was taken, the authorities would play safe and propose a larger devaluation than was really needed, so as to minimize the danger of having to repeat the same process two or three months later in the event of a further deterioration in their balance of payments.

This explains in part the choice of an unexpectedly low rate for sterling in September 1949. The wholesale cascade of devaluations proposed to the Fund, and accepted by it with record speed during that month, proved a most fateful and fatal test for the efficacy and prestige of the institution.

It is no longer a secret that the British, irked by a previous American-led Fund campaign in favor of sterling devaluation and uneasy about news leaks from the unwieldy Executive Board sessions, did not propose a new par value for sterling in accordance with the Fund's Articles of Agreement. They merely told the Board one tense Saturday afternoon that the British Chancellor of the Exchequer would broadcast to the world on the following day the Cabinet's decision to devalue the pound from $4.03 to $2.80. The Chancellor would "appreciate it" if he could announce at the same time the concurrence of the Fund with this "decision."

The Fund's Agreement provided that the Fund would have seventy-two hours to declare its attitude when a proposed change in par value did not exceed 20%. The British request left the Fund less than twenty-four hours to agree or disagree with a 30.5% devaluation, deemed unquestionably excessive by most Fund members.[18] The Board agreed, in fact, the very same Saturday afternoon.

The speed with which the Fund had agreed with the British proposal precluded any serious discussion of the flood of devaluation requests which fell upon it during the following few days. Britain had had weeks and months in which to consider its decision and the Fund had meekly agreed in a matter of hours. How could the Fund delay its approval of decisions suddenly forced upon other countries by the British move, when such delays might give rise to all sorts of rumors and speculation about the final rate to be adopted?

There was indeed no discussion, the staff and the Board agreeing in each case that the precise rate of devaluation proposed by each country was, in accordance with Article IV, Section 5-f, "necessary to correct a fundamental disequilibrium."

The only exception to such smooth approvals came when Belgium requested, "in view of the exigencies of the situation," Fund approval for a floating exchange rate until a period of experimentation would allow it to propose a new and stable par value. This was also agreed to in the end, but only after a heated debate and by an extremely narrow margin in the Board. Fortunately or unfortunately, the decision came in the early hours of the morning, the newspaper reporters had gone home, and no announcement of this revolution in the Fund's policy was ever made to the world. Belgium had reconsidered during the night and announced before morning that a few hours of experimentation with a fluctuating rate now allowed her to propose to the Fund a new and stable par value of fifty Belgian francs per U.S. dollar.

The September 1949 debacle amply demonstrated the futility of the Fund's par value provisions as an effective weapon to control and harmonize widespread changes in exchange rates.[19] Once again the Fund had passively registered the precise rates proposed to it by each of its members, as it had done in the establishment of initial par values three years earlier.[20]

18. The general expectation at the time was that the sterling devaluation would not exceed 20% to 25%.

19. It did not, however, prove their inefficacy in handling individual exchange rate problems against a background of general currency convertibility and exchange rate stability. See below, p. 137.

20. The conflict which opposed the Fund to France in January 1948 did not arise from any disagreement between France and the Fund about the official parity proposed by that country to the Fund. The main objection of the Fund was addressed

One may finally reflect on the ludicrous debasement of the par value concept which resulted from the Fund's handling of multiple and floating exchange rates. The definition of initial par values in December 1946 had posed a rather ticklish problem to the countries—most of them in Latin America—which maintained a whole gamut of multiple exchange rates, widely different from one another, for various types of transactions. A solution of this riddle was quickly discovered, the Fund sanctioning as par value any single rate proposed to it by the member, and the member continuing to apply a wide variety of other rates to many, or even most, of its exchange transactions. As many as fifteen Fund members have operated under this kind of system, often for excellent reasons [21] and sometimes upon the advice of the Fund itself. In the course of time, and in spite of later parity revisions, one witnessed actual—and often fluctuating—rates for some transactions ranging up to ten times the Fund's par value in Paraguay, more than fifteen times the par value in Bolivia and Brazil, and more than twenty times the par value in Chile. The Fund itself candidly admits that the present par value of Bolivia—190 bolivianos per dollar, as against effective rates up to thirty-eight times as great for imports—"has no application." [22] In many other cases only minor transactions, such as government remittances and student and medical expenses, can be effected at the official par value. In the words of the Fund's 1955 *Annual Report* (p. 101): "For several . . . members the proportion of their total international transactions that is carried on at exchange rates governed by the established par value is small." The par value thus becomes a purely mythical concept, practically divorced from actual exchange rates and exchange transactions.

---

to the refusal of France to guarantee the cross-rate of inconvertible currencies, on the French market, for trade transactions. France refused to modify its proposals and was declared ineligible to use the Fund's resources. The Fund "welcomed as an appropriate step in the right direction" the unification of French rates for trade transactions in October of the same year, and the later unification and stabilization of all rates on the basis of 350 francs per dollar in September 1949. Bizarrely enough, however, it took the Executive Board another five years (until Oct. 15, 1955) to conclude that France had again become eligible to use the Fund's resources.

21. None of these reasons, however, could justify the absurd spreads mentioned below. Even when a good case could be made for multiple or floating rates, their adoption made nonsense of the par value concept as such.

22. See "Country Notes" on exchange rates for Bolivia in any 1956 issue of *International Financial Statistics*.

This, clearly, could not have been the intention of the Fund's founders. I cannot agree, however, with the economists who argue that no attempt should be made to stabilize exchange rates and who favor completely flexible exchange rates as a normal and permanent feature of the international monetary system.[23] The Fund's basic philosophy on par values is not wrong. It was, however, inapplicable to the highly abnormal and fluid circumstances of the early postwar years, and was implemented by unrealistic provisions for parity revisions even in more normal times. Instead of requesting the communication of a par value and accepting automatically any par value proposed to it by its members, the Fund should recognize a *de facto* exchange rate as par value only when it is satisfied as to the meaningfulness and prospective stability of such a rate. The maintenance of a par value with the Fund should not constitute an obligation imposed upon members, but it should entail the international recognition of a successful currency stabilization, carrying with it some advantages with respect to the use of the Fund's resources by the country concerned. The acceptance by the Fund of a proposed parity should be made conditional upon the assumption by the member of its normal convertibility obligations under the Articles of Agreement. At the very least, the member should renounce the right to retain and modify at its own discretion, under Article XIV, pervasive systems of exchange restrictions on current transactions. Any such restrictions should be brought under Article VIII, and made subject to the approval of the Fund. To facilitate acceptance of this condition, the Fund would probably have to agree on some escape clauses authorizing the member, in case of disagreement with the Fund, to resume its freedom and renounce the benefits associated with the maintenance of an official par value.[24]

Such a procedure should have implied in 1946 the postponement of initial par values for a large number of countries. It should also

23. See particularly Milton Friedman, "The Case for Flexible Exchange Rates," in his *Essays in Positive Economics*, Chicago, 1953.

24. This will probably be regarded by most readers as an unnecessary and undesirable concession. The experience of OEEC, however, leads me to believe that it is both more difficult to avoid and less damaging than would appear at first. (See below, pp. 250–1.) It should at least have been accepted as a way to minimize actual recourse to Art. XIV as long as the Fund found itself unable to bring to an end the applicability of the "transitional" provision of the Agreement.

imply, even in more normal times, that the modification of an existing par value could proceed in two stages. The Fund and the member could agree first on the immediate abandonment of a par value which has become incompatible with fundamental equilibrium. Exchange rates would then be allowed to fluctuate for some time, and agreement on a new parity postponed, until de facto stabilization has confirmed the achievement of a new equilibrium.[25] Until this was done, the Fund and the member would remain "in consultation" with one another, the Fund being empowered to assist the member financially—under some waiver clause similar to that of Article IV, Section 4, or Article XX, Section 4-d-ii—but being also entitled to enjoin excessive fluctuations of a competitive, beggar-my-neighbor character.

Such a system would probably be incompatible with a strict interpretation of the Fund's Articles of Agreement and would make it desirable, therefore, to undertake the difficult process of revision of its Charter. Yet this is true for many other Fund provisions, and the Agreement has rightly and inevitably been interpreted in a very flexible manner in a multitude of other cases. Moreover, a trend in the direction suggested here is already discernible in many Fund decisions and pronouncements. In recent years the Fund's *Annual Report* has repeatedly and forcefully argued the case for flexible rates in exceptional circumstances. Floating rates are widely condoned by the Fund as part of multiple exchange rate systems. Flexible rates have been applied to all transactions by Canada, Mexico, Peru, and Chile without formal objection by the Fund. The Fund has concluded stand-by credit arrangements with the latter three countries while they were operating such a system. It even adopted, on June 15, 1954, a specific set of rules "making it possible for the Fund to engage in transactions in the currencies of [fluctuating currency] members on an equitable basis and to make the computations required by the Fund Agreement." [26] Finally, the initial establishment of par values has often been postponed for a considerable period after the acceptance of membership by some countries. At the time of this writing, nine countries,

25. It need hardly be mentioned that in the gold standard days legal stabilization, after a devaluation, was similarly preceded by a protracted period of de facto stabilization.

26. See *Annual Reports, 1955,* pp. 87 and 125-7.

including four original members of the Fund, have not yet declared a par value to the Fund. One of these is Italy, whose exchange rate has been one of the stablest in the world since 1947.

2. Exchange Restrictions and the Scarce Currency Clause

The Articles of Agreement list as one of the major objectives of the Fund: "To assist in the establishment of a multilateral system of payments . . . and in the elimination of foreign exchange restrictions which hamper the growth of world trade" (Art. I-*iv*). They leave, however, two enormous loopholes which could not but handicap progress toward that objective.

The first is the exclusion of trade restrictions from the jurisdiction of the Fund. Trade restrictions and exchange controls are largely interchangeable techniques to achieve the same results, and the Fund noted in its first *Annual Report* (p. 38): "The progress achieved even through the total elimination of exchange restrictions on current transactions would be illusory if direct controls were to take their place." One of the main concerns of the Fund thus became to achieve a close coordination with the stillborn ITO, and later with the GATT and the proposed OTC (Organization for Trade Cooperation), so as to harmonize international action on trade and exchange measures. A reasonable degree of success has been achieved in this respect, but the consultative procedure which has been established clearly remains far inferior to the much closer integration which characterizes the OEEC Code of Liberalization in Europe.[27]

The second major loophole is the sweeping latitude granted to members, for an ill-defined postwar transitional period, to "maintain and adapt to changing circumstances . . . notwithstanding the provisions of any other articles of this Agreement . . . restrictions on payments and transfers for current international transactions" (Art. XIV, Sec. 2). Twelve years after the end of the war, all but ten Fund members [28] were still availing themselves of these postwar transitional arrangements. In its 1955 *Annual Report*, the Fund pointed out for the first time that "most of the members of the Fund that still have balance of payments difficulties requiring

27. The liberalization rules of OEEC apply both to trade and exchange techniques of restriction.

28. The United States, Canada (since Dec. 1951), Mexico, Cuba (since Dec. 1953), and six other small countries in the Caribbean and Central America.

the use of exchange restrictions no longer have to face problems related to war-caused conditions, and . . . the question has arisen whether the maintenance of transitional arrangements is still justified. . . . At the time of writing this Report, the issues raised by these considerations were still being studied by the Fund." [29]

They still are.[30]

The existence of Article XIV, however, should not have precluded all Fund activity in this field. First of all, as already indicated above,[31] the parity provisions and the lending powers of the Fund could have been used to elicit from some countries an earlier and voluntary renunciation of Article XIV and the acceptance of a certain degree of Fund control over remaining restrictions under Article VIII. Secondly, the Fund could encourage some other members to shift from direct, quantitative controls to market forms of control such as exchange surcharges and multiple rates. The Fund should properly be credited with a certain degree of courage in this respect. Multiple rates and floating exchange rates were, of course, anathema to many of the Fund founders and were mistakenly regarded by the public at large as even worse and more directly contrary to the Fund's objectives than other forms of exchange restrictions. Yet the very first mission sent to a country by the Fund to advise it on exchange control matters recommended, with the approval of the Fund's Executive Board, a system of exchange surtaxes—tantamount to multiple rates—and of a floating, free market exchange rate for luxury imports and all invisible transactions. This was in picturesque Ecuador, in the spring of 1947. The country had lost about half of its monetary reserves in the previous six months and had accumulated a foreign exchange backlog [32] totaling about four times its remaining gold and foreign assets. In four weeks' time a new exchange control legislation was enacted, eliminating all quantitative restrictions and allowing any firm or individual to buy abroad whatever they pleased, in any country or currency they wished. To make this possible, a 30% surtax had

29. *Annual Report, 1955,* pp. 81–2.

30. "The issues that may arise in connection with the termination of the transitional period and of the transitional arrangements which have been maintained during this period continue to be under study by the Fund." *Annual Report, 1956,* p. 97.

31. P. 122.

32. Foreign exchange committed by the Central Bank as cover for outstanding import permits.

to be paid on all nonessential imports, the proceeds of the tax being earmarked for amortization of the state's debt to the Central Bank, stabilization operations in the market for government securities, and the financing of production loans. Capital transactions and all other uncontrollable transactions were, moreover, to be channeled into a free market, where exchange had also to be bought, at higher and fluctuating rates, for luxury imports.

The results were instantaneous and spectacular. The huge windfall profits made by the lucky importers favored with official licenses were now recouped by the Central Bank, which amortized over a few months about one third of its outstanding loans to the state. Prices ceased to rocket upward. Exchange reserves doubled before the end of the year, and the exchange backlog was reduced to one fourth of its former amount. The new free rate for capital movements and uncontrolled transactions dropped immediately below the previous black market rate and continued to decline progressively.

This success was all the more impressive as the deterioration in the external situation, fully reversed in Ecuador, continued to plague its two neighboring countries of roughly comparable foreign trade structure, Colombia and Peru. The Colombian and Peruvian currencies were sharply devalued in 1948 as a result of these continuing difficulties, while the effective rate for the Ecuadorean sucre has remained practically unchanged to this date.

The Ecuadorean reform attracted considerable attention in Latin America, and was imitated, with less boldness but still with a considerable degree of success, by later Fund missions in the area.

A third type of action, of more general applicability, would have been to encourage and to support with Fund resources multilateral negotiations aiming at a mutual relaxation of controls among countries closely interdependent in their trade relationships. The effects of such relaxation on the individual countries' balance of payments would, under such conditions, be largely self-offsetting—as were indeed the controls themselves—since they could be expected to lead to a simultaneous expansion of both exports and imports. The Fund made some feeble and ineffectual moves in this direction when European countries initiated such a program within the framework of the Organization for European Economic Cooperation. There was, however, considerable opposition within the Fund to such an approach, on the ground that regional arrangements of this kind would be discriminatory in character, and therefore contrary to the Fund's objectives.

Most of the discriminations involved in these arrangements related to the maintenance of tighter restrictions against imports payable in dollars, and approximated in their effects a declaration of dollar scarcity under Article VII of the Fund Agreement. The scarcity of the dollar was indeed at that time a credo of monetary and economic policy in every country of the world, not excluding the United States itself. Certainly the demand for dollars would have seriously "threatened the Fund's ability to supply that currency" [33] if the Fund had not adopted, at an early stage, a negative attitude toward members' drawings. Given this policy, however, dollars were never scarce in the Fund. Its dollar holdings never fell substantially below $1.3 billion, and could at all times be replenished by gold holdings ranging from $1.3 billion to $1.8 billion.

Moreover, the only practical result of an official declaration of dollar scarcity would have been to authorize Fund members to impose restrictions on their dollar transactions. This was totally superfluous, since such restrictions and discrimination were freely allowed anyway under Article XIV of the Agreement.

Yet the refusal of the Fund to recognize a dollar scarcity had two important and unfortunate consequences.

First of all, it precluded the application of a provision designed to relieve the United Kingdom, in the case of a dollar scarcity, of her nondiscrimination commitment to the United States under the Anglo-American Financial Agreement. This forced the United Kingdom into a formal breach of contract in August 1947, even though the inevitability of her action was tacitly or openly recognized in all quarters.

Secondly, it made it much more difficult for the Fund to press its members to abandon, as soon as feasible, their freedom of action under Article XIV or to limit its use to whatever restrictions could be regarded as reasonably justified in the early postwar years. Countries remained free to restrict and discriminate as they wished, against weaker as well as against stronger countries than themselves, and to use their full bargaining power in the negotiation of bilateral trade and payments agreements.

It was left to the OEEC and the EPU to remedy this situation and themselves put into practical operation the scarce currency

33. Art. VII, Sec. 3.

clause of the Fund through a preferential system of trade and payments liberalization in Europe. Nobody will deny that the OEEC has thus achieved much greater results than those which have so far transpired from the one-by-one consultation procedures initiated by the Fund in 1952, under Article XIV of the Agreement.[34] The "Policy Decision on Bilateralism," adopted by the Executive Board on June 22, 1955,[35] indicates the intention of the Fund to "explore with all countries which are parties to bilateral arrangements which involve the use of exchange restrictions the need for the continuation of these arrangements, the possibilities of their early removal, and ways and means, including the use of the Fund's resources, by which the Fund can assist in this process." While wondering whether such "explorations" could not have begun long ago, one may hope that they will lead to concrete results, supplementing and broadening the successful fight of OEEC and EPU against intra-European bilateralism in trade and payments.

The published record may, however, give too gloomy an impression of the Fund's activities in this field. Consultations under Article XIV have developed, quietly and without publicity, a better understanding by each member country of the problems and policies of others, of the real costs and practical limitations of exchange restrictions as a mechanism for balance of payments adjustments, and of possible alternatives to excessive reliance on their use. They may well have exercised a far greater impact on actual decisions and policies than would be suspected from information available to the outsider. In this, as well as in other areas of the Fund's jurisdiction, slow but real progress has probably been achieved in recent years toward more flexible and realistic methods of international cooperation than those formally embodied in the Fund's Articles of Agreement.

3. Lending Policies (see Chart XVII and Table X)

Three very distinct phases have marked the lending policies of the Fund.

The first was one of fairly active lending, particularly in Europe, during its initial year of operations. The second was one of progres-

---

34. The progress thus made possible toward a greater volume and a better pattern of trade, and toward the ultimate objectives of world-wide trade liberalization and currency convertibility, will be reviewed below, Chap. 5, pp. 204–8.

35. See 1955 Annual Report, 1955, pp. 123–4.

CHART XVII

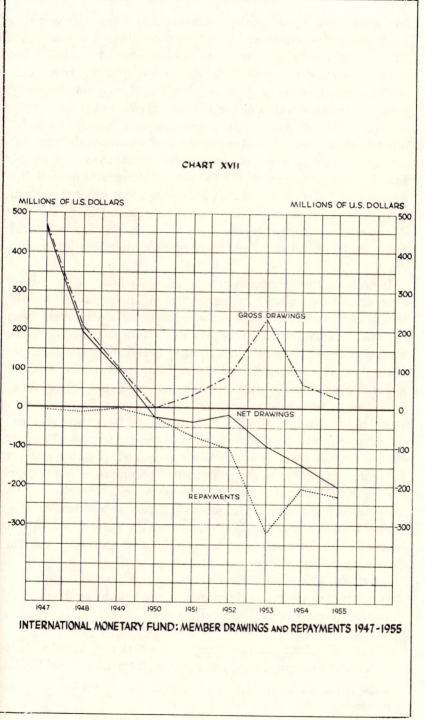

MILLIONS OF U.S.DOLLARS   MILLIONS OF U.S. DOLLARS

GROSS DRAWINGS

NET DRAWINGS

REPAYMENTS

INTERNATIONAL MONETARY FUND: MEMBER DRAWINGS AND REPAYMENTS 1947-1955

sive withdrawal from activity, culminating—if one may use this word—in a total cessation of lending throughout the year 1950. This period was marked by a series of decisions of the Executive Board in relation to the use of the Fund's resources.[36] A large number of such decisions adopted in March 1948 gave an extremely restrictive interpretation of the borrowing rights of members under the Articles of Agreement. These were now revealed to be far less automatic than one had suspected, and a member's request for assistance could in effect be discouraged or turned down by the Board without recourse to the formal and dangerous ineligibility procedure of Article V, Section 4. A separate decision, on April 5, 1948, stated that "the attitude of the Fund and ERP members should be that such members should request the purchase of United States dollars from the Fund only in exceptional or unforeseen cases."

In both instances the position adopted by the Board had considerable merit. I have already criticized [37] as highly unrealistic any system of large and automatic borrowing rights as a permanent basis for international monetary cooperation. As for the ERP decision, there can be little doubt that a country benefiting from the European Recovery Program would have been most unwise to draw simultaneously on the Fund, in this manner depleting resources which might become invaluable to it in the event of a sudden and premature curtailment in the ERP program. Both the Fund and its European members should conserve these resources as long as American assistance on a large scale remained available to meet current needs. Moreover, the amounts appropriated by Congress for the ERP program were based on estimates of Europe's needs and the United States' capacity for assistance. It was not unlikely, therefore, that any dollar loan granted by the Fund to a recipient of ERP aid might lead Congress to reduce its aid appropriations by an equivalent amount.

The third phase in the Fund's lending policies was timidly ushered in in May 1951 with the adoption of a resolution designed to encourage members to take greater risks

in undertaking practical programs of action designed to help achieve the purposes of the Fund Agreement . . . which in-

36. See 1948 *Annual Report, 1948,* pp. 97–9 and 74–5.
37. Above, pp. 106–7.

clude the achievement of monetary stability, the adoption of realistic exchange rates, the relaxation and removal of restrictions and discrimination, and the simplification of multiple currency practices. Arrangements would be worked out appropriate to the particular situation of the member concerned and intended to ensure that use of the Fund's resources would be available if the implementation of the proposed program required such assistance. When a program is found acceptable, the member would be assured that the Fund's resources would be available if the implementation of the proposed program required such assistance.[38]

This procedure developed gradually, after lengthy discussions, into a permanent system for so-called "stand-by arrangements," initially concluded for a period of six months to a year, but which may be renewed before expiration. It might be regarded as a way to restore, but for a limited time and under specified terms and conditions, the presumption of automaticity which previous decisions had in effect reversed as a normal expectation for Fund borrowings. Stand-by arrangements totaling $117.5 million were concluded in 1952 and 1954 with Belgium, Finland, Mexico, and Peru. By the end of 1955, only $27.5 million of this amount had been used—and repaid—and $62.5 million remained unused and still available to Belgium and Peru, the arrangements with Finland and Mexico having expired in the meantime.[39]

Other decisions of the Fund during this period aimed at hastening the repayment of Fund loans. Charges were lowered on credits repaid by members within a short period, and raised on credits remaining outstanding for longer periods. Moreover, drawings might be arranged in some cases with specified repurchase provisions within a period not to exceed eighteen months, and in all cases repayment should be expected within an outside range of three to five years.

Members were also assured that requests for drawings within their "gold tranche"—i.e. up to the amount of their gold subscription—would receive "the overwhelming benefit of any doubt," [40] that the Fund's attitude toward further drawings up to one fourth

38. *Annual Report, 1951,* pp. 81–2.
39. New stand-by arrangements were concluded in 1956 with Chile ($35 million) and Iran ($17.5 million).
40. *Annual Report, 1952,* p. 42.

of the quota "is a liberal one," and that "should the need arise, and should the justification be substantial, members need not doubt that drawings on subsequent tranches will be permitted." [41] They were told that the Fund was prepared to authorize, under the waiver clause of Article V, Section 4, drawings or stand-by arrangements in excess of 25% a year. In fact this was done on several occasions in 1953 and the following years. Finally, a special procedure was established in June 1954 for drawings on or by members with fluctuating currencies.

Repeated references were made to the need to facilitate "the transition from a period of relatively modest use of the Fund's resources to one of more active use," to the fact that "an increased use of the Fund's resources might contribute to the solution of the payments problems now confronting some of its members and could at the same time promote the achievement of the purposes of the Fund." [42] The 1955 *Annual Report* even expressed veiled regrets at "the continued lack of use of the Fund's facilities" (p. 86).

Drawings on the Fund have indeed remained extremely modest since 1948 and have been exceeded by repayments in every single year since 1949. Borrowings by OEEC Europe during this whole period were confined to small credits to Turkey, but other European countries amortized $490 million of the $535 million credits obtained by them in 1947 and 1948. Repayments by outer sterling area countries also exceeded new borrowings. Net lendings to Latin America and other countries offset only a fraction of these repayments, and total outstanding credits to the world at large fell from $757 million at the end of 1949 to $234 million at the end of 1955.

The improvement in the world payment situation undoubtedly accounts in large part for the current lack of response to the Fund's calls for larger drawings by members. Paradoxically, a resumption of Fund lending might nevertheless be expected if this improvement continued and induced some countries, particularly the United Kingdom, to accept the risks involved in a return to currency convertibility.

The main criticism to be leveled at the Fund's lending policies is closely related to the one made above concerning its policies on exchange restrictions. The Fund should not be blamed so much for having lent so little, but rather for its failure to develop and

41. *Annual Report, 1955,* p. 85.
42. *Annual Report, 1952,* pp. 39–40.

Table X. INTERNATIONAL MONETARY FUND: MEMBER DRAWINGS AND REPAYMENTS, 1947–55

(in millions of U.S. dollars)

	Total	1947–49	1950–52	1953–55
I. *Gross Drawings*	1,216	777	120	320
II. *Repayments*	982	20	200	763
A. *Repurchases*	779	2	172	605
B. *Drawings in debtor currencies*	203	17	28	158
1. Sterling	192	6	28	158
2. Belgian francs	11	11	—	—
III. *Net Drawings*	234	757	−80	−443
A. *Western Europe*	60	540	−81	−399
1. Belgium	—	21	−21	—
2. Denmark	—	10	—	−10
3. France	45	125	—	−80
4. Netherlands	—	75	−27	−48
5. Norway	—	10	−10	—
6. Turkey	15	5	5	5
7. U.K.	—	294	−28	−266
B. *Outer sterling area*	13	130	20	−137
1. Australia	—	20	30	−50
2. India	13	100	—	−87
3. South Africa	—	10	−10	—
C. *Latin America*	106	69	−29	66
1. Brazil	65	37	—	28
2. Chile	12	9	−7	11
3. Colombia	25	—	—	25
4. Mexico	—	23	−23	—
5. Other Countries	3	—	1	2
D. *Other countries*	56	19	9	27
1. Czechoslovakia	4	6	—	−2
2. Egypt	—	3	−3	—
3. Ethiopia	—	1	−1	—
4. Finland	—	—	4	−4
5. Indonesia	15	—	—	15
6. Iran	17	—	9	9
7. Philippines	10	—	—	10
8. Yugoslavia	9	9	—	—

Source:
International Financial Statistics.

implement special lending techniques designed to support desirable and feasible steps toward multilateralization in trade and payments and the mutual relaxation of mutually offsetting restrictions. This objective could not be served by dissipating its inadequate dollar resources on individual salvage operations of the kind undertaken in its first year of activity. The Fund could have encouraged, however, the multilateralization of payments agreements attempted in Europe in the fall of 1947, which finally culminated in the setting up of the European Payments Union.

The first step in this direction would have been to allow each country to use over as wide an area as possible—rather than only bilaterally—its current earnings or accumulated balances in inconvertible currencies. The second would have been to replace bilateral credit margins in inconvertible currencies by multilateral credit facilities usable, again, over as wide an area as possible. The third step would have consisted in building upon the first two a determined attack against bilateral controls and discrimination and against mutually offsetting restrictions on reciprocal trade.

Such a program would have involved a distinction between credit assistance in inconvertible currencies on the one hand, and in convertible currencies on the other. The latter would necessarily have had to be more narrowly circumscribed than the former. Or, to express the same thing in different words, the former could have been made more generous than the latter. This was precisely the intent of the scarce currency clause, which foresaw a rationing of the Fund's loans in the scarce currency and a correlative discrimination by members on payments involving that currency.

Inconvertible currency credits had in fact been made available to many countries under bilateral payments agreements. Many of these could have been merged into multilateral credit margins if some way could have been found to restrain or finance a convergence of drawings against one or a few lending countries in excess of the total credit margins granted by them to all other participants. I suggested to the Fund, as early as September 1947, that any such excess be financed from existing Fund holdings in the currency of these countries. Under the Articles of Agreement, this would have allowed the lending countries to increase by an equivalent amount their access to the Fund's dollar resources. On the other hand, the corresponding indebtedness of the borrowers would have imposed upon them a repurchase obligation in gold or convertible currencies—in practice the dollar—irrespective of the currency borrowed by them.

Such obstacles were not insurmountable, as was demonstrated later by the creation of the European Payments Union. I suggested that the extreme creditors' right to dollar repayments or additional dollar drawings be limited to 50% of the net credit balances accumulated by them and that the debtors' net balances be similarly made subject only to partial dollar repayment.[43] These suggestions were in effect very close to the arrangements later instituted by EPU and accepted by its members. That they would not have overtaxed the resources of the Fund is demonstrated by the fact that total EPU credits never exceeded $1,200 million in members' currencies, and that the Union's gold and dollar payments to the creditor countries have been more than covered by its gold and dollar receipts from the debtor countries.[44]

One might object that part of the intra-European deficits of these years was covered by American aid, but there is no reason to think that such aid would not have been forthcoming also if the Fund had helped in the setting up of a multilateral system of payments in Europe. Indeed, bolder initiative on the Fund's part might well have channeled through it some of the amounts of aid specifically assigned for the support of the intra-European payments system before and after the creation of EPU.

In fact, however, the Fund made only half-hearted gestures in this direction in 1948 and 1949. It "informed" the European countries in 1948 of its

> hope that an arrangement can be made for multilateralizing European payments and of its hope that a moderate rise in the credit margins of payments agreements can be made available by the European creditor countries as their further contribution to European recovery. The Fund also indicated that it would not object to the use of its European resources in moderate amounts by ERP members eligible to draw on the Fund to assist in the multilateralization of European payments provided the conditions and purposes of the Fund Agreement relating to the use of its resources are met.

43. The netting of balances, for both creditors and debtors, implied, of course, the right for the debtors to discharge their debts in any of the participating currencies, and the obligation for the creditors to accept repayment in their own currency or in any other participating currency usable by them to reduce their gross deficits.

44. The liquid gold and dollar assets of the Union have fluctuated between a low of $179 million and a peak of $544 million, as compared with an initial capital contribution by the United States of $350 million gross, but only $271.6 million net after deduction of initial grants by the United States to some of the weaker members of EPU.

It also decided that the financing of its European surpluses by an ERP member would justify requests by that country to purchase foreign exchange—including dollars—from the Fund to the extent necessary to avoid a decline in its monetary reserves. Finally, "the Fund also indicated its willingness to place its advice and technical facilities at the disposal of its members in connection with the formulation and administration of any multilateral payments arrangements." [45]

Little was done, however, to implement these cautious declarations, and particularly to exercise effective leadership in a field so close to the most basic purposes and objectives of the Fund. The friendly attitude initially evidenced by the Fund changed gradually, under the influence of the United States Treasury, into one of increasing reserve and hardly veiled hostility. The conflict of views between the Treasury and the Economic Cooperation Administration (ECA) manifested itself in strong American support for EPU by the latter in the OEEC negotiations in Paris, but in fierce opposition to it by the former in the Fund's Executive Board in Washington.

The following paragraph was inserted, at the request of the Fund, in the Agreement for the establishment of a European Payments Union:

> The functioning of EPU will be of great interest to the International Monetary Fund of which many participating countries are members, and these countries will be concerned to ensure that obligations incurred by them as Members of the EPU should be consistent with obligations which they may have as members of the International Monetary Fund. Close co-operation and consultation with the International Monetary Fund are desirable, and it will be necessary for the Management Committee to examine and report to the Council what shall be the appropriate relationships.

In reporting on this, one year later, the 1951 *Annual Report* stated that the "nature of the relationship" was still under consideration at that time. Presumably it still is, the only progress reported so far being the admission, three years after the creation of EPU, of the Fund representative in Paris to the meetings of the EPU Managing Board.

45. *Annual Report, 1948*, pp. 35 and 75.

4. Conclusions

The over-all failure of the Fund to affect significantly the course of events in the postwar world should not make us forget the steps taken in recent years to overcome the heavy handicaps placed upon it by its excessively rigid Articles of Agreement. In the previous pages we have repeatedly noted Fund decisions and interpretations permitting greater flexibility and realism in the institution's operations and policies.

Moreover, the most glaring defects of the Fund's charter relate to its handling of the widespread but temporary disequilibria inherited from the Second World War. The Fund Agreement was generally silent on these short-run problems, except for the practical denial of any Fund jurisdiction over exchange restrictions during the transitional postwar period. It dealt with the setting up and revision of par values, the elimination of exchange controls, and the Fund's lending operations as if these problems could be handled with each country individually against a background of general convertibility and stability in world trade and currency arrangements. These defects will continue to limit the Fund's effectiveness unless they can be remedied through further revisions or interpretation of the Articles of Agreement. They were, however, particularly damaging during the period of widespread dislocation and disequilibria from which the world is now emerging.

Even then they could have been remedied by supplementing the Fund's jurisdictional powers and legal machinery with mutually negotiated agreements and commitments among the Fund members. The Fund's administrative structure unfortunately constitutes the worst possible instrument for the negotiation of such international agreements and compromises among sovereign countries. Permanently in residence in Washington, cut off from regular policy-making responsibilities in their own countries, the members of the Executive Board inevitably tend to become little more than glorified messenger boys, dependent on instructions from their home countries for all substantive matters submitted to the Board. This does not create an effective forum for negotiation, and the Fund often finds its role confined to that of passively registering the decisions on exchange rates and exchange controls independently made by each national government and officially communicated to the Fund through its Executive Director.

The OEEC type of organization has proved its superior effectiveness in this respect and should inspire the necessary reform of the Fund's administrative structure. It is based primarily on committee work by permanent national experts and technicians advising their own governments and receiving instructions from them, assisted by suggestions and research work from an international staff. All issues on which these permanent delegates have been unable to reach agreement are submitted to periodic meetings of high-level representatives, with continued responsibility and influence at home and empowered to make on the spot the mutual concessions necessary to reach international agreement.

Last but not least, the administrative organization of the Fund could profit greatly from a certain degree of decentralization and from cooperation with regional institutions on all matters which do not vitally affect the interests of the world at large. The respective roles of regional and world-wide cooperation in the reconstruction of an international system of trade and payments will be examined in Chapter 7 of this study.

IV. THE ANGLO-AMERICAN FINANCIAL AGREEMENT AND THE FAILURE OF STERLING CONVERTIBILITY

The vagueness and laxity of the Fund's provisions respecting the transitional postwar period began, at an early stage, seriously to worry its founding fathers. At the same time, some of the Fund's opponents—particularly Professor John H. Williams—were propounding as an alternative to the Fund plan a "key currency approach" aimed primarily at restoring the status of the pound sterling as an international currency alongside of the United States dollar.

The Anglo-American Financial Agreement of 1946 met both points of view. It tightened the Fund's provisions with respect to the United Kingdom's commitments to trade and exchange liberalization, and at the same time provided the United Kingdom with a sizable amount of special credits necessary to bolster the ability of the pound to resume its traditional role in international trade.

A $3,750 million line of credit was opened to Britain, and an additional amount of $650 million agreed upon to cover the final settlement of Lend-Lease and other claims arising out of the war.[1] The United Kingdom accepted, in return, a series of far-reaching trade and exchange commitments to be implemented in full within a year, i.e. by July 15, 1947.

In the trade field, the United Kingdom would remain free to impose trade and import restrictions upon her own residents, but without any discrimination against the United States.

In the exchange field, no restrictions would be placed by the United Kingdom on payments and transfers for authorized current transactions, not only with the United States but with other countries as well. A second series of exchange commitments related to the convertibility of sterling balances held by or accruing to non-residents of the United Kingdom. These should be freely usable for the settlement of current transactions anywhere in the world and would be freely convertible into dollars when paid out to American residents. The dollar pool arrangements governing sterling area members would also be modified so as to permit the free use of dollar, as well as sterling, earnings by the members.

Some exceptions and escape clauses modified somewhat these sweeping commitments. Exchange *restrictions*—or equivalent trade restrictions—could be imposed in agreement with the Fund, under Article VIII of the Fund Agreement, but the United Kingdom renounced its right to retain or modify them, at its own discretion, under Article XIV of the Agreement. Trade or exchange *discrimination* could also be imposed against a currency declared scarce by the Fund, or in order to use, for the purchase of needed imports, balances in inconvertible currencies accumulated before December 31, 1946, or in order to assist "by measures not involving a substantial departure from the general rule of non-discrimination, a country whose economy had been disrupted by war." Finally, convertibility obligations would not apply to outstanding sterling balances. These could be readjusted, funded, or blocked, but any amounts released for use under such arrangements would be assimilated to current sterling accruals and would therefore be freely usable for

1. It may be worth emphasizing that this contribution to the key currency approach was far larger than the United States contribution to the IMF ($2,750 million) and that it was effectively disbursed in its entirety, while actual dollar drawings from the IMF never exceeded cumulatively about $750 million, most of which was repaid fairly promptly. By the end of 1955, our effective contribution to the IMF had dropped to about one tenth of that to the Anglo-American Agreement.

the settlement of current transactions in any currency area without discrimination.

The United Kingdom met with only limited success in her negotiations regarding the readjustment or funding of these outstanding sterling balances, but proceeded nevertheless to implement its commitments under the Agreement. So-called "American accounts" had already been set up previously with the United States and other dollar area countries such as Mexico, the republics of Central America, the Caribbean islands, and the northern coast of South America. All sterling paid into an American account was convertible, upon demand, into United States dollars.

In the first half of 1947, the United Kingdom proceeded to renegotiate its bilateral agreements with other countries outside the sterling area on the basis of "transferable" rather than "bilateral" accounts. Transferable account countries undertook to accept sterling from all other countries in settlement of current transactions, but were also authorized to draw on their sterling accounts—except for previously accumulated balances in blocked sterling—for the settlement of current transactions virtually anywhere in the world, including the American account countries. The United Kingdom would thus be exposed to a gold or dollar drain whenever transferable sterling was paid into an American account. On the other hand, transferable sterling was not directly redeemable into gold or dollars, but would be retained as monetary reserves to the extent that it was not needed for current payments. Its status was not unlike that of the bancor accounts of the Keynes plan, but it gave Britain, rather than an international Clearing Union, the benefit of the implied loans by the holders of such accounts.

By the fateful date of July 15, 1947, transferable account agreements had been signed with eighteen countries, and the United States had granted a two-month postponement to permit the completion of other negotiations still in process with another fourteen countries. The drain on Britain's gold and dollar reserves, however, was also mounting at an appalling pace. The monthly rate of loss had climbed from $75 million in 1946 to $315 million in the first half of 1947, $500 million in July and $650 million in August. Over the five weeks from July 15 to August 20, the amount lost was about a billion dollars.

On the latter date, convertibility was suspended. Technically, this decision affected only transferable account sterling, which could henceforward be used only for payments to other transferable account countries or to the sterling area, the prior approval of the British exchange control authorities being required for all other sterling transfers. The transferable account agreements had, of course, to be renegotiated as a result, and a number of countries reverted to their previous "bilateral" status, meaning that they could freely make or receive sterling payments only in settlement of transactions with the sterling area alone, but that they were no longer committed to accept such inconvertible sterling in payment, except from the sterling area and within the limits of agreed "swings" or "credit margins."

The return to currency inconvertibility was, of course, accompanied by a parallel reversal to discrimination and bilateralism in trade as well as in payments. The United Kingdom restricted severely its own imports both from the American account countries and from the bilateral account countries whose surpluses exceeded the agreed credit margins. Licenses were granted more liberally, on the other hand, for imports from countries which were willing to accumulate inconvertible sterling or to spend their sterling earnings for purchases only from the sterling area or from transferable account countries. These countries, in turn, could not but discriminate also against imports requiring payment in scarce dollars, and in favor of imports which they were allowed to pay in sterling.

The disastrous failure of this premature experiment would bar, for many years to come, any attempt at restoring sterling convertibility. It was also to discourage and slow down the more modest and realistic efforts at regional monetary cooperation in Europe initiated some months earlier under the spur of the Marshall Plan.

V. SUMMARY AND CONCLUSIONS

The early blueprints for international monetary reconstruction failed utterly to cope with the real problems confronting the postwar world.

The Keynes plan's sweeping logic dealt boldly and imaginatively with the problem of restoring a multilateral system of trade and payments providing adequate safeguards against the international spread of depression and deflation. The methods proposed for its implementation, however, remained vague and ambiguous in many respects and were rightly regarded by the creditor countries, particularly the United States, as making insufficient provision against the unleashing of inflationary forces damaging to their own economies. Indeed, the plan reflected almost exclusively the national interests and preoccupations of the United Kingdom and other war-impoverished countries.

These defects of the Keynes plan had to be corrected, and were in fact corrected, before agreement could be reached on the setting up of an International Monetary Fund. Unfortunately, some of the most essential and totally unobjectionable suggestions of the Keynes plan were also lost in the process. The Articles of Agreement set up an administrative structure which unrealistically neglected mutual negotiation in favor of legal jurisdiction. In their excessive concern with exchange stability, they encouraged in practice undue reliance on trade and exchange controls as an alternative tool for balance of payments adjustments. They failed to distinguish between over-all restrictions compatible with a multilateral system of trade and payments, and bilateral restrictions based on the exploitation of bargaining power by stronger countries against weaker countries. These defects soon deprived the Fund of any effective influence on its member countries' policies, and left a large void which had to be filled by other attempts at international cooperation in the monetary field.

The key currency approach, embodied in the Anglo-American Financial Agreement of 1946, was more realistic in many respects. It was too niggardly, however, to allow war-impoverished Britain to bear alone the burden placed on its shoulders. American aid, on a much larger scale—of the order of magnitude suggested in the Keynes plan—and to many countries besides Britain, proved still insufficient to bring about an early restoration of currency convertibility.

The first postwar years thus witnessed the gradual extension and consolidation of bilateralism in trade and payments over the largest part of the world. We shall review in the next two chapters the efforts made by Europe to palliate the worst absurdities and wastes of such a system and, later on, to escape from it through the creation of a broader framework for trade and payments.

CHAPTER 4

Bilateralism and Its
Palliatives: 1945-50

THE BRETTON WOODS conference had indulged in the luxury of drawing up blueprints for a far distant future. The Articles of Agreement of the International Monetary Fund were adopted on July 22, 1944 and entered into force on December 27, 1945.[1] The Fund, however, was not actually organized until the summer of 1946 and did not begin exchange transactions until March 1947. The convertibility provisions of the Agreement were to be held in abeyance for a transitional period which should theoretically have terminated on March 1, 1952, but is still operative today for most of the Fund's members.

In the meantime, European countries had to live and to find some basis on which to resume their international trade and payments in an inconvertible world. All foreign transactions being subjected to national systems of controls and restrictions, none could take place without the concurrence of the licensing authorities of at least two countries. It was to facilitate this process that European countries began to negotiate with their major trade partners bilateral trade and payments agreements which were to constitute, for several years to come, the keystone of their postwar international monetary system.

I. BILATERALISM TRIUMPHANT: 1945–47

The first of these agreements, signed in London on October 21, 1943 by the governments-in-exile of Belgium, the Netherlands, and

1. The Agreement "entered into force" after it had been signed on behalf of governments having 65% of the total of the quotas, and after the corresponding instruments of acceptance had been deposited with the Government of the United States of America (Art. XX).

Luxembourg, was largely used as a model for the more than two hundred agreements negotiated in Europe in the following four years. The bilateral payments agreements usually included the following provisions:

1. The determination of an official exchange rate for the settlement of authorized transactions between the residents of the two countries. This rate could be modified only by prior agreement —as in the Belgo-Dutch Agreement, for instance—or, more frequently, after mere consultation or prior notification between the partners;

2. The payment by importers in their national currency and to their own central bank of the amount due to the foreign exporters; and the payment of this sum to the foreign exporters, in their national currency and by their own central bank;

3. The bilateral offsetting between the two central banks of the mutual claims and debts arising from these operations;

4. Agreed procedures for the financing or settlement of the residual debt—and reverse claim—subsisting between the two banks after the above offsets had taken place;

5. Consultation between the two governments in the event of implementation difficulties, and particularly in the case of an excessive or persistent imbalance in the two countries' bilateral transactions.

These payments agreements were accompanied by trade agreements guaranteeing a certain volume of import and export licensing by both countries to their residents for the various categories of goods of interest to their trade.

The financing procedures mentioned in paragraph 4 above usually took the form of "mutual credit margins" between the partner countries. No immediate settlement would be required by the creditor country from the debtor country as long as the latter's debit balance did not exceed an agreed margin (or "ceiling"). In the case of denunciation or nonrenewal of the agreement, the debt would be funded into medium-term treasury notes, repayable over a period of, usually, three to five years.

When the bilateral balance exceeded the agreed margin, the debtor country was often committed to settle the difference in gold or dollars. Such was notably the case in most or all of the agreements concluded by Belgium, Switzerland, and the Allied Zone of Occupation in Germany. In other cases, and particularly in the agreements between the United Kingdom and the Scandinavian countries, the credit margin was more loosely defined and became a "talking point" rather than a "gold point" in the above sense. Both countries merely undertook to rediscuss the whole of their trade and financial relations in order to check the disequilibrium whenever the ceiling was reached.

The characterization of these agreements as "bilateral" naturally evokes the connotation of an artificial and uneconomic balancing of trade and payments on a bilateral basis. This is true only in part. Under the conditions prevailing at the end of the war, the bilateral agreements constituted in effect a first and concrete step away from national autarky and toward the resumption of international trade and payments. National and divergent trade and exchange control legislations, regulating exports as well as imports, receipts as well as payments, would often have blocked all possibility of international economic intercourse in the absence of agreed procedures for trade and payments making the regulations of a country compatible with those of its partners.

Moreover, in view of the depleted level of monetary reserves in most countries, the resumption of trade on a cash basis—i.e. on the basis of immediate payment in gold or in gold-convertible currencies—would have been confined almost inevitably to such imports as could be paid for immediately by equivalent exports in the reverse direction. Paradoxical as it may seem, the bilateral payments agreements served the essential function, through their mutual credit provisions, of avoiding or at least postponing the danger of a strict bilateral balancing of exports and imports on a barter basis.

Their effectiveness in this respect is amply demonstrated by the size of the credits which reflected the lack of such bilateral balance. From the end of the war to the end of 1947, known intra-European payments credit lines rose to the huge total of $1.5 billion.[2] Intra-European trade at first revived rapidly under this stimulus, but the rate of progress began to slacken in 1947, long before the prewar level had been regained.[3] This could be attributed in part to the size and persistence of over-all disequilibria, but also to the bilateral character of the payments agreements machinery. The credits absorbed by the system were much larger than the net imbalance to

2. BIS, *Eighteenth Annual Report* (Basle, 1948), p. 174.

3. Intra-European trade in 1947 was still at only 60% of its 1938 volume. See OEEC, *Foreign Trade by Areas. 1928, 1937-53* (Paris, 1954), p. 24.

be financed, since the same country simultaneously accumulated bilateral credit claims on the countries in deficit toward it and bilateral debts to the countries with which it was itself in deficit. As long as payments agreements remained operative, repayment would not take place and total credits would continue to grow, unless and until the pattern of trade reversed itself totally, deficits being replaced by surpluses and surpluses by deficits in each bilateral relationship.

This would occur only rarely in the normal course of events, but at some point the creditor country would refuse to extend further credits, or the debtor refuse to accept further increases in its indebtedness. The payments agreements machinery then became paralyzed, and the deficit countries, unable or unwilling to pay gold, would abruptly reimpose or tighten bilateral restrictions in order to avoid further bilateral deficits. These restrictions went so far, at times, as to impose a sudden and complete cessation of imports by the debtor country from the creditor country until export proceeds had reconstituted some credit facilities under the existing payments agreement.

In order to escape such restrictions on its imports, or to avoid the indefinite piling up of frozen credits, the surplus country would itself try to reverse artificially its pattern of trade and to increase through trade discrimination its imports from the debtor country.

These opposite pressures on debtors and creditors thus converged to stimulate, through discrimination, the bilateral balancing of accounts from which the payments agreements credits had provided a temporary escape. The same country could find itself subject to such pressures from both sides. Even if it were itself in over-all equilibrium in Europe, it would be unable to pay its bilateral creditors because it was unable to collect payment from its bilateral debtors. It would thus find itself inexorably pushed toward discrimination against its creditors and in favor of its debtors, in order to avoid gold payments to the first and either an indefinite piling up of frozen credits on the latter or the application of discriminatory restrictions on its exports to them.

The payments agreements had provided a breathing spell, but no permanent stop, in Europe's drift toward discrimination and bilateralism.

This outcome had indeed been anticipated by the framers of the agreements. These had been initially conceived as short-term expedients to be submerged later into more comprehensive agreements among all the countries concerned. In the months preceding Bretton Woods, the view had often been put forth by Europeans that one of the most urgent tasks confronting the conference would be to harmonize and coordinate existing bilateral agreements into a multilateral framework, facilitating the transferability or convertibility of bilateral credit and debit balances.[4] The world monetary organization could then be made a very simple and streamlined affair designed only to regulate and harmonize relations among several regional monetary groups.

This approach was regarded by others as too pedestrian and cumbersome, and as threatening to bring about the emergence and consolidation of autarkic monetary and trade blocs. The latter danger was undoubtedly a real one, but the short-cut road to a truly international monetary institution led to a mere blueprint rather than to an actual shelter. For many years to come, Europe would be unable to find in it an operative substitute for the payments agreements system, and the only effective progress toward the multilateralization and liberalization of trade and payments would come from gradual improvements of the existing agreements rather than from the implementation of the International Monetary Fund's charter.

II. THE FIRST AGREEMENT ON MULTI-
LATERAL MONETARY COMPENSATION: 1947–48

The first initiative toward the broadening of bilateral payments agreements into a multilateral system of intra-European payments came in the summer of 1947 from the same Benelux countries which had concluded the first postwar bilateral payments agreement.[1]

4. Most of the bilateral agreements concluded before Bretton Woods contained a specific clause contemplating their revision in case either contracting party adhered to a more general monetary agreement. This clause was all but forgotten when it became obvious that the IMF would not provide, for many years at least, any practical alternative to the bilateral payments agreements as a method of international settlements.

1. Mr. Hubert Ansiaux, Director of the National Bank of Belgium, and Dr. F. A. G. Keesing, Adviser to the Dutch Finance Minister, played a leading role

They boldly proposed that each country be allowed to offset its bilateral debit balances with some of its European partners against its bilateral credit balances with the others. This would reduce greatly the net settlements to be made under existing payments agreements. Beyond the credits available in such agreements, gold settlements would be required but could be financed through the earmarking for this purpose of a portion of Marshall aid to the debtor countries.

The conference called upon to deal with these proposals unfortunately met in the latter part of 1947—i.e. upon the heels of the convertibility crisis in Britain. The British were in no mood to accept the risks of a new experiment in convertibility or even in more limited transferability commitments, and the conference was deadlocked from the start.

In the atmosphere of discouragement which followed, a more modest step was nevertheless taken on November 18 with the signature by Belgium, Luxembourg, the Netherlands, France, and Italy of the First Agreement on Multilateral Monetary Compensation.[2] These countries—joined shortly thereafter by the Anglo-American Bizone of Germany—agreed to accept the automatic application among themselves of simple offsetting operations. Such offsetting operations—which were dubbed "first-category compensations"—were limited to those compensations of outstanding credit and debit balances which involved only a reduction in such balances, but no increase whatsoever in any of the intervening accounts. That is to say, each country agreed to settle its indebtedness to a second country by abandoning its claim on a third country, but not by increasing its indebtedness to a third country. Thus, in practice, first-category compensations could apply only to "closed" circuits, i.e. to a chain relationship in which each country was a creditor of the preceding one and a debtor of the following one.

This was, of course, a very severe limitation, and automatic first-category compensation remained extremely modest in amount, even after all other OEEC countries joined the machinery in

in this attempt as well as in the endless discussions on the multilateralization of payments, credits, and drawing rights which occupied the Intra-European Payments Committee of OEEC until the establishment of the European Payments Union, three years later, in the summer of 1950.

2. This salvaging operation must be credited primarily to the dogged persistence of Mr. Le Norcy, Adviser to the Governor of the Bank of France.

October 1948 under the 1948–49 Agreement for Intra-European Payments and Compensations.[3] Their total turnover reached only $5 million under the 1947–48 Agreement, and $160 million from October 1948 through June 1950. The latter figure represents less than 2% of the gross surpluses incurred during that period.

Table XI. TURNOVER OF INTRA-EUROPEAN COMPENSATIONS, DECEMBER 1947—JUNE 1950

(in millions of U.S. dollars)

	Automatic	Nonautomatic	Total
I. First Agreement on Multilateral Monetary Compensation, Dec. 1947—Sept. 1948	5	47	52
II. Intra-European Payments and Compensations Agreements			
A. Oct. 1948—June 1949	99	4	104
B. July 1949—June 1950	63	86	149
III. Total	167	137	305

Source:
BIS, Twenty-First Annual Report (Basle, 1951), p. 219.

Second-category compensations, i.e. those which would necessitate an increase in any of the participating accounts, remained optional for all members under the three successive agreements. The approval of all parties concerned was required before any operation could be carried out. Although the opportunities for second-category compensations were obviously much larger than for first-category compensations, they were rarely accepted in practice and totaled less than $140 million for the whole period from November 1947 through June 1950.[4]

Second-category compensations involved indeed for the debtor country the substitution of one creditor for another, and for the creditor country the substitution of one debtor for another. These substitutions would, in general, replace debts in relatively weaker

3. Portugal and Switzerland, however, never accepted automatic participation in the compensation agreements. They joined only as "occasional members," reserving their decision on each compensation proposed to them. The same status, involving no advance commitment, had been accepted at a much earlier stage by the other OEEC countries.

4. All in all, the formal compensation machinery established under these Agreements cleared only about 4% of the positions which would have been cleared under a system of full and automatic multilateral compensation such as was adopted later under the EPU Agreement. The imperfection of the system left 96% of these positions to be settled by bilateral credits and by drawing rights financed by American aid.

currencies by debts in relatively stronger currencies, and claims on relatively stronger currencies by claims on relatively weaker currencies. This would always tend to be the case, since the carrying out of all possible compensations would wipe the slate nearly clean for intermediate countries—i.e. those whose bilateral claims closely approximated in over-all amount their bilateral debts—but leave the net creditors with claims on the net debtors, and the net debtors with debts to the net creditors. Intermediate countries would benefit from second-category compensations, but extreme creditors and extreme debtors would both worsen their position. The only way out lay in a system of joint guarantees of all debts and claims so as to preserve the participation of the more nearly balanced countries in the credit risks involved. Such a provision was indeed essential to the agreement reached later on the automaticity of all compensations in the European Payments Union.

Credit risks were not the only objection to monetary compensation and the restoration of a multilateral system of settlements in Europe. Each country could exploit more fully its bargaining strength by dealing bilaterally with each of its partners, in isolation from one another, than by negotiating a multilateral trade and payments agreement with all of them collectively. The country in deficit could hope to extract from its bilateral creditors special trade or credit concessions by threatening to restrict severely all imports for which gold or dollar payment was demanded. Conversely, the granting of bilateral credits to one's debtors could be used by the creditor country as a weapon for obtaining preferential treatment for its exports or, at least, for avoiding discriminatory restrictions against them.

The credit and trade advantages gained by one country in such negotiations were, of course, necessarily offset by corresponding disadvantages for its partners in the negotiation—in the form of compulsory lending to it or of higher prices paid to it for imports obtainable more cheaply elsewhere—and for other countries whose more competitive exporters were being displaced by the spread of discriminatory restrictions. Globally, the waste of a trading pattern based on bilateral discrimination rather than price and quality competition undoubtedly constituted a net loss for the group. The resulting increases in the cost pattern and lowering of productivity of European countries also handicapped them more and more in trade relations with nations outside Europe. These arguments for a return to a multilateral system of trade and payments were obvious enough, but a number of countries were more mindful, in those days, of the immediate advantages they derived from bilateralism than of its long-term costs to them, and particularly to others. Such advantages were particularly marked for countries with large deficits, uncompetitive prices, and a vast market for so-called "unessential" imports, i.e. goods for which competition was keener among the selling countries than among the buying countries.

III. THE TWO AGREEMENTS FOR INTRA-EUROPEAN PAYMENTS AND COMPENSATIONS: OCTOBER 1948–JUNE 1950

The intra-European payments debate took an entirely new turn in the summer of 1948 with the initiation of the Marshall Plan. The bilateral payments agreements remained in force, but their role was greatly diminished by the availability of Marshall aid as an alternative means for the settlement of intra-European surpluses and deficits. The debate over multilateralization centered now on the multilateral use of such aid, rather than of the payments agreements credits.

The exact manner in which American aid could be used for intra-European settlements was not specified in the European Recovery Act. Congressional appropriations were based on annual forecasts of Europe's deficits with the Western Hemisphere alone, after deduction of some other resources—such as International Bank and private loans, etc.—available to cover such deficits. The financing of European deficits with nonparticipating countries outside the Western Hemisphere was hopefully expected to "be met basically by cooperative efforts of the participating countries and the affected non-participating countries." Finally, it was pointed out that intra-European settlements should not require any additional outside aid to Europe as a whole, since intra-European deficits would be matched, by definition, by equivalent intra-European surpluses. Vague references were made to the steps already taken by the Europeans themselves to improve, and multilateralize, intra-European settlements, and to the possibility of allocating a portion of Marshall aid in such a way as to contribute to the success of these undertakings. The European Recovery Administration, therefore, "should have the authority to finance procurement for one participating country from another participating country. In using such authority to help balance European clearing accounts . . . the Administrator would have greater control over any United States contribution to European multilateral clearing than would be the case if dollars were made available directly to settle these accounts." [1]

This ruled out the suggestion advanced some months earlier by the Committee of European Economic Cooperation (CEEC) that a portion of United States aid be set aside to underwrite a European clearing mechanism allowing each country to use its bilateral surpluses on some countries to offset its bilateral deficits with others, and guaranteeing the conversion into dollars of any residual amounts due to creditors in excess of the credit margins provided for in the payments agreements. [2]

Bilateral payments agreements were therefore left untouched until the Europeans had agreed among themselves—and with the Americans—on a new system of intra-European settlements. Dollar aid was allotted to the various countries on the basis of their respective deficits toward the Western Hemisphere alone, but a

1. See U.S. Senate, *Outline of European Recovery Program. Draft Legislation and Background Information*, submitted by the Department of State for the use of the Senate Foreign Relations Committee, 80th Congress, 1st Session (Washington, D.C., 1948), pp. 42, 50, and passim.

2. This proposal bears a great deal of resemblance to that which I presented to the IMF in September 1947, and which has been briefly outlined above, pp. 134–5. It differs from the latter in two respects. First of all, it substituted direct dollar payments to excess creditors, financed by United States aid, for the Fund's sales of the excess creditor's currency to the debtors and the consequent addition to the creditor country's drawing rights on the Fund. Secondly, it did not contemplate any multilateralization of the payments agreements credit margins and therefore did not determine the manner in which existing credit margins would be used for the settlement of net surpluses and deficits. Would France, for instance, use its surpluses on Norway to offset its deficits with Belgium, and its credit margin to finance its deficits with Britain, or would it, on the contrary, use its Norwegian surpluses to offset its deficits with Britain and its credit margin to finance its deficits with Belgium? The Benelux delegation later proposed to solve this question by apportioning net debts among net creditors in proportion to their share in the total intra-European surpluses, regardless of the actual pattern of bilateral surpluses and deficits. This plan, however, met with the objections described above (pp. 149–50) in connection with second-category compensations and was not accepted by the Committee as a whole. See the *General Report* of the CEEC (Washington, D.C., U.S. Department of State, 1947), *1*, 129–36, and *2*, 523–37.

portion of such aid might be allotted to them by ECA, not as a free gift but in payment for so-called "offshore" procurement of goods to be delivered by them to other participating countries.

The administrative machinery of offshore purchases was heavy and cumbersome, involving for each transaction a joint decision by three countries: the buying country, the selling country, and the United States itself. Intra-European offshore purchases totaled less than $245 million during the first six months of operations, and were replaced after October 1948 by new techniques, embodied in the two successive *Agreements for Intra-European Payments and Compensations,* of October 16, 1948 and September 7, 1949. American dollar aid remained based on advance estimates of each country's Western Hemisphere deficit, but part of this aid was labeled "conditional," the condition consisting in equal grants by the recipient country—in the form of "drawing" rights in its own currency—to be made "available" to other participating countries to finance their forecast bilateral deficits with the former.

It might seem that the final outcome of this new technique would be practically identical with that of the offshore system but would offer the advantage of greater simplicity and flexibility, since the intra-European financing involved would be related to the net balance arising from all transactions between each pair of countries rather than to specific export-import transactions. In fact, however, this new system considerably modified the relative bargaining strength of the various countries in their trade negotiations, stimulated bilateralism at the expense of competitive forces as the determinant of the intra-European trade pattern, paralyzed and discouraged successful readjustment policies, and led in a number of cases to a further aggravation of the intra-European payments problem.

From a financial point of view, the functioning of the system appears to have been as unpredictable and haphazard as that of the better known Monte Carlo roulette. The initial allotments of drawing rights, over its twenty-one months of operation, totaled about $1,700 million. In spite of multiple and complex revisions and adjustments (upward and downward), $260 million of the drawing rights "finally established" remained unused at the expiration of the Agreements. The proportion of the bilateral deficits financed by drawing rights ranged from 0% for Italy to 89% for Austria, and the proportion of the bilateral surpluses from 0% for Greece to 68% for Belgium. On a net basis, the proportion ranged even more widely from 14% of the Portuguese deficit to 100% of the Danish deficit, and from 26% of the Italian surplus to 92% of the Belgian surplus. Even more puzzling is the fact that the utilization of drawing rights increased—rather than reduced—the net surplus of France and the net deficit of Germany, and shifted the United Kingdom from a small creditor position to a much larger debtor position (see Table XII).

Table XII. DRAWING RIGHTS GRANTED AND USED AND THEIR IMPACT ON NET POSITIONS, OCTOBER 1948—JUNE 1950

(in millions of U.S. dollars)

| | Drawing Rights Granted a | | Drawing Rights Received a | | Net Surpluses (+) or Deficits (−) | | Net Impact of Drawing Rights |
	Established	Used	Established	Used	Before Drawing Rights	After Drawing Rights	
I. *Net Grantors*	1,508	1,258	356	197			−1,061
Belgium	618	494	11	9	+526	+40	−486
U.K.	488	382	122	62	+27	−293	−320
Germany	238	216	187	118	−69	−166	−97
Italy	78	82 b	27	—	+305	+224	−82
Sweden	86	85	10	8	+149	+72	−77
Switzerland	—	—	—	—	+108	+108	—
II. *Net Beneficiaries*	166	155	1,318	1,216			+1,061
France	51	58 b	446	358	+43	+344	+300
Greece	—	—	210	204	−232	−28	+204
Netherlands	31	32 b	226	226	−262	−67	+195
Austria	6	4	157	157	−158	−5	+153
Norway	24	11	135	134	−226	−104	+123
Turkey	43	34	88	85	−79	−28	+51
Denmark	12	9	36	35	−28	−3	+26
Portugal	1	8 b	21	18	−104	−94	+10
III. *Totals*	1,674	1,413	1,674	1,413	±1,159	±788	—

Notes:

a. Including a special credit line of $87.5 million granted by Belgium to the Netherlands ($38 million), the United Kingdom ($28 million), and France ($21.5 million), of which $39.1 million were actually used by the Netherlands ($38 million) and the United Kingdom ($1.1 million); but excluding minor readjustments posterior to the expiration of IEPA.

b. The use of multilateral drawing rights led, in a few cases, to drawings in excess of the drawing rights established by the grantor country.

These paradoxical consequences were the combined result of *faulty forecasting* in the assignment of drawing rights and of the fact that these were actually used for the settlement of *monthly* surpluses and deficits in each *bilateral* relationship, rather than applied to the much smaller net cumulative imbalance which would have remained after full compensation of mutually offsetting surpluses and deficits of each country with its various trade partners over a longer period of time than a single month.

Thus close to $500 million of drawing rights was absorbed by the financing of successive monthly deficits and surpluses in the same bilateral relationship and prevented their cancellation against one another (see Table XIII). The use of drawing rights resulted, in such cases, in an increase rather than a decrease in the cumulative bilateral surpluses and deficits, or even in a reversal of the initial creditor or debtor positions.[3]

Further and even greater wastes and absurdities resulted from the fact that the system operated on a purely bilateral basis, thus completely disregarding the evolution of each country's over-all creditor or debtor position in Europe. More than $300 million of conditional aid was apparently "wasted" in compensating countries for the granting of drawing rights that were in fact already compensated by drawing rights received by them from other participating countries. All in all, the haphazard forecasts and bilateral criteria used in the establishment and use of the drawing rights resulted in increasing *net* creditor and debtor positions by nearly $700 million; they added $300 million to France's net surplus, deepened Germany's deficit by nearly $100 million, and shifted the United Kingdom from a small surplus of $30 million to a large deficit of $290 million (see Tables XII and XIII).

If the system had been operated on a cumulative and multilateral basis—as in the European Payments Union that succeeded it—less than $1,200 million of conditional aid would have sufficed to finance completely all intra-European surpluses and deficits. Operating as it did on a monthly and bilateral basis, it absorbed a substantially larger amount of aid to finance only one third of the total net imbalance (see Table XII). Moreover, the system of settlements, after drawing rights, also remained essentially bilateral in character, so that means of financing or settlement were in fact

3. Thus Belgium used $9 million of drawing rights to finance occasional monthly deficits with Italy, even though it emerged from the 21-month period of the Intra-European Payments System with a net cumulative surplus on that country. In this case, the use of drawing rights increased the Italian debt to Belgium from $11 million to $20 million. In the Franco-British relationship, drawing rights led to the even more paradoxical result of replacing a French deficit of less than $53 million by a much larger claim of nearly $135 million against the United Kingdom.

Table XIII. Intra-European Surpluses and Deficits and the Impact of Drawing Rights, October 1948—June 1950

SUMMARY OF OPERATIONS

	In Millions of U.S. Dollars			In % of Gross Positions		
	Before Drawing Rights	After Drawing Rights	Impact of Drawing Rights	Before Drawing Rights	After Drawing Rights	Impact of Drawing Rights
I. *Bilateral Monthly Positions (surpluses = deficits)*	4,395	4,395	—	100	100	—
II. *Financed by:*	2,070	3,001	+931	47	68	+21
A. Gross drawing rights a	—	1,413	+1,413	—	32	+32
B. Reversals in bilateral positions	2,070	1,588	—482	47	36	—11
III. *Cumulative Bilateral Positions (I–II)*	2,325	1,393	—931	53	32	—21
A. Compensable multilaterally	1,165	605	—560	27	14	—13
B. Uncompensable net positions	1,159	788	—371	26	18	—8

THE IMPACT OF DRAWING RIGHTS

	In Millions of U.S. Dollars		In % of Gross Drawing Rights	
	Bilateral Positions	Multilateral Positions	Bilateral Positions	Multilateral Positions
I. *Reduction of Imbalance*	931	371	66	26
II. *Absorption by:*	482	1,042	34	74
A. Offsets between drawing rights granted and received by the same country	39	352	3	25
B. Reduction of compensable positions	443	690 b	31	49
III. *Gross Drawing Rights* a	1,413	1,413	100	100

Notes:

a. Including $39.1 million of Belgian credits, but excluding some minor readjustments subsequent to the expiration of IEPA.

b. Drawing rights increased the French surplus by $300 million and the German deficit by $97 million. They shifted the U.K. from a small surplus to a deficit of $293 million. See last two columns of Table XII.

required for the $1,400 million of cumulative bilateral positions, rather than for the $800 million of net positions to which they would have been reduced by multilateral compensations. The very limited compensations system embodied in the Intra-European

Payments Agreements (IEPA) cleared only about $100 million, leaving about $1,300 million to be covered by gold payments and, most of all, by the movement of credit balances under existing payments agreements. This is not to say, however, that this latter form of financing increased by a corresponding amount the bilateral claims and debts of the participating countries with one another. There were a number of cases in which the claims or debts incurred during the IEPA era were applied instead to amortization of previous debts or claims accumulated before October 1948.

The financial results of IEPA cannot be fully appraised on the basis of their impact on net creditor and debtor positions within Europe alone, and only during the twenty-one months from October 1948 through June 1950. Some of the distortions noted above may have helped compensate—or have been compensated by— other and opposite sources of imbalance in the European countries' over-all position. These distortions resulted, for instance, in a desirable strengthening of France's monetary reserves. They did, on the other hand, impose an additional drain on the United Kingdom's resources. There is certainly no reason to believe that either the ECA or the OEEC foresaw, planned, or welcomed these wild discrepancies between the drawing rights and the surpluses or deficits which they were supposed to finance.

The financial results of IEPA were merely arbitrary. Its impact on economic incentives and the competitive allocation of European resources was not only arbitrary but positively harmful.

The allocation of drawing rights required a complicated process of bilateral forecasts and negotiations in order to reach agreed estimates of the probable imbalance to be financed by drawing rights. Each country had, of course, a major interest in forecasting deficits and obtaining drawing rights from its partners. Such drawing rights would add to its economic resources and constitute at the same time a free grant to its often hard-pressed national treasury, providing noninflationary means of financing budgetary deficits. Once the drawing rights had been agreed upon, the beneficiary countries would have a definite incentive to make use of them, even if better or more essential imports were obtainable from other countries at lower prices. Imports financed by drawing rights amounted to a gift, while imports from other countries would involve immediate or deferred payment in goods, gold, or convertible currencies. The danger of losing the benefit of such free gifts also acted as a deterrent to readjustment policies which might reduce a country's deficits below the level of the drawing rights available to it. The large amount of drawing rights left unused under both Agreements thus appears highly puzzling when one considers only the incentives created by the system for the deficit countries.

If "conditional" aid had been really and truly conditional, prospective creditors would have had a powerful incentive to grant drawing rights to their partners and to ensure that they be fully used by them. The status of conditional aid was, however, very ambiguous from the beginning, and it became increasingly apparent that "conditional" aid was in fact very nearly unconditional. The initial allotments of global aid to each country were based on its Western Hemisphere deficit and "had been agreed upon before the intra-European payments plan was drawn up. 'Conditional' dollars for the creditors were, therefore, not additional dollars but part of the original dollar aid they expected to get in any case." [4] Secondly, the drawing rights left unused did not in fact involve an actual loss of dollar aid to the grantor countries, but merely a semantic transfer of aid from so-called "conditional" or "indirect" aid to "direct" aid.

The surplus countries, therefore, had little incentive to grant drawing rights and every incentive to discourage or prevent their use—through high prices or export controls—after they had been granted. This was not so apparent at the start as it became later on, however, and the discretion retained by ECA to revise at frequent intervals the total aid to be "firmly" allotted to each country could be used at any time as a club to deter niggardly policies in respect of drawing rights by the creditor countries.[5] Yet complaints on this score were frequently voiced, openly or privately, by the recipients of unused drawing rights. What is clear is that the allocation of drawing rights by the creditor countries placed in their hands a powerful bargaining weapon in their negotiations with the deficit countries, considerably strengthening bilateral pressures and incentives, as against competitive market forces, in intra-European trade and payments.

This account still fails to give a correct impression of the com-

4. See BIS, *Nineteenth Annual Report* (Basle, 1949), p. 202, and the ECA *Report on Recovery Progress and United States Aid* (Washington, D.C., 1949), pp. 99-100 and 211.

5. This club was openly used in negotiations with Sweden and particularly with Belgium, as these countries were soon declared ineligible for "direct" aid in view of their relative prosperity and over-all balance of payments strength.

plexity of the two Intra-European Agreements and of the actual operation of the system.[6] Numerous legal provisions, revisions, and readjustments were introduced in an attempt to avoid or minimize the disadvantages noted above. Three of these are worthy of at least a brief mention.

Large claims and debts had been accumulated, previous to the first Intra-European Agreement, under the bilateral payments agreements which had preceded it. Some of these claims were in liquid form, while others were frozen in blocked accounts. A number of agreements were reached concerning the manner in which such "existing resources" would be used in lieu of drawing rights, or before drawing rights could be exercised. A minimum of $300 million to $400 million of such resources was released for use by the debtors, but not all these resources had been effectively used by the time the Agreements expired. Most of these releases concerned sterling balances held on the United Kingdom. Together with the large drawing rights granted by that country, they contributed to the shift in the United Kingdom's position from a net creditor to a net debtor in the IEPA.

A second complication arose from the fact that Belgium's intra-European surpluses far exceeded its estimated Western Hemisphere deficit and, therefore, the amount of aid which the United States was willing to assign to that country. In the Second Intra-European Agreement, a compromise was reached on this issue. Of the forecast $400 million surplus of Belgium, the first $200 million would be covered by drawing rights fully compensated by conditional aid. A further $125 million would be covered half by conditional aid and half by special Belgian credits. The last $75 million of the forecast surpluses would also be covered by matching conditional aid with Belgian credits, but in the proportion of two to one.[7]

Finally, a minor step toward the multilateralization of drawing rights emerged from the bitter and protracted discussions which

6. An excellent and detailed account of the negotiation and development of the intra-European system during this period may be found in William Diebold, *Trade and Payments in Western Europe*, New York, 1952.

7. I had vainly defended for many months this "matching credit" or "fractional settlement" formula as a solution for reaching a more general agreement on the multilateralization of drawing rights. This suggestion was later incorporated in the EPU Agreement, as a keystone of the system.

The Belgian surpluses turned out in fact to be much smaller than had been anticipated. More than $70 million of the Belgian drawing rights and $48 million of the Belgian credits were left unused at the expiration of the Agreement.

preceded the renewal of the Agreement in September 1949. One fourth of the total drawing rights established under the Second Intra-European Agreement were made multilateral, i.e. they could be used to settle deficits with other participating countries as well as with the grantor itself, a corresponding amount of conditional aid being allotted to the country against which the drawing rights had been effectively exercised. Since, however, the bilateral portion of the drawing rights—75%—had to be fully used before any recourse could be had to their multilateral portion, the system was bound to remain highly bilateral for most of the Agreement's life. Because of these limitations, the use of drawing rights against countries other than the initial grantor amounted only to 9% of the total drawing rights used under the Second Agreement, although it represented as much as 41% of the multilateral drawing rights, for which alone such transfers were authorized by the Agreement.

The limping compromises of September 1949 did very little, therefore, to correct the financial and economic absurdities of the bilateral system of drawing rights. Moreover, the ink had hardly dried on the new Agreement when the cascade of devaluations which took place before the end of the month threw into further confusion the balance of payments forecasts on the basis of which the new drawing rights had been established.

The spectacular improvement which followed in the economic position of the major European countries contributed greatly to allaying the fears which had blocked until then all efforts to multilateralize the intra-European payments system. The United Kingdom, particularly, which had adamantly opposed all such efforts since August 1947, was rapidly regaining confidence in its ability to meet the test of competition in intra-European trade. Its gold and dollar reserves were increasing rapidly, and its net position in Europe had shifted from monthly deficits of more than $150 million on the eve of sterling devaluation to surpluses of $20 million to $90 million a month in the latter part of 1949 and the first half of 1950. Opinion in the United Kingdom thus moved gradually away from the frightened, defensive attitude induced by the collapse of the 1947 convertibility experiment to a growing willingness to return, although cautiously and progressively, to a multilateral system of trade and payments.

The first step in this direction was taken with the establishment, in the summer of 1950, of the European Payments Union.

CHAPTER 5

The European Payments Union: 1950-55

I. A DIFFICULT PREGNANCY

THE FIRST MOVE toward a radically new approach to the problem of intra-European settlements was officially launched by the Economic Cooperation Administration in December 1949. Nine months of arduous negotiation were to elapse before the signing of the European Payments Agreement on September 19, 1950.

Rarely has an international negotiation been so successful in reaching its objectives rather than hiding its failures behind Platonic declarations of intent, nullified in effect by mountains of exceptions, transitory provisions, or escape clauses. The EPU Agreement was a remarkably clean and simple document, embodying sweeping and precise commitments of a revolutionary nature, which drastically shifted overnight the whole structure of intra-European settlements from a bilateral to a multilateral basis.

Among the many reasons which might be marshaled to explain this success, three appear particularly worthy of the attention of anyone interested in the mechanics of international negotiations.[1]

The first lies in the realism of the initial ECA proposals and objectives, and in their immediate applicability to the concrete situation with which they dealt. The EPU plan did not propose an ideal model or ambitious blueprint, to be implemented only gradually after numerous and still far distant "prerequisites" had been met. It was designed to bring limited but immediate improvements to a system of settlements whose defects were by then universally recognized by the participating countries. It did not aim, therefore, at

1. Other readers may skip this section, and turn immediately to sec. II, below, p. 168.

161

substituting a new and permanent mechanism for that already agreed upon at Bretton Woods. Its purpose was merely to define a system of mutual rights and commitments which would effectively reduce or eliminate the unnecessary trade and exchange restriction, discrimination, and bilateralism which had flourished under the famous postwar "transitory" provisions of the IMF Agreement. The Preamble of the EPU Agreement thus stated clearly that the Union should facilitate "a return to full multilateral trade . . . , to the general convertibility of currencies . . ." and operate only "until it is possible to establish, by other methods, a multilateral system of European payments."

Scathing criticisms of the Agreement were often heard in those days, particularly on this side of the Atlantic, for its failure to restore immediately full and world-wide liberalization and currency convertibility. In fact, however, this was not then a real alternative, susceptible of international agreement and implementation. To insist on such objectives at that time, as a prerequisite for agreement, could only have meant the perpetuation of the *status quo*, i.e. of unrestricted bilateralism in European trade and payments.

The success of the EPU negotiation must also be credited to the admirable negotiating machinery set up under the aegis of the OEEC. Ministers of Foreign Affairs, Economics, or Finance from all the European countries assembled in Paris once a month or every other month to seek agreement on the most intractable questions at issue. The hard bargaining that took place on those occasions could often win assent, not through limping compromises on these issues themselves, but through other concessions on which conflicts of national interests had arisen. Most of all, however, these meetings were carefully prepared by national experts permanently stationed in Paris by their governments, meeting daily in the OEEC technical committees but acting under instructions from their national Administrations and keeping in very close contact with them. In the course of time, such experts inevitably developed a broad understanding of other countries' problems and policies and a sincere urge for concrete achievements in their work. Their task was not merely to defend in Paris the initial points of view of their own country but also to report and explain to their government the points of view of others, to seek new instructions, and to suggest policy changes and compromises which would facilitate agreement without seriously damaging vital national interests. The test of their success would lie, to a great extent, in their ability to ease the task of their Minister at the Council meetings, by leaving as few questions as possible unresolved at the technical level, and by informing him fully about the probable standpoint of other countries on such questions and the ways in which final compromises could be worked out.

Finally, the strong and imaginative leadership of ECA helped crystallize the vague and often conflicting aspirations of a score of countries around a coherent plan of action, based on only a few, but strategic, principles. The ECA showed the utmost flexibility in devising ways and means to meet legitimate fears and objections without sacrificing or compromising any of the fundamental features of its plan.[2]

The key provisions of the ECA project were derived from previous proposals, already mentioned in the preceding chapters, and originating for the most part in IMF studies and discussions. They were primarily aimed at creating a fully multilateral system of intra-European settlements that would remove, in one clean swoop, all bilateral techniques and incentives in intra-European payments. Their second and third objectives were to facilitate a gradual but rapid elimination of quantitative trade and exchange restrictions in intra-European trade, and to provide thereby a transition toward world-wide trade liberalization and currency convertibility.

The first step in this direction had already been outlined in CEEC and IMF studies dating back to the summer and fall of 1947. It lay in the automatic multilateral offsetting of all bilateral surpluses and deficits incurred by each country toward all the other participating countries in the system. The second step lay in defining equally multilateral means of settlement for the net claims and debts that would emerge from such offsets. It had been suggested, both at the CEEC and at the Fund, that the credit margins of existing bilateral payments agreements be multilateralized for this purpose. Balances in excess of the credit margins would then be settled by means of Marshall Aid dollars (according to the CEEC proposals), or by drawings on the Fund's resources (in the IMF proposals). The Fund's staff had later developed, during the fall and winter of 1948–49, alternative formulas under which intra-European credits would be used *pari passu* with ECA conditional aid dollars and gold or Fund drawings in the settlements of net intra-

2. See, for instance, below, pp. 166–7.

European deficits and surpluses. This matching credits or fractional gold and credit settlements formula was the keystone of the EPU plan. It offered a workable compromise between the viewpoints of creditor and debtor nations, and a realistic transition between the bilateral credits of the payments agreements and an eventual return to full convertibility.

Numerous hurdles still had to be surmounted, however, before agreement could be reached. The exact amounts of credit to be made available, the precise proportion of gold to credit in the settlements, the guarantees to be provided against default and exchange rate fluctuations, the provisions for withdrawal and liquidation, etc. were the subject of long and difficult debates in which the opposite viewpoints of prospective creditors and debtors had to be harmonized with one another and with those of ECA itself. Special provisions were also necessary to deal with so-called "structural" creditors and debtors, since it would have been absurd to envisage or enforce, even in the long run, any strict balancing of each country's regional transactions within the EPU area alone. The use or liquidation of outstanding claims arising from previous payments agreements had also to be regulated in such a way as not to perpetuate bilateral incentives under the new system. It would be tedious to review here the manner in which agreement was finally hammered out on all these questions, but the reader should be aware of the conflicts of interest which each of them raised, in order to appraise fairly the solutions given to them and summarized in section II of this chapter.

Only the most crucial aspect of these negotiations will be mentioned here by way of example. It concerns the participation of the United Kingdom in the proposed EPU system. The negotiation had progressed remarkably smoothly when it was suddenly brought to an abrupt stop in February 1950 by a British memorandum submitted by the Chancellor of the Exchequer, Sir Stafford Cripps, to the OEEC Council. The United Kingdom, affirmed Sir Stafford, could never accept the multilateral clearing system which was the starting point and the keystone of the ECA plan. Surplus countries should be required to grant substantial credits free of any gold payments or amortization provisions, which could be repaid only through a shift in their position from surpluses to deficits in their intra-European trade. Every country should retain the right to use quantitative controls, and even discriminatory restrictions, in order to protect its monetary reserves. Finally, the authority of the Managing Board should be narrowly circumscribed and the operations of the Union should be largely automatic in character.

This memorandum was followed in March by new British proposals which would have led, in effect, to a total subordination of the EPU mechanism to whatever agreements the United Kingdom chose and was able to negotiate bilaterally with her creditors and debtors. All sterling claims and debts would continue, in principle, to be financed under bilateral agreements, and automatic compensations would apply only to the continental countries' surpluses and deficits with one another. Sterling claims would be brought into the compensations only insofar as (1) this would reduce a continental country's net indebtedness to the clearing system, or (2) such claims exceeded the credit margins granted to the United Kingdom, normally entitling the creditor country to demand gold payment from Britain.

The resulting indebtedness of the United Kingdom to the clearing system would be settled fully in gold, but only after it had been reduced by a similar transfer to the clearing system of all British claims on continental countries in excess of payments agreements credit margins.

The main point of the system was, of course, to allow the United Kingdom to pick and choose the claims and debts which she would handle bilaterally and those which she would pass on to the Union, in accordance with her bargaining strength in bilateral payments agreements. She could build up surpluses with the Union by granting only small credit margins to her weaker debtors, such as Greece, Turkey, and Austria, and by transferring to the Union her claims on such countries in excess of these margins. Her deficits with other countries would be kept out of the clearing system whenever she could induce net creditor countries—Italy and Sweden, for instance—to accept sterling balances in settlement. On the other hand, she would avoid gold payment to the creditor countries— Belgium, Switzerland, and Germany, for example—with which adequate credits could not be negotiated, by settling her indebtedness to them through her surpluses in the clearing system.

These proposals, however, were ingeniously presented and appeared plausible on the surface. Many people tended at first to regard them as a great British concession, and were inclined to accept them as the only way open to break the deadlock which had stalled the negotiations ever since the intervention of Sir Stafford Cripps at the February meeting of the OEEC Council. The ECA team in Paris rejected this course of action, pointed out the real implications of the plan, and showed concretely how its application during the previous year and a half would have allowed Britain to finance bilaterally her deficits with Italy and Sweden, to cover her deficits with Belgium, Switzerland, and Germany by unloading upon the clearing system her claims on Austria, Greece, and Turkey, and to emerge as a net creditor in the Union in spite of the large net deficits incurred by her during that period with the participating countries as a group. This analysis was never rebutted and the British made no further effort to defend their proposals.

The deadlock was finally broken in two different ways. First of all, the United States announced that $600 million [3] of European aid funds would be set aside to support EPU even if it were not joined by all the participating countries of OEEC. The old "Fibenel" plan for a closer trade and payments association between France, Italy, Belgium, the Netherlands, and Luxembourg was also dusted off as an indication to Britain that her continued opposition would merely isolate her from, but would not kill, the proposed payments union.

At the same time, however, ECA made a determined attempt to clarify the underlying sources of British opposition to EPU and to eliminate all objections which could be met without sacrificing the fundamental objectives of the plan. British opinion was indeed far less unanimous on the issue than appeared on the surface. There existed a hard core of opposition, adamantly attached to bilateralism as the best way to promote full employment objectives while avoiding the difficult readjustments necessary to restore the country's external balance under a freer system of trade and payments. This, however, remained a minority view, and many influential circles in Britain herself were sincerely desirous to escape from the strait jacket of bilateralism, if this could be done without sacrificing the future status of the pound as a component of other countries' international reserves and without causing an immediate and unbearable drain on Britain's slender gold and dollar holdings.

One of the by-products of the EPU plan which most worried the British was the fact that any sterling balances that would ac-

3. Later reduced to $500 million in the congressional appropriations act.

crue in the future to any continental country would be automatically wiped out in the monthly compensations and replaced
by a claim on the Union—or a reduction of debt to the Union
—even though the country acquiring such sterling balances
might itself have been willing to hold them as an integral part of
its monetary reserves. The United Kingdom also feared the additional gold losses to EPU which might result from the multilateral
use in EPU settlements of the large bilateral sterling balances previously accumulated by European countries, and particularly by
Italy and Sweden.

Two suggestions were developed and discussed within ECA to
deal with these problems, and were officially endorsed in April by
the Fibenel group. The first of these was to authorize surplus countries to exchange the credit—but not the gold—portion of their
EPU claims for equivalent sterling balances, provided that these
remained fully usable in future EPU settlements with any participating country, and not only for the settlement of deficits with
the sterling area. This amendment did not, therefore, modify in
any way the multilateral system of EPU settlements nor the respective proportions of gold and credits in such settlements. It did,
however, remove a real roadblock to the resumption of sterling's
traditional role as a component of international currency reserves.

The second ECA suggestion related to existing sterling balances
accumulated by European countries previous to the entry into
force of the EPU Agreement. The use of such balances by the creditor, or their amortization by Britain, could no longer be restricted
bilaterally, but would have to be channeled through the Union. On
the other hand, all balances on which a specific amortization schedule would not be agreed upon between Britain and her creditors
could be freely used by the latter, but only to the extent necessary
to cover their net deficits toward the Union. The ECA would reimburse the United Kingdom for any gold which it might be called
upon to pay to the Union as a consequence of such use.

Both of these proposals were accepted by the United Kingdom in
the first days of May 1950 as a workable basis for its participation
in EPU,[4] and the Paris negotiations then moved rapidly toward a

4. In spite of their crucial role in the negotiation itself, both proposals remained
meaningless in practice. The "sterling option" clause was broadened at the request
of the Scandinavian countries to apply to all currencies, rather than to sterling
alone. It had, however, been previously redrafted by the British themselves and
given a needlessly complex and limiting formulation which deprived it of any prac-

successful conclusion. All substantive provisions of the Agreement were adopted unanimously by the OEEC Council on July 7, and the legal instrument embodying them was signed on September 19, with retroactive effect to July 1, 1950.

II. THE STRUCTURE OF THE AGREEMENT

Three broad objectives dominate and explain the basic provisions of the EPU Agreement. The first was to eliminate all monetary incentives to bilateralism in trade and payments and to effect at the same time a maximum economy of resources in intra-European settlements. This was achieved through the clearing of all bilateral surpluses and deficits—multilaterally and over time—and through the full multilateralization of all the means of settlement used to cover residual surpluses or deficits: gold or dollars, intra-European credits, debt amortization, and American aid.

The second was to induce countries to accept the risks involved in such a system and those inherent in the concomitant program for the liberalization of intra-European restrictions, by providing "cushioning" credits, with adequate guarantees against default and exchange risks, for moderate disequilibria in intra-European payments.

The third was to stimulate readjustment policies and check the development of excessive or permanent disequilibria in the Union. This was the purpose of the graduated system of gold settlements, and of the powers conferred on the Managing Board to make recommendations to member countries and to back up such recommendations with special credits in support of agreed readjustment programs.

A. MULTILATERAL CLEARING OF BILATERAL SURPLUSES AND DEFICITS

The core of the EPU system lies in the full and automatic offsetting of all bilateral surpluses and deficits incurred by each participating

---

tical use for the countries concerned (Art. 16 of the EPU Agreement). As for the ECA reimbursements to Britain for gold payments arising from the use of "existing resources," they merely came out of dollar funds which would have been appropriated for British use anyway under the ECA aid program.

country [1] with all the others, whether for current or for capital transactions. These compensations take place once a month, and are carried out by the Bank for International Settlements (BIS) acting as Agent for the OEEC. Each central bank reports the balances held by it in favor of each of the other central banks, and on this basis the Agent determines the net deficit or surplus incurred by each during the month.[2] A single settlement of this net amount between each country and the Union thus takes the place of separate settlements of bilateral positions between each pair of countries separately. This has the effect of economizing about half the means of settlement that would be required otherwise. Far more important is the fact that this system destroys at the very roots most of the balance of payments incentives to discrimination among members. A deficit country may still feel impelled to tighten its over-all restrictions on intra-European imports in order to check a drain on its reserves or the increase of its indebtedness, but it no longer has any monetary incentive to discriminate in favor of its bilateral debtors and against its bilateral creditors. Its settlements will be determined exclusively by its over-all position toward all of them taken together, regardless of the bilateral pattern of its earnings and expenditures.

This basic change in incentives was probably more important than the formal commitment, simultaneously accepted by members, to eliminate all discriminatory practices in their mutual trade and other transactions. It constituted the first, but essential, step toward the abolition of the bilateral barriers which had previously been stifling competition in Europe.

1. EPU includes as members all the participating countries of OEEC. The transactions of Ireland, Luxembourg, and Trieste, however, are merged with those of the United Kingdom, Belgium, and Italy, respectively. Operations also cover all European transactions with the monetary area of the participating countries, including in the British case the whole sterling area and other authorized sterling transfers.

2. EPU compensations and settlements thus bear only on the reciprocal claims and debts of *central banks* vis-à-vis one another. As will be noted later (pp. 213-4), growing numbers of transactions are now effected directly between traders and private banks and do not concern EPU in any way, except for each member's commitment to "use its best endeavors to ensure that abnormal balances in the currencies of other Contracting Parties are not held by banks other than central banks or otherwise placed so that they are excluded from the calculation of bilateral surpluses or deficits" (Art. 4-f). It should also be noted that the exclusion of direct settlements between central banks involved a commitment by them to finance fully, through credits, the bilateral claims accumulated by them between two settlement dates (Art. 8).

B. FRACTIONAL SETTLEMENT OF NET CUMULATIVE POSITIONS

Full gold or dollar settlement of the net monthly positions would never have been accepted at that time by the debtor countries. Substantial credits were still available to them under their bilateral payments agreements, and their debtor position gave them a trump card in the negotiation of new credits or special trade preferences, under the bilateral trade and payments system which they were asked to give up. Moreover, the sudden elimination of all credits in intra-European settlements would undoubtedly have unleashed a new spiral of trade restrictions, while the fundamental objective of the Union was to promote greater progress toward trade liberalization.

The EPU system combined, therefore, fractional gold payments [3] with fractional credits in all intra-European settlements. Previous bilateral credit margins were discontinued and replaced by a single, multilateral payments agreement under which each country gave and received a line of credit to help cover its net surpluses or deficits with the Union. In further contrast with the former payments agreements, this line of credit was not to be used exclusively until the credit ceiling was reached, and then replaced abruptly by gold settlements. Such a shift from 100% credits to 100% gold payments would have provided excessive facilities at the outset and probably stimulated a sudden relapse into trade and exchange restrictions once the credits were exhausted.

Credits and gold were thus to be used simultaneously in settlement, and the proportion of gold to credit was to increase gradually for the debtors as their deficit rose within the Union. The credits would thus provide a shock absorber for moderate or temporary deficits, and particularly for those which some countries would incur as a result of their trade liberalization commitments. The rising schedule of gold payments, on the other hand, would place increasing pressures on persistent debtors to adopt readjustment policies. These pressures would be further reinforced by the administrative authority conferred on the Managing Board to foster and support

3. The term "gold payments" is used throughout as a short cut for payments in either gold, or United States dollars, or any other currency acceptable to the payee (Art. 14).

national or mutual policies aiming at the correction of excessive surpluses or deficits within the Union.

The over-all lines of credit were fixed at 60% of each country's quota, and the quotas themselves at 15% of each country's total visible and invisible trade with the EPU area in 1949.[4] Provision was made for later revisions, in accordance with future changes in the turnover of transactions, but this procedure was used only twice. In July 1951, the Dutch quota was raised from $330 million to $355 million, and the German quota from $320 million to $500 million.[5]

Small surpluses or deficits—up to 20% of the quotas—were covered fully by credits to or from the Union. As deficits increased, gold payments by debtors would rise gradually to 20%, 40%, 60%, 80%, and finally 100% when the quota was exhausted. For the creditors, a uniform percentage of 50% would apply for all surpluses above 20%, but within the limits, of the quota (see Appendix Table 20). No advance rules could be agreed upon for the settlement of surpluses beyond quota, and the problem was left for future decisions of the Organization.[6]

The adoption of a graduated system of gold and credit settlements implied, of necessity, a further complication in the Union's accounting procedures. The surpluses and deficits of a country with the Union, determined *monthly* by the multilateral compensation of its bilateral surpluses and deficits, would have to be offset against each other in order to establish its *cumulative* position toward the Union. The graduated scale of gold and credits applied to the settlement of this cumulative position. Thus previous gold and credit settlements would be reversed when a cumulative position was re-

4. Except in the Swiss and Belgian cases. The Swiss request for a larger quota was indeed welcomed by the Organization, but the Belgian insistence on a lower quota gave rise to a bitter fight in the last stages of the negotiations. (Initial quotas may be found in Appendix Table 19.)

5. Large, uniform quota increases were effected in 1954 and 1955 but were purely nominal, their purpose being to maintain unchanged each country's credit line in spite of the rise in the gold fraction of settlements to 50% in 1954 and 75% in 1955.

6. An automatic approach to convertibility would have suggested 100% settlements beyond quotas for creditors as well as for debtors. Few countries, however, were ready to accept automaticity in this respect, and most of them rejected any rule of settlement which might induce countries to seek a solution for their dollar problem through an expansion of their intra-European surpluses. See below, pp. 187–8 and 192–3.

duced, i.e. when the monthly compensation established a net surplus in favor of a debtor, or a net deficit on the part of a creditor, of the Union.

C. THE UNION'S CAPITAL AND LIQUID RESOURCES

The asymmetry between the creditors' and the debtors' settlement rules exposed the Union to the threat of considerable gold drains, at least during the initial phase of its operations. These drains were to be financed from a $350 million capital fund contributed to the Union by the United States.[7] This contribution would serve, at the same time, as a guarantee to the creditors against possible defaults by the debtors.

This $350 million capital fund was, however, reduced in effect to $271.6 million by other ECA decisions under which the Union made initial grants of $279 million to so-called "structural debtors" balanced only in part by corresponding grants of $200.6 million to the Union by "structural creditors." [8]

D. EXCHANGE RATE GUARANTEES AND LIQUIDATION PROVISIONS

The compensation machinery of the Union and the multilateralization of the net debts or claims of the participating countries in the Union required the adoption of a single monetary unit in which all accounts could be uniformly denominated. The choice of this unit would determine at the same time the exchange rate guarantee attaching to the credit operations of the Union.

Rumors about a possible revaluation of gold with respect to the

7. If each country's cumulative surplus or deficit rose in uniform proportion of the established quotas, the Union would lose $160 million in the second and third "tranches" of quota utilization, as the 50% payments to creditors exceeded the 20% and 40% payments received from debtors. These losses would later be recouped by the Union when debtors' payments rose to 60% and 80%, in the fourth and fifth quota tranches. The gold drain could, however, theoretically reach a maximum of $350 million if widespread deficits concentrated on a few creditors only. On the other hand, the Union might gain gold in the opposite case of few but large deficits balanced by many but small surplus positions.

8. See below, pp. 175–7. These arrangements, proposed at the last minute by ECA, were bitterly fought by the creditor countries, but quickly accepted by them when the ECA representative pointed out that the discrepancy would easily be remedied by increasing their grants to the Union and "compensating" them by labeling as "conditional" rather than "direct" a further portion of their Marshall Aid allocations.

dollar were still rampant at the time, and the prospective creditor countries therefore wished all EPU claims and debts to be expressed in terms of gold. The prospective borrowers, on the other hand, were reluctant to adopt gold, or even the dollar, as a unit of account, since European currencies might still depreciate later with respect to both.

It was finally agreed that all accounts would be carried out in a special EPU unit, *initially* defined by a gold content equal to that of the 1950 U.S. dollar. This gold content could be changed at any time by a decision of the OEEC Council, but the unanimity rule governing the Council's decisions made it highly improbable that any such change would intervene, since the creditors would always have an interest in vetoing a devaluation and the debtors an interest in vetoing an appreciation of the EPU unit. It was further provided, therefore, that no country could oppose its veto to a change equivalent to, or smaller than, the appreciation or depreciation of its own currency with respect to gold since the inception of the Agreement.

The economic meaning of this legal language amounted in effect to a definition of the EPU unit—and an exchange rate guarantee for EPU claims and debts—in terms of whichever member currency remained most stable in the future in terms of gold.[9]

The liquidation provisions of the Agreement embodied further guarantees for the creditor countries against defaults on the part of the debtors. We have already noted [10] the objection of both extreme creditors and debtors to any system of automatic compensations which would wind up with bilateral claims of the first against the latter. This difficulty was solved by associating all participating countries in the credit risks involved. During the life of the Agreement, all net claims and debts would be channeled through the Union itself, eliminating all bilateral credit relationships. These would reappear at the time of liquidation, but all countries would share in the risks involved in proportion to their quota in the

9. The European country which devalued least—or not at all—would probably be a creditor of EPU and could veto any devaluation greater than its own. In the more improbable case of a proposed appreciation of the unit of account, any debtor country could veto an upward revaluation greater than that—if any—of its own currency. My own objective in proposing and defending this formula was not only to facilitate agreement between creditors and debtors. It was also to define a form of exchange guarantee that might be used later to encourage a resumption of capital movements in Europe, and a monetary unit that might be adopted in future agreements on European economic integration.

10. See above, pp. 149–150.

Union. This result would be achieved through an ingenious, if complex, formula first proposed by Dr. Posthuma of the Netherlands Bank, and under which all residual claims and debts of the Union would be split up, at liquidation, among all members—whether net creditors or debtors—in proportion to their respective quotas. The net claim of a creditor country on the Union would then be reflected in the excess of its bilateral claims on all other members over its bilateral debts to all other members, and the net debt of a debtor country in the Union by the excess of its bilateral debts over its bilateral claims.

The prospective creditor countries regarded the EPU capital fund and liquid dollar resources as a further guarantee for their claims at the time of liquidation. A few of them favored, for that reason, an early liquidation of EPU and a prior claim of net creditors upon the outstanding convertible assets. Most countries, however, wished to prolong the Agreement until further progress toward full convertibility became possible, and the Economic Cooperation Administration was anxious to retain intact, even in that event, the United States capital contribution as a collective fund to be used only to promote European cooperation and integration.

Compromise was reached on an initial two years' life for the Agreement, but for its later continuation among the countries which agreed to its renewal—with or without amendments—as long as those countries accounted together for at least half of the total quotas. The United States, moreover, reserved to itself the right to block the distribution of EPU's convertible assets contributed by it, if it objected to the liquidation decision.

E. Other Transitional Means of Settlement

These basic provisions of the Agreement were essentially simple and easy to operate. The main complexities of the EPU system—outside of the liquidation provisions—relate to the settlement of bilateral claims and debts outstanding when the Union was created, and to the channeling of American aid to so-called "structural" debtors and creditors.

1. Outstanding Claims and Debts

Outstanding indebtedness under the previous system of bilateral agreements had to be dealt with before EPU could come into operation. More than $850 million of claims and debts had accumulated in this manner and could be used by the creditor countries only to finance later bilateral deficits with their debtors. If such bilateral use remained authorized, it would preserve powerful discriminatory incentives whose elimination constituted one of the most fundamental objectives of the new multilateral payments system. Italy, for instance, held large sterling balances and would be tempted to discriminate in favor of imports payable in sterling, both in order to get rid of such balances and to avoid gold payments to the Union. In order to avert this danger, the Union ruled out any bilateral use of such balances but left a choice between two methods of amortization, both of which were fully multilateral in fact:

1. The creditor country and the debtor country could agree to amortize such balances either by a lump payment or by contractual, periodic installments. Such repayments would then be channeled into the accounts reported monthly to the Agent and netted multilaterally by the Union prior to actual settlements.

2. An alternative—or supplementary—technique of amortization lay in the definition of all or part of such balances as "existing resources." Such resources could then be used freely by their holders to cover all or part of their net cumulative deficit in the Union, regardless of their current bilateral surpluses or deficits with the debtors of the balances.[11]

2. Initial Balances and Special Resources (see Appendix Table 21)

The financing of structural disequilibria raised another kind of problem, which was handled primarily by bilateral U.S. negotiations rather than through OEEC discussions as such. The term "structural" was unfortunately used to cover—and in part to confuse—two types of situation very different from one another.

A structural creditor was a country with persistent surpluses with the other OEEC countries, offset by parallel deficits outside Europe.

11. This alternative method originated in the discussion of sterling balances referred to above, p. 167. Even before the Agreement was signed, the United Kingdom notified all its creditors in EPU that their sterling balances could be used in this fashion, irrespective of the amortization agreements concluded. The subsequent use of sterling balances as "existing resources" decreased the United Kingdom's surpluses with the Union during the first year of operations, but increased correspondingly its later cumulative deficits. The resulting increase in the United Kingdom's gold payments to the Union thus brought into operation the "reimbursements" discussed above, p. 167 and n. 4.

A structural debtor was a country with persistently large deficits in Europe, *not* offset by surpluses outside Europe. It was therefore in over-all deficit in its balance of payments, while the structural creditor was not in over-all surplus.

It was emphasized in EPU discussions that these structural surpluses and deficits could not be financed through the EPU credit system. The structural creditor countries were not able to grant such financing without finding themselves an outside source of finance for their extra-European deficits. The structural debtors, on the other hand, were in too weak a position to commit themselves either to fractional gold settlements for their deficits or even to later reimbursements of the credits which the Union might extend to them.

The technique adopted by ECA to solve both problems simultaneously was a hangover from the preceding drawing rights and conditional aid system. Six countries received "initial credit balances" totaling $314 million—$279 million as grants and $35 million as long-term loans—in order to cover expected deficits with the Union, prior to any gold or credit settlements under the quota system. Two of them renounced, in exchange, their normal right to EPU credits.[12] Three countries were assigned, on the other hand, "initial debit balances" in EPU, meaning that they would receive no gold or credit settlement for a corresponding portion of their net surpluses. These debit balances constituted, in effect, an initial grant by them to the Union, compensated by equivalent allotments of conditional aid to them by the United States.

As distinct from the former drawing rights and conditional aid, however, these initial balances would be used multilaterally to finance net over-all disequilibria, rather than bilaterally between each pair of countries. Another difference was that, contrary to everyone's expectation, the ECA announced at a late stage of the negotiation its intention to grant much larger initial balances to the deficit countries than the amount of conditional aid allotted to the creditor countries. The difference would have to be borne by the Union, thus reducing its capital fund by an equivalent amount.

The repetition of a similar procedure in later years threatened to deplete gradually the modest capital fund assigned to the Union.

12. Greece's borrowing quota has remained blocked to this day under these arrangements, but Austria's quota was unblocked on July 1, 1953. Iceland's quota was also blocked temporarily from April through September 1951.

After June 1951, therefore, the initial balances procedure was replaced by a so-called "special resources" procedure under which the United States bought in fact from the Union itself, rather than from the creditor countries, the EPU resources which it wished to put at the disposal of the structural debtors. These operations no longer affected the capital of the Union, but contributed to a considerable strengthening of the Union's gold and dollar reserves.

The allotment of special resources to debtor countries tapered off gradually and came to an end in 1953–54 with a final grant of $19.4 million of special resources to Greece.

F. ADMINISTRATIVE STRUCTURE

In spite of the immense responsibilities entrusted to it, the European Payments Union has no staff or organization of its own.

The various operations described above are carried out, economically and efficiently, by the Bank for International Settlements in cooperation with the central banks of the participating countries. The Bank acts as Agent for the OEEC, to which it reports periodically and to which it submits the accounts of the Union.

The Union operates, in all other respects, as an integral part of the OEEC, under the supreme authority of the OEEC Council. The Council elects each year a Managing Board of seven members which supervises the operation of the system, determines the interest rates to be paid by the debtors to the Union and by the Union to the creditors,[13] and periodically reviews the development of each country's position in the Union. The Board is empowered to recommend to members or to the Council the measures or policy readjustments called for by the development of excessive or persistent deficits or surpluses. It is also charged with the task of studying the conditions under which the Agreement—initially concluded for only two years—should be renewed, and to suggest the amendments which it may deem desirable in the light of previous experience, or in view of the evolution of the international situation and balance of payments of members.

The influence of the Managing Board on the debtor countries' policies is strengthened by its ability to grant special credits, of a nonautomatic character, to help such countries in the adoption and implementation of agreed programs of financial and economic re-

13. See Appendix Table 22.

adjustment.[14] Although this authority was used only very sparingly, the skill with which it was used to overcome the German payments crisis in the first months of the Union's operations strengthened immensely the influence and prestige of the Managing Board.[15]

The creditor countries have, of course, a direct interest in co-operating with the Board in all decisions and recommendations aiming at reducing disequilibria in the Union and, therefore, their own lending to it. Direct pressure may also be brought to bear on them when their surplus quota is exhausted, since at this point they become dependent on new Council decisions for the settlement of their further surpluses. Their refusal to accept such decisions would exclude them from EPU settlements and relieve other members from their trade liberalization commitments to them.

In its advisory functions to member countries, the Board has consistently tried to avoid as far as possible the cumbersome and dangerous procedure of public and spectacular discussion of a country's difficulties in the OEEC Council and technical committees. In many cases, the advice or warnings of the Board are communicated to the countries concerned informally and without any publicity whatsoever, either by the Board members for countries directly represented, or by the Board's chairman, or by special invitation to send representatives to a meeting where the country's problems are to be discussed.

Finally and paradoxically, the influence of the Board can be ascribed to the very precautions initially taken to minimize its legal powers and importance. First of all, the Board is barred, in most cases, from adopting final decisions, binding on all members. Its recommendations must be adopted by unanimous vote of the OEEC Council before they can have any executive force. As a consequence, the Board has been allowed to vote by simple majority—a provision without precedent or parallel in OEEC—and its members are usually left a large degree of discretion, instead of being rigidly bound by their government's instructions. Its recommendations carry, however, an enormous weight in the Organization. If unanimity is required for their adoption, unanimity is also

14. The Agreement contemplated the allocation of additional U.S. funds for the financing of such "special assistance" programs. The $150 million of Marshall aid theoretically earmarked for this purpose was in fact never released by ECA to the Union and was used for other ECA operations in Europe.

15. See below, pp. 180–2.

required to modify them in any way. A country may often be opposed to some aspects of the Board's recommendations, but still prefer their adoption to the absence of decision which would result from its veto.

Secondly, the Board members are not in permanent session in Paris, but most of them continue to carry primary responsibilities in their own countries for the daily preparation or formulation of policies in the monetary and exchange field. They bring to the meetings a full knowledge of their countries' current and prospective position and problems, and then return to their daily tasks with a keener realization of the prospects and problems of other countries, and of the measures necessary to avoid later crises or open conflicts in OEEC. Their advice carries great weight with their respective governments. As a result, necessary harmonization of policy can often be effected quietly at the technical level, or greatly facilitated even in the more difficult cases calling for decisions by the Council itself at the ministerial level.

In brief, the absence of jurisdictional powers has produced a most effective machinery for effective cooperation and successful negotiation of conflicts of interests and policies among the members of EPU.

III. THE EPU IN OPERATION

A. THE KOREAN UPHEAVAL: 1950–52 (see Charts XVIII and XIX and Appendix Tables 23 and 26

The EPU experiment could hardly have been launched under more inauspicious circumstances. The feeling of optimism generated by the rapid economic improvements of 1949–50 had induced some liberalization of internal and external controls in most member countries and, at the same time, sharp cuts in Marshall Aid allotments. Over-all assistance to Western Europe as a whole was reduced by one third from the fiscal year 1949–50 to the fiscal year 1950–51, and by as much as two thirds for the United Kingdom.

Hostilities broke out in Korea on June 25, 1950, that is, a few days before the entry into force of the EPU Agreement. A wave of panic buying surged throughout the world during the following months, defense programs were stepped up sharply, and new inflationary forces quickly reversed previous progress toward better balance in international payments.

Within Europe itself, the monthly deficits and surpluses now channeled into EPU rose rapidly from the previous average of $200 million a month to $260 million in 1950–51 and $360 million in the following year. The peak level of $550 million was reached in October 1951. It was fortunate that the new compensations system was established by EPU in time to cover the largest portion of the settlements involved in intra-European trade. Yet the net surpluses and deficits—after compensation—reached within a year an amount roughly equivalent to that experienced over the previous twenty-one months of the IEPA system.

The newly born EPU was thus confronted, at a much earlier stage than had been anticipated, with two equally difficult problems: that of excess debtors and that of excess creditors.

1. The Settlement of Excess Deficits

The German crisis developed so rapidly as to confront the EPU Managing Board with a most formidable test at its very first meeting in October 1950. Germany had absorbed within the previous three months three fourths of the quota credits which were supposed to last it for at least two years. Its total quota was indeed exhausted by the end of November, and deficits continued to mount at an appalling rate throughout the winter of 1950–51.

The normal outcome of such a situation would have been the immediate reimposition by Germany of drastic restrictions on its imports. Such restrictions would have hit with particular force two neighboring countries, the Netherlands and Denmark, which were highly dependent on "unessential" vegetable and dairy exports to the German market, and which were already themselves in a very shaky balance of payments situation. These countries, in turn, would have become unable to finance their most essential imports needs. A spiraling of restrictions, spreading from country to country, threatened the complete collapse of the trade liberalization program of OEEC, and a severe setback to European production and recovery.

Faced with this situation, the Board acted with unexpected speed and energy. In spite of all emotional prejudices toward a former enemy country and deep conflicts of interest among its members,[1] the Board agreed in record time to offer Germany a temporary line of credit of $120 million, if a strong program of financial and economic readjustment were put into effect by the German authorities under the continuous supervision of the Board. These recommendations were accepted by Germany and the OEEC Council, and the plan entered into operation at the beginning of November.[2]

In sharp distinction to the economic policies prevalent in those days throughout Europe, Germany resorted to a wide variety of fiscal and credit measures, rather than to trade and exchange controls, in order to check its external deficits. The turnover tax was increased in order to hold back internal consumption, and various modifications were introduced in income and corporate taxes in order to curtail the volume of self-financed investments. Most of all, however, the stockpiling boom was restrained through a long series of bank measures, including a 50% increase—from 4% to 6% —in the discount rate, sharp rises—up to 100%—in the legal reserve requirements of the banking system, the compulsory deposit in blocked accounts of 50% of the national currency equivalent of the foreign exchange applied for by importers, direct ceilings and cutbacks in the volume of rediscounts and of commercial bank credits to the private sector of the economy, etc. These measures did not actually curtail the outstanding volume of credit, except for a very short period, but the rise in net credits to the economy was held down to about 7% in the first half of 1951, as against 30% in the second half of 1950.

The results of this program on the balance of payments were, at first, disappointing, and the OEEC had to agree to the temporary suspension of trade liberalization by Germany in March 1951. The continuous expansion of German production and exports made it possible, nevertheless, to sustain imports at a relatively high level, even during this period. Moreover, Germany and all the participat-

1. France and the United Kingdom were averse to increasing their loans to the Union and to facilitating further stockpiling of scarce raw materials by Germany. On the other hand Denmark, Italy, and the Netherlands had opposite financial and commercial interests, since a loan to Germany would sustain their export markets for fruit and vegetables and reduce their deficits in EPU.

2. Messrs. A. K. Cairncross, Director of the OEEC Trade and Payments Division, and Per Jacobsson, Director of Research of the BIS, played a vital role in the preparation of this program and its discussion with the German authorities and the Managing Board.

ing countries agreed to place the distribution of German import licenses under the supervision of a mediation group of three independent experts appointed by the OEEC Council.[3] The task of this group was to preclude a scramble for German licenses through bilateral bargaining and to ensure an allocation of licenses which would minimize the harmful impact of German restrictions on the weaker members of OEEC.

The situation improved shortly thereafter. The special EPU loan was fully repaid by the end of May, five months before maturity, and Germany soon changed its position from that of an extreme debtor to that of an extreme creditor in the Union. German dollar reserves also increased to more than twice their previous level before the end of 1951, reaching their highest point in more than twenty years. Industrial production increased by 20% in a single year, and exports rose by more than 40% in volume and 75% in value. The over-all trade deficit was cut from more than $700 million in 1950 to less than $30 million in 1951. At the end of that year, Germany began to remove progressively the trade and exchange controls restored in March.

This dynamic and successful handling of a major crisis endowed the young Managing Board with a prestige and authority far beyond the most optimistic expectations of the promoters of the EPU Agreement. The manner in which the crisis had been surmounted through the combination of national monetary policy and international cooperation also made a deep impression on other countries. The Netherlands' position in the Union closely paralleled that of Germany and received close attention from the Managing Board during the course of 1951. By June the Netherlands had exhausted its $30 million initial grant from the Union and 90% of its normal credit facilities—$198 million—with the Union. The only action taken by the Board was a slight revision in the Dutch quota, in effect increasing the credit ceiling by $15 million. The Dutch government, however, introduced on its own initiative a drastic fiscal and monetary program aiming at a 25% cut in investment and a 5% cut in consumption expenditures. By the end of the year, its position had shifted radically from extreme debtor to extreme creditor in the Union.

3. The revolutionary character of this decision is worth pointing out, as it involved a renunciation by each country of its bilateral bargaining strength and sovereignty for protecting its national interests in the middle of a dangerous crisis.

Four other countries—Turkey, Greece, Austria, and Iceland—also exhausted at an early stage their facilities in the Union. An application from Turkey for special assistance was turned down by the Board in June, mainly on the ground that the Turkish deficits were not due to temporary balance of payments fluctuations, but were the planned and fully anticipated result of an investment program for which the Union could not be regarded as a proper source of financing. By August 1951 Turkey had exhausted both its initial credit balance ($25 million) and its quota facilities ($50 million) in EPU. It has remained ever since on a full gold basis for the settlement of its EPU deficits.[4] By June 1955 its gold payments outside quota totaled $274 million, of which $69 million was financed by the United States under the "special resources" procedure described above (p. 177).

Greece, Austria, and Iceland had also exhausted their "initial credit balances" well before the end of the first year of EPU operations. Their later deficits were also fully covered by special resources allotted by the United States—$153 million to Greece, $45 million to Austria, and $11 million to Iceland—and by additional 100% gold payments in the case of Greece, until the unfreezing of Iceland's quota in October 1951 and Austria's quota in July 1953.[5]

The worst of the EPU crises occurred in the second year of operations with the alarming growth of French and British deficits and Belgian surpluses.

France and the United Kingdom had both experienced initial surpluses in EPU at such a rate as to threaten an early exhaustion of their surplus quota. Their persistent creditor position had been investigated by the Managing Board in the winter and spring of 1951, and trade and exchange liberalization had been stepped up by both countries in order to slow down the accumulation of further surpluses.

The situation reversed itself dramatically at the end of the spring. The slow deterioration in the United Kingdom's position had been masked at first by the boom in the outer sterling area's exports of raw materials. The post-Korean collapse in the market for primary products greatly aggravated the British position in EPU. Surpluses

4. Except for short-term credits of $20.3 million used in September and October 1952, and fully repaid in January 1953.

5. By June 1955, Greece had paid $50 million to the Union. Austria, however, has been a creditor of the Union ever since November 1952.

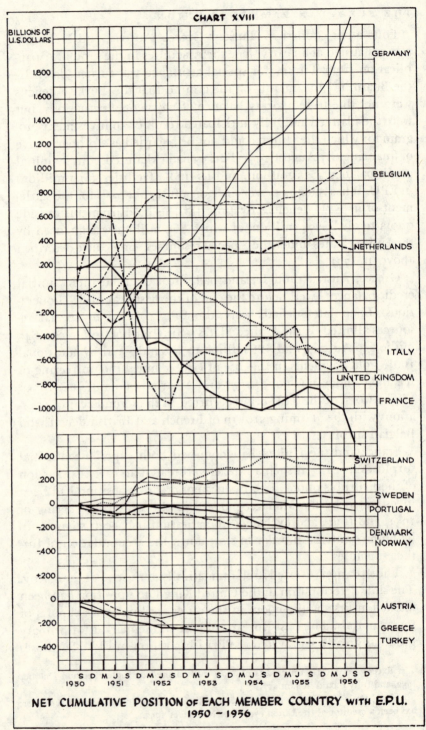

CHART XVIII

BILLIONS OF
U.S.DOLLARS

1.800
1.600
1.400
1.200
1.000
.800
.600
.400
.200
0
-.200
-.400
-.600
-.800
-1.000

GERMANY
BELGIUM
NETHERLANDS
ITALY
UNITED KINGDOM
FRANCE

.400
.200
0
-.200
-.400

SWITZERLAND
SWEDEN
PORTUGAL
DENMARK
NORWAY

+.200
0
-.200
-.400

AUSTRIA
GREECE
TURKEY

S D M J S D M J S D M J S D M J S D M J S D M J S D
1950   1951   1952   1953   1954   1955   1956

NET CUMULATIVE POSITION OF EACH MEMBER COUNTRY WITH E.P.U.
1950 – 1956

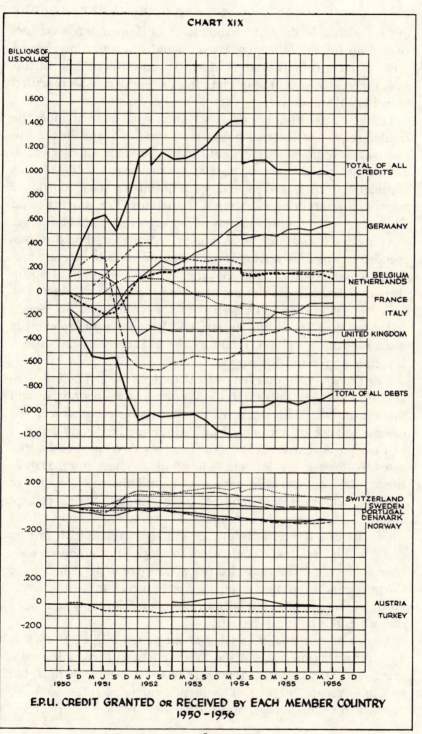

CHART XIX

BILLIONS OF
U.S. DOLLARS

TOTAL OF ALL CREDITS

GERMANY

BELGIUM
NETHERLANDS

FRANCE

ITALY

UNITED KINGDOM

TOTAL OF ALL DEBTS

SWITZERLAND
SWEDEN
PORTUGAL
DENMARK
NORWAY

AUSTRIA

TURKEY

S D M J S D M J S D M J S D M J S D M J S D M J S D
1950   1951   1952   1953   1954   1955   1956

E.P.U. CREDIT GRANTED OR RECEIVED BY EACH MEMBER COUNTRY
1950 - 1956

of $670 million in the first ten months of EPU operations were succeeded during the following sixteen months by an uninterrupted series of large deficits totaling about $1,700 million. The British quota was exhausted in May 1952, and further deficits were settled fully in gold and dollars.

Yet the British situation was slowly improving by then under the double impact of internal policy measures—increases in the discount rate from 2% to 4%, debt funding, investment cuts, etc.—and of a sharp tightening of trade and exchange controls. As in the German case, fiscal and monetary readjustments acted too slowly to avoid a resumption of external restrictions. The proportion of liberalized trade was brought down from 90% to 61% in November 1951 and 44% in March 1952, while the Managing Board recommended to the United Kingdom various measures to increase production and exports and urged other OEEC members to step up their own liberalization of imports from the United Kingdom.

From $236 million in October 1951, the monthly sterling deficit fell to less than $50 million in May and June 1952, and soon made room for large surpluses, totaling close to $500 million, between September 1952 and June 1953.

The French crisis was even worse than the British. The inflationary impact of the Korean war, the Western rearmament drive, and the war in Indo-China destroyed the remarkable progress achieved toward balance of payments equilibrium and monetary stability in 1949–50. A new flight from the currency developed and aggravated the French predicament. The efforts to check internal inflationary developments did not succeed until the early months of 1952. French prices were stabilized at that time and have been kept at about the same level ever since. This is unfortunately a level which appears dangerously uncompetitive in relation to foreign markets. The frequent examinations to which French policies have been subject in OEEC have led to a fair degree of agreement as to the policies which should be pursued by France, but the implementation of these policies has been thwarted or delayed by continued difficulties of a political character.

French deficits in EPU totaled about $1,100 million from May 1951 through June 1953. A short-term credit of $100 million was granted to France by the Managing Board in February 1952, but was fully repaid in June. The French quota facilities were exhausted in October 1952, and further deficits have been covered ever since by 100% gold payments to EPU. The pressure which such a drain of reserves would normally have exercised upon French policies was obviated, however, by large receipts of American aid—including $89 million of special resources in April and May 1953—and by substantial dollar earnings arising from United States military expenditures and offshore contracts.

The worst aspect of the French crisis from the OEEC point of view was the consequent setback in its trade liberalization program. French liberalization measures were totally suspended at the beginning of 1952, and were not resumed until the end of 1953. Even then progress was extremely slow, and the gradual resumption of trade liberalization was partly offset by a simultaneous recourse to export subsidies and "compensatory" import taxes, designed to make up for the admittedly uncompetitive level of French prices and costs.

2. The Settlement of Excess Surpluses

The EPU Agreement itself had laid down the presumptive rules applicable to the settlement of excess deficits. Deficits beyond quotas were to be settled fully in gold, "unless the Organization decides otherwise" (Art. 13-a). No agreement had been reached, however, on the settlement of excess surpluses, this being left entirely to future decisions of the Organization (Art. 13-b).[6]

The first line of attack adopted by the Managing Board was to make every effort to slow down the accumulation of surpluses by urging persistent creditors, well before their quota was exhausted, to adopt more expansionary policies and particularly to step up the liberalization of their trade and exchange restrictions. Such action had been successfully pressed, during the first year of operation, upon France, the United Kingdom, Portugal, and Belgium. These countries had shown themselves receptive to the Board's advice, and by June 1951 had liberalized 75% to 90% of their intra-European trade.

Although these policies were continued and amplified in the following months and years, they did not prevent the accumulation of surpluses well in excess of the EPU quotas. Belgium exceeded its surplus quota in August, Portugal in September, and Italy in November 1951. The settlement rules to be applied were the sub-

6. See above, p. 171 and n. 6.

ject of long and difficult negotiations throughout the second year of operation of EPU.

The arrangements arrived at as a result of these negotiations were of a highly precarious nature. Only limited and temporary quota "rallonges" could be agreed upon between these countries and the Board, on the basis of 50% gold and 50% credit settlements.[7] These settlement rules were preceded, or accompanied, by further policy measures designed to slow down the accumulation of surpluses. Efforts were made by all three countries to stimulate imports from the EPU area. They included, for instance, the liberalization of restrictions on imports (up to 99% in Italy and 85% in Portugal) and invisible transactions, the liberalization of imports of overseas territories, tariff reductions, expanded credit facilities to importers, and so on. Capital exports to other EPU countries were encouraged, while tighter controls were established on imports of flight capital and on the re-export of goods in transit. Belgium and Portugal also imposed a temporary blocking of a part of the proceeds of exports to the EPU area, in order both to discourage such exports and to slow down the internal inflationary impact of their EPU surpluses. Finally, Belgium even resorted to direct licensing of export goods for which alternative markets could be found in the dollar area.

These measures, together with the opposite policies followed by the deficit countries and the post-Korean changes in the international situation itself, contributed to arresting—and reversing—the accumulation of surpluses by Belgium, Portugal, and Italy. The first two countries experienced moderate, and Italy very large, deficits in the Union in 1952–53.

7. The Italian rallonge was equivalent to about 50% of the initial quota. Those successively established in the face of growing Portuguese and Belgian surpluses totaled before the end of the second EPU year 80% and nearly 150%, respectively, of these countries' initial quota commitments. The 50% rule mentioned in the text is only a rough approximation of the actual, and more complex, arrangements negotiated with Portugal and Belgium. Portugal received, in fact, a little less, and Belgium a little more, than 50% gold for their excess surpluses in 1951–52.

Sweden's creditor quota came within a hairsbreadth of total exhaustion in March 1952, but since an early reversal was expected—and indeed soon took place—Sweden herself offered to finance fully her excess surpluses by additional credits to the Union.

3. First Renewal of the Agreement

In the meantime the EPU Agreement, initially concluded for two years, had to be renewed from July 1, 1952. The 1952 revision of the Agreement was aimed primarily at avoiding the uncertainties and time-consuming negotiations associated during the previous year with the attempt to reach only limited and short-term agreements with the excess creditors on an ad hoc basis, and only after their quota was already exhausted or on the point of being exhausted.

Uniform arrangements were therefore made with the major creditors at that time for 50% gold and 50% credit settlements beyond quotas up to certain amounts designated as "quota rallonges." Similar arrangements were reached in December 1952 with Germany and the Netherlands, and no difficulties were encountered for the settlement of excess surpluses during the year 1952–53.

The acceptance of these additional credit commitments by the excess creditors, and particularly by Belgium, was linked with the partial settlement and consolidation of the credits in excess of quota reluctantly granted during the previous months under strong pressure from the Managing Board. Belgium received an extraordinary gold amortization of $80 million and consolidated an additional $50 million of its credit claims on EPU into a medium-term loan, repayable in five yearly installments.[8] Another $50 million of Belgian credits to the Union was transformed into bilateral claims of $25 million on France and $25 million on the United Kingdom, and used for purchases of defense equipment by Belgium from these countries, whose debt to the Union was reduced by a corresponding amount. Other bookkeeping adjustments[9] had the effect of retroactively generalizing the 50% settlement rule for surpluses beyond quotas, up to the amount of the agreed rallonges. The final result of these various adjustments was to settle fully in

8. A stand-by credit for an equivalent amount was simultaneously negotiated with the IMF, in order to facilitate the financing of this credit by the National Bank of Belgium as a "bankable" asset.

9. Some previous gold payments to Belgium and Portugal were also excluded from these countries' "accounting position" in the Union, meaning in effect that they would no longer be subject to reverse payments to the Union to finance later deficits under the "cumulative principle."

gold, outside the normal quota mechanism, $315 million of the $458 million of Belgium's surpluses beyond quota.[10]

Finally, some minor modifications were introduced into the Agreement, in order to reduce the strain on the Union's convertible assets.[11] These had fallen in October 1951 to a low of $179 million, as a result of the concentration of diffused deficits upon a few major countries,[12] but had risen by June 1952 to $460 million as a result of the large amount of full gold settlements ($349 million) of deficits beyond quotas. The $207 million allotted as "special resources" by the United States to cover such payments were not subject to reversals under the "cumulative principle," but the $142 million received directly from the United Kingdom, Turkey, and Austria might be lost rapidly in 100% settlements to these countries if and when they reduced their cumulative deficit with the Union through later monthly surpluses. Yet the concern shown by the Managing Board at the time certainly erred on the side of caution. The quota credits available to debtor countries were close to exhaustion, and the special resources contributions of the United States were still to continue for some time, even though on a declining scale. The convertible assets of the Union could only have been endangered by a complete reversal in the countries' current balances with the Union, coupled with a radical change of policies with respect to debtors' or creditors' settlements.

The convertible assets decreased in fact from $459 million to

10. The adjustments may be summarized as follows (in millions of U.S. dollars):

	Surpluses	Gold	Credit
Financed under the quota	330.6	129.3	201.3
Financed under the rallonges	85.2	42.6	42.6
Excluded from accounting position	372.9	272.9	100.0
Previous gold settlements	192.9	192.9	–
New gold amortization	80.0	80.0	–
Five-year credit to the Union	50.0	–	50.0
Credits to France and the United Kingdom	50.0	–	50.0
Total	788.7	444.8	343.9

11. Gold payments by debtors were stepped up in the initial quota tranches, without modifying, however, the over-all 40–60 ratio of gold and credit settlements. Member countries also agreed to make temporary contributions to the Union whenever necessary to ward off a decline of its convertible assets below a level of $100 million.

12. See above, p. 172, n. 7.

Table XIV. EVOLUTION OF EPU GOLD AND DOLLAR RESOURCES

(*in millions of U.S. dollars*)

July 1:	1951	1952	1953	1954	1955	1956
I. *Capital Fund*	271.6	271.6	271.6	271.6	271.6	271.6
A. *U.S. contribution* a	350.0	361.4	361.6	361.6	361.6	361.6
B. *Plus initial debit balances* a	200.6	189.2	189.0	189.0	189.0	189.0
C. *Minus initial grants*	−279.0	−279.0	−279.0	−279.0	−279.0	−279.0
II. *Unused Swedish Initial Debit Balance* (−)	−21.2	—	—	—	—	—
III. *Excess of Creditors' Claims Over Debtors' Borrowings*	102.0	78.7	161.1	138.9	125.1	164.2
IV. *Operating Profits or Losses* (−)	−0.4	1.0	3.4	3.2	2.7	2.1
V. *Total = Gold and Dollar Resources*	352.0	351.2	436.2	413.6	399.4	437.9
A. *Gold*	—	149.5	153.0	153.0	153.0	290.6
B. *Dollars*	352.0	201.7	283.1	260.6	246.4	147.3
1. Treasury bills	—	—	142.5	92.4	72.3	5.9
2. Current account	65.9	78.4	17.1	44.7	50.6	17.9
3. Undrawn balance at U.S. Treasury	286.1	123.3	123.5	123.5	123.5	123.5

Note: a. The U.S. contribution was increased by the amounts of conditional aid renounced by Sweden against the cancellation of an equivalent portion of its initial debit balance.

$351 million as a result of the June 1952 adjustments,[13] but rose again to $436 million in the course of the following year, and remained uninterruptedly at comfortably safe levels afterward (see Table XIV).

B. POST-KOREAN SETTLEMENTS: 1952–55
(*see Charts XVIII and XIX and Appendix Tables 23 and 26*)

The problems raised by the financing of intra-European settlements abated greatly after the first two years of operation. First of all, the gross monthly deficits and surpluses fed into the Union's mechanism declined considerably from $4.3 billion in 1951–52 to $2.7 billion in 1953–54, and less than $1.9 billion in each of the following years. Moreover, compensations continued to absorb and

13. Belgium received $80 million, the United Kingdom $25 million, and France $16 million as a result of the amortization arrangements described above, while the Union itself received about $13 million in consequence of the modification in the schedule of debtors' gold payments.

finance the lion's share of this imbalance. Net cumulative deficits and surpluses increased by a lesser amount over the four years 1952–56 than in the preceding two years. Previous extreme creditors—particularly Sweden, Italy, and Portugal—experienced substantial deficits which could be financed in large part through the amortization of their former EPU claims, while the United Kingdom's current surpluses could be absorbed in full by reimbursements on her outstanding EPU debt. Germany alone continued to accumulate persistent surpluses at an alarming rate.

Payments problems were further eased by the spectacular improvement in the EPU countries' gold and dollar position. The estimated gold reserves and dollar holdings of Western Europe rose uninterruptedly from $8.4 billion at the end of 1949 to $17.2 billion in June 1956. This spectacular improvement made it possible to reconcile a considerable hardening of EPU settlement rules with further progress toward trade liberalization.[14] Recourse to EPU credits has remained extremely moderate ever since June 1952, $340 million of new credits to Italy, Norway, Denmark, Iceland, and Austria being more than offset by $508 million of debt amortization by France and the United Kingdom. Total credits to the debtor countries thus declined by $170 million over the four years 1952–56, as against an increase of $1,000 billion in the first two years of operation of the Union.

As mentioned above,[15] special provisions had been made in June 1952 for the continuation of fractional settlements of prospective surpluses beyond quotas on a 50% gold and 50% credit basis. The special rallonges established at that time were revised periodically, upward or downward, in the course of the following two years, and maintained in all cases a sufficient margin for the settlement of actual surpluses. All four of the original excess creditors—Belgium, Portugal, Italy, and Sweden—were indeed running current deficits with the Union. New rallonges, however, had to be established to cover the rising surpluses of the Netherlands (in the latter part of 1953), Austria, Switzerland, and particularly Germany.

The initial lack of agreement on the settlement of surpluses beyond quotas had been responsible for most of the difficulties encountered by EPU in later years. Actual cases had been solved on

14. See below, pp. 193–7.
15. See p. 189.

a precarious and ad hoc basis by the extraordinary reimbursements to Belgium and Portugal in 1952 and the rallonge decisions of 1952–53. The problem was finally tackled in a bolder manner by the radical amendments introduced in 1954 and 1955 in the original EPU Agreement. It is largely as a consequence of these amendments that the huge surpluses of Germany in 1954–56 could be handled without difficulty and that outstanding credit claims on EPU declined by about $450 million, from $1,446 million on the eve of the 1954 revision to $996 million in June 1956.

IV. THE 1954 AND 1955 REVISIONS OF THE AGREEMENT

The European Payments Union had been initially established for two years only, and its early demise was freely predicted each spring from 1952 on. Those forecasts were uniformly confounded each June, the Agreement being renewed in every case on a precarious year-to-year basis.

The first two of these revisions, in June 1952 and June 1953, have already been discussed. Neither involved any fundamental change in the normal operating rules of the system. The 1954 revision, on the other hand, introduced into the operation of the Union an entirely new principle which had been debated at length in the negotiation of the 1950 Agreement, but had then been rejected by the prospective debtor countries. This was the provision for contractual amortization of at least a portion of the EPU claims and debts which would not be extinguished in fact by the reversal of previous cumulative positions. Although such reversals had been substantial (see Appendix Tables 23 and 26), they had only slowed down the growth of cumulative imbalance. By June 1954 the normal quota facilities established in June 1950 were indeed close to exhaustion. Of the seven creditor countries at that time, four had long exceeded their quotas, and only $70 million of quota credits (out of an initial amount of $1,100 million) remained available for settlements with the other three creditor countries. Of the eight debtor countries, three had far exceeded their quota facilities and had therefore been for some time on a 100% settlement basis with the Union. Only $200 million of quota credits (out of an initial amount of $1,350 million) remained available to the other five debtor countries for further EPU settlements (see Appendix Table 25, col. a).[1]

Moreover, a growing portion of the credits previously granted to cushion "temporary" disequilibria failed to be amortized through the EPU mechanism itself, as some countries remained persistent creditors or persistent debtors in the Union.[2] By June 1954, 60% of the credits granted to and 76% of the credits granted by the Union had been outstanding for more than two years (see Table XV).

The main objective of the June 1954 revision was to solve both of these problems together by providing a regular mechanism of debt amortization which would, at the same time, reopen fractional credit facilities for future EPU settlements.

Bilateral amortization agreements, concluded directly between creditor and debtor countries along general lines suggested by the Managing Board, provided for immediate repayment of $226 million of outstanding debts and claims in EPU, and for further amortization of $637 million by periodic installments over an average of seven years. Each bilateral payment actually made or received would cancel an equal amount of the debtor's liability to, and the creditor's claim on, the Union. The Union itself repaid an additional $130 million to the main creditor countries on July 1, 1954 from its own gold and dollar funds, which by then had risen to $544 million, i.e. by nearly $200 million over the amount initially received by it from the United States.

Additional agreements, along the same general lines, were negotiated during the following two years, particularly on the occasion of the fifth renewal of the EPU Agreement in June 1956. Together with the 1954 agreements, they provided for $1,120 million of contractual repayments, $480 million of which had already been effected by July 1, 1956. Voluntary cash repayments of $130 million by France and $12 million by Italy to EPU itself

1. Much larger facilities would be reopened, of course, in the event of a reversal of positions, i.e. for the settlement of future deficits by current creditors and of future surpluses of current debtors. Such reversals did indeed take place, but on a limited scale, in the following months, and helped meet the deficits of Sweden, Switzerland, Austria, and Portugal in 1954–56.

2. No amortization of claims or debts was provided for in the Agreement except through the reversal of previous cumulative positions.

Table XV. EPU CREDITS AND REPAYMENTS, JULY 1950—JUNE 1956

(in millions of U.S. dollars)

	Total 1950–56	1950–51	1951–52	1952–53	1953–54	1954–55	1955–56
I. Creditors							
A. *Yearly changes*	996	649	432	91	−80	−59	−36
1. Lending	3,233	773	1,108	360	417	312	263
2. Repayments	−2,237	−124	−676	−268	−498	−372	−299
B. *Credit outstanding, end of year*		649	1,081	1,172	1,092	1,032	996
1. One year or less		649	927	368	200	155	125
2. One to two years		—	154	650	231	123	87
3. Two to three years		—	—	154	523	195	123
4. More than three years		—	—	—	138	559	661
II. Debtors							
A. *Yearly changes*	832	547	456	9	−58	−46	−75
1. Borrowing	2,677	735	1,083	174	259	243	184
2. Repayments	−1,845	−188	−627	−165	−317	−289	−259
B. *Credit outstanding, end of year*		547	1,002	1,011	953	907	832
1. One year or less		547	938	140	164	182	83
2. One to two years		—	64	807	68	162	111
3. Two to three years		—	—	64	657	68	162
4. More than three years		—	—	—	64	495	475
III. *Amortization (−) of Pre-EPU Payments Agreements Debts*	−812	−319	−268	−72	−76	−47	−30
IV. *Net Credit Expansion (+) or Contraction (−): IIA + III*	+20	+228	+188	−63	−134	−93	−105

were also distributed among the creditors, bringing to $750 million the total of special amortization payments to EPU creditors over the two financial years 1954–56 (see Appendix Table 24). All creditor countries' claims, except Germany's, were brought back in consequence well below the limits of their lending commitment under quotas. Provisional credit rallonges totaling $618 million had been established in July 1954 for the six major creditor countries. Most of these could be discontinued in the 1955 and 1956 revisions.

Cash repayments by the debtors had also reopened equivalent borrowing facilities for them under the initial quota provisions of the Agreement. Moderate credit rallonges totaling $160 million were granted to them in 1954, in return for their acceptance of the amortization agreements negotiated at that time. Only two countries—Italy and Denmark—have ever had occasion to draw upon these additional credits, and by July 1, 1956 the only rallonge credit outstanding was a credit of $39 million to Italy. The United Kingdom and France, on the other hand, had reduced their outstanding indebtedness to the Union through current surpluses combined with large amortization payments.[3] No new rallonges were established in the 1955 and 1956 revisions, but a special two-year line of credit of $50 million was made available to Italy in recognition of her high level of trade liberalization and in order to give her more time for the negotiation of the long-term loans necessary for the financing of the Vanoni plan.[4] It was left to Italy's discretion to decide whether deficits beyond her quota and rallonge would be financed fully—within the $50 million limit established —by drawing on this credit line, or partly by credits and partly in gold.

The credit facilities available as of July 1, 1956 totaled $580 million for settlements to the creditor countries[5] and $760 million for settlements by the debtor countries.[6] They were sufficient to

3. Including voluntary amortization payments of $130 million by France and $12 million by Italy, which were distributed pro rata among the creditors.

4. The Vanoni plan contemplates large-scale investments for economic development and the reabsorption of Italy's structural unemployment over a period of ten years.

5. For simplicity's sake, Portugal and Austria are still regarded here—and in Appendix Tables 24 and 25—as creditor countries, although their position has shifted from cumulative surpluses to cumulative deficits in the Union. Both countries have so far opted to settle such deficits fully in gold, thus avoiding recourse to EPU credit except for an insignificant amount of credit—less than $0.7 million —in the case of Austria.

6. See Appendix Table 25. Future amortization installments would, moreover, reopen equivalent borrowing and lending commitments within quotas—except in the case of Germany, where they would be applied first to the amortization of outstanding credits beyond quota. It has also been agreed that EPU could, in case of need, call anticipatively on lending commitments expected to be reopened by future amortization installments (but only with respect to those deriving from the July 1, 1954 amortization agreements) and on additional amounts corresponding to the rallonge credits outstanding on the eve of the 1954 EPU revision. On July 1, 1956, these contingent lending obligations totaled $228 million.

cover fractional settlements four times larger than these amounts, owing to a second major reform in the EPU settlement system. The graduated schedule of gold settlement previously in existence was abolished on July 1, 1954, and was replaced by a uniform schedule of 50% gold and 50% credit at first and 75% gold and 25% credit after July 30, 1955. This led to a considerable simplification of the accounting mechanism of the Union. It eliminated, in particular, a number of complications arising from the application of different ratios of gold settlement to different countries on the same date, and to the same country at different dates, depending on the development of their cumulative position. The graduation of gold payments had served a useful purpose in the early years of the Union, but had become more and more arbitrary and artificial as the cutoff date of June 30, 1950, used in the determination of cumulative surpluses and deficits, receded into a dim and distant past.

The current operating rules of the Union have thus become extremely simple. Bilateral amortization installments are included, together with other monthly balances, in the reports made by each country to the Agent. Each country's bilateral surpluses are offset against its bilateral deficits to arrive at its net monthly position toward the rest of the group. This is then settled, in principle, 75% in gold and 25% in credit. There remain, however, three exceptions to this principle:

1. Deficits in excess of quotas and rallonges are settled 100% in gold by the debtors. Turkey (whose cumulative deficits are far in excess of its quota) and Greece (whose quota is blocked) have long been operating under this rule. Current surpluses of these countries are also settled 100% in gold under the cumulative principle, as long as their previous 100% payments to EPU have not been fully reversed. France also remains entitled to such 100% settlements for its surpluses—up to the net amount of $196 million previously paid by it beyond quota and not yet recovered as of July 1, 1956—although recent surpluses and amortization payments have brought it back well within its quota facilities and entitle it to 25% credit for the settlement of its deficits.

2. Debtor countries may elect not to exercise their borrowing rights in EPU and to settle instead their deficits 100% in gold. In this case, however, they may reverse their decision at any time and substitute EPU credits for these voluntary gold payments. France, Portugal, and Austria have generally chosen this course of action

for the settlement of their deficits in the last two years of operation of the Union (1954–56).

3. Italy's $50 million special line of credit may be drawn upon to settle all or part of any deficit in excess of quota and rallonge.

The adoption of a flat rate of gold settlements, uniform for creditors and debtors, has also had the effect of removing previous uncertainties concerning possible fluctuations in the gold and convertible assets of the Union. These totaled $438 million at the end of June 1956, and would remain unchanged in later months, up to liquidation, if it were not for the three exceptions to normal settlement rules just mentioned.[7] The maximum impact of these exceptions can, however, be calculated in advance. Under present operating rules, gold and convertible assets could not fall below a floor of $245 million.[8] They could, on the other hand, rise far above their current level as a result of further deficits beyond quotas and rallonges paid 100% in gold by the debtors and giving rise only to 75% gold payments by EPU to the creditor countries.

Reference might finally be made to some accounting changes associated with the 1954 and 1955 increases in the gold settlement schedule. All quotas were raised uniformly by 20% above their previous level in June 1954, and quadrupled as from August 1, 1955. This was merely a bookkeeping device, however, designed to maintain intact the amount of EPU credit lines as the proportion of credit in EPU settlements fell from the previous average of 60% to 50%, and then 25%, of the surpluses or deficits to be financed.[9]

The negotiation of the 1955 EPU renewal was concerned only in part, however, with the provisions discussed in this chapter. The major controversies and accomplishments of this negotiation

7. Minor variations would also result from the current excess or deficiency of interest earned over interest payments and administrative expenses.

8. They could be reduced by withdrawals of the voluntary "excess" gold payments of France, Portugal, and Austria ($83 million) and by one fourth of the "recoverable" 100% payments of France, Greece, and Turkey ($379 million) and of the special credit line of Italy ($50 million).

9. The so-called "gold settlement adjustment" in current accounting reports similarly constitutes a mere bookkeeping entry designed to bring the "cumulative accounting surplus or deficit" of each country to a level equal to four times the amounts of credit effectively granted by it to the Union or received by it from the Union. I have found it more convenient to ignore this concept in the text and tables of this chapter, and to speak therefore of "credit rallonges" or "credits in excess of borrowing rights and lending commitments" rather than of "quota rallonges" or "surpluses—or deficits—in excess of quotas."

related to the adoption of a new code of trade and settlement rules to be put into effect in the event of Europe's return to full convertibility.[10] Before turning our attention to these issues, as we shall in chapter 6, we shall try to appraise the over-all results of the EPU experiment over the first five years of operation of the system.

V. A TENTATIVE APPRAISAL

Many appraisals of the European Payments Union experiment are vitiated by a total misunderstanding of its basic nature and objectives. As distinct from the IMF Charter, the EPU Agreement was never conceived as a permanent system of monetary organization, designed to replace, and improve upon, the defunct gold standard of former days. Criticisms of the Agreement for its failure to restore full convertibility in Europe as of July 1, 1950 forget that other instrumentalities were already at hand for this purpose if agreement could have been reached for its implementation. The European Payments Agreement was merely designed as a temporary expedient to "permit the maintenance of desirable forms of specialization in trade, while facilitating a return to full multilateral trade and . . . to the general convertibility of currencies."[1]

The relevant comparison with the Monetary Fund, therefore, is between the so-called "Transitional Provisions" of Article XIV of the Fund Charter, on the one hand, and the whole EPU Agreement and Code of Liberalization on the other. The significance of the latter two instruments lay, first of all, in their immediate outlawing of the most destructive techniques of restriction in trade and payments, left to the discretion of the member countries by Article XIV of the Fund Agreement. There is little question as to the success attained in this respect. Discrimination and bilateralism in intra-European trade were not merely outlawed. They became technically impossible to implement for the wide and growing portion of formally liberalized trade, i.e. trade which could

10. The amortization of outstanding EPU credit and the steep rise in the schedule of gold payments were also intended to provide a transition toward full convertibility, as well as to solve the more pressing problems raised by the current operations of EPU.

1. Preamble to the *Agreement for the Establishment of a European Payments Union* (Paris, OEEC, Sept. 1950), p. 4.

now be carried out freely by individual traders without requiring any import or exchange licensing by the state. Moreover, the immediate suspension of the former bilateral payments agreements and their transformation into a multilateral payments agreement destroyed the major instrument and financial incentive to discrimination and bilateralism among member countries, even over the remaining area of nonliberalized trade. Finally, the introduction of gold settlements on a fractional basis tended to lessen—although not to eliminate—discrimination toward third countries, particularly toward the dollar area.

The radical nature of these changes in the former machinery of intra-European payments did, indeed, elicit considerable opposition. Many economists and statesmen, particularly in Scandinavia and the United Kingdom, foresaw export losses and reserve drains to EPU for the countries least able to sustain intra-European competition. They predicted a consequent tightening and spiraling of import restrictions, an over-all contraction in European trade, a slowdown of investment expenditures, and a rise in unemployment. These gloomy forecasts were soon refuted by the sustained growth of European trade and economic activity. Intra-European trade more than doubled in volume between 1949 and 1955, industrial production increased by 56%, and GNP—at constant prices—by 37%.

Paradoxically enough, the elimination of intra-European bilateralism was also regarded as a backward step by the most sanguine advocates of trade liberalization and currency convertibility. They brandished the specter of a "sheltered, soft currency area" increasingly isolated from competitive pressures in trade with non-member countries. On these grounds they attacked the "excessive" credit facilities made available for intra-European settlements and the "discrimination" toward outsiders implicit in the OEEC program of intra-European trade liberalization. Regional monetary arrangements of the EPU type might well be preferable, from a short-run point of view, to nationalistic restrictions and bilateralism, but they would slow down or permanently impede further progress toward *world-wide* competition and currency convertibility.

The first argument advanced in favor of this thesis was that the large credits placed by EPU at the disposal of the deficit countries would weaken the mechanism of balance of payments adjustments, by removing the pressures otherwise exercised by reserve losses upon national monetary policies. Inflationary policies could be continued for a longer time, and exchange rate readjustments postponed, if the resulting deficits could be financed automatically by EPU credits.

Let us note, first of all, that EPU credits could only play a very minor role in this respect. The breathing spell which they might offer to deficit countries did not differ in substance from the breathing spell normally provided by gold and foreign exchange reserves under the traditional functioning of the gold standard itself. And it was universally recognized that the level of such reserves in 1950 was far below desirable or "normal" levels. Even if the theoretical maximum of borrowing facilities created by EPU [2] could actually have been used, they would have replaced only a small fraction of the $10 billion loss of gold and dollar reserves—measured at constant, 1950 prices—suffered by European countries since prewar days. The new credit facilities created were, moreover, offset to a substantial extent by the suspension of previous credit margins under bilateral payments agreements.

It could hardly be argued, therefore, that excessive reserves or borrowing facilities were responsible in 1950 for the postponement of desirable policies of monetary readjustment by the deficit countries. The unavailability of reserves or credits was less likely to enforce domestic readjustments than to be met by a tightening of trade and import restrictions. The automatic credit facilities of the EPU Agreement were designed to break up this spiral of restrictions and to stimulate a gradual liberalization of intra-European trade, on the basis of reciprocal commitments among member countries. Any persistent debtor, however, would be subject to an increasing schedule of gold settlements rising progressively to 100% beyond quota. Only minor or temporary relaxations of this provision were ever granted by the Managing Board. In the first six years of operation, more than $700 million of deficits beyond quota were fully settled in gold or dollars by France, Turkey, the United Kingdom, Greece, Austria, and Iceland (see Appendix Table 27).

Advantage was taken of the general improvement in the international payments situation and reserve position of members to

2. Half the total of borrowing rights and lending facilities under quotas, i.e. about $1.2 billion.

Table XVI. EPU SETTLEMENTS, JULY 1950—JUNE 1956

	Total 1950–56	1950–51	1951–52	1952–53	1953–54	1954–55	1955–56
I. *In % of Bilateral Monthly Balances*							
A. *Compensations*	75	66	74	92	70	86	64
1. Multilateral	46	49	40	55	48	47	37
2. Over time	30	17	34	37	22	39	27
B. *Net settlements*	25	34	26	8	30	14	36
II. *In % of Net Settlements*							
A. *Gold and dollars*	66	21	51	46	110	121	108
B. *EPU credits*	23	57	39	22	—12	—21	—8
1. Current settlements	44	57	52	22	38	51	22
2. Amortization	—21	—	—13	—	—50	—72	—30
C. *American aid*	11	22	10	32	2	—	—

Source:
Appendix Table 26.

harden the settlement rules through both the increase in the gold-credit ratio and contractual amortization of outstanding debts and claims.

The over-all record of EPU transactions clearly reveals the minor and decreasing role of credit facilities in EPU settlements. The major significance of EPU operations lay indeed in its compensation machinery rather than in the financing of net settlements. More than three fourths of the $32 billion of surpluses and deficits incurred over the years 1950–56 was cleared through multilateral and cumulative offsetting, leaving only 25% of net surpluses and deficits to be settled. Of these, 66% was paid for in gold and dollars, but this proportion rose gradually from 21% in the first year of operations to more than 100% in each of the last three years. U.S. aid declined simultaneously from 22% to zero, and for the last three years the amortization of past credits has exceeded the small amounts of new credits granted by EPU (see Table XVI).

Account must finally be taken of the large repayments of pre-EPU debts effected during this period. All but 6% of the $861 million of debts previously accumulated under bilateral payments agreements was repaid, leaving only $49 million of such debts outstanding at the end of June 1956. If these repayments are deducted from the new credits extended by EPU itself, one arrives at a net increase of $415 million of intra-European credits in 1950–52, but at a net contraction of $395 million over the four following years. For the six years as a whole, the financing of $15,787 million of bilateral deficits and $3,936 million of net deficits after compensation involved a net increase of only $20 million in intra-European credits (see Table XV). These figures should effectively dispose of any impression that EPU credit facilities established a "soft" system of settlements, destructive of the classical system of balance of payments adjustments.

The objections raised against the discriminatory features of the EPU system have far greater validity. The EPU enthusiast can point to the elimination of intra-European discrimination and bilateralism as the most solid achievement of the system, but must concede that it also entailed a certain degree of discrimination against non-EPU members. Financial aid was made available to help debtor countries meet their EPU deficits, while deficits with the dollar area had to be settled fully in dollars. Moreover, the liberalization commitments of members applied to imports from other member countries, but left them free to restrict as they wished all imports from other countries.

In practice, however, account should be taken of the fact that settlements with third countries were by no means free of similar discriminatory elements. Imports from the dollar area certainly benefited also from the enormous financing associated with Marshall aid, under "procurement authorization" techniques which barred the use of such aid for the financing of imports from the EPU area. Settlements with other countries were regulated by bilateral payments agreements which were often softer in effect than EPU settlements themselves.

As for the intra-European liberalization commitments, they were subject to sweeping escape clauses for countries in balance of payments difficulties. Liberalization was, as we have seen, severely slashed, or even entirely suspended for a considerable period of time, by the countries which experienced such pressures during the Korean crisis.

A stronger argument can be made against the discriminatory incentives of the system for the creditor—rather than the debtor—countries, particularly in the years 1952 and 1953. The claims accumulated by them in EPU could be freely used to finance imports from the EPU area, but not to meet deficits with other countries. Yet it should not be forgotten that these countries were also receiving very large gold payments from EPU, totaling, on a net basis, more than $2,700 million over the years 1950–56, against a mere trickle of $200 to $300 million over the twenty-one months of the IEPA system. Their gold and dollar holdings were rising steeply and uninterruptedly—by about $3.8 billion, or more than 100%—over this period. The credits extended by them to EPU did not, therefore, seriously affect their ability to import from the dollar area or other non-EPU markets.

The incentive to discrimination by the creditors was not so much the result of inadequate gold reserves or settlements as of their reluctance to pile up an indefinite amount of EPU credits. Three methods were simultaneously used by them to reduce their intra-European surpluses. The first was to encourage capital exports and repayments to other EPU countries and to step up their rate of intra-European liberalization far beyond the formal requirements of the Code of Liberalization. The second was to restrict imports from non-EPU sources in an effort to force traders to seek substitute sources of supply within the EPU area. The third—and the most absurd from a collective point of view—was to impose restrictions on their exports to other EPU members. The dogmatic adherence to the 50% settlement rule for surpluses beyond quotas remains, to my mind, one of the most questionable decisions of the Managing Board.[3] This rule was indeed modified in effect by special ad hoc settlements to Belgium and Portugal, but through an ex post amortization of past credits rather than by a gradual increase in the gold schedule or an agreed limit on credits beyond quotas. This preserved the presumption and the fear of limitless credit accumulation for future surpluses, and at times stimulated the adoption of totally irrational and indefensible policies on the part of some creditor countries.

On balance, it is clear that the EPU system included some built-in incentives toward discrimination, or rather toward preferential liberalization of trade within the area, tantamount to a declaration of dollar scarcity under Article VII of the IMF Agreement. This was the price paid for the gradual elimination of restrictions over reciprocal trade among the member countries. In theory this could have led to a gradual increase in production costs, a deterioration

3. Let it be noted, in passing, that this decision was strongly encouraged by ECA technicians bent on forcing European surplus countries to grant larger credits to the European deficit countries and decrease the latter's need for dollar assistance.

of these countries' ability to compete in third markets, and to an indefinite postponement of convertibility.

At first view, the differential increases in imports from OEEC countries and from the rest of the world would confirm these forebodings. The first rose by 97%—(from $8.7 billion to $17.1 billion) between 1949 and 1955, while the second increased only about 33% (from $16.2 billion to $21.5 billion). This comparison, however, is not really the most relevant one for our purpose. Imports from non-OEEC sources were abnormally boosted in 1949 by temporary reconstruction needs and shortages of production in Europe itself, and by the large amount of American aid available to finance Europe's dollar deficit. A more direct test of the validity of the "sheltered, high cost area" theory of discrimination lies in the comparative evolution of exports rather than of imports. Is there any evidence that OEEC discrimination has resulted in a weakening of competitive pressures upon European costs and in a diversion of European exports from unsheltered third markets to the OEEC area itself? OEEC exports to other OEEC countries increased by 97% from 1949 to 1955. Exports to third countries increased 60%, but exports to the dollar area 158%, and to the United States 184% (see Chart XX and Appendix Table 28).

Large balance of payments surpluses, on current account, replaced the heavy deficits of earlier years, and in spite of the curtailment of U.S. aid to Europe most EPU countries were thus enabled to extend gradually to other areas the liberalization measures initially applied only to imports from European sources. The OEEC Council has recommended increased efforts toward dollar liberalization, and in December 1954 instituted a periodic review of the measures adopted by each country, the obstacles to further progress, and the development of supporting policies of trade liberalization by the United States and Canada. By September 1956 only 59% of the OEEC countries' dollar imports had been formally liberalized under this procedure, but licenses were granted far more freely than before for other, nonliberalized, categories of imports. Purchases from the dollar area increased by one third from 1954 to 1955. The growing competitiveness of Europe with the dollar area was also manifest in the disappearance or near disappearance of the wide discounts at which European currencies were previously traded against dollars on the free or black exchange markets.

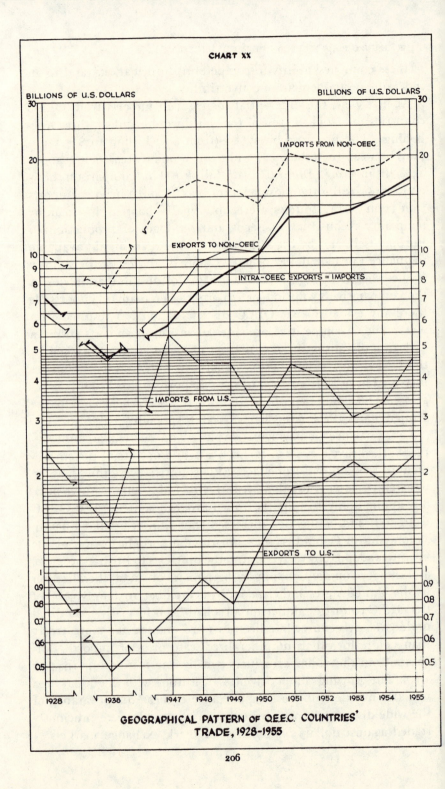

CHART XX

BILLIONS OF U.S. DOLLARS

BILLIONS OF U.S. DOLLARS

IMPORTS FROM NON-OEEC

EXPORTS TO NON-OEEC

INTRA-OEEC EXPORTS = IMPORTS

IMPORTS FROM U.S.

EXPORTS TO U.S.

1928   1938   1947   1948   1949   1950   1951   1952   1953   1954   1955

GEOGRAPHICAL PATTERN OF O.E.E.C. COUNTRIES'
TRADE, 1928-1955

206

It would be absurd, of course, to ascribe to EPU the whole merit of an improvement which springs from a variety of factors and policies, and particularly from the large investments which have speeded up postwar increases in European production and productivity. It may at least be asserted that the creation of EPU restored competitive pressures which accelerated balance of payments readjustments.

First of all, the elimination of bilateralism reintroduced competitive forces among all OEEC members on their European export markets. The highest cost exporters could no longer be protected outside their borders by bilateral monetary arrangements stimulating import discrimination in their favor and against lower cost exports from other members. In order to hold these markets—accounting in most cases for 75% or more of their total export trade —they were forced to readjust their prices and costs. And for many categories of goods, the lowest European prices which they had to meet—Swiss prices for some goods, Belgian or German prices for others, etc.—were probably as competitive as those of any third country, including the United States.

Secondly, the gradual liberalization of trade increased competition not only among exporters but also between foreign and domestic producers on the latter's home market, and led to further price and cost readjustments. By the end of August 1956, 89% of intra-European imports had been freed of all quantitative restrictions, and the OEEC had initiated consultations on the lowering of tariff barriers among its members. For twelve of the seventeen member countries, the liberalization percentage exceeded 90%, and only two countries—Iceland and Turkey—had failed to reach 75% (see Table XVII). Licenses, moreover, were granted increasingly freely for the remaining, nonliberalized, categories of imports, state trading had dropped from more than 10% to less than 5% of total imports, and most current invisible transactions— which account for about one fourth of total visible and invisible trade—had been fully liberalized among all member countries and even, in a number of cases, in relations with the dollar area.

Finally, in the absence of a uniform pattern of trade and exchange discrimination against dollar goods, intra-European trade liberalization often weakened, through transit trade and triangular transactions, the effectiveness of dollar discrimination itself. The wide diversity in the intensity and structure of dollar restric-

Table XVII. INTRA-EUROPEAN TRADE LIBERALIZATION,[a]
JUNE 1950—AUGUST 1, 1956

	June 1950	1950	1951	1952	1953	1954	1955	August 1, 1956
End of:								
I. *Number of Countries Having Liberalized:*								
A. 90% to 100% of imports	—	—	—	2	7	7	10	12 [b]
B. 75% to 90% of imports	1	3	8	8	6	7	5	3 [c]
C. *Subtotal*	1	3	8	10	13	14	15	15
D. 60% to 75% of imports	2	10	4	2	—	1	—	—
E. 50% to 60% of imports	10	2	1	—	1	—	—	—
F. Less than 50% of imports	4	2	4	5	3	2	2	2 [d]
II. *Average Liberalization Percentage for OEEC as a Whole*	56%	67%	62%	65%	77%	83%	86%	89%

Notes:

a. Each country notifies the OEEC of the categories of merchandise imports from other members which have been freed for all quantitative trade or exchange restrictions. The liberalization percentage indicates the relative weight of those commodities in the total intra-European imports of the member country in the reference year 1948. A shift to a more recent year is now under study, but would have only a minor impact on these calculations, except in the French case.

b. Italy (99%), Portugal and the United Kingdom (94%), Switzerland and Sweden (93%), Germany (92%), Benelux (Belgium, Netherlands, and Luxembourg, 91%), Austria (91%), and Ireland (90%). Greece is also in this group, although the OEEC has not been officially notified of her de facto liberalization percentage (95%).

c. Denmark (86%), France (82%), and Norway (78%).

d. Iceland (29%) and Turkey (0%).

tions in the various countries of OEEC constituted from the start a most formidable obstacle to the much feared development of a sheltered, high cost European area.

Few people would deny today that the EPU experiment has served, with a considerable degree of success, the two objectives assigned to it from the start. It loosened overnight the stranglehold of bilateralism on intra-European trade and payments, and stimulated gradual adjustments in institutions and policies which paved the way toward the resumption of multilateral trade and currency convertibility.

The main opposition to EPU is based today not on its failure but on its success. Many people feel that sufficient progress has been achieved under such transitional arrangements to permit their liquidation, and to call for a return to full convertibility on a world-wide scale. The steps already taken in this direction will be considered in Chapter 6 of this study.

CHAPTER 6

Current Approaches
to Convertibility

I. THE COLLECTIVE APPROACH AND
BRITISH LEADERSHIP

THE EPU AGREEMENT had clearly outlined the initial stages of the transition from bilateralism to convertibility. These lay primarily in the immediate multilateralization of intra-European trade and payments agreements, and the gradual liberalization of intra-European trade and invisible transactions from all quantitative restrictions. Secondly, the increasing proportion of gold or convertible currencies in intra-European settlements would progressively remove a major incentive to discrimination toward nonmember countries, and stimulate the extension to them of the liberalization measures already adopted with respect to intra-European trade. Half-hearted efforts were also initiated in 1952 to broaden EPU clearing operations by the inclusion, on a voluntary basis, of triangular compensations with nonmember countries, mainly in Latin America.[1]

There existed, however, basic disagreements about the final steps that would usher in a formal return to world-wide currency convertibility. These steps would have to include fundamental shifts in national trade and exchange control regulations, and the uneven recovery of the various EPU countries raised difficult questions of timing in this respect. Some countries could be expected to

1. Actual results were disappointingly small. Most EPU countries uniformly tended to accumulate surpluses under their bilateral agreements with nonmembers, and compensation possibilities were therefore extremely limited. Moreover, some member countries—particularly the United Kingdom—preferred to carry out such compensations through an increase in their own currency's transferability, rather than through recourse to the EPU machinery.

be ready to assume full convertibility obligations long before others felt capable and desirous of doing so. They could hardly move ahead of their EPU partners, however, without playing havoc with a settlement machinery based on regional payments imbalance within the EPU area alone. The "collective" approach to convertibility, on the other hand, would force the more progressive countries to wait for the more laggard ones, and might delay indefinitely their "dash" toward convertibility.

Finally, certain functions now performed by EPU and fully compatible with—even indispensable to—the resumption of convertibility were functions normally performed, in prewar days, by the major foreign exchange markets, particularly by the London market. Some proponents of the collective approach were in favor of retaining these functions in a revamped but permanent EPU framework, while the United Kingdom and certain other countries wished to liquidate EPU altogether and to reassume fully and independently their own prewar role in world markets, without EPU competition or supervision.

Combined opposition on the part of the weaker countries—opposed to a hardening of settlements—and of some of the stronger countries—opposed to a permanent EPU—thus defeated for a time all attempts to adjust the EPU machinery to the radical improvement of Europe's balance of payments since 1950, and tended to perpetuate some obsolete features of the system. Actual progress toward convertibility, in 1953–55, was primarily associated, therefore, with national plans and decisions taken outside EPU itself.

A first, and spectacular, indication of this "new look" came in early March 1953, with a unilateral attempt on the part of the United Kingdom to negotiate directly with the United States a broad plan for the restoration of sterling convertibility. The major feature of this plan lay in the restoration of sterling convertibility for "nonresidents." Current sterling earnings of nonresidents would be made convertible into any other currency, including the United States dollar, but exchange or trade restrictions would continue to be applied to sterling area residents. The elimination of such restrictions would be undertaken gradually, and would center initially on the elimination of their discriminatory features, particularly with respect to the dollar area. This plan would have to be discussed further with other countries, but it depended first of all on adequate support on the part of the United States and the

International Monetary Fund. The United States would be expected to reduce its own tariff barriers and discriminatory practices,[2] to stabilize its purchases of raw materials, to encourage private investments abroad, to provide stabilization credits to the United Kingdom, and so on. Further and substantial support from the International Monetary Fund would also be necessary to supplement the slender gold and dollar reserves of the sterling area.

The young Republican Administration was far from ready to undertake such sweeping trade and financial commitments. Moreover, many officials in the State Department and the Mutual Security Agency—which had succeeded the Economic Cooperation Administration—were fearful of the political and economic consequences of the United Kingdom's intended withdrawal from its commitments to EPU and the OEEC Liberalization Code. The Washington conversations ended in early March with a platitudinous communiqué in praise of "sound internal policies . . . freer trade and currencies," etc., but relegating any concrete measures to further study by interested governments and international organizations.[3]

The British views on convertibility were finally disclosed to the OEEC Council by the Chancellor of the Exchequer immediately after his return from the disappointing Washington visit. The accent was now placed on a "collective approach to a wider system of trade and payments," stressing the link between financial convertibility and freer trade, the need for "sound" internal policies, the balancing of dollar accounts, the problem raised by the inadequacy of gold and dollar reserves, and the role of world-wide international institutions.

The British initiative thus ushered in a period of protracted studies and discussions of the convertibility problem, both in the United States and in Europe. The main conclusion that emerged in both cases was that progress toward financial convertibility—or convertibility for nonresidents—would remain purely formal if it were achieved through the maintenance of trade restrictions: "The removal of restrictions upon payment and upon trade should go hand in hand." As far as the European Payments Union was con-

2. Such as the Buy American Act, discrimination in favor of U.S. shipping, etc.

3. See National Advisory Council on International Monetary and Financial Problems, *Semiannual Report to the President and to the Congress for the Period October 1, 1952–March 31, 1953* (Washington, D.C., 1953), pp. 64–5.

cerned, the Randall Commission felt that "it should not sponsor any measures that might wreck the Union before there is something better to put in its place." The Commission's recommendations as to the liberalization of United States trade barriers were rather disappointing, on the whole, and were implemented only in part by Congress. The International Monetary Fund seemed ready to heed its plea for more flexible lending and exchange rate policies, but nothing came out of the Commission's recommendation that "the Federal Reserve System explore with foreign central banks the possibilities of standby credits or line of credit arrangements." [4]

The OEEC stressed in addition the need for continued cooperation among its members and with other major countries in the field of trade, payments, and long-term capital movements, in order to permit not only the resumption but also the future maintenance of a satisfactory system of convertibility, compatible with the growth and liberalization of world trade.[5] More than two years were to elapse, however, before the divergent points of view of EPU members could be reconciled around a concrete agreement of permanent monetary cooperation that should take the place of EPU in the event of a return to convertibility.[6]

In the meantime, actual progress toward convertibility centered primarily on national measures and policies, adopted by individual countries outside the EPU framework itself and moving steadily toward de facto convertibility.

II. NATIONAL PROGRESS TOWARD DE FACTO CONVERTIBILITY

The first step in this direction lay in the resumption of foreign exchange arbitrage, as from May 18, 1953, among eight of the EPU countries (Belgium, Luxembourg, Denmark, France, Germany, the Netherlands, Switzerland, and the United Kingdom, joined by Norway in December 1953 and by Italy in August 1955). Authorized

4. All quotations in this paragraph from Commission on Foreign Economic Policy, *Report to the President and the Congress* (Washington, D.C., Jan. 1956), pp. 73–5.

5. EPU, *Fourth Annual Report of the Managing Board* (Paris, 1955), pp. 113–14.

6. See below, sec. IV, pp. 220–33.

banks in those countries were permitted to carry out freely with one another arbitrage operations for spot transactions in any of the participating currencies. In order to enable the arbitrage settlements to take place, balances on the accounts of the authorized banks were made fully transferable among all the participating currencies. Finally, each participating country's central bank undertook to intervene in the market to prevent its currency from appreciating or depreciating by more than 3/4 of 1% above or below its official parities with the others.

Arbitrage facilities were later (as from October 5, 1953) extended to forward operations up to three months and then up to six months, but were limited in principle to the settlement of firm commercial contracts and without advance commitment by central banks to stabilize forward rates.[1]

These arbitrage operations displaced a considerable amount of multilateral compensations previously performed by EPU itself. No direct data are available on the amount of arbitrage transactions cleared through the market, but their importance may be gauged from the fact that EPU compensations among the arbitrage countries fell by $1.2 billion, or 57%, in the following twelve months, while remaining practically unchanged with respect to the bilateral positions for which arbitrage operations were not authorized (see Table XVIII). Theoretically, the effect of arbitrage operations should have been to reduce equally the amount of bilateral positions reported to EPU and the amount of multilateral compensations cleared by it, leaving unchanged the net positions of each country in the system. The decline in net positions shown in Table XVIII was due to other causes, such as an underlying trend toward better balance in intra-European transactions or the growing use of EPU currencies in settlement outside the EPU area.[2]

The main significance of the new arrangements lies in their attempt to revert to traditional mechanisms in exchange transactions. The EPU system had been superimposed, in 1950, upon a network of bilateral payments agreements under which the total amount of bilateral imbalance between any two countries was reflected in bookkeeping accounts between their two central banks.[3] Under

1. Except for the French franc, the relation of forward to spot rates has nevertheless remained very stable, reflecting, in the main, interest rate differentials among the various markets.

2. See below, pp. 214–15 and 218.

3. Except mostly for small working balances.

Table XVIII. EFFECT OF ARBITRAGE ON EPU OPERATIONS

	In Millions of U.S. Dollars		
	May 1952– April 1953	May 1953– April 1954	% Change
I. *Monthly Bilateral Positions* *Reported to EPU*			
A. Among the arbitrage countries	3,756	2,100	−44
B. Other	1,978	1,926	−3
C. Total	5,734	4,026	−30
II. *Multilateral EPU Compensations*			
A. Among the arbitrage countries	2,052	888	−57
B. Other	1,117	1,107	−1
C. Total	3,169	1,995	−38
III. *Net Positions*			
A. Among the arbitrage countries	1,704	1,212	−29
B. Other	861	819	−5
C. Total	2,565	2,031	−21

these conditions, EPU compensations between reported central bank balances were the only channel through which a country's bilateral surpluses on some partner countries in EPU could be used to finance its bilateral deficits with others. The aim of the new arrangements was to return as many of these operations as possible to the private arbitrage markets. Central banks would enter the market only to the extent necessary to prevent excessive exchange rate fluctuations, and would do so systematically only at some predetermined "buying" and "selling" rates, reminiscent of the gold points in the good old days of the gold standard.

A different and more substantive approach to convertibility lay in a number of measures designed to open up new possibilities for currency transfers with non-EPU countries. The first of these was the reopening of international commodity markets in various European centers—particularly in London—and the acceptance of inconvertible currency payment for re-exports of commodities sold in such markets, even when these commodities originated in imports from other currency areas and had to be paid for by the re-exporting country in dollars or other convertible currencies. The second measure was the direct broadening of transferability privileges for some major EPU currencies, particularly sterling and the Deutsche mark. The most momentous step in this direction was taken by the United Kingdom in March 1954, with the enlargement of the transferable account area to include practically all countries outside the dollar and sterling areas, and the relaxation of restrictions on the use of such accounts by their foreign holders. Transferable accounts were made available to individuals as well as banks, could be used for capital transactions as well as current payments, and could be bought and sold legally at any exchange rates resulting from the functioning of the market mechanism. Transferable sterling could in fact be converted freely into dollars through the free exchange markets, especially in Zurich and New York. Such transactions increased considerably in volume during the following months, and the margin between the official rate and the transferable sterling rate for dollars widened from about 1% in March 1954 to a peak of about 3% toward the end of the year. In February 1955, however, the Exchange Equalization Account received authority to intervene at its own discretion in the free sterling markets. The rate for transferable sterling was rapidly brought back to about 1% below the official rate and has fluctuated ever since very close to that level.

A further liberalization of capital movements resulted from the relaxation of restrictions on transactions in blocked sterling accounts and in foreign securities held by sterling area residents.[4] While such transactions do not permit a net outflow of capital that would expose the United Kingdom to actual gold or dollar losses,[5] they nevertheless establish a market in which individuals can transfer capital between sterling and dollar assets. Market quotations for such "security sterling" are tantamount to the establishment of a free exchange rate for capital movements, but have in fact remained within a margin of about 2% or 3% below the rate for official sterling. The freedom of transactions in transferable and security sterling amounts to a de facto convertibility of sterling, but at a slight and fluctuating discount with respect to the dollar, and with the maintenance of significant restrictions and discrimination on merchandise imports (see Table XIX).

These British moves toward broader transferability privileges and the relaxation of capital controls were immediately and closely paralleled by Germany. A Deutsche mark with limited converti-

4. In the latter part of 1955, blocked sterling balances and sterling securities owned by nonresidents outside the dollar area were made transferable to residents of the dollar area itself.

5. The monetary authorities, however, may intervene—and have at times intervened—in the market, to buy or sell foreign securities in order to minimize fluctuations.

Table XIX. Sterling and Deutsche Mark Discounts in
New York, 1947–55

(in % of official parity)

| End of: | Pound Sterling | | Deutsche Mark | |
	Transferable	Security	Limited Convertibility	Capital Account
1947	−37	......	......	......
1948	−24	−57	......	......
1949	−11	−42	......	......
1950	−7	−29	......	......
1951	−12	−15	......	−47
1952	−2.5	−5	......	−37
1953	−1	−2	......	−24
1954	−3	−2	−3	−3
1955	−1	−2	−1	−1

Sources:
International Financial Statistics and BIS *Annual Report.*

bility was introduced on March 31, 1954, in order to give nonresidents a type of account freely transferable outside the dollar area in the same way as transferable sterling accounts. Since December 1954 it has been possible to effect payments between Germany and nearly all the countries outside the dollar area in transferable Deutsche marks or in any foreign currency, except that Germans may not pay dollars to nondollar countries. A similar choice between the use of transferable sterling and of certain foreign currencies—convertible currencies and most OEEC currencies—in payment for imports from the sterling area was granted in April 1955 by the United Kingdom to all countries in the transferable account area.

Blocked Sperrmark balances were also transformed, in September 1954, into "liberalized capital accounts" transferable into Deutsche marks with limited convertibility, or directly into the holder's currency, except for residents of the dollar area and the Eastern countries. The discount on liberalized capital Deutsche mark accounts moved at first very close to that on transferable sterling, and disappeared entirely in 1956 (see Table XIX). [6] A free market for capital and invisible transactions also operates in Belgium, whose exchange regulations are now about the most liberal in Europe. Exchange rates on this market fluctuate, in fact, within a similarly narrow range from official parities.

6. While capital exports from Germany are now practically free of restrictions, the import of new capital into Germany remains subject to limitations designed to combat the inflationary impact of balance of payments surpluses.

These measures are now gradually being imitated by other OEEC countries. Relations with inconvertible currency countries are increasingly placed on a transferable, rather than strictly bilateral, basis. Credit margins under payments agreements are gradually reduced. Restrictions on capital movements are progressively relaxed through the extension of free markets. Free or grey market discounts with respect to the dollar have largely disappeared or fallen close to the vanishing point, or even been replaced at times by slight premia. Trade liberalization continues also to move forward in Europe—although at a slower pace as full liberalization is approached—and is gradually extended, at least on a de facto basis, to imports from the dollar area. Finally, several countries have even begun to relax the keystone of any exchange control system, i.e. the compulsory surrender by residents, within a specified period, of foreign exchange proceeds from exports or other international transactions.[7] A detailed review of the current stage of trade and capital liberalization in the various European countries would be a complex and tedious undertaking and would almost certainly be largely out of date by the time it appeared in print.

A last and significant development might nevertheless be mentioned, as it is likely to spread in the very near future. In August 1955, Germany, the Netherlands, and the United Kingdom agreed to coordinate their payments agreements with Brazil in such a way as to permit all settlements to take place in any one of their respective currencies. This so-called "Hague Club" was joined later by Austria, Belgium, Luxembourg, Italy, and France. Taken together with the wide facilities for sterling, Deutsche mark, and Belgian franc transfers, this arrangement enables Brazil, in effect, to spend its export proceeds from any of its European partners, not only for imports from other participants but also throughout most of the nondollar world.[8] A similar arrangement, on a much wider geographical basis, was negotiated in the late spring of 1956 between Argentina and all the major EPU countries.[9]

7. The obligation to surrender foreign exchange was completely abolished by Germany in May 1956, and residents were allowed to maintain foreign exchange accounts of any size for any period of time and to acquire foreign market-paper and quoted foreign shares and bonds, in any currency whatsoever.

8. The existence of free markets for transferable sterling or Deutsche mark accounts would even permit such spending in the dollar area itself, but such operations would probably be contrary to the spirit, if not the letter, of the Agreement.

9. Including, in addition to the members of the Hague Club, Switzerland and the

The extension of currency transferability and of the Hague Club type of agreement constitute, to date, the broadest and most promising attack against bilateralism in trade and payments relations between the OEEC countries and the nondollar world. Together with the EPU Agreement and the use of the dollar in settlements with dollar area countries, they are rapidly eliminating bilateralism from the world trade and payments pattern.

III. THE IMPACT ON EPU

The measures reviewed in section II of this chapter did not, by themselves, require any formal modifications of the EPU Agreement. They had nevertheless a considerable impact upon its operation.

The displacement of EPU compensations by market arbitrage has already been discussed above. Far more significant are the relaxation of capital controls and the growth of transferability privileges between European currencies, particularly sterling, and those of non-EPU countries. Such transfers strike indeed at the root of automatic credit arrangements ostensibly related to the development of net payments imbalance within the EPU area alone. Any EPU country can now increase, decrease, or even reverse at will its accounting surplus or deficit with EPU by accepting or paying out another EPU currency for the settlement of non-EPU transactions, or by selling or buying it against dollars at free market rates. It is an open secret that France carried out substantial operations of this sort in 1954–55 in order to build up surpluses in EPU, while benefiting from the discount at which transferable sterling could be bought for dollars on the free market. A country which wished to borrow from EPU could just as easily—even though at a slight cost rather than at a profit—undertake similar operations in the opposite direction. Borrowings from EPU have therefore become discretionary rather than automatic, and can be used not only to settle deficits with non-EPU members but even to build up a country's gold and dollar reserves.

Such discretion removes the last shred of plausibility for the per-

three Scandinavian countries. German participation was delayed for several months, however, by separate negotiations on the amortization of the huge Argentine debts to Germany.

petuation of a system of automatic credits governed by the development of EPU accounting positions. Such a system was adopted in June 1950 as a temporary expedient to replace former bilateral payments agreements, encourage intra-European trade liberalization, and provide some cushioning credits by the stronger EPU countries to the weaker. It was never more than an expedient, however, although some enthusiasts initially saw in it an implementation of the Keynes proposal for automatic lending commitments by the surplus countries to the deficit countries. Whatever the merits or demerits of the Keynes proposal,[1] there is certainly no logic in a system that might compel a capital-poor country, such as Italy or Portugal, to lend to a richer country, such as France or the United Kingdom, merely because it is in regional deficit in Europe and regardless of its over-all balance of payments position with the world as a whole.

The development of transferability privileges strengthened further the case against automatic credits, repayable only through a reversal of EPU accounting positions. It hastened the long overdue hardening of EPU settlement rules from 40% to 50% and finally 75% gold, and the adoption of contractual amortization agreements for outstanding claims and debts.[2]

Both these measures were, of course, of considerable interest to the major creditor countries in the Union, but the second was also strongly supported, paradoxically enough, by its major debtor, i.e. the United Kingdom. The reason for this is that the restoration of convertibility by Britain and its withdrawal from the Union would have involved otherwise difficult and uncertain negotiations with every other EPU member for the repayment of its indebtedness to EPU, amounting at the time to $485 million. The consolidation of more than 80% of this debt clarified in advance the repayment burden confronting the United Kingdom, and made it, moreover, independent of its decision to restore convertibility.

The United Kingdom also wished to gain a freer hand in the timing of its convertibility decision. It was handicapped in this respect by the fact that the EPU Agreement was renewed from year to year and could be terminated only on a renewal date— normally on June 30—unless all countries unanimously agreed to such termination. The United Kingdom had to wage a long battle

1. See above, pp. 106–7.
2. See above, pp. 194–9.

to gain other countries' assent to more flexibility with respect to this termination clause. It received only a rather Platonic satisfaction in June 1953, through a Council decision providing that the obligations assumed by member countries could be "re-examined" at any time during the year "at the request of any Contracting Party if, in the opinion of that Contracting Party, this is necessary to enable progress to be made towards a system of freer trade and payments, including convertibility of currencies." This could hardly satisfy the United Kingdom, since this so-called "re-examination" remained subject to the unanimity rule.

It is only in the July 1955 revision that the EPU Agreement was modified so as to provide for a termination of the Union *at any time* on the joint demand of countries whose combined quotas represent at least 50% of the total amount of EPU quotas, provided, however, that a new Agreement come simultaneously into force. The new Agreement in question is the European Monetary Agreement (reviewed in the next section of this chapter) which, after protracted negotiations extending over more than two years, provided a reconciliation of views, or at least an acceptable compromise, between the proponents of world-wide convertibility and the defenders of monetary cooperation within the framework of OEEC.

IV. THE EUROPEAN MONETARY AGREEMENT

The European Monetary Agreement, adopted on July 29, 1955, embodies the "collective approach" to convertibility for which the OEEC had been groping ever since March 1953. It remains, as of now, a mere blueprint embodying a series of reciprocal commitments designed to replace the present EPU Agreement and to bolster up the convertibility of European currencies, if and when major countries decide to return to full, *de jure* currency convertibility.[1]

The major provisions of the Agreement relate to the establishment of a European Fund, shifting the credit provisions of EPU from an automatic to a nonautomatic basis, and of a Multilateral

1. The Agreement would come automatically into operation only if EPU were terminated under the special termination clause discussed at the end of sec. III. As long as this does not occur, its provisions may be amended on the occasion of the annual negotiations regarding the prolongation of the EPU Agreement.

System of Settlements, to take the place of the present EPU machinery for compensations. The substitution of the European Monetary Agreement for EPU would, in addition, be accompanied by important and closely related amendments to the OEEC Code of Liberalization.

A. THE EUROPEAN FUND

Agreement was reached relatively easily on the desirability of preserving, into the convertibility era, an access to short-term credits to help member countries meet temporary difficulties in their balance of payments. As distinct from the EPU credits, the European Fund credits will be granted on a nonautomatic basis, will have a maximum maturity of two years, and will be subject to such other terms and conditions as the Fund may decide in each case. Basically divergent views as to the general purpose of the Fund [2] were finally resolved through a limping compromise providing that credits would be given to aid the borrowers "to withstand temporary *over-all* balance of payments difficulties" but only "in cases where these difficulties endanger the maintenance of the level of their *intra-European* liberalization measures" (Art. 2-*i*). The granting of a credit may be subordinated to the the acceptance by the borrower of specific recommendations regarding trade liberalization and to the various aspects, internal as well as external, of its financial economic policies. Recommendations may be issued simultaneously to other members to adopt measures that would alleviate the difficulties of the country concerned.

Another compromise designed to rally support from the countries favoring an automatic credit system provided that some lines of credit might be committed even before the Fund comes into operation, particularly to countries with low gold and convertible currency reserves.[3] In the opinion of the Managing Board, the total amount of these initial credits should not exceed 20% or 25% of the Fund's resources.

The capital of the European Fund was fixed at $600 million, $272 million of which will be derived from the transfer to the

2. Some countries wished to restrict Fund assistance to the support of intra-European liberalization, while others wished to broaden it into general support for currency convertibility.

3. Only a few countries, such as Denmark and Norway, could still be regarded as falling within this category.

Table XX. Capital of the European Fund and
Interim Finance Limits

(in millions of U.S. dollars)

	Capital of Fund	Interim Finance Limits
I. *Transfer of EPU Capital*	271.575	
A. *Immediately available*	148.037 a	
B. *Obligated by the U.S.*	123.538 b	
II. *Contributions of Members*	328.425	263
A. *Callable pro rata*	271.575 b	
1. U.K.	86.575	64
2. France	42.0	32
3. Germany	42.0	30
4. Belgium	30.0	20
5. Netherlands	30.0	22
6. Switzerland	21.0	15
7. Sweden	15.0	16
8. Portugal	5.0	5
B. *Deferred*	56.850 b	
9. Italy	15.0	13
10. Norway	15.0	12
11. Denmark	15.0	12
12. Austria	5.0	5
13. Turkey	3.0	7.5
14. Greece	2.850	7.5
15. Iceland	1.0	2
III. *Total*	600.000	263

Notes:

a. Including $113.037 million in gold and $35 million of long-term claims (initial balance loans) on Norway and Turkey.

b. To be called up, as needed for current and expected drawings, but in any case whenever liquid assets fall below $100 million:

(1) $148.037 million will be subject to first call upon countries listed under IIA in order to match the amount of EPU capital already paid in by the United States.

(2) The next $247.076 million will be called in *pari passu* from the U.S. and from the countries listed under IIA.

(3) The residual $56.850 million will be called in last from the countries listed under IIB. These are countries with relatively low reserves, generally in deficit in EPU.

Fund of the present capital of the European Payments Union. The other $328 million will be contributed by members (see Table XX). Interest on paid-up contributions will be determined every six months.

Finally, the capital of the Fund will also be used to advance—and underwrite up to $50 million—outpayments due to creditor countries under the operation of the Multilateral System for Settlements discussed below.

B. The Multilateral System for Settlements

The granting of credits was not the sole, nor even the major, objective of the European Payments Union. Its major purpose was to protect countries against bilateral pressures by guaranteeing the free transferability of member currencies into one another through the multilateral compensation and settlement of their bilateral surpluses and deficits. The preservation of similar guarantees under convertibility conditions proved a far more difficult task than the preservation of the Union's lending facilities.

The United Kingdom had always tended to regard the EPU machinery for compensations and settlements as a threat to a full resumption of the traditional role played in this respect by sterling in prewar days. It argued for many months that any compensation system would become both superfluous and unworkable under convertibility conditions. Compensations would be effected, in fact, through arbitrage operations carried out by the exchange markets themselves. The United Kingdom wished, moreover, to broaden substantially the exchange margins within which sterling would be allowed to fluctuate in accordance with market forces. It might be prevented from doing so, however, if the central bank of any EPU member retained the right to compensate and cover monthly in EPU, at fixed par values, its positions in sterling and other EPU currencies. Central banks would, indeed, have an interest in buying sterling in the market whenever it tended to drop below the official par of $2.80 per pound and to sell it to EPU at the $2.80 rate. Such operations would prevent the sterling rate from falling substantially below the $2.80 parity. Opposite operations could also interfere with any tendency for the rate to appreciate above parity.

A number of continental countries—particularly Switzerland— took very strong exception to these views. They granted that EPU compensations would be unnecessary and could be replaced by arbitrage operations so long as all European currencies remained fully convertible. Not all countries, however, would necessarily return to convertibility on the same day, nor would all of them necessarily remain convertible forever in the face of a later renewal of balance of payments difficulties. The dismantlement of the EPU compensation machinery might therefore be accompanied or followed, sooner or later, by a relapse into bilateralism. The current functioning of multilateral arbitrage among EPU countries and the gradual extension of transferability between EPU and other currencies depended essentially on the intervention of central banks in the exchange markets, and such interventions rested, in turn, on the assurance that any balance purchased by them from the market during the month was guaranteed by EPU against any exchange losses or inconvertibility risks. Even if all countries became convertible, any of them could change its decision at any moment, return to inconvertibility, or change unilaterally the rate at which it would support its currency on the exchange markets. A multilateral agreement among the EPU countries remained, therefore, indispensable to the satisfactory functioning and preservation of a multilateral system of payments in Europe.[4]

The compromise finally reached involved a substantial endorsement of the latter view in principle, but also a minimization of the practical scope of compensation operations under the new agreement. Particular stress was placed on the need to allow participation both by countries with inconvertible currencies and those with convertible currencies, and by countries whose currencies would fluctuate within relatively wider margins as well as by those who would limit these fluctuations within a very narrow range.

1. Exchange Rate Margins

Each country will notify the Agent (i.e. the Bank for International Settlements) and other central banks of fixed buying and selling rates at which it is prepared to sell or redeem its own currency against gold, dollars, or some other currency.[5] These rates may be freely chosen and modified by the country concerned—after consultation with the International Monetary Fund, if necessary—but

4. These arguments had been defended by the author at a private meeting of central bank experts from a number of European countries, held in Neufchatel in August 1954. They were accompanied by an ambitious proposal to replace EPU by a Clearing House for Central Banks, along the lines discussed below, pp. 284–6.

5. This obligation does not apply to a country whose currency is not officially quoted on the market of any other participating country. Since the U.S. dollar will, in principle, be the currency used in monthly settlements, any country which links its currency to gold or a currency other than the United States dollar must also declare the relationship between that standard and the United States dollar to be used in calculating these settlements.

will remain valid until the other central banks and the Agent have been notified of the change. The Agreement records the intention of all member countries to keep the margins between buying and selling rates as moderate and as stable as possible [6] and notes that no country is precluded from fixing the same rate for buying as for selling. While committed to buy and sell its currency at these rates, each central bank will remain free to do so, either on its own or on any other market, at any intermediate rate between the buying and selling points of which the Agent has been notified.

2. Interim Finance

In the interval between monthly settlements, each country will be under obligation to place at the disposal of any other participating country the amounts of its currency which the latter may request. This obligation is similar to that currently in effect under Article 8 of the EPU Agreement, but with an important difference. In the early days of EPU, the amounts of interim finance were directly governed by the development of the bilateral accounts entered in the books of central banks under their payments agreements. The return of exchange operations to free markets in which arbitrage transactions and central bank transactions are freely authorized will deprive—and has indeed already deprived in part—interim financing of any such clear-cut and bilateral limits. The currency of a member may be used to settle deficits with other countries, and central banks may buy or sell any currency they choose in order to prevent an excessive appreciation or depreciation of their own currency on the exchange markets. It might even be difficult, in practice, to make sure that central banks do not use interim finance for the mere purpose of earning an interest profit either in the market of the lending country or elsewhere, although it is agreed that this would constitute a clear abuse of the system.[7]

It was necessary, therefore, to fix agreed limits on the total

6. This declaration of "intention" constituted a concession by the United Kingdom to the majority opinion in favor of stable rates and narrow exchange margins. It might be noted, in passing, that the 3% margin on either side of parity—which widespread rumors described as the goal of the British authorities during the initial phase of the negotiations—would permit, in effect, a swing of 12% in the exchange rate between any two currencies. See below, p. 282.

7. The interest charge on interim finance will be uniform and moderate, a rate of $1\frac{1}{2}\%$ per annum being mentioned, by way of example, as appropriate under the circumstances prevailing in July 1955.

amount of interim finance that a country is allowed to draw from all the others, or that it may be required to grant to them. These limits were fixed, in general, at about 10% of the EPU credit quotas, but were increased for the countries with the lowest quotas (see Table XX). They may be revised later if circumstances and experience appear to justify a change.

3. Monthly Settlements

Each central bank will report monthly to the Agent the bilateral claims and debts which should be brought into the multilateral system of settlements. Each country's claims and debts will be re-calculated by the Agent in terms of the United States dollar—used as a common unit of account—compensated against each other, and converted into a single net claim on, or debt to, the European Fund. This net position will then be settled with the Fund in dollars, and this settlement will discharge all the bilateral debts and claims of which it is composed.

Three major distinctions emerge between this new compensation and settlement system and that of EPU. First of all, the settlements will be made fully in cash, rather than partly in cash and partly in EPU credits. Secondly, the settlements will usually take place at the notified buying or selling rates for dollars rather than at a single, uniform par value. Finally, and largely for that reason, very few balances are in fact likely to be reported for settlement.

Three main cases are distinguished in the Agreement: (1) balances acquired by a central bank from the exchange market in the course of stabilization operations; (2) balances due from a central bank to another as a consequence of "interim finance" lending and borrowing; and (3) balances on an account kept under a bilateral payments agreement of which the OEEC has been notified.

1. The first case should be the most normal and frequent one under convertibility conditions. The bulk of international settlements would then be effected through the private exchange and arbitrage markets, rather than through the central banks themselves. The latter would normally buy or sell foreign currencies on such markets—rather than directly between one another—only as a means to prevent an undue appreciation or depreciation of their own currency. They might also do so at the request and for

the account of a partner central bank, under ad hoc instructions or arrangements concluded between the two banks for the support of their currencies, either inside or at the buying and selling rates of which the Agent has been notified.

In either case the balances acquired need not, but may, be reported for settlement at the discretion of the holder, in which case they will be settled at the debtor country's selling rate for dollars.[8] Since this is the least favorable rate for the holder of the balances, they are far more likely to be disposed of by him in the market or settled directly between the two central banks concerned in accordance with the ad hoc arrangements concluded by them. Convertible currency balances may also, of course, be retained indefinitely by a central bank as a component part of its gold and foreign exchange reserves.

2. The second case is that of claims and debts—always expressed in the lender's currency—arising from the use of the "interim finance" facilities provided for under the Agreement. These *must* be reported, but will be settled at the lending country's *buying* rate for dollars, i.e. the most disadvantageous rate for the borrower. Central banks will therefore have an interest in buying from the market the foreign currency required—either in lieu of interim finance borrowing, or in order to repay such borrowings before the end of the month—unless market rates for that currency remain throughout at the upper margin corresponding to the country's buying rate for dollars.

3. The third case would be that of balances on an account kept under a bilateral payments agreement with an inconvertible currency country which has not notified the Agent of buying and selling rates for its currency. The Organization should be notified of any agreement of this kind, with full details as to its duration, the amount of credit margins, the currency of account, the rate agreed for settlements, etc. The balances outstanding under such agreements must be reported and settled monthly at the rate for the dollar agreed upon between the two parties. The Organization may, however, without the concurrence of the two parties concerned, issue recommendations to them to modify any provision

---

8. Balances acquired under ad hoc arrangements, however, can be settled through the Fund only if the contracting parties have notified the Organization of these arrangements, and they must be reported separately from those acquired for the buyer's own account.

that might prejudice the satisfactory operation of the settlement system or is contrary to the broad objectives of the European Monetary Agreement. If the two countries do not give effect to such recommendations, however, the only sanction provided for by the Agreement is the right for the Organization to exclude the balances from the monthly compensations and settlements.

4. Guarantees against Defaults and Exchange Risks

An important objective of the Multilateral System of Settlements is to give the contracting parties some guarantees of last resort against defaults or currency depreciation by the debtor countries.

The exchange rate guarantee provided is, normally, in terms of the United States dollar. If a country changes its buying and selling rates, the Agent and the other central banks will have to be notified of the change; and the calculations for the monthly settlements will be carried out separately, as far as that country is concerned, for the periods before and after the change, on the basis of the buying and selling rates notified in respect of each of these periods.

This system does not provide any general guarantee against losses resulting from a change in the United States price for gold or from the introduction of restrictions by the United States on its present policies with regard to gold sales and purchases in relation to any contracting party. Such a guarantee is provided, however, with respect to interim finance claims which will be separately calculated and settled in gold, rather than dollars, on the basis of the previous United States gold price. The Organization would, moreover, carry out as soon as possible a comprehensive review of the operation of the System in order to adjust it to the new circumstances.

The capital of the European Fund will be used to make the outpayments due to creditors in the monthly settlements, on the same day as the inpayments are due from the debtors. Delays or defaults will therefore be borne by the Fund, unless the defaults exceed an aggregate of $50 million, in which case the excess will be repaid pro rata to the Fund by the bilateral creditors of the defaulting countries. The countries in default will be automatically suspended, both from the Fund and from the System, and the Fund will use all means at its disposal to secure repayment and reimburse the creditors. Debts still in default at the time of liquidation will be converted back into bilateral claims on the defaulting countries.

C. Amendments to the Code of Liberalization

It is agreed in advance that the Code of Liberalization will in due course have to be reviewed in the light of conditions prevailing after the adoption of convertibility. It will nevertheless be maintained in full force in the meantime and for an unspecified period, with a number of amendments already agreed upon in advance.

1. Suspension of Liberalization Measures

A compromise, somewhat similar to the one reached with regard to borrowings from the European Fund,[9] had to be reached on the criteria governing recourse to the escape clauses of the Code. A country would now be allowed to suspend its liberalization measures if its *general* balance of payments—rather than its deficit with the Union—were developing adversely at a rate and in circumstances which it considers serious in view of the state of its reserves.[10] Regard should be paid principally, however, "to the incidence of specifically European factors on the balance of payments position of that Member country, unless it is a Member country whose balance of payments is fundamentally influenced by its relations with non-Member countries." Finally, in formulating its recommendations to the Member country concerned, the Organization will "take into consideration the desirability of maintaining intra-European liberalization and the advantages of reciprocity."

The conflict of views between the proponents of world-wide convertibility and the defenders of European integration is hardly resolved by these ambiguous and partly contradictory formulas. The balance of payments position of a country within the EPU region alone could hardly be maintained as a relevant criterion under convertibility conditions and might, moreover, be extremely difficult to determine factually under the new payments

9. See above, p. 221.

10. The general balance of payments of a country was previously taken into account also, but only as a secondary criterion, in determining whether a country was justified in suspending its liberalization commitments.

system. The exact wording of the Council's decision will probably remain of little significance for future decisions by the members or by the Organization. Countries will certainly continue to consider all the relevant factors in the situation, including both their reluctance to discriminate in favor of others—particularly under convertibility conditions—and their desire to avoid retaliatory restrictions against them by their partners. The preferential treatment of intra-European imports will certainly be weakened under the new system, but countries will be deterred from adopting intra-European restrictions by the fear of losing the benefits of reciprocal liberalization and by the availability of credits from the European Fund in support of their intra-European liberalization measures.

2. Conflicts with Other International Commitments

Most OEEC countries are already committed to the principle of nondiscrimination by the IMF and GATT Agreements. If this principle came to be more strictly applied in the future, some countries might feel impelled to decrease their OEEC liberalization to a level allowing them to offer the same treatment to countries which are not members of OEEC. This implication has been officially recognized by the Council as justifying, as a last resort, the suspension of intra-European liberalization measures. The Organization, however, will first review such problems when they arise and "take active steps to seek methods of cooperation" which would make it possible to avoid or minimize the recourse to deliberalization in such cases.

Here again, the wording of the Council's decision reflects a general awareness of possible conflicts between convertibility and liberalization and the intention to seek cooperative solutions for them, rather than any advance and concrete agreement on the nature of such solutions.

3. Assistance to Economically Underdeveloped Countries

Conflicts between liberalization and economic development would already be covered by existing escape clauses based on balance of payments considerations. Provision is now made for a more specific escape clause in this context, together with an undertaking to examine jointly ways in which the member countries could cooperate with a view to assisting the economic development of a country in this situation.

D. ADMINISTRATION

The shift from EPU to the European Monetary System will involve very few administrative changes. Great stress was placed throughout the negotiation on the need to preserve the practice of mutual discussion and confrontation of economic policies and on the right of the Organization to issue recommendations in this respect. The role of the Managing Board of EPU in these examinations will be continued by the Board of Management of the European Fund.

This Board will be selected and will operate in the same way as the EPU Managing Board. It will supervise the execution of the Agreement, make its reports and recommendations to the OEEC Council, and exercise such other powers as may be delegated to it by the latter. The Bank for International Settlements will continue to act as Agent for the execution of all financial operations under the Agreement, and the OEEC Steering Board for Trade will continue its functions in relation to the Code of Liberalization.

There will be set up, in addition, a special Consultative Committee of high-level officials charged with examining problems arising out of the working of the new system, and particularly the incidence of the exchange rate policies of any member country upon the trade of other members. This constitutes a mild concession to the countries—particularly Switzerland—which insisted on narrower exchange margins and a greater stability of exchange rates than are guaranteed under the Agreement.

E. ENTRY INTO FORCE, DURATION, AND LIQUIDATION

The new Agreement will enter into force, and EPU will be terminated, when countries whose combined quotas are at least 50% of the total of EPU quotas notify the Organization of their intention to liquidate EPU and, at the same time, countries responsible for at least 50% of the contributions to the European Fund's capital express their intention to bring the European Fund into being. All member countries of OEEC are committed in advance to participate, in this case, in the new system, even though the notification mentioned above might emanate from only three or four [11] of the seventeen member countries.

The EPU Agreement was a temporary agreement, concluded initially for two years and renewed subsequently on a year-to-year basis. The European Monetary Agreement is designed, on the contrary, to establish a permanent system of cooperation, and to remain in force for an indefinite period. The Agreement may be reviewed, however, from time to time in the light of experience, and in consultation with the U.S. government. A first comprehensive review of the operation of the Multilateral System will take place before the end of the first year, and of the operation of the Agreement as a whole before the end of its third year. Thus the Multilateral System will remain in force for a minimum period of one year and the European Fund for a minimum period of three years, after which they will continue under conditions to be decided on the occasion of each review. A country may withdraw only on such renewal dates [12] and the Agreement can only be terminated either by unanimous decision or upon notice of withdrawal by countries responsible for at least 50% of the Fund's capital.

In the event of such termination, the Fund will remain in existence, for purposes of liquidation, at least until the date on which the last repayment of its credits falls due. It may be continued, in the event of defaults or delays, until such payment is effectively made. The members' contributions will be repaid in the reverse order in which they were made (see Table XX) and the residual capital transferred from EPU will be distributed as foreseen in the EPU Agreement.

F. Brief Appraisal

The European Monetary Agreement represents a first attempt to reconcile the current and prospective progress of OEEC countries toward world-wide convertibility with the maintenance and development of intra-European cooperation in trade and payments.

11. Germany, Belgium, and the Netherlands are generally thought to be most favorable to a return to convertibility and to be waiting only for British initiative to do so themselves. The entry into force of the European Monetary Agreement would deprive other countries of most of the advantages of inconvertibility "for nonresidents," and most of them would therefore be expected to follow suit, even though reluctantly in some cases.

12. Except with the unanimous agreement of the Organization.

The mechanisms established since the war, particularly the European Payments Union, had proved their worth in a period of transition between bilateralism and convertibility. It is now agreed that they should be modified rather than scrapped, and that regional cooperation can assist in the maintenance, as well as in the resumption, of viable convertibility in the postwar world.[13]

The general acceptance of this thesis by the European countries is of much greater significance than the precise provisions of the present European Monetary Agreement, which will necessarily be subject to considerable revision in the light of future developments. The Agreement, as it now stands, constitutes a tour de force in that it is supposed to be equally and simultaneously applicable to countries with inconvertible or with convertible currencies, with fluctuating or with fixed exchange rates, and with varying degrees of trade and exchange restrictions. This tends to reduce the members' commitments to the lowest common denominator among the heterogeneous policies pursued by them. It is very likely, however, that the resumption of convertibility will be followed more or less rapidly by a greater harmonization of policies than exists today, and by a greater willingness to stabilize such policies through amendments to the present Agreement.

The major shortcomings of the European Monetary Agreement will be discussed in the concluding chapter of this study, together with an ambitious proposal to remedy them through the broadening of the Multilateral Settlements System into a clearing house for the central banks of member countries.[14] The implications of such a proposal, however, far transcend the limited scope of past and present forms of monetary cooperation in Europe. It could, on the one hand, constitute a first step toward full monetary integration; and this explains the resistance deployed against it by all those who fear rather than welcome further progress toward that goal. On the other hand, it would also solve some of the major problems raised today on a world-wide scale by the present drift toward a mere return to a gold exchange standard, whose vulnerability was amply debated by economists in the late 1920's and tragically proved by events in the early 1930's, but which has been all but forgotten in postwar discussions of international convertibility.[15]

13. The reasons for this conclusion will be discussed in Chap. 7 of this study.
14. See below, pp. 284–6.
15. See below, pp. 296–301.

CHAPTER 7

Toward Viable Convertibility

EUROPE'S PROGRESS toward an orderly system of international trade and payments is usually identified with its progress toward convertibility, and its crowning achievement is taken to be the restoration of convertibility. The concrete meaning of this goal, however, is less easy to define than its emotional connotation. It is associated in people's minds with all the prestige of a monetary system which, more than any other, came close to the "invisible hand" dear to Adam Smith, and which effectively provided the nineteenth century with a relatively smooth and unquestioned system of international settlements.

It was not a static system, however, and much of its success in those days was due to its adaptability to a changing environment. This process of evolutionary adaptation was brusquely interrupted by the First World War and, later on, by the world depression and the Second World War. Radical readjustments in the 1913 convertibility techniques are certainly indispensable to ensure their viability under present-day economic and political conditions. Any attempt merely to dig up and dust off the pre-1914 convertibility model would almost certainly kindle only a brief bonfire, such as that which followed the reconstruction of the gold standard in the late 1920's.

Economic theorizing cannot provide a complete answer to the problem. What is essentially at stake is the restoration of a certain degree of stability in the institutional framework of international trade and payments, and such stability unavoidably involves corresponding limitations on national sovereignty—or on the use to be made of it—in the broad field of economic policy. We must therefore first define the various objectives which might be deemed desirable in this respect from the economic viewpoint; and consider secondly to what extent each of them is likely to prove acceptable and susceptible of effective implementation from political and administrative viewpoints.

I. SCOPE AND LIMITATIONS OF TRADITIONAL CONVERTIBILITY

A. Exchange Rate Stability

"Currency convertibility" was easily defined by our fathers as the maintenance of a fixed parity or exchange rate with relation to gold or to foreign currencies convertible themselves into gold at a fixed parity. A currency was regarded as inconvertible as soon as it was permitted to fluctuate from this parity by more than a small margin, approximating the cost of gold shipments. Viewed in this perspective, the advocacy of fluctuating exchange rates as the cornerstone of some recent convertibility plans might seem highly paradoxical.

And yet the paradox is only apparent. It is symptomatic of the enormous changes in economic philosophy, policies, and institutions which we have inherited from two world wars and a major economic depression. The traditional definition of convertibility in terms of exchange rate stability took for granted the freedom of transactions. The criterion of exchange stability becomes highly academic when stability is preserved only through pervasive restrictions limiting, more or less severely in different countries or at different times, freedom of access to the international commodity and exchange markets. True inconvertibility, i.e. the impossibility of legally converting the national currency into foreign goods or currencies at any exchange rate whatsoever, is a relatively modern phenomenon whose consequences can be incomparably more destructive of international competition than those of mere exchange fluctuations in a free market.

B. Capital Controls

Present-day convertibility discussions thus center around the removal of administrative controls and restrictions over international transactions. It is generally admitted, however, that the freedom of current transactions is far more important, in this respect, than that of capital movements. Thus Article VI of the International Monetary Fund Agreement leaves each country free "to regulate international capital movements" as it wishes,[1] and even gives positive encouragement to such controls by denying access to the Fund's resources to a member which "fails to exercise appropriate controls" over "a large or sustained outflow of capital." In keeping with this philosophy, the Fund has generally taken a dim view of free gold markets, on the ground that they permit a dispersal among individuals of international gold reserves which ought to be concentrated in the hands of the national monetary authorities.

The maintenance of capital controls necessitates, however, a continued supervision over current transactions as well, and such supervision may be difficult to reconcile with market techniques of currency convertibility. It is noteworthy that this distinction was given up in the European Payments Agreement, whose provisions were applied equally from the start to all intra-European settlements, whether on current or capital account. Recent trends in exchange control relaxation also reveal a growing tendency to liberalize capital movements, even in advance of trade, and to relax or eliminate the obligation of individuals to turn over to the monetary authorities their foreign exchange earnings or assets.[2]

Capital controls are indeed extremely difficult to enforce through administrative regulations. Their disincentive effect on capital imports are often more patent than their effectiveness in preventing capital exports. New techniques of control, based on market forces, have been developing recently and may well become a characteristic feature of future convertibility systems. Capital exports may be discouraged, and capital imports or repatriation encouraged, by channeling such operations into a free exchange market with fluctuating rates. Such a system has been formally adopted by a number of countries, and approximated in others through the liberalization of transactions in securities or currency notes. Central banks may intervene in such markets, but do not commit themselves in advance to any definite pegging at or close to the official parity of their currency.

1. "Payments of moderate amounts for amortization of loans or for depreciation of direct investments" and "moderate remittances for family living expenses" are classified, however, under current rather than capital transactions (Art. XIX).

2. See above, pp. 212–17.

In any case, postwar discussions have generally narrowed down the concept of convertibility to that of convertibility for current transactions. Divergencies of views still remain, however, between those who would define convertibility as implying the total elimination of all restrictions on current transactions and those who would require only the elimination of discriminatory or bilateral restrictions on such transactions.

C. LIBERALIZATION OF CURRENT TRANSACTIONS

Let us note, first of all, that the liberalization of current transactions implies, of necessity, an immediate broadening of the convertibility concept to encompass trade as well as monetary aspects of convertibility. The need for such a broadening results from the fact that trade and exchange techniques of restriction are largely interchangeable. The right to convert freely, let us say, sterling into dollars to pay for merchandise imports from the United States would remain Platonic if the state reserved the right to forbid or limit these imports themselves. This is precisely the case today with respect to the use of sterling in trade settlements with the dollar area. "American account" sterling is freely available to pay for authorized imports from the United States, and can be converted at will into U.S. dollars. It is the imports themselves which are controlled, and it is these controls which effectively limit the convertibility of sterling into dollars for current transactions.

To be at all meaningful, the restoration of convertibility would therefore require the removal of trade restrictions as well as of exchange restrictions. This principle was indeed applied from the start to the OEEC trade liberalization program. No category of merchandise is regarded as liberalized until both imports and payments are freed from all licensing restrictions.

The word "restrictions" is, however, interpreted in a very peculiar sense. All *exchange* restrictions are usually considered as incompatible with convertibility, this incompatibility applying equally to quantitative restrictions—licensing—and to market restrictions—multiple or differential exchange rates—which preserve, but at a cost, the freedom of transactions. In the field of *trade* restrictions, on the other hand, market restrictions are regarded as perfectly compatible with convertibility: customs duties and tariffs can be maintained or even increased, as long as quantitative restrictions are abolished.

This curious distinction appears untenable for several reasons. The practical significance of multiple exchange rates is often equivalent to that of tariff duties. Little does it matter to the importer if the tax collected from him is dubbed "exchange surcharge" or "customs duty." Secondly, while the internal incidence of quota restrictions [3] is infinitely more serious than that of tariff restrictions, their external incidence on partner countries and on the actual volume of trade may be very similar as long as the quotas are nondiscriminatory in nature. High and unstable tariff levels can indeed be as damaging, or more, to international trade as moderate, nondiscriminatory systems of trade or exchange control. Convertibility would hardly be worth while if it were achieved through a shift from trade quotas and exchange licensing to simultaneous and equivalent increases in tariff protection.

Shall we therefore be pushed into a definition of convertibility which equates it with the old free trade ideal of classical economists? In this case, progress will indeed have to be gradual, and full convertibility is unlikely to reward our most dogged efforts or even those of our children and grandchildren.

D. NONDISCRIMINATION

Clarity of thought and effectiveness of policy both require a less ambitious definition of immediate convertibility goals. Such a definition can be found in the restoration of a *multilateral system of trade and payments* rather than in the removal of all protection for domestic production against imports from abroad. This was indeed the meaning of nineteenth-century convertibility, which accommodated itself to varying degrees of national protection. The major difference between these age-old techniques of protection and modern inconvertibility lies in the fact that the former extended protection only to the national producers and only within the protecting country's boundaries, while the latter discriminates in favor of certain exporting countries at the expense of others and tries to protect domestic producers not only within the country's boundaries but in all foreign markets as well. Once adopted by a major country, such techniques inevitably spread from trading partner to trading partner, each country trying to

3. Distortion of prices and profits in favor of license holders, lack of any disinflationary effect on incomes and liquidity, etc.

secure special advantages to itself or at least being forced to defend its exporters against the discriminatory actions of others. International trade is then forced more and more into the strait jacket of bilateral negotiations, increasingly relegating to the background all considerations of price or quality competition and the underlying pattern of comparative costs and advantages.

The key to "workable" convertibility is not free trade, desirable as this might be, but the maintenance of full competition in third markets. Professor MacDougall's study of United States and United Kingdom exports in 1937 showed ample verification for the classical theory of comparative costs, but found that it depended essentially on third market competition rather than on direct trade between the two countries.

> Before the war, American weekly wages in manufacturing were roughly double the British, and we find that, when American output per worker was more than twice the British, the United States had in general the bulk of the export market, while for the products where it was less than twice as high the bulk of the market was held by Britain. . . . But while in the normal text-book examples the exports of each country go to each other, the great bulk of the exports of the United States and the United Kingdom in 1937 went to third countries—more than 95 per cent of British exports of our sample products but three, more than 95 per cent of American exports of all the products but six. It is true that each country was nearly always a net exporter to the other of products in which it had a comparative advantage, but this is of limited interest, since trade between them was in general a negligible proportion of their total consumption.[4]

Thus, the preservation or restoration of traditional competitive forces in international trade depends essentially on the equal access of all foreign exporters to each national market rather than on the elimination of all protection for domestic producers within a country's own territory. The latter objective has never been achieved, and one can hardly expect it ever to be fully achieved

4. G. D. A. MacDougall, "British and American Exports. A Study Suggested by the Theory of Comparative Costs," Pt. I, *Economic Journal* (Dec. 1951), pp. 697–724, particularly pp. 697–9.

without a political as well as economic merger among the countries concerned. Equal access to third markets has always constituted the bulk and the core of international competition.

Convertibility is not incompatible, therefore, with a certain amount of protection and restrictions. The past is, in this case, a guide to the future. The restoration of convertibility depends essentially on the elimination of discrimination and bilateralism—rather than of over-all protection or restrictions—from the trade and payments mechanism. In the payments field, such a system presupposes the full interconvertibility of currencies, i.e. the right for each country or its residents [5] to convert their earnings in some foreign currencies into other currencies needed for the settlement of their deficits with other countries. In the trade field, convertibility does not presuppose the immediate elimination of all restrictions, nor even of all quantitative restrictions, but only the absence of any discrimination in the administration of remaining restrictions.[6]

Yet this argument cannot be pushed too far. If the definition of convertibility were to be narrowed down to nondiscrimination,

5. The convertibility of the pound would imply, for instance, that the United Kingdom would authorize the free conversion of French sterling earnings into dollars or other currencies. Whether such conversion privileges would be exercised by French residents or only by the French monetary authorities would depend on whether or not France retains exchange controls and forces its residents to surrender their exchange earnings to the monetary authorities.

6. The "convertibility for nonresidents" proposed by the United Kingdom in the spring of 1953 satisfied the first, but only the first, of these two conditions. It covered the payments aspect of convertibility, and would have allowed foreigners to convert freely into other currencies the sterling balances earned by them. The United Kingdom would have been left free not only to maintain quantitative restrictions on British imports—so as to limit the over-all acquisition of convertible sterling by foreigners in general—but also to apply such restrictions in discriminatory fashion, so as to influence the trade policy of its partners or the actual use made by them of their convertibility privileges. The United Kingdom considered such discretion necessary to allow her to force her creditors to follow what she called "a good creditor policy," but other countries could hardly agree to let England be the sole judge in matters in which she was also a vitally interested party. They feared the use of discrimination by England to shift her imports from those countries which would actually convert their sterling earnings into dollars to those countries which would agree to retain them in the form of sterling balances or to use them for purchases in the sterling area.

The British proposals are still today at the center of all convertibility discussions, but they have evolved in a much more acceptable direction by admitting, in all such matters, the intervention of international institutions such as GATT and the IMF.

convertibility could be technically restored by aligning all restrictions upon the highest level of restrictions in existence. It could even be compatible, in pure logic, with the adoption of such high levels of nondiscriminatory restrictions as would in fact eliminate international trade altogether. The acceptance of convertibility as a desirable and feasible aim of international economic policy requires, therefore, a delicate balancing of the twin objectives of trade liberalization and nondiscrimination.[7] It is precisely the possible conflict between these two objectives which in recent years has dampened the former enthusiasm of many economists and statesmen for the restoration of convertibility in a way which might endanger the progress already and simultaneously achieved, on a regional basis, toward nondiscrimination and trade liberalization.

E. Historical Basis of Traditional Convertibility

The most striking feature of nineteenth-century convertibility was that it was maintained internationally without any international agreements or commitments whatsoever. International convertibility was never juridically organized. It was a de facto system, dependent at all times upon the spontaneous and simultaneous adoption and maintenance of national convertibility policies by all—or most—trading countries. Each country retained its full national sovereignty with respect to its own monetary and economic policy, but chose—or happened—to exercise it in such a way as generally to eschew recourse to exchange rate fluctuations or trade and exchange restrictions, as willful, or even involuntary, methods of preserving or restoring equilibrium in its foreign transactions. Such equilibrium was thus made dependent on other forms of adjustment abundantly described in the classical literature of international trade.

In this respect much stress is usually placed on the flexibility of internal prices and wages and their responsiveness to international competitive pressures, transmitted to the domestic economy through the impact of balance of payments disturbances upon

7. The relative emphasis placed by British policy on the former objective to the neglect of the latter, and by American policy on the latter to the neglect of the former, lies at the root of the most untractable difficulties in postwar economic negotiations between the two countries.

national income and money flows. I would be tempted to put at least equal emphasis on the fact that economic institutions and policies tended to limit in advance the probable size of such disturbances as well as to facilitate later internal adjustments to them. We noted in Chapter 2 that an external deficit on current account necessarily coincides with an over-all excess of expenditures over current income. The ability of a country's residents to finance such an excess of expenditure over income is limited by their ability to liquidate their own foreign assets, to borrow capital from abroad, to borrow funds from their own national banking system, or to convert into foreign exchange liquid claims previously accumulated on the monetary and banking system. The first two procedures restrict the size of the possible excess of expenditures over income to the means of foreign financing available to the community as a whole, excluding any decrease in the international reserves of the banking system. Neither of them involves any conversion of the national currency into foreign exchange, and neither can give rise to convertibility problems for the monetary authorities.[8]

Conversion difficulties could arise only in connection with the last two procedures mentioned above. Liquid claims on the banks can be presented to them for conversion into foreign exchange, and such conversion may become impossible if large liquid claims have been created previously by the banking system—or are currently created by it—through its lending operations rather than through purchases of gold and foreign exchange.

The willingness of the commercial banks to follow such expansionary policies, however, was narrowly limited by their own concern for survival. They would be deterred from excessive lending by the fear of being forced into liquidation if they became unable to reimburse their depositors in gold, foreign exchange, or legal tender money. When this happened, only the depositors of the liquidated banks would suffer, but the convertibility of the currency proper would remain unaffected thereby.

The growth of central banking somewhat modified this situation for two reasons. The first is that the central bank itself might now consider it its duty to intervene in some cases—and gradually

8. They may, of course, create internal deflationary pressures which the authorities might decide to fight by expansionary credit policies. This would bring us into a consideration of the third procedure mentioned in the text.

in nearly all cases—to support, through its own credit, commercial banks in difficulties. Secondly, central banks might be unable or unwilling to reject demands for credit on the part of the state or of other state-backed borrowers.[9] The expansion of central bank credit might, however, in contrast to that of private banks' credit, lead to a depletion of the central bank's international reserves and endanger the free convertibility of the country's legal tender money into gold or foreign exchange.

Even then, however, true currency inconvertibility remained the exception rather than the rule. Modern trade and exchange control techniques were virtually unknown, and would have been, in any case, deeply repellent to the liberal philosophy of the age. Extreme reserve losses were thus followed, in practice, by currency devaluation or temporary recourse to floating exchange rates, rather than by currency inconvertibility in the modern and stricter sense of the word. Even this was a rare occurrence, outside of Latin America and a few other underdeveloped countries exposed to particularly violent balance of payments fluctuations or to political instability and civil strife. In the older and more diversified economies of Western Europe, balance of payments fluctuations were much milder in amplitude, international capital movements would often respond to small differentials in discount and interest rates—particularly in the case of a capital-exporting country—and credit expansion was rarely allowed to proceed to the point where convertibility at the current exchange rate might have to be suspended. This occurred only in national emergencies, such as a protracted and costly war, but hardly ever under peacetime conditions. In the liberal climate of opinion which pervaded political as well as financial circles, the economic activities and objectives of the state were narrowly circumscribed, its financial procedures were kept close to business standards of "soundness," and large recourses to central bank credit or the printing press were both unnecessary and impossible.

These institutions and traditions thus held down within a modest range the financing, and thus the development, of balance of payments deficits in excess of private capital imports. Correspondingly small fluctuations in prices and wages could suffice to

9. This danger was even more direct, of course, in countries where paper currency was issued by the state itself rather than by a banking institution endowed with some degree of independence and subject to legal limitations on its right of issue.

restore equilibrium and did not meet the institutional resistance which they would evoke today. These readjustments might nevertheless be accompanied at times by temporary unemployment, but again the severity of such unemployment and the political and economic power of the working classes were not such as to force large-scale intervention, deficit financing, or other measures likely to bring about a convertibility crisis.

In brief, nineteenth-century convertibility was essentially the product of historical circumstances. It rested on the spontaneous restraints upon the objectives and instrumentalities of internal and external economic policy imposed upon the state by tradition, the structure of society, the prevailing doctrine of liberalism, and the ignorance of modern techniques of monetary management and controls.

It hardly need be said that these historical circumstances have all but disappeared today. The authorities of each country are keenly conscious of a much wider range of objectives which can be pursued by the exercise of their national sovereignty in economic matters. They are equally conscious of a much wider range of policy instruments at their disposal for the attainment of these objectives. And, finally, some of the traditional methods of balance of payments adjustment—budgetary and credit restraints, price and wage flexibility, unemployment—elicit far greater resistance today than they did in the nineteenth century. Their practical implementation, whether desirable or not in the abstract, is often regarded as politically impossible or, at least, as far less palatable than alternative forms of adjustment involving a greater or lesser departure from traditional convertibility policies.

The liberal ideal of an optimal allocation of employed resources now has to vie with other policy objectives, such as those of a high and stable level of activity and employment, a rapid rate of economic development, a greater equality in income distribution, some protection of the weaker sectors of national production, and so on. These various objectives of modern governments are not necessarily incompatible with one another, but neither is their compatibility necessary and automatic. The larger the number of policy "targets," the larger the number of policy "instruments" which need be used to satisfy them simultaneously.[10] Exchange

10. Professor Jan Tinbergen has done more than any other economist to clarify both the theoretical and the policy implications of the expanding horizons of gov-

readjustments and trade and exchange controls are foremost among the new instruments of policy to which governments have had recourse in the last forty years, both in order to implement new and broader ranges of policy objectives and to make up for increasing institutional rigidities interfering with more traditional methods of international adjustment such as price and wage flexibility. These new techniques were often adopted hurriedly, under the pressure of circumstances, and with wildly exaggerated hopes as to their long-run effectiveness as an antidote to persistent inflationary policies. The disappointment of these excessive hopes may well prompt a partial return to more traditional policies and stimulate the search for other readjustment techniques less lethal to the maintenance of international convertibility.

Yet it would be totally unrealistic to expect a spontaneous and permanent rejection of inconvertibility techniques by each country, acting independently under the spur of purely national pressures and interests. There exist many circumstances—even though less numerous than has been claimed at times—when restrictions, discrimination, and even bilateralism would better serve the true interests of an individual country than practicable alternative policies. There are other cases in which this would not be true, but in which public opinion and political leadership may be unwilling or unable to accept and implement such alternative policies. Progress toward viable convertibility thus involves of necessity a "collective approach," totally different from the "national approach" of the nineteenth century.

II. SCOPE AND FEASIBILITY OF INTERNATIONAL CONVERTIBILITY AGREEMENTS

The collective approach to convertibility involves essentially the acceptance and implementation by the participating countries of voluntary restraints upon the free exercise of their monetary and economic sovereignty. It would be foolhardy, however, to base such an approach only on Platonic appeals and exhortations to in-

---

ernmental economic decisions. See particularly his booklet *On the Theory of Economic Policy*, Amsterdam, North-Holland Publishing Co., 1952.

ternational cooperation. Sovereign countries should not be expected to undertake and respect international commitments which come into conflict—real or even imaginary—with powerful national pressures or interests. In the words of Keynes, any convertibility plan "must operate not only to the general advantage but also to the individual advantage of each of the participants." [1] Barring the use of coercion, the efficacy of international commitments depends primarily on the provisions that make their implementation both feasible and attractive, and their breach unnecessary and damaging, from the national points of view of the countries concerned. National interests should be made to coincide, through a double mechanism of deterrents and incentives, with the collective interests of the group. Reciprocity and mutual help are the keystones of such a construction.

Great difficulties are encountered, however, as soon as one tries to spell out in detail the practical implications of this broad principle. Most of them have to do with the conflict between ideal and workable models of international organization. An ideal model should encompass *all* the trading countries of the world and involve *extensive* commitments by each in support of the system. Since, moreover, there always exist several alternative methods of setting up such a system, it becomes necessary to reach agreement on the selection of some of these methods in preference to others. In view of these problems, workable models of a less ambitious nature will remain the only practical alternative to economic nationalism, unless and until world government becomes itself a feasible goal of international organization. The more sanguine defenders of economic liberalism and internationalism will merely succeed in blocking the path to actual progress as long as they continue to reject as inadequate or discriminatory any plan which falls short of full and world-wide convertibility.

A. NATURE AND TIMING OF COMMITMENTS

The ideal convertibility model would involve both the stabilization of exchange rates and the permanent stabilization or dismantlement of all forms of trade and exchange restriction. Workable convertibility models will aim instead at exploiting fully, at any

1. *Proposals by British Experts for an International Clearing Union*, Preface, Sec. (5).

given point of time, existing opportunities for actual agreements, limiting arbitrary and unilateral action in either respect. Two criteria should determine the order of priority in which these problems should be attacked. The first is the relative harmfulness of the practices to be banned, the second the actual prospects for agreement among the countries concerned. These criteria will often coincide, as countries will be most anxious to reach agreement on the outlawing of those forms of restrictions from which they suffer most in their international relations.

This ordering of priorities is of extreme importance, since renunciation of one type of control may often result in stimulating or forcing greater reliance upon the other types of control left to the discretion of the participating countries. A premature stabilization of exchange rates may thus result in a tightening of restrictions, and a tightening of restrictions in the spread of bilateral agreements designed to preserve a minimum level of mutual trade. This was indeed the unhappy pattern of the early postwar years, when concrete commitments with respect to exchange rates and tariff levels were combined with mere declarations of intention concerning the elimination of quantitative restrictions and discrimination.

The success achieved by OEEC is largely due to the adoption of a radically different order of priority for cooperative international action. All OEEC countries were keenly conscious of the absurdities and waste involved in the bilateral administration of trade and exchange restrictions under existing agreements. Bilateralism was therefore made the first target of attack, and its rapid elimination, or near-elimination, restored the full force of intra-European competition among exporters and contributed to the readjustment of excessive national cost levels. Minimum liberalization commitments were, however, simultaneously agreed to, lest intra-European discrimination be removed on the basis of a tightening of restrictions all around. These commitments applied equally to all forms of quantitative restriction but not to tariffs, and were gradually stepped up from 50% to 60%, 75%, and finally 90% before any attempt was made to reduce market forms of restriction, particularly tariffs. Finally, the problem of exchange rate stabilization has been left, up to now, outside the scope of OEEC action, although it is not clear whether this was due to a realization that exchange rate stabilization should follow—rather than precede—the removal of restrictions, or merely to the fact that this field of activity had been most obviously pre-empted by the International Monetary Fund.

B. Acceptance and Implementation of Multilateralization and Liberalization Commitments

A wise choice and ordering of multilateralization and liberalization targets is a necessary, but not a sufficient, condition for their acceptance and implementation by national governments. An international agreement must also aim at creating conditions which make it possible and attractive for the participating countries to accept and observe the commitments necessary to its successful operation. Here again, the OEEC experience offers a valuable guide to the type of techniques which may achieve this objective.

The restoration of a multilateral trading system among the members of the Organization required, first of all, that each of them relinquish its right to negotiate bilateral trade and payments agreements with the others. Such agreements, however, retained a great deal of attraction for many countries as long as they remained the only, or the most effective, channel through which they could protect their exports against the threat of trade or exchange restrictions by their customers, or through which they could hope to secure credit assistance for the financing of temporary deficits in their international transactions. The mere outlawing of bilateral agreements would have been unnegotiable from the start if no alternative guarantees had been provided for the defense of these two interests. The elimination of intra-European bilateralism, in 1950, was made possible by the prior or simultaneous negotiation of trade liberalization guarantees under the Code of Liberalization, and of multilateral lines of credit under the EPU Agreement.

The gradual removal of trade restrictions constituted, therefore, an indispensable basis for the elimination of intra-European discrimination and bilateralism, as well as an independent objective of OEEC cooperation. The acceptance and implementation of liberalization commitments by the member countries required, in turn, the adoption of a wide range of techniques necessary to gain and retain the assent of member countries to the system.

The first and most crucial of these techniques was that of reciprocity. Countries were not exhorted to abandon their restrictions unilaterally, but induced to do so by the simultaneous adoption of similar commitments by their main trading partners. The simultaneous removal of reciprocal restrictions by all countries would be far less dangerous to the balance of payments of each, since one could expect the consequent increase in imports to be matched to a considerable extent—or more than matched for some countries—by a parallel expansion of exports. Yet the net result of this double movement was, of course, unpredictable, and would vary greatly from country to country.

Automatic borrowing rights and lending commitments, related to the evolution of each country's intra-European payments, were thus inserted into the Agreement in order to induce the weaker countries to accept the residual risks involved. Additional assistance could be provided, on a negotiated basis, when required by the deterioration of a country's position and justified by the adoption of an agreed program of balance of payments readjustment.

The resources needed to finance these credits could be derived in part from the United States' contribution to the EPU capital fund, but the largest portion was furnished by EPU creditors under initial quota and later rallonge commitments. The first inducement to the acceptance of these lending commitments was similar to that which had prompted the granting of bilateral credit margins under payments agreements, i.e. it lay in the protection which liberalization commitments would assure them against the application of trade or exchange restrictions to the bulk of their export trade. Moreover, the substitution of EPU credits for bilateral credits would be of great benefit to them, as the former would be usable multilaterally throughout Europe and the sterling area while the latter were narrowly confined to the financing of subsequent deficits toward the very countries on which they were currently accumulating surpluses. Finally, the EPU Agreement assured the creditors of gold—or convertible currencies—settlement of at least a portion of their intra-European surpluses, and the EPU capital provided them some guarantees against ultimate defaults by the debtors.

Nevertheless, the surplus countries could not be expected to grant unlimited credits to EPU. The deficit countries, on the other hand, might also be reluctant to assume a large burden of indebtedness in order to maintain a given level of liberalization, and might be unable or unwilling to carry out quickly the internal corrective measures necessary to limit the size of their external deficits. Broad escape clauses authorized, in such cases, the temporary reimposition of restrictions by countries in difficulties, but the Agreement continued to protect them against retaliation by their stronger partners, thus preventing the spread and spiraling of reciprocal restrictions from one country to the others.

These escape clauses constituted a dangerous exception to the reciprocity principle on which the Agreement was based. If widely resorted to by the weaker OEEC members, they would have led other members to withdraw, as their membership would no longer carry any benefit to themselves. Thus, any recourse to escape clauses had to be justified to the Organization. The consultations which took place on such occasions ranged over the whole field of the restricting country's policies, and extended to internal financial and economic measures as well as to external trade and exchange measures. Each country knew that its unwarranted recourse to restrictions, or undue delays in the adoption of measures allowing it to resume liberalization, would probably, in the last resort, be penalized by its exclusion from the benefits of other countries' trade and credit commitments.

Similar negotiations were also forced upon persistent creditor countries. No method of settlement having been agreed upon in advance for the financing of surpluses beyond quotas, the continuation of fractional gold and credit settlements became dependent on ad hoc rallonge agreements, acceptable to both creditors and debtors. In order to gain assent to this solution and at the same time limit the piling up of further credits to the EPU, the creditor countries were led to step up their liberalization far beyond the minimum levels jointly agreed upon and, in a number of cases, to impart a more expansionist direction to their internal financial and economic policies.

The element of compulsion involved in the EPU commitments was thus largely overshadowed by escape clauses and negotiations which left each country essentially free to determine its policies in the light of its own national interests. The success of the system did not rest on the willingness of its members to sacrifice national advantages to international objectives, but on the reconciliation of both through built-in incentives and deterrents. The availability of credit assistance to debtors, of fractional gold payments to creditors, and of guarantees against default, restrictions, and discrimination were all contingent upon continued participation in the system. They constituted powerful incentives to cooperative policies and loaded the dice heavily against unilateral, disruptive action by any of the participating countries.

C. TRANSFERABILITY OF SETTLEMENTS AND NONDISCRIMINATION IN TRADE

The applicability of these techniques to world-wide agreements will be discussed in section III of this chapter. It must first be recognized, however, that they involve considerable departure from tradition and orthodoxy. The two cardinal sins of these OEEC methods, in the eyes of their opponents, lie in the subordination of nondiscrimination to reciprocity and in the provision of automatic credits in international settlements. The need for both features does not arise from abstract economic reasoning but from the attempt to reconcile national sovereignty with international cooperation. They might be considerably reduced, or even eliminated, if a supranational authority were established over member states, with sufficient power to dictate and effectively enforce ideal norms of internal and external economic policy. Each country would then be required, in its own interest as well as in that of others, to maintain high and expanding levels of employment, but to refrain at the same time from inflationary policies conducive to price instability and balance of payments disequilibria at home and abroad.

This would imply, essentially, the adoption of fiscal and credit policies aiming at stimulating a level of consumption and investment demand sufficient, but no more than sufficient, to elicit and absorb a maximum use of each country's productive capacity. Richer countries, however, would be directed to maintain and finance—through private or official capital exports—a balance of payments surplus on current account [2] to the extent needed to accelerate the rhythm of economic development throughout the world and, possibly, to reduce present crying inequalities in national production and consumption levels. Conversely, the under-

2. And thus an excess of domestic production over domestic expenditures.

developed countries would be encouraged to finance in this way a larger flow of production investment than could be financed from domestic savings alone.

Secondly, each country would be required to carry out the readjustments in internal cost levels or exchange rates necessary to maintain, on the above basis, long-run equilibrium in its balance of payments and to absorb the net impact of mutual trade liberalization by itself and by others, as well as the impact of other structural changes in the international pattern of resources, tastes, and technology.

Finally, each country would be expected to cushion through so-called "compensatory policies" the disequilibrating impact of short-term, temporary balance of payments fluctuations upon domestic prices and economic activity. Fundamental price, income— or even exchange rate—adjustments should not be allowed, or wilfully resorted to, in order to eliminate such fluctuations, since they would have to be reversed later and would therefore introduce unnecessary disturbances in international as well as in domestic economic relations.

Most countries would probably agree, in theory, on the desirability of such policy prescriptions, and any international organization, whether supranational or not, should certainly bend its efforts to stimulate their adoption and implementation by all its members. It is painfully obvious, however, that no international organization or national government can trust to the full success of such policies.

First of all, some governments are likely to insist on their right to retain or restore restrictions for a variety of good or bad reasons, such as the old infant industry argument, the desire to protect certain sectors of the economy, the political pressures exercised by powerful vested interests, and so on. This is a fact of life which should indicate a first exception to the nondiscrimination rule—or the famed most-favored-nation clause—whenever it conflicts with the alternative principle of reciprocity as an effective technique for securing international commitments to trade and exchange liberalization. Neither technique should be entirely sacrificed to the other. First of all, no country should be allowed to block feasible liberalization agreements, or to claim indefinitely the benefit of other countries' liberalization commitments, if it persistently refuses to accept and honor reciprocal commitments toward others. On the other hand, a country should not be automatically excluded from the benefits of the agreement if compelling reasons prevent it from applying the same degree of liberalization as some of its stronger partners. Continued membership in the organization may be reconciled with different degrees of liberalization by the participating countries, and each member should be protected by the group against discriminatory restrictions as long as it can persuade the organization of the sincerity of its efforts to participate as fully as possible in the collective undertaking for trade and exchange liberalization.[3]

Secondly, the maintenance of compensatory policies may prove difficult for the deficit countries if their reserve level is insufficient and if adequate credits cannot be obtained from the creditor countries. This could, of course, be obviated by an additional rule of good behavior, requiring all countries to maintain, on an average of years, a persistent surplus in their balance of payments sufficient to feed the gradual increase in their international reserves necessary to keep them in line with the growth of production, money supply, and volume of foreign trade. Such a suggestion, however, would raise the further question as to whether current and prospective levels of gold production are adequate for this purpose or whether further provisions need be made to meet this problem.[4]

Surplus countries are not subject to the same limitation, since compensatory policies accelerate here the growth, rather than the depletion, of international reserves. The application of compensatory policies by surplus countries tends, indeed, to exercise a deflationary influence on other countries' reserves, export levels, and economic activity, while its application by deficit countries tends to exercise an expansionist effect on others. The fact that financial limitations may prevent a country from spending more than it earns, but not from spending less than it earns, imparts to the gold standard what has often been dubbed a "deflationary bias," in that it gives greater scope for compensatory policies by the surplus countries than by the deficit countries. This becomes particularly unfortunate if surplus countries resort to compensa-

3. It may be noted that this exception to nondiscrimination has been incorporated from the start in the OEEC Code of Liberalization, and was recognized by GATT as a valid justification for the discrimination against non-OEEC members implicitly authorized by the Code.

4. See below, pp. 297–301.

tory policies—improperly and against their own interests as well as the interests of others—at times when deflationary tendencies still prevail in their own economy and may indeed be in part responsible for their surpluses. Discrimination might be authorized, or even encouraged, in these cases, in order to put pressure on the creditor country to change its policies, or at least in order to enable other countries to preserve trade liberalization in their relations with one another.

All balance of payments disequilibria, however, cannot be blamed on the surplus countries. Inflationary excesses are indeed more attractive and difficult to resist than deflationary policies. Creditor countries are therefore on solid ground when objecting to any proposed system of automatic credits to deficit countries. They cannot escape—even though they may be able to offset—the impact of inflationary pressures from abroad insofar as other countries meet their deficits from their own gold and foreign exchange reserves. Automatic credits, however, would aggravate these pressures by increasing the size of the foreign deficits and, therefore, of the creditor countries' surpluses.

In the absence of external assistance, the deficit country will be forced by the depletion of its international reserves either to stop its inflation, or to devalue its currency, or to resort to trade or exchange restrictions. The first of these solutions will generally be deemed preferable to the second, and the second to the third. This is particularly true, however, for the deficit country itself. Its trade partners have a far smaller stake in the matter than is usually believed. They should not, for instance, object to an exchange rate devaluation which merely cancels the impact of cost inflation upon the devaluing country's exports and import levels and restores equilibrium in its balance of payments. The same reasoning would also apply in part to trade restrictions which reduce an inflated level of imports, although specific countries may in this case be hit harder than others by the nature of the import restrictions and by the fact that the restricting country will have to keep its over-all import level below that which it could afford if cost or exchange rate readjustments had stimulated a recovery of its exports. The reciprocity rule might again have to be invoked here to release other countries from their nondiscrimination commitments to the restricting country.

In general, however, the main danger arising from such a situation does not lie in resort by the deficit countries to exchange devaluation or to over-all trade and exchange restrictions, but in their use of bilateral bargaining power to extract special trade or credit concessions from their weaker partners. International monetary and trade agreements should erect the strongest possible safeguards against such tactics and the chain reaction which they might trigger. Mere prohibitions may prove unavailing in the face of powerful national interests. Far more important is the adoption of provisions designed to reduce the possibility of their being successful and to offer alternative and more promising forms of assistance to a country in difficulty. Member countries should band together to reject any bilateral trade or credit deals at one another's expense. Any unilateral resort to discrimination and currency inconvertibility should automatically release all other countries from their liberalization commitments toward the delinquent member. Finally, the international organization should be in a position to offer adequate credit assistance to its members to facilitate the adoption of agreed programs of balance of payments readjustment. This would not, of course, involve any automatic borrowing rights by the deficit countries, but would require some advance commitments by other members to make funds available for this purpose. The implications of this proposal will be discussed, in a broader context, in the last chapter of this study.

D. Conclusions

To conclude, world-wide trade and exchange cooperation should aim, first of all, at a maximum degree of liberalization, on a reciprocal and nondiscriminatory basis. Full currency transferability would be an indispensable component of such a program and a major deterrent to discrimination and bilateralism, either as a deliberate policy or as a defense against other countries' pressures for preferential treatment in trade or credit matters. The preservation of such transferability should not be left to each country's unilateral decisions, but should be collectively guaranteed through institutional arrangements enabling each country to make full multilateral use of its foreign exchange earnings to cover its foreign exchange payments, irrespective of the bilateral pattern of its external transactions.

Maximum efforts should be made to tide individual countries

over temporary difficulties and give them time to implement non-restrictive policies of balance of payments readjustment. If adequate credit facilities cannot be made available to them for this purpose, they should continue to enjoy the benefits of other countries' liberalization commitments even though they may themselves be forced to resort provisionally to nondiscriminatory trade or exchange restrictions, in accordance with some generally agreed escape clauses.

Two exceptions to the nondiscrimination rule, however, should be foreseen as an instrument of last resort, in order to preserve a maximum degree of liberalization. First of all, no country should be able to claim the benefit of other countries' liberalization commitments if it refuses to accept and implement reciprocal commitments consonant with the strength of its own balance of payments position. In other words, nondiscrimination should not be invoked in such a way as to block feasible progress toward liberalization on the basis of reciprocity.

Secondly, discrimination against a persistent creditor country may, under certain circumstances, become the only feasible alternative to generalized deflation or restrictions. In the next and final chapter of this study we shall explore various ways and means by which this principle might be more realistically implemented in practice than it has been so far under the scarce currency clause of the International Monetary Fund Agreement.

These suggestions remain disappointingly short of any ideal system of international economic organization. Any closer approximation to such an ideal, however, will depend essentially upon the slow development of political attitudes and administrative instruments appropriate to an international community, rather than to the coexistence of national sovereignties in an interdependent world.

III. REGIONAL COOPERATION AND WORLD-WIDE CONVERTIBILITY

A workable and viable system of monetary convertibility in the modern world must rest, therefore, on a network of reciprocal commitments, embracing positive as well as negative forms of cooperation and extending beyond the field of trade and exchange measures alone. The maintenance of convertibility is inseparable from a minimum degree of integration of national economic policies in general, and this integration can no longer be expected to flow automatically from spontaneous restraints by all countries on the use of their national sovereignty.

A. Regional and World-Wide Agreements

Ideally, the geographical framework of such integration should be that of the world itself. Under the *ceteris paribus* assumption dear to economic theorists, there can be no doubt that world-wide agreements would always be preferable to regional agreements. "Other things," however, are not equal, and rigid adherence to the universality rule would often slow down feasible progress by blocking agreements altogether or by limiting their actual content to a much lower common denominator than could be attained among a smaller number of participating countries.

We must recognize, first of all, the practical, administrative difficulties of negotiating agreements requiring unanimous acceptance by several scores of sovereign nations. Indispensable compromises would often be difficult to arrive at among "instructed" delegates, and would require the physical presence of top-level officials or statesmen retaining responsibility for daily management of their countries' affairs. Such meetings could be arranged only infrequently and would, even then, become extremely unwieldy in view of the sheer number of participants.

Secondly, these administrative problems are further complicated by deep-seated ideological divergences, reflecting wide variances in the economic evolution and real problems confronting, let us say, the U.S.S.R., Paraguay, the United States, and Switzerland. Common solutions are difficult to arrive at, and might often be objectively undesirable in view of the heterogeneity of national conditions confronting the various countries concerned. The monetary policies suitable to the United Kingdom are most unlikely to suit Bolivia.

Thirdly, provisions for mutual help, and particularly for credit assistance, will be difficult to negotiate among countries which have little or no contact with one another, little or no faith in the observation of each other's commitments, and little or no understanding of each other's problems and policies.

The degree of feasible cooperation and integration among sovereign countries will thus long remain highly dependent on the number and homogeneity of the participating countries. The larger and the more heterogeneous the group, the more modest the results that can realistically be aimed at.

This common-sense conclusion need not, however, be as disturbing to the internationally minded as they might think at first. Actual possibilities for cooperation and integration need not be sacrificed to the myth of systematic universalism. Internationalism is not desirable per se; it is desirable only insofar as it corresponds to real needs and problems. The difficult and time-consuming nature of world-wide negotiations is such that these should be reserved for truly world-wide conflicts rather than wasted on issues which can be solved at a more modest level. In many cases, the centralization of negotiations and decisions at the world level would constitute a handicap, an element of paralysis, and a source of international friction rather than an effective contribution to the solution of our problems.

Numerous difficulties involve a limited number of countries, and not the world as a whole. If a fishing conflict in the Baltic can be resolved by agreement among the countries concerned, it is hardly necessary to insist on the full participation of Bolivia and Australia before the agreement can be signed or put into force. Nor is it indispensable that a conflict in the Indian Ocean be resolved along exactly the same lines as in the Baltic Sea.

Many issues of trade and exchange policy also arise in their most acute form among a limited number of countries, and can be most fruitfully explored first through regional negotiation. Considerable progress may often be achieved with greater ease and speed by direct discussion among the countries most vitally concerned, and should not be delayed or impeded unnecessarily by rigid insistence on a world-wide negotiation of all the issues involved. The IMF consultations on the September 1949 devaluations, for instance, could have been less purely formal, if they had been preceded and prepared by more careful exploration at the regional level before being brought up to the Fund's Executive Board for decision. World-wide cooperation and agreements are certainly essential to avoid or resolve world-wide conflicts of interest, but they should not be overburdened with issues which can best be handled by a more limited negotiation among the countries most directly concerned.

The advantages of the regional approach are all the more evident when, as indicated above, agreements are dependent upon the acceptance by all participants of positive, long-range commitments about financial assistance, coordination of domestic monetary and fiscal policy, etc. To insist here upon world-wide agreements will often be tantamount to blocking action altogether.

To conclude: We should recognize the infinite diversity of real needs and possibilities for an effective coordination of individual or group decisions and activities. Many decisions in our daily life can be left without any inconvenience whatsoever to the individual. Others require only a coordination within the family or the business firm. Still others demand a broader coordination within the framework of a trade union, a business group, a city or township, or a state. A nearly complete liberalization of all obstacles to trade and payments has hardly proved possible up to now except on a national level, supported and sanctioned by the authority of a sovereign state. Regional agreements and organizations have nevertheless demonstrated their ability to solve pressing conflicts and to achieve intimate, even though incomplete, integration of economic policies among countries highly interdependent on one another, keenly conscious of their interdependence, and easily amenable to close cooperation because of similar national viewpoints resulting from a common geographical and historical background and a relatively homogeneous stage of economic development. Finally, looser forms of coordination on a world-wide scale remain both feasible and necessary as a framework for national or regional decisions and policies giving rise to conflicts of interest, real or imagined, which cannot be arbitrated on the regional level.

These various forms of integration are by no means alternative or exclusive of one another. They can, on the contrary, support and help one another. Their respective roles and fields of action should be delimited in each case in the light of a careful weighing of the concrete advantages, feasibility, and urgency of centralized decisions against the real costs, difficulties, and friction inseparable from such centralization.[1] This principle, long recognized by free nations in the delimitation of personal freedom, minority rights, and state powers, should be applied equally to the delimita-

1. See Tinbergen, *Centralization and Decentralization in Economic Policy,* Amsterdam, North-Holland Publishing Co., 1954.

tion of the respective fields of action of regional and world-wide integration. Within the regional framework itself, the close integration achieved by the three Benelux countries in the postwar years has proved perfectly compatible with the lesser integration of the six countries united in the European Coal and Steel Community and the more flexible integration still of the seventeen countries grouped in the Organization for European Economic Cooperation.

B. DISCRIMINATION AND TRADE DIVERSION

Regional forms of economic cooperation still meet adamant opposition from orthodox economists devoted to the higher ideal of universal free trade. This opposition is not based merely on a preference for world-wide liberalization over regional liberalization. It also implies a preference for *nondiscriminatory restrictions* over *discriminatory liberalization*. Nondiscrimination is regarded as a higher goal of policy than liberalization itself.

Rigid adherence to the principle of nondiscrimination raises, however, some very puzzling questions, as it would condemn not only regional liberalization agreements but also customs unions, and even the absence of internal barriers to trade within the national borders of a country. Any tariff wall or other import restriction discriminates against foreign trade and in favor of internal trade. Each one of our forty-eight states discriminates in favor of the other forty-seven, and against imports from foreign countries. The pure logic of nondiscrimination would require the partition of the United States into separate tariff areas, corresponding to our forty-eight states or to our three thousand counties, or to even smaller geographical units. It would deplore the gradual elimination, in the nineteenth century, of internal barriers to the movement of goods within each country's national borders, and applaud the breaking up, after the First World War, of the economic unity of Austria-Hungary and the erection of separate tariff walls around each one of the successor states in the Danubian basin.

The stillborn ITO Charter and the proposed OTC Charter both shuddered at such absurd conclusions and approved any regional lowering of tariffs or other trade barriers, provided that they be intended as preliminary stages toward the ultimate goal of a full customs union. This left many people puzzled as to why a little discrimination—i.e. tariff preferences—is bad, but a lot of it—i.e. a customs union—becomes good, at least according to these provisions.

Professor Viner had proposed, many years ago, a clear-cut economic criterion which would lead to different conclusions. Customs unions—and, presumably, trade preferences—can be good or bad depending on whether or not their "trade-creating" impact outweighs their "trade-diverting" impact. A customs union between France and Germany would be good insofar as it induced Frenchmen to buy the more economically produced German cars instead of manufacturing cars themselves, but bad insofar as it induced them to substitute German cars for the still more economically produced American cars. The world pattern of trade and production would improve in the first case, but deteriorate in the second, as a result of the customs union.[2]

Professor Haberler later made use of the same criterion to justify the ITO distinction between trade preferences and customs unions. The reduction of duties under preferential regimes is likely to be predominantly trade-diverting, "because there is a natural tendency to reduce trade barriers only for those commodities which do not actively compete with domestic production." On the other hand, "a customs union will always be to some extent, possibly to a large extent, trade creating." Yet Professor Haberler recognized that "in Europe the policy of regional trade liberalization (implying though it does discrimination against the United States, Canada, Latin America, Japan and others) has had some success and has gone beyond trade diversion, creating additional trade between the European countries. Fortunately [italics supplied], however, the discrimination against the United States, Canada, Latin America, has become progressively less severe because restrictions on imports from dollar countries have been reduced and currencies have become more freely convertible."[3]

This latter observation illustrates, to my mind, the fact that the main argument for regional economic integration lies outside the scope of mere economic reasoning of a static character. The lowering of restrictions on imports from nonmember countries

2. See Jacob Viner, *The Customs Union Issue*, New York, Carnegie Endowment for International Peace, 1950.

3. *Foreign Economic Policy:* Hearings Before the Subcommittee on Foreign Economic Policy of the Joint Committee on the Economic Report, 89th Congress (Washington, D.C., 1955), pp. 501, 505, and 507–8.

and the gradual extension of currency convertibility may well be a by-product of regional integration rather than an independent and fortunate accident. The trade-creating and trade-diverting effects of regional integration cannot be fully appraised by looking only at the immediate and direct trade concessions incorporated in a regional agreement. Indirect policy and incentives are far more significant for arriving at a broad judgment of the over-all impact of the agreement on future trade patterns.

Trade restrictions are not desirable per se, and it is not in a country's interests to divert its imports from cheaper to costlier sources of supply. The main spur to restrictive or discriminatory policies lies in the difficulties which a country may encounter in reconciling full employment with equilibrium in its balance of payments. Insofar as regional agreements are trade-diverting rather than trade-creating, they tend to increase each participating country's exports while leaving its imports unchanged, to improve the over-all balance of payments of the group as a whole, and to stimulate a fuller employment of its resources. This should decrease incentives to restrictions against imports from third countries; and the liberalization of such restrictions should, in turn, offset part of the initial trade-diverting impact of the agreement. Only as full employment is approached will these favorable effects disappear, as larger exports to member countries would then tend to create inflationary pressures, increase production costs, and lower export capacity and price competitiveness in trade relations with non-member countries.

The lowering of trade barriers among the member countries, moreover, does not merely increase trade within the area itself. It also results in a lowering of production costs, and therefore in greater price competitiveness in world markets as well.[4] The elimination of discrimination among member countries also tends in the same direction, even if it does not create trade within the area, but merely reshuffles existing trade into a more economic pattern.

Thirdly, the conclusion of a regional agreement does not merely

4. This will always be true as far as the trade-creating impact of the agreement is concerned. Trade-diverting liberalization measures will also lower production costs for individual importers if such measures operate through tariff reductions rather than through a geographical redistribution of import or exchange licenses, but this may be offset by the consequent reduction in customs revenue and the incidence of budgetary deficits or new taxes upon internal prices and costs.

ensure an immediate lowering of trade barriers within the area. It usually introduces certain safeguards against future unilateral recourses to trade and exchange restrictions by member countries against one another and therefore introduces a greater degree of security in foreign trade within the area. This security may be as significant as liberalization itself as an incentive for the prospecting and development of export markets by the lower cost producers in the area. It may also play a vital role in limiting the spread of deflationary tendencies and trade restrictions from one country to another in the event of an international recession.

Finally, the substantive content of regional agreements can hardly be confined to trade liberalization alone. Trade liberalization will have to be supported by mutual credit commitments, and these in turn will have to be supported by an increasing willingness of members to consult with other members on various aspects of their monetary and economic policies, internal as well as external. Regional agreements may thus become a driving force for the development of an increasing administrative and political cohesion among their members, eroding gradually outworn concepts and institutions of economic sovereignty and providing a flexible transition toward broader forms of economic and political organization better adapted to modern needs and conditions.

These various considerations seem to me to create a far stronger presumption in favor of regional agreements than that which might emerge from a purely static and exclusively economic interpretation of the balance between their immediate trade-creating and trade-diverting impacts. Yet it is still no more than a presumption, which may be strengthened or weakened by the concrete circumstances surrounding actual experiments in economic integration. If, for instance, regional integration tended in fact to divide the world into rival blocs bent on protectionist, autarkic policies, we would view it with much greater misgivings than if it created instead a large and stable area of freer trade, gradually drawing nonmember countries into its orbit.

Postwar integration has clearly developed in the latter, rather than the former, direction. Formal cooperation among OEEC countries was extended through EPU to an area whose total trade accounts for nearly 60% of world trade. Harmonization of this area's trade and payments policies with those of the United States and Canada would cover about 80% of world trade, and would be tantamount to establishing a universal framework for world trade and monetary settlements. The regional approach would blend, in this case, into the world-wide approach to economic co-operation.

Regional economic integration is indeed unlikely to lead to the formation of rival autarkic blocs for the simple reason that this would require a most radical upheaval in the world trade pattern. The formation of EPU was greatly enhanced by the fact that exports to the EPU area have long accounted for 70% to 75% of the total exports of most EPU countries. This was already true in pre-war days at a time when currency convertibility prevailed and trade and exchange restrictions were at a minimum over most of the present EPU area.

Trade patterns in other parts of the world are very different indeed. A Latin American union, for instance, would regulate only 10% of the total exports of its members. Even a Western Hemisphere bloc would include only 53% of the participating countries' exports, and substantially less than this (43%) for the southern countries of the group, whose main export markets (47%) are in the EPU area itself (see Table XXI and Appendix Table 29). For reasons amply discussed above, effective regional agreements are likely to be concluded only among countries closely interdependent on one another, and this would seem to preclude the duplication of EPU types of arrangement in other parts of the world.[5]

Let us, therefore, limit our further discussion to the quantitative significance of EPU discrimination toward third countries, and of third countries' discrimination in their mutual trade and in their trade with EPU.

We should remark first of all that the trade-creating impact of the EPU Agreement is likely to be far larger than its trade-diverting impact, owing to the fact that the first may affect favorably the much larger volume of intra-area trade (about three fourths of total trade), while the latter can apply unfavorably only to the much smaller volume of extra-area trade (one fourth). Secondly, every extension of trade liberalization makes it more and more difficult to apply it only to such commodities as were previ-

---

5. This is not to say, however, that other countries might not find it useful to conclude different types of arrangements aiming primarily at strengthening their bargaining position in trade negotiations with nonmember countries.

ously imported from third countries, and to exclude from it the categories of merchandise domestically produced under the spur of existing restrictions. Thirdly, imports from nonmember countries, particularly from the dollar area, were already so severely restricted in 1949 that there remained little scope for further trade diversion measures as a result of the EPU Agreement.

Actual data on trade movements from 1949 to 1955 are, as always, difficult to interpret. The over-all trade of OEEC countries expanded by about 65%, in dollar terms, following the adoption of the EPU Agreement. Exports increased 77% and imports 56%. The changes in the geographical pattern of imports would suggest, at first view, a substantial amount of trade diversion, since imports from EPU sources rose by 64% while those from other sources rose only by 19%. This difference, however, can be more than accounted for by the contraction of extraordinary foreign assistance and abnormal import needs for reconstruction, and by the recovery of Europe's productive capacity. The bogey of a "high cost, sheltered area," raised against EPU in 1949, is directly contradicted by the fact that the increase in European exports to the dollar area over these six years (159%) was more than twice as large as the increase in exports to the EPU area itself (76%).

To conclude, the opponents of regional integration must reconcile their criticisms and forebodings with the following evidence:

1. The elimination of the huge balance of payments deficits of 1949 Europe, and the achievement of substantial surpluses on current account throughout the years 1953–56;

2. The abatement of internal inflationary pressures and the considerable stability of prices which has prevailed, in most countries, during the recent years;

3. The maintenance throughout of an exceptionally high and growing volume of economic activity and employment;

4. The elimination of bilateralism in intra-European trade, the liberalization of trade and exchange restrictions within the OEEC area, and the gradual extension of these liberalization measures to trade and exchange transactions with nonmember countries;

5. The enormous expansion of intra-European trade and the even larger growth of European exports toward the dollar area;

6. The steep increase in OEEC imports from non-OEEC sources (10%), particularly from the dollar area (40%), in 1953–55.

The implications of these achievements for the restoration and maintenance of *world-wide* convertibility will be explored presently.

C. De Jure Commitments and De Facto Policies

The de jure consolidation of nondiscrimination, trade liberalization, and currency transferability within the EPU area necessarily exerts a powerful impact outside that area itself. The absence of similar de jure commitments in trade relations among or with third countries by no means precludes an abatement of discriminatory practices outside the jurisdiction of the EPU Agreement itself. There are, on the contrary, many reasons why contractual convertibility among EPU members should spur progress toward at least de facto convertibility outside the EPU area.

No country has a direct interest in discrimination, i.e. in shifting its imports from less costly to costlier sources of supply, except as a means to extract from its trade partners similar discrimination in its own favor, or to protect its exports against unfavorable discrimination by them. The EPU Agreement, however, together with the nondiscriminatory policies generally pursued by the dollar area, effectively safeguard against discrimination 85% of the EPU countries' exports, and preclude the use of discrimination as a weapon for expanding these exports. All other countries together absorb only 15% of EPU countries' exports, and their own exports account for only 16% of total world exports (see Table XXI). This leaves relatively little room for discrimination, particularly if one considers that profitable discrimination requires in each case mutual action by at least two countries.

EPU countries have, moreover, an interest in avoiding discriminatory arrangements concluded with third countries at one another's expense. Recent EPU consultations have been dealing with this problem and have already led to a substantial contraction of credit margins in payments agreements with nonmember countries, to a large decline in the number of such agreements, and to the adoption of transferable EPU currencies for settlements with inconvertible countries. The main concern underlying residual bilateral payments provisions is to guarantee debt repayment by the partner country rather than to promote a further expansion of exports through discriminatory trade and payment practices.

The increasing reluctance of EPU countries to perpetuate bilateral trade and payments agreements makes it correspondingly difficult for third countries to maintain such agreements with their major trading partners. Since the overwhelming bulk of their own trade is with the EPU countries, the United States, and Canada, the remaining opportunities for discrimination and bilateralism are becoming so scant as to be of little significance for world trade and payments in general. The essential point is that the broad direction of the international trade and payments system toward or away from convertibility is determined by the policies of the major trading nations. These can force their weaker partners into convertibility as well as into inconvertibility, but the smaller countries cannot exercise the same influence upon the larger ones.

Table XXI. REGIONAL DISTRIBUTION OF WORLD EXPORTS IN 1954

		Exports to		
Exports from	*World*	*EPU Area*	*Dollar Area*	*Other Countries*
EPU Area	58	73	11	15
Dollar Area	27	34	50	16
Other Countries	16	51	22	27
World	100	60	23	17

Note:
Exports to (first column) and from (last row) the world are given in % of world totals. The other data are given in % of each area's total exports to the world.

Source:
For further details, see Appendix Table 30, and *International Trade, 1955* (Geneva, GATT, May 1956), pp. 201–3 and 222–3.

This is why firmer, de jure arrangements among the latter are both necessary, under modern conditions, and sufficient to restore and maintain international convertibility. Trade and payments relations not covered specifically by these agreements will depend on the de facto policies pursued by the countries concerned, but will offer few opportunities, incentives, or pressures for discrimination and bilateralism, except as a protection of last resort against the international spread of deflation or restrictions.

Such a mixture of de jure and de facto convertibility may not be sufficient, of course, to ensure the continued progress of trade liberalization and exchange rate stability among all the countries of the world. Broader negotiations, within the framework of the OTC and the IMF, will retain a major role in this respect, but it will be helped rather than hindered by the closer degree of cooperation and integration which may be achieved under regional agreements. It should finally be noted that even nineteenth-century convertibility rested essentially on the maintenance of convertibility policies by European countries and the United States, but did not preclude varying degrees of trade restriction and protectionism by individual countries, and of exchange rate instability in Latin America and Asia. Similar limitations on any ideal pattern of international economic institutions are likely to remain with us as long as political and administrative difficulties make it utopian to contemplate a merger of national sovereignties into an effective world government.

CHAPTER 8

Current Prospects and
Conclusions: The Tasks Ahead

THE PRACTICAL conclusion of this study may be expressed in a nutshell: Convertibility is around the corner, but we must still turn that corner and, most of all, make sure that the next storm will not push us back too easily and inevitably into the path of deflation, restrictions, and bilateralism.

I. THE RETURN TO CONVERTIBILITY

It would be difficult to imagine more favorable circumstances for the restoration of international convertibility than those that prevail today. Indeed, they are so exceptionally and abnormally auspicious as to make it highly unlikely that such an opportunity will last indefinitely, and highly desirable to strike while the iron is hot.

The dollar shortage of the early postwar years has been succeeded by a large and growing outflow of dollars from the United States to the rest of the world, far in excess of total dollar disbursements by foreign countries. Excluding foreign aid, this outflow is nearly seven times as large in current dollars, and more than three times as large in constant purchasing power, as it was in the late 1930's (see Chart V, p. 15, and Appendix Table 6). Foreign countries' purchases from the United States have risen to record levels, but our current account surplus has nevertheless been reduced to an order of magnitude roughly equivalent to that of our private capital exports. Most of our foreign aid and official lending, as well as most of the current additions to the world gold stock, have thus gone into an unprecedented build-up of gold reserves and dollar holdings outside the United States. These have risen from $19 billion at the end of 1949 to $32.5 billion in mid-1956, while our own gold holdings declined by $2.7 billion and our short-term liabilities abroad increased by $7.9 billion. Foreign countries' dollar holdings now exceed total sterling balances, and are twice as large as the sterling balances held outside the British colonies (see Table XXII).

Table XXII. FOREIGN-HELD DOLLAR AND STERLING BALANCES, 1939–55

(in billions of U.S. dollars)

	1939	1945	1946	1947	1948	1949	1950	1951	1952	1953	1954	1955
I. *Dollar Balances* a	3.2	6.9	6.0	4.9	5.9	6.4	8.4	8.3	9.9	10.8	11.9	13.0
A. *Official* b	1.0	4.2	3.0	1.9	2.9	3.2	4.6	4.2	5.5	6.3	7.3	8.4
B. *Private*	2.2	2.7	3.0	3.0	3.0	3.2	3.8	4.1	4.4	4.5	4.6	4.6
II. *Sterling Balances*	2.1	14.9	15.0	14.5	13.8	9.6	10.5	10.7	9.6	10.4	10.9	10.5
A. *U.K. Colonies*	(0.5)	1.8	2.0	2.1	2.2	1.6	2.1	2.6	2.9	3.1	3.4	3.6
B. *Other*	(1.6)	13.1	13.0	12.5	11.5	7.9	8.4	8.1	6.7	7.3	7.5	6.9
1. £ area countries	(1.0)	8.1	7.8	7.2	7.3	5.0	5.6	5.2	4.6	5.1	5.1	4.7
2. Other countries	(0.6)	5.0	5.2	5.3	4.3	3.0	2.8	2.9	2.1	2.2	2.4	2.2
III. *Total*	5.3	21.8	21.0	19.4	19.7	16.0	18.9	18.9	19.5	21.2	22.8	23.5

Notes:
a. Excluding international institutions, but including EPU and BIS holdings and, after 1948, U.S. government bonds and notes with original maturities of more than one year.
b. As estimated in *International Financial Statistics* (Aug. 1956), p. 19, and former issues.

Sources:
Federal Reserve Bulletin and *International Financial Statistics.*

This vast redistribution of international reserves from the United States to foreign countries has probably established a better over-all reserve pattern with relation to needs than could be found at any previous time in history (see Chart IV, p. 13, and Appendix Table 5). The main exception to this generalization—and a very important one indeed—is the persistent inadequacy of the reserve position of the United Kingdom, whose gold reserves and dollar holdings continue to fluctuate widely from year to year and provide only a fractional cover for foreign-held sterling balances. Yet these are less worrisome today than they were at the end of the war. Sterling liabilities to the independent sterling area countries have dropped from $8.1 billion in 1945 to $4.7 billion at the end of 1955, and those to nonsterling area countries from $5.0 billion to $2.2 billion.

Chart XXI and Table XXIII give a rough indication of the relative progress of the major world areas toward better balance in their over-all gold and dollar transactions. The basic recovery of Western Europe's balance of payments is shown by the fact that the rise in its gold reserves and dollar assets in the last three years ($5.8 billion) exceeded its total receipts of United States economic aid and net official capital ($2.6 billion) by as much as $3.2 billion. Most of this amount ($3 billion), however, is attributable to the continental OEEC countries, and only $200 million to the European sterling area. Nevertheless, the only region of the world which experienced substantial deficits—before aid—was the motley group of countries outside the Western Hemisphere and the EPU area. This includes such countries as Nationalist China, South Korea, and Vietnam, whose balance of payments remained overwhelmingly influenced by political disturbances, military operations, and a growing volume of American assistance.

The vanishing of the world dollar gap and the large surpluses currently accumulated by Western Europe constitute a most favorable environment for a return to currency convertibility, in the sense defined in the previous chapter. The data reviewed above also explain the recent slowing down of the convertibility drive in the United Kingdom and the incipient shift of British opinion away from a unilateral dash into convertibility toward the maintenance—and possible tightening—of the sterling area's association with the continental OEEC countries.

Most encouraging of all is the fact that the strengthening of Europe's balance of payments was not achieved at the cost of renewed deflation, nor even of any slowdown in the rate of economic growth. The years 1952–55 have witnessed, indeed, a sustained increase in Europe's GNP, averaging in volume terms 5% to 6% annually, i.e. more than twice that of the United States.

This progress has been accompanied by a remarkable degree of price stability and by a considerable relaxation of bilateralism, discrimination, and trade and exchange controls in general. The quantitative significance of the remaining obstacles to de facto convertibility is now small, or even negligible, in nearly all countries of Western Europe.

Finally, public opinion is far more aware today than it was in the 1930's or 1940's of the disadvantages and limitations of trade and exchange restrictions, and particularly of discrimination and

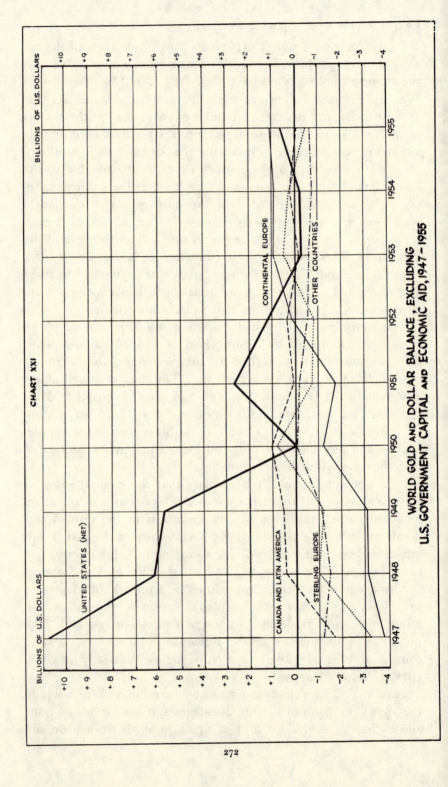

CHART XXI

BILLIONS OF U.S. DOLLARS

UNITED STATES (NET)

CANADA AND LATIN AMERICA

STERLING EUROPE

CONTINENTAL EUROPE

OTHER COUNTRIES

WORLD GOLD AND DOLLAR BALANCE, EXCLUDING
U.S. GOVERNMENT CAPITAL AND ECONOMIC AID, 1947-1955

ECONOMIC AID, 1946-55

(in billions of U.S. dollars)

	United States (1) = -(3+4-2)	Gold Monetization Outside the U.S. (2)	International Institutions (3)	Foreign Countries					
				Total (4 = 5 + 8 + 9)	Western Europe and Dependencies			Canada and Latin America (8)	Other Countries (9)
					Total (5 = 6 + 7)	Continental (6)	Sterling (7)		
I. Years									
1946	+6.9	+0.4	-1.4	-5.1	-3.3	-3.1	-0.2	-0.5	-1.3
1947	+10.8	+0.4	-0.4	-9.9	-7.1	-3.8	-3.3	-1.7	-1.2
1948	+6.1	+0.4	-0.4	-5.3	-4.2	-3.2	-1.1	+0.4	-1.5
1949	+5.7	+0.5	-0.2	-5.0	-4.3	-3.1	-1.2	+0.5	-1.1
1950	—	+0.4	-0.1	+0.5	-0.4	-1.2	+0.8	+1.0	-0.1
1951	+2.7	+0.1	+0.1	-2.6	-2.5	-1.7	-0.8	+0.2	-0.2
1952	+1.1	+0.3	+0.1	-0.9	-0.7	+0.1	-0.8	+0.4	-0.6
1953	-0.3	+0.4	—	+0.7	+1.5	+0.9	+0.5	-0.1	-0.6
1954	-0.2	+0.6	+0.2	+0.6	+1.1	+0.9	+0.2	+0.2	-0.7
1955	+0.7	+0.6	+0.1	-0.2	+0.6	+1.1	-0.5	-0.1	-0.7
II. Totals									
1947-49	+22.6	+1.3	-1.1	-20.2	-15.6	-10.1	-5.6	-0.8	-3.8
1950-52	+3.7	+0.9	+0.1	-3.0	-3.7	-2.8	-0.8	+1.6	-0.9
1953-55	+0.2	+1.7	+0.3	+1.2	+3.2	+3.0	+0.2	—	-2.0

Sources:

U.S. government capital and economic aid (from the U.S. balance of payments estimates of the *Survey of Current Business*) are deducted from the increase—or added to the decrease—in foreign countries' gold reserves (from the *Federal Reserve Bulletin* estimates) and other dollar assets (from the *Survey of Current Business*), to arrive at this over-all gold and dollar balance exclusive of net official U.S. grants and loans.

The over-all balance for the U.S. (col. 1) corresponds, with reverse sign, to the surpluses or deficits of the rest of the world (cols. 3 + 4) *plus* current gold monetization (col. 2). Estimates for the latter are derived from the comparison of U.S. gold sales and purchases (from the *Survey of Current Business*) with the estimated changes in gold reserves outside the U.S. (from the *Federal Reserve Bulletin*).

bilateralism. The impact of these measures on resource allocation, production costs, and living standards had always been recognized; but bitter experience has dispelled earlier illusions about their efficacy in controlling international capital movements and channeling savings into socially desirable investments. A minimum degree of exchange freedom as well as of exchange stability is now admitted to be indispensable for a satisfactory functioning of capital markets, domestically as well as internationally. In the situation of acute scarcities which prevailed during the war and the early postwar years, rationing had inevitably displaced monetary and fiscal policies as a main weapon for the adjustment of expenditures to available resources. The postwar recovery of production has been accompanied by an opposite trend toward the rehabilitation of monetary and fiscal policies, and convincing evidence has piled up everywhere as to the efficacy of these policies in dealing with "normal" strains and pressures on a country's internal and external equilibrium in an expanding world economy.

Very little remains to be done today to return the world—although not every single country—to international convertibility. Most European countries are prepared to follow immediately any British initiative in this direction, and some have indeed moved far ahead of Britain already.[1] Britain herself has made abundantly clear her determination to restore convertibility at the earliest opportunity, and will undoubtedly do so if she succeeds, as now appears likely, in further strengthening her balance of payments position and her international reserve level.

Convertibility thus appears possible today. The main question at issue is whether it would be capable of weathering tomorrow a resurgence of deflationary trends or restrictive policies in the United States, or inflationary pressures and unilateral inconvertibility decisions in other parts of the world. As long as these uncertainties persist, some countries will remain reluctant—and all would be unwise—to dramatize their de facto progress toward convertibility by spectacular de jure proclamations or commitments unilaterally mortgaging their future freedom of action.

1. When questioned last year about the timing of a rumored convertibility move, Herman J. Abs, President of the Deutsche Bank, answered that with luck, wisdom, and courage, Germany would restore convertibility five minutes after England. See *Deutsch-Englisches Gespräch 1954*, Deutsch-Englische Gesellschaft E.V., p. 36.

II. THE MAINTENANCE OF CONVERTIBILITY

The maintenance of international convertibility, once restored, will depend primarily on the national policies that the major trading countries will follow in the future. Its successful operation, however, will require in addition some further strengthening of the regional and international institutions and agreements governing trade and payments relations among independent countries in an interdependent world.

Each country has a national interest in the promotion of a high and expanding level of employment and economic activity for its people, in the most economic allocation of its resources in accordance with their needs and desires, and in the avoidance of inflationary monetary pressures on domestic prices and the balance of payments. These objectives of national policy coincide with those of the international community itself. If they were unflinchingly pursued and successfully implemented at all times by all the major trading nations, there would remain relatively few problems requiring international cooperation and agreements in the monetary and trade field.

In practice, however, a variety of other motives, good or bad from the national point of view itself, have the nasty habit of interfering with the benevolent "invisible hand" of Adam Smith, and of initiating international disturbances which tend to spread from country to country. International agreements and institutions should try to prevent the emergence of such disturbances, but one can hardly expect them to be fully successful in this respect. Their efficacy will often have to be measured, more modestly, by their ability to circumscribe the damage. Firebreaks and fire engines have often proved useful, even in the middle of fire prevention week.

In any case, the strains which a convertibility system must be ready to face depend, first of all, on future economic developments and policies in individual countries, particularly in the United States. The special position occupied by the United States in this respect derives from the fact that it is by far the major economic power in the world today. Its national production is about twice that of all the OEEC countries combined, and eight times as large as that of the second largest production in the free world, that of the

United Kingdom.[1] While its importance in world trade is far less overwhelming (about 20% of world exports, against 30% for the continental OEEC countries, 25% for the sterling area as a whole, and 10% for the United Kingdom alone), it is a major source of supply for commodities essential to other countries' economic life and development.

This gives the United States considerable leverage on other countries' trading policies. Its willingness and ability to expand its imports through tariff reductions and the maintenance of a high level of domestic economic activity greatly facilitate the adoption of similar policies by other countries. U.S. leadership in trade and tariff negotiations can hasten this process and consolidate the progress already achieved toward the promotion of mutually profitable international trade. On the other hand, any outburst of deflation or protectionism in the United States could quickly reverse this progress and lead the world back into depression and trade restrictions, unless further safeguards can be erected against nationalistic, beggar-my-neighbor policies abroad.

Our postwar policies have fortunately followed the first, rather than the second, of these two patterns. We have been remarkably successful in maintaining a high and expanding level of economic activity, and both the Truman and the Eisenhower Administrations have pursued, with only minor blemishes and concessions to pressure groups and political expediency, the tariff liberalization policies initiated by Cordell Hull some twenty years ago. We have assisted through enormous grants and loans the restoration of war-destroyed economies and have initiated, even though on a modest scale as yet, a policy of active support for economic development in other areas of the world. Finally, the persistent upward trend in our price and wage levels, our rapidly growing imports of goods and services, and the dramatic shift of international reserves from the United States to foreign countries in the last six years all testify to the absence of any deflationary pressure by the United States on the rest of the world economy. If anything, we may at the moment be straining our own resources and

1. Dollar terms comparisons, however, probably exaggerate the discrepancy between GNP in the United States and abroad. For an interesting attempt at more realistic comparisons, see Milton Gilbert and Irving Kravis, *An International Comparison of National Products and the Purchasing Power of Currencies*, Paris, OEEC, 1954.

sailing dangerously close to the Charybdis of domestic inflation and the Scylla of excessive reserve losses.

None of these observations can rule out the possibility of a later resurgence of the dollar shortage. They are sufficient, however, to justify the adoption of trade and exchange policies predicated on the probability that such a shortage can be avoided if other countries succeed in controlling inflationary pressures on their own economies. The main threat to the maintenance of convertibility by the European countries lies indeed in their own policies rather than in those of the United States. This should be obvious when one reflects that total exports of the OEEC countries to the United States represent no more than 14% of their combined gold and dollar holdings, 7% of their world exports, and 1% of their Gross National Product. Their exports to the EPU area are more than ten times as large as their exports to the United States, and account for three fourths of their total exports to the world. Balance of payments pressures are therefore overwhelmingly dominated by their mutual trade rather than by fluctuations in their exports either to the United States or even to non-EPU countries in general. The devastating impact which United States recessions or restrictions have exercised at times upon the European economy has been due, to a major extent, to internal weaknesses within the area itself, and particularly to the rapid spread of balance of payments pressures from one country to another owing to the divergent pace of national inflationary or deflationary developments and to the simultaneous adoption of mutually defeating restrictions, discrimination, and bilateral deals in the conduct of their trade and payments relationships with one another.

Regional cooperation and reciprocal commitments among the OEEC countries have played a vital role in their progress toward convertibility and trade liberalization. They have tended to strengthen these countries' resistance to outside deflationary pressures and may have been an important factor in preventing the spread of the 1954 American recession to Europe and even to third countries. Continued prosperity and relaxation of restrictions in Europe are generally regarded as having contributed to the mildness of this recession in the United States itself.

There can be no question that the OEEC-EPU system of trade and financial commitments has also strengthened the resistance of European countries to the spread of intra-European disequilibria, restrictions, and bilateralism, and has helped consolidate and enlarge the advances toward more liberal trade and payments policies.

These institutional changes should therefore facilitate the restoration and maintenance of workable convertibility in Europe. Protracted controversies have arisen, however, between those who would integrate these arrangements within a modernized system of workable convertibility and those who regard their abandonment as an essential step for the restoration of world-wide convertibility. The triumph of the latter thesis would probably have postponed the general acceptance of convertibility commitments by European countries. It would certainly have restored convertibility under conditions leaving it highly vulnerable to future unfavorable developments in the world economy.

The European Monetary Agreement has succeeded in reconciling these divergent views by admitting the need for some permanent forms of trade and financial cooperation and commitments among the OEEC countries. The concrete details of that Agreement, however, mark in some respects a retrogression with respect to the EPU system. Most of all, they fail to take full advantage of the progress achieved since 1950 in order to harmonize more fully the methods by which European countries can simultaneously pursue the complementary objectives of regional integration and world-wide convertibility. The periodic revisions contemplated in the Agreement fortunately keep the door open for the improvements necessary to its future viability and success.

The shortcomings of the European Monetary Agreement, in its present form, illustrate the limitations placed upon OEEC by British participation in the Organization. The reluctance of Great Britain to associate itself too closely with Europe accounts, in large part, for the timidity and hesitancy of OEEC's progress toward permanent forms of integration, and for the parallel development of a bolder approach to the problem among the six countries of the European Coal and Steel Community. When, however, the six countries announced their intention to draft, in the latter part of 1956, treaties setting up a European Atomic Authority and a European Common Market, the United Kingdom announced its support for an alternative or complementary OEEC arrangement for cooperation in the atomic field, and began to explore with its

European partners the possibility of joining them into a so-called "free trade area." [2] The delayed acceptance of EPU itself by Britain in the spring of 1950, when that country was similarly presented with the prospect of an alternative Fibenel Agreement, was in a sense a forerunner of what may be happening today. Britain, however, insisted at that time, and continued to insist until June 1955, on the temporary nature of the EPU Agreement and on the need to terminate it as soon as circumstances would permit. Its last-minute conversion to a permanent European Monetary Agreement, in the summer of 1955, marked the first breach in a well-established policy, but was still tempered by a strong emphasis on world-wide rather than regional objectives and by a minimization of the effective role entrusted to European institutions in the technical operation of the Agreement. The formation of a free trade area encompassing all of Western Europe and closely allied with the rest of the British Commonwealth would certainly constitute a revolutionary break with the past and carry momentous implications for the future.

Two world wars have sapped the financial and economic strength of the United Kingdom to such an extent as to cast growing doubts everywhere about its ability to resume its traditional position as the sole core and support of the enormous superstructure erected, in former days, upon sterling trade and sterling financing. A closer association with continental Europe would, however, provide an immeasurably stronger center for the system, while at the same time considerably reducing the fluctuations impinging upon it. It might even be, in the long run, the only way to combat the centrifugal tendencies which have manifested themselves from time to time since the war and have threatened the survival of the financial and economic links between the independent countries of the Commonwealth.

Official American policy has, so far, welcomed and encouraged this line of development. The desire to strengthen the free world against the Communist menace has generally stilled our relentless opposition to all forms of preference and discrimination in trade

2. As distinct from the common market, the free trade area would not require the uniformization of member countries' tariffs toward nonparticipating countries, and would permit the maintenance of Commonwealth preferences in non-European trade. The exclusion of agricultural products from the scope of the free trade area would also preserve such preferences even with respect to British imports from Europe.

and payments. The conflict between political and economic motivations continues, however, to smolder under the surface of official pronouncements and to foster interagency squabbles and policy vacillations in Washington. A broader understanding of the economic as well as of the political issues involved is very much to be desired. Regional cooperation and agreements need not spell out a withdrawal into regional autarky. They may, on the contrary, help weed out nationalistic interferences which are damaging to competitive forces within the area and hinder its ability to withstand competition from the outside. They may also help combat the international spread of deflation and restrictions and introduce "built-in stabilizers" indispensable to the satisfactory performance, and therefore to the effective maintenance, of a relatively free international economic system. By decreasing the vulnerability of foreign economies to American recessions, they would also tend to moderate, rather than intensify, economic fluctuations here, and reduce the need for United States assistance abroad. Our self-interest in a true internationalization of the gold exchange standard [3] is particularly evident in this respect.

It has been argued above [4] that further progress toward regional integration is both more essential and feasible within the EPU area than among other countries whose economic interdependence is more diffuse and does not lend itself, therefore, to regional agreements of this character. Regional integration must, in any case, be inserted into world-wide cooperation if it is to be truly beneficial to all concerned. The next two sections of this study will therefore explore the needs and possibilities for further progress toward European integration and world-wide cooperation in trade and payments.

III. THE INSTITUTIONS OF REGIONAL MONETARY INTEGRATION IN EUROPE

A. The European Monetary Agreement

The role of regional integration in the consolidation of convertibility can first be discussed most realistically with reference to

3. See below, pp. 296–301.
4. See Chap. 7, pp. 263–8.

existing institutions and already agreed-upon plans, i.e. with reference to EPU and the European Monetary Agreement.

The availability of short-term stabilization credits to help a country meet temporary difficulties in its balance of payments is a most important feature of both Agreements. The EMA improves considerably on EPU in this respect by making these credits discretionary rather than automatic, and by subordinating them to agreed criteria with respect both to needs and to the readjustment policies to be pursued by the borrowing country. Automatic credits, governed by regional balance of payments criteria alone, have long been totally absurd and unrealistic, particularly when account is taken of the growing size of transferable European currencies in settlement outside the EPU area. The EMA reform on this point is very much overdue, and there is no reason why it could not be implemented immediately in advance of the other provisions of the European Monetary Agreement. The substitution of full cash payments for the present system of 75% cash and 25% credit would, of course, be welcomed by the creditor countries (Germany, Belgium, the Netherlands, Switzerland, and Sweden). Among the present debtors, five already settle all or most of their deficits on a 100% gold basis, either because their quota is blocked (Greece) or exhausted (Turkey) or because they have freely elected to do so in view of their over-all reserve position (France, Portugal, and Austria). The total amount of automatic credits available on July 1, 1956 to all other debtors together, the United Kingdom excepted, was only about $100 million, i.e. less than one fourth of the gold and dollar assets of EPU and one sixth of the capital assigned to the European Fund. The only debtor country which still had at its disposal a substantial amount of automatic credits in EPU ($350 million) was the United Kingdom. The timing of a shift from automatic to discretionary credits thus depends primarily on the agreement of the United Kingdom, and this agreement in turn is likely to be influenced by the future course of the United Kingdom's balance of payments.

Another reform of EPU contemplated in the European Monetary Agreement would essentially make more explicit, rather than modify, the recent evolution toward the restoration of free exchange markets. In the early days of EPU, the balances communicated to the Agent at the end of each month by the European central banks had been accumulated by them during the month under the operation of bilateral payments agreements. With the reopening of free exchange markets, however, and the introduction of multilateral arbitrage agreements, a growing portion of central bank balances result from stabilization interventions of central banks in the market rather than from direct bookkeeping transactions between them. The European Monetary Agreement takes for granted that this new procedure will become the more normal and general one, but it still leaves room for bilateral payments agreements with the countries which do not make their currencies convertible.

The desirability of the additional EPU reforms contemplated in the European Monetary Agreement is more debatable.

The first of these would open the door to much wider fluctuations around parity in the market exchange rates of member currencies. Each country would be left free to fix and modify the margin between its official buying and selling rates, and to let its currency fluctuate within these limits. While the Agreement states the intention of the members to keep these margins as moderate and as stable as possible, it is generally known that a margin of 6%—3% below and 3% above par—was often mentioned as illustrative of the United Kingdom's intentions. This would permit a maximum discount of 6% of, let us say, the French franc vis-à-vis the pound, and this discount might later be reversed through an appreciation of the franc and a depreciation of the pound, allowing for a total fluctuation, over time, of 12% between the two currencies. Under the present arbitrage scheme, the maximum spread allowed between the strongest and the weakest currency is only ¾ of 1%, and the maximum fluctuation over time 1½%. The EMA might thus increase these spreads and fluctuations to eight times those allowable under the present arbitrage system.

Secondly, EPU compensations and settlements are now based uniformly on the par value of the currencies involved. Under EMA, they would usually take place at either the official buying rate or the official selling rate communicated to the Agent, whichever is most unfavorable to the country requesting the settlement. This would reduce the compensation machinery to a clearing of last resort only, since central banks could instead buy and sell their balances on the private market at rates which could not be worse, and would often be far more advantageous to them, than

the clearing rate. This new procedure for settlements reflects primarily the British desire to enlarge the margin of fluctuation for
sterling, a desire which might be thwarted by other central banks
if these were assured, as they are now, of being able to sell or buy
sterling from the clearing system at par in the monthly settlements.
This assurance now gives them, indeed, a profit incentive to buy
sterling from the market as soon as it falls below par, and to sell
it to the market as soon as it rises above par. It should be hoped,
however, that sufficient confidence now exists among European
central banks for them to trust a gentlemen's agreement outlawing
such operations whenever they run counter to the policies of the
country concerned. Uniform par settlements among central banks
have raised little difficulty so far. They contribute to the effective
stabilization of exchange rates. They protect the central banks
themselves against the risks and temptations of speculation on the
future course of exchange rates. And, finally, they would greatly
simplify the accounting and operations of an expanded clearing
machinery.

A third modification of the EPU Agreement is the abandonment of the EPU unit of account and its replacement by an exchange guarantee in terms of gold or the U.S. dollar, depending
on the nature of the settlements to be effected. This substitution
introduces new complications and uncertainties into the system [1]
and is difficult to explain except on the basis of British fears that
the EPU unit might enjoy greater prestige than the pound sterling, displacing it gradually as a key currency in world trade and
settlements.

A fourth modification lies in the ceiling placed by the new
Agreement on each country's rights and commitments with respect
to "interim finance." Such limits are indeed logically called for
by the abandonment of payments agreements procedures in the
intervals between settlement. Yet it would not be difficult to improve upon the "first-come, first-served" rationing system implicit
in EMA.[2]

An even more controversial change proposed by EMA would
authorize the revival of bilateral payments agreements and the

1. Particularly in the event of a change in the United States gold price or policy.
The provision calling for an urgent and comprehensive review of the Agreement
in such a case is only a thin disguise for a total lack of agreement at this stage as
to the way in which the situation should be handled.
2. See below, p. 286.

exclusion of bilateral balances from monthly compensations if
OEEC disapproves the terms of such agreements. Under EPU,
all bilateral balances *must* be cleared multilaterally each month.
OEEC might still ensure that this be done, by approving agreements to which it would otherwise object. It would seem, however, that further progress toward currency convertibility would
be better served by strengthening OEEC supervision and controls
over agreements which are directly contrary to convertibility objectives. And there is no reason why the small amounts of credit
which it might be deemed desirable to preserve in settlements
with inconvertible countries could not be maintained on a multilateral, rather than bilateral, basis and handled through the
European Fund.

There remains, finally, the most revolutionary change of all in
EPU operations. Central banks will no longer be required to
bring into the monthly compensation all the balances acquired
during the month. They may, at their own discretion, bring such
balances into compensation or retain them as part of their monetary reserves.[3] Some change of this sort would, of course, become
well-nigh unavoidable when European currencies became convertible. One could hardly allow European central banks to retain
convertible U.S. dollars or other third currencies, but forbid them
to keep convertible pounds or Deutsche marks as a component
of their monetary reserves. Yet this return to a multicurrency
gold exchange standard carries with it very great dangers for
future monetary convertibility and trade liberalization. Now, as
in the 1920's, sudden and often speculative shifts from one currency into another or into gold may greatly endanger the stability
and convertibility of the key currencies actually used as foreign
exchange reserves by central banks. Moreover, some countries may
again use trade concessions or the threat of trade restrictions as a
weapon to induce other countries to accumulate their currency or
to spend it exclusively within their own currency area.[4]

The above defects of EMA could not all be fully obviated
within the scope of a regional agreement. They could be very

3. Except balances resulting from interim financing or bilateral payments agreements.

4. See, for instance, the Roca-Runciman Agreement concluded in the early 1930's
between the United Kingdom and Argentina, at a time when sterling was more fully
convertible than is envisaged in any of the present plans for the restoration of convertibility.

largely eliminated, however, if advantage were taken of the next EPU revision to transform EPU into a clearing house for all European central banks, and to require these to hold all their European currency reserves—and possibly a specified portion of their overall gold and foreign exchange reserves—in the form of EPU deposits. All settlements among member countries' central banks would then be made by crediting and debiting, respectively, the EPU accounts of the receiving and of the paying central bank. The EPU accounts would be fully convertible into gold or dollars for settlements outside Europe, and a member bank would have to settle with EPU in gold or convertible currencies—other than its own—any overdraft appearing on its account. Settlements would take place daily, rather than monthly, and there would be no need to liquidate forcibly all accounts at fixed monthly dates, as is now done in EPU. Finally, the EPU unit would be retained as the most logical form of exchange rate guarantee for the operation of the system.[5]

This would not involve any substantive changes in the operations of EMA's European Fund, but it would immeasurably strengthen the EMA Multilateral System of Settlements. It would also, in time, open up new and vast possibilities for stabilization intervention in international exchange markets, approximating the open market operations of a national central bank in its domestic market. Deposits with the European Clearing House would constitute a particularly safe and attractive form of investment of a country's foreign exchange reserves, since they would be fully protected against both any inconvertibility decision on the part of any other country and any currency devaluation greater than that experienced by the stablest European currency, including that of the depositing country itself.[6] If we assume, for the sake of illustration, that European central banks developed the habit of holding—or agreed to hold—with the European Clearing House about 20% of their total gold and foreign exchange reserves,[7] the Clearing House's assets would be of the order of $3 billion. Part of these assets would probably be retained in gold, but a substan-

5. Except as mentioned below, p. 286.
6. See above, p. 173 and n. 9.
7. The OEEC countries as a group currently hold about 50% of their international reserves in the form of foreign exchange rather than gold. This proportion is much higher for most countries and is substantially less than 20% only in the case of the United Kingdom.

tial proportion of them could be used for investment in various currency markets. Investments in member countries' markets should be subordinated to an exchange guarantee in terms of the EPU unit and to the member's commitment that such investments would not be subject to any future and unilateral inconvertibility decision on the part of that member. Investments in nonmember markets might be guaranteed instead in gold or dollars, the OEEC decision authorizing such investments implying in this case the acceptance by members of the exchange risk involved in relation to the value of the EPU unit.

Little purpose could be served by a lengthier discussion of the details of such a hypothetical agreement. Let us merely mention that members could also agree in advance to authorize limited overdrafts in their favor and in favor of the clearing system, repayable within a specified period of time presumably not to exceed one month. These overdrafts would replace the interim finance provisions of the European Monetary Agreement, but could always be drawn upon in the currency of any member, rather than requiring a first-come, first-served rationing procedure.

A European Clearing House of the type proposed here could become a most powerful instrument for a collective European approach to convertibility, and for the future and collective defense of European convertibility against speculative currency movements or balance of payments difficulties. It would probably have been agreed upon several years ago, when first proposed in informal discussions with EPU officials, if it were not for the immense weight of inertia which always blocks international action and for the jealous zeal with which many central bank officials insist on safeguarding their full—even though often merely formal—independence of decision against international institutions as well as against their own governments. Another powerful obstacle lies in the imagined rivalry between sterling and EPU as a focus for international settlements. Yet Britain would undoubtedly be the greatest beneficiary of a system which could not but greatly strengthen international confidence in the pound itself, enabling it to resume its former role in international settlements and arbitrage transactions on the private exchange markets of the world.

B. THE EUROPEAN COMMUNITY

Far closer forms of integration than those exemplified by OEEC, EPU, and EMA have been proposed and discussed repeatedly in recent years among the six countries of the European Coal and Steel Community. The ECSC itself is a concrete, and on the whole remarkably successful, example of this approach, but it has suffered greatly from the rejection of the European Defense Community project by the French Parliament in 1954. It has recently been given a new lease on life, however, by the endorsement given by the six countries to the drafting of a Euratom treaty and a common market treaty.

This latter project would eliminate, in three or four stages extending over a period of twelve to fifteen years, all customs duties as well as other trade restrictions now existing among the participating countries. At the same time, a common tariff would be introduced vis-à-vis third countries, and would approximate initially the arithmetical average of existing tariff rates. A common market organization would be set up to deal with certain products, particularly in the agricultural field, which could not realistically be left to the operation of supply and demand in private markets free of all government intervention. Other provisions are designed to control or remove major sources of distortion upon competitive pricing within the Community, such as cartels, monopolies, governmental subsidies, and the discriminatory impact of taxation, social legislation, freight rates, and so on. An Investment Fund of $1 billion, financed by loan issues, would promote economic development in the poorer regions of the Community, and an Adaptation Fund, fed by contributions from the member countries, would combat, through the adaptation and retraining of workers, the unemployment pockets that might accompany the formation of the common market. Finally, necessary exchange rate adjustments would be smoothed out during the transition period through additional tariff cuts, quota increases, and credits in favor of countries experiencing difficulties in their balance of payments.

The treaty would be open to other countries, and there are indications that the six countries might be joined by others, although in a looser kind of association. Britain herself has recently shown an increasing interest in the project and might seek a special status in the Community, permitting her to maintain some preferential treatment in her trade with the Commonwealth.[8]

The prospects for ratification of this ambitious project by the parliaments of the six countries of the Community are still uncertain. If such ratification occurred, it would bring into the realm of realistic planning the matter of a full currency merger among the participating countries. To dismiss such an objective as a mere utopian dream would be particularly irrational on the part of those who advocate as an alternative to it the restoration of full currency convertibility on the basis of stable and unchanging exchange rates. Indeed, this second objective would, if anything, present greater *economic* difficulties than the first.

In order to clarify our ideas on the matter, let us eliminate at the outset some widely held misconceptions as to the obstacles to monetary unification. Monetary unification would not require, in any manner, a full unification of national levels of prices, costs, wages, productivity, or living standards. Price differentials would indeed be limited by transportation and other transfer costs, but this would be equally true under a system of independent but convertible currencies. Wages, incomes, living standards, and productivity would nevertheless continue to differ from one country to another just as they differ enormously today among different regions of a single country. In the 1930's, for instance, average wage and income levels were two to three times as high in the North of the United States as in the South. What monetary unification involves is rather the adaptation of monetary income levels to productivity levels through the absence of state interference with the normal processes of economic adjustment.[9]

---

8. See above, pp. 278–9. The accession of Britain would undoubtedly also rally the Scandinavian countries to the project. Current discussions point toward the creation of a "free trade erea" embracing all OEEC members, but involving a lesser surrender of sovereignty to supranational authorities than that accepted by the signatories of the "common market" treaty.

9. It is sometimes asserted that fiscal redistribution between richer and poorer regions of a single country plays a major role in regional balance of payments adjustments. This is extremely doubtful if one reflects that: (a) such redistribution was extremely limited in scope in all countries until 20 or 25 years ago and is still very limited in many countries with poorly developed fiscal and social security systems; (b) this redistribution is not designed primarily to smooth out balance of payments disequilibria and may often aggravate them rather than reduce them. Relatively rich regions subject to high taxation—such as New England, for instance —may experience greater pressures on their balance of payments than poorer re-

Neither does monetary unification require a uniformization of the budgetary, economic, or social policies of the member countries. The United Kingdom, India, South Africa, and Australia belong to the same monetary area in spite of widely divergent policies in all these respects. The same diversity—as between Swiss and Greek expenditures on education and defense, for instance—certainly existed within the pre-1914 Latin Union in Europe. This diversity constitutes indeed, in many cases, a factor of equilibrium rather than of disequilibrium, insofar as it corresponds to differences of economic structure, resources, and productivity.

From an economic point of view, the prerequisites for the successful preservation of monetary unification are practically identical with those for the successful preservation of free and stable exchange rates. The participating regions or countries must, in either case, subordinate their internal monetary and credit expansion to the maintenance of equilibrium in their balance of payments. Let us note that the maintenance of such an equilibrium is not itself in question. This is not a prerequisite for exchange stability or monetary unification but a completely unavoidable element in the situation, irrespective of the monetary policy adopted, since in any case deficits cannot exceed the foreign resources available for their financing.

The significance of monetary unification, like that of exchange stability in a free market, is that both exclude the resort to any other corrective techniques except those of internal fiscal and credit policies. From an economic viewpoint, monetary unification would even impose a somewhat less stringent monetary discipline on the participating countries, since the elimination of exchange risks would be even more complete than under a system of free and stable exchange rates, and would therefore stimulate the cushioning of temporary deficits through readjusting capital movements rather than aggravate them through speculative capital flight.

The problem of monetary unification is therefore a political rather than an economic problem. The incentives and obstacles to it are essentially political in nature.

---

gions with a low demand for consumption and investments. The regional pattern of federal expenditures on military production is also very likely to disturb rather than equilibrate regional balances of payments.

First of all, a national currency is one of the symbols of a country's national unity. Monetary unification will thus be desired insofar as political unification is accepted as an objective, but resisted as long as such an objective is not yet acceptable to governments and public opinion.

Secondly, the major economic advantage of monetary unification over free and stable rates lies in the irreversible character of such a decision. The adoption of convertibility at stable rates can never rule out the possibility of a subsequent devaluation or a later relapse into inconvertibility. Monetary unification is much harder to undo and therefore gives greater security to the lender and more incentives for equilibrating, as against speculative, capital movements. By the same token, however, national authorities will also hesitate to surrender so fully and irrevocably their monetary sovereignty if they are not yet ready themselves—or if their partners are not yet ready—to forego the use of devaluation or restrictions as an alternative to internal monetary readjustments.

Finally, monetary unification implies administrative and institutional changes on which agreement must also be reached. This is particularly true with relation to the rules governing the issue of currency proper and the control of bank credit and deposits. The restraints imposed in this respect by anonymous market forces in a system of free and stable rates may be more easily accepted on an ad hoc basis than negotiated and agreed to in advance in the form of definite commitments, similar legal or administrative provisions, and the setting up of joint institutions and authorities.

Monetary unification should be regarded, therefore, as the culmination, rather than the starting point, of the process of economic integration. The economic obstacles to be overcome are identical with those of currency interconvertibility at stable exchange rates. Exchange rate readjustments, however, are one of the least damaging forms of adaptation to the disequilibria arising from a divergent evolution of national monetary policies and national price and cost levels. As long as such divergencies persist, exchange rate flexibility should be encouraged rather than discouraged. The interplay of competitive forces throughout the area requires, first of all, a joint renunciation of increases in trade and exchange restrictions. It requires, secondly the gradual elimination of these restrictions themselves and the formation of a common market. Some degree of flexibility in exchange rates will be helpful or even indispensable during the transition period for the attainment of these two objectives. This is undoubtedly the reason the present draft for the establishment of a common market among the six countries of the European Coal and Steel Community does not contemplate any additional commitments to exchange stability until the common market is achieved.

Many countries, however, and particularly the six countries of the Community, are deeply attached to the concept of exchange stability for reasons of national interest, regardless of the leeway which international agreements may give them in this respect.[10] It is highly likely, therefore, that a stable exchange rate pattern will remain one of their policy objectives, and it may prove attainable after completion of the adaptations required by the elimination of present exchange, trade, and tariff restrictions. The consolidation of this pattern through reciprocal de jure commitments may become a realistic aim of integration policy after an experimental period of de facto stability.

Institutional arrangements may be usefully resorted to when this stage is reached, to reinforce public resistance to exchange instability and the internal policies leading to it in the various member countries.

A first step in this direction might be to legalize the use of exchange guarantees in terms of the EPU unit, in the writing of private as well as public contracts. This could aid greatly in the revival of capital markets, now paralyzed by exchange fears and risks.

A second and more spectacular step, already implying in practice the acceptance of full monetary unification as a future goal, would consist in the overhauling of the present national currency systems whose basic units, such as the French franc or the Italian lira, have become too small for the convenience of transactions, and in the adoption of new national currency units, still independent of one another but equivalent in value. Each central bank would remain responsible for its own currency issue, but the new national units could be granted the privilege of intercirculation throughout the Union's territory. Foreign notes returned by the public to the central bank of the country in which they circulated

10. This is precisely one of the reasons trade and exchange controls have usually been preferred to exchange rate adaptations throughout the postwar era.

would be redeemed by the issuing bank, and corresponding settlements between the two banks would be effected immediately through their respective accounts with the joint clearing house discussed above. Such a system of intercirculation would bear a great deal of resemblance to the old Latin Union under which silver coins of France, Belgium, Italy, Switzerland, etc. circulated at par throughout most of Europe, irrespective of fluctuations in the value of their silver content in relation to gold.[11]

The intercirculation privilege, together with the equivalence in the exchange value of the member currencies, would greatly strengthen the opposition of governments, parliaments, and public opinion to later exchange readjustments. A shift from European parity to 90% of this parity, for instance, would in fact deprive the devaluing currency of the intercirculation privilege, and would in addition elicit far greater psychological reactions than a similar fluctuation from an arbitrary rate of, let us say, 314 per dollar to another arbitrary rate of 349 per dollar. This psychological factor certainly explains in part the stability of those various Latin American currencies which have a simple relationship to the U.S. dollar, in contrast with the persistent instability of other currencies in the same region.

The final stage of monetary unification would require the setting up of a European Monetary Authority, entrusted with sole issue rights for all the participating countries. The participating central banks would simultaneously transfer to the European Monetary Authority their liability for outstanding currency issues and equivalent amounts of their own assets backing such issues. The new monetary system thus instituted would require, of course, a level of gold and foreign exchange reserves sufficient to cushion temporary fluctuations in the balance of payments of the area with the rest of the world. This would not be difficult to achieve, since the gold and dollar holdings of the ECSC countries already covered, at the end of 1955, 44% of their total annual exports, 74% of their exports to non-ECSC countries, more than 160% of their exports to non-EPU countries, and nearly 500% of their exports to the dollar area. One of the by-products of mone-

11. This historical precedent would suggest the adoption of one fifth of the present EPU unit as an anchor for the system. This would restore the convenient and traditional relationship of these monetary units—all based on the so-called "germinal franc"—to the U.S. dollar and to each other, as it existed for more than a century and until the First World War.

tary integration would be to increase considerably the adequacy of international reserves with respect to foreign trade.[12]

The ratio of monetary reserves to monetary liabilities varies enormously, however, from country to country. An equitable distribution of the burden associated with the constitution of adequate monetary reserves for the new institution would probably require that each country contribute at the outset a more or less equivalent—or at least minimum—ratio of gold and foreign assets to the liabilities transferred by it to the Union. This could be done through preliminary stabilization loans in gold or dollars with medium- or long-term maturities, to be granted by the high reserve countries to the low reserve countries.

It should finally be possible to organize the European Monetary Authority on a largely decentralized basis, retaining the individuality of the national central banks as member banks of the new system. Each bank could conduct its own credit and monetary issue operations under broad statutory limitations,[13] subject only to the general supervision of a joint managing board. Temporary reserve deficiencies could be covered by stabilization loans, advances, and open market operations conducted between the national central banks and the European Monetary Authority. Many of the substantive features of such a system would already have been put into operation by the previous functioning of the European Fund and the European Clearing House suggested above as a desirable revision of the present EPU and European Monetary Agreements. The unlikelihood of full participation of the United Kingdom would, however, require the establishment of a special relationship between a continental European Monetary Union on the one hand, and the United Kingdom and the sterling area on the other.

To pursue further the exploration of the technical details of such a hypothetical project would be an idle exercise at this stage. Let us merely note that they could not raise major difficulties,

12. The monetary integration of the ECSC countries would thus raise from 44% to 74% their ratio of gold and dollar holdings to foreign trade. The United Kingdom already enjoys a great deal of this advantage through the integration of the sterling area itself. The gold and dollar holdings of the sterling area at the end of 1955 were equivalent to only 20% of the member countries' total exports, but to 40% of their exports to the nonsterling world, and 75% of their exports to non-EPU countries.

13. These limitations could take the form of national ceilings not to be exceeded without previous authorization, or of minimum reserve requirements, or both.

given the will to proceed with a monetary unification program within the broader context of a political federation of European states. Both the advantages of and the obstacles to such a program are essentially political rather than monetary or even economic.

In any case, there can be little divergence for a long time to come between the proponents of European monetary integration and the proponents of convertibility with stable exchange rates. The immediate steps required for the ultimate achievement of either of these two objectives are practically identical. They demand both further progress by the weaker countries toward basic monetary equilibrium—internal and external—and further progress toward closer cooperation and integration among all the participating countries.

IV. THE ROLE OF WORLD-WIDE AGREEMENTS

For reasons abundantly discussed in previous chapters of this study,[1] the role of world-wide agreements in the restoration and preservation of international convertibility should remain suppletory or complementary rather than pre-emptive at this stage of the world's political and administrative evolution. The existence of a hard core of convertible currencies in the major trading nations of the world would, by itself, remove many of the incentives to and opportunities for discrimination and bilateralism in world trade and payments. National and regional convertibility policies, supplemented by ad hoc agreements of the Hague Club type, will probably remain, for some time to come, the main instruments for realistic progress toward world-wide convertibility and trade liberalization.

Institutions such as the IMF and the proposed OTC will then have a far better opportunity than they have had so far to consolidate, harmonize, and enlarge this progress by joint action and decisions of a world-wide character. This line of development would require, however, substantial modifications in the present philosophy and policies of these institutions.

The first reform, strongly suggested by the OEEC experience,

1. See particularly above, pp. 256-8.

would be to establish a much closer coordination between the regulation of restrictive exchange techniques by the IMF and of equivalent trade restrictions by the OTC. Such an integration between the two institutions should, secondly, lean toward the OTC concept of reciprocal negotiation rather than the IMF concept of universal jurisdiction, as the most fruitful method to ensure general support for and compliance with their objectives. This, in turn, would imply a considerable decentralization in the Fund's administrative organization and the replacement of the Fund's permanent board of instructed delegates by periodic meetings of high-level officials or representatives from the countries mainly concerned in a particular negotiation.

The Fund and the OTC should also lean heavily on the regional organizations and agreements that promote their basic objectives, and should openly recognize the justifiable exceptions to the rule of nondiscrimination which may be inseparable from progress toward trade and exchange liberalization. The Fund's procedures for exchange transactions should not ignore the existence of regional monetary agreements such as the sterling area, the EPU, or the EMA. Such agreements should normally be used—in preference to the Fund—for the financing of transactions among their own members, the Fund intervening only, in principle, in the financing of transactions between such members and third countries. Finally, new procedures should be devised to facilitate direct transactions with a regional institution rather than with its individual members, in order to permit greater flexibility and economy of operation. There is no reason, for instance, why the Fund could not purchase EPU units from the European Union [2] and place them at the disposal of a borrowing Fund member in lieu of national European currencies. Such transactions could be undertaken initially through joint agreements among the countries concerned, pending a much overdue but politically complex and difficult revision of the IMF Articles of Agreement. Their incidence on the structure of Fund quotas, and the advantages of a pooling of certain members' quotas, might be considered whenever such a revision appears feasible.

Other changes in the Fund's philosophy have been suggested above [3] and need not be repeated here. Of fundamental impor-

2. As was done by the U.S. under the "special resources" procedure.
3. See pp. 116–38.

tance in the long run, however, is a frontal attack by the Fund on the well-known deficiencies of the gold exchange standard. The vulnerability of this system to sudden shifts from one key currency to another or from foreign exchange balances into gold itself was amply demonstrated in the early 1930's. Massive conversions of foreign-held sterling assets into gold and dollars—particularly by the Bank of France—played a large role in the sterling crisis of September 1931 and did not prevent heavy exchange losses on the residual sterling balances still held at that time by foreign central banks. These events induced a generalized flight into gold and a drastic contraction in the foreign exchange component of international monetary reserves.[4]

History might easily repeat itself tomorrow if convertibility were to be restored today on the same unorganized gold exchange standard basis. Short-term dollar and sterling liabilities to foreigners ($23.5 billion at the end of 1955) are now about twice as large as total gold holdings outside the United States and the United Kingdom ($12.4 million). Their partial conversion into gold, in the event of renewed currency fears, could easily wreck sterling convertibility [5] and might even create serious, although still manageable, financial problems for the United States itself. Our short-term dollar liabilities had risen to 70% of our gold reserves by the end of 1955 and have been growing in recent years at an annual pace of roughly $1 billion. The possibility of substantial conversions into gold is enhanced by the fast growth of dollar holdings in relation to gold reserves outside the United States. The dollar holdings of France, Germany, Italy, and Japan ($4.5 billion at the end of 1955) present a particular threat in this respect, as they appear most unlikely to be maintained indefinitely at such high levels (see Table XXIV).

Even more striking is the fact that the enormous improvement of foreign countries' reserves which has taken place in recent years has been primarily the result of a vast redistribution of net re-

4. Dollar balances held by foreigners dropped from $2.7 billion at the end of 1929 to less than $400 million at the end of 1933, a contraction of more than 85%. Comparable data on sterling balances are not available, but official foreign exchange reserves for 24 European countries contracted by 80% from 1928 to 1932. See R. Nurske, *International Currency Experience* (Geneva, League of Nations, 1944), pp. 234–6.

5. At the end of 1955, the United Kingdom's gold and dollar holdings were equal to only 27% of her short-term sterling liabilities, and were $600 million larger than sterling balances held outside the sterling area.

serves from the United States to the rest of the world. Gold and dollar holdings outside the United States have risen by more than $12 billion since 1949, but only 21% of this increase was derived from current additions to the world's monetary gold stock. The

Table XXIV. RATIO OF DOLLAR HOLDINGS TO GOLD RESERVES, 1938–55

	1938	1949	1955
Dollar Holdings, in % of:			
A. World gold reserves	8	23	40
B. U.S. gold reserves (−)	−15	−33	−70
C. Gold reserves outside the U.S., of which:	18	76	94
1. France	7	39	154
2. Germany	62	(no gold)	159
3. Italy	10	119	176
4. Japan	37	214	716

Source:
Derived from Federal Reserve Bulletin tables on estimated gold reserves and dollar holdings.

overwhelming portion of the increase—nearly $10 billion—reflected gold losses and increases in short-term liabilities on the part of the United States (see Table XXV). It is evident that such a movement could not continue indefinitely without eventually undermining confidence in the dollar itself.

And yet the world could hardly return to a pure gold standard without gravely endangering the continued expansion of production and international trade. A minimum relationship between the level of international reserves and the level of world trade must be preserved if the former are to play their normal role in the cushioning of temporary fluctuations in national balances of payments, and to provide a practical alternative to unnecessary and damaging measures of internal deflation, exchange rate instability, or trade and exchange restrictions. A similar relationship needs also to be maintained, for similar reasons, between the level of international reserves and the growing money supply and other liquid liabilities of the monetary and banking system which are the normal accompaniment of higher production and income levels in an expanding economy.

Industrial production and the volume of world trade have both been rising, in the last five or six years, at an annual rate of about 6%. With all proper disclaimers as to the feasibility of thus arriving at a quantitative appraisal of reserve needs, it is still suggestive to note that a parallel expansion of international reserves would require an increment of roughly $3 billion a year. The current contribution of gold production to the growth of monetary reserves ($400 million to $600 million in recent years) is only a small fraction of this amount.

Table XXV. SOURCES OF INCREASE IN GOLD AND DOLLAR HOLDINGS OUTSIDE THE UNITED STATES, 1950–55

	In Millions of U.S. Dollars				In % of Total			
	1950–55	*1953*	*1954*	*1955*	*1950–55*	*1953*	*1954*	*1955*
I. *Additions to World Gold Reserves*	2,575	420	645	615	21	16	29	33
A. *Gold production*	5,320	865	915	965	43	33	41	52
B. *Gold sales by U.S.S.R.*	225	75	75	75	2	3	3	4
C. *Private Absorption* (−)	−2,970	−520	−345	−425	−24	−20	−15	−23
1. Industrial uses	(−1,070)	(−170)	(−190)	(−210)	(−9)	(−7)	(−9)	(−11)
2. Private hoarding	(−1,900)	(−350)	(−155)	(−215)	(−15)	(−13)	(−7)	(−12)
II. *Decrease in Net U.S. Gold Reserves*	9,790	2,180	1,580	1,230	79	84	71	67
III. *Total Increase in Gold and Dollar Holdings Outside the U.S.* (I +II)	12,360	2,600	2,225	1,845	100	100	100	100

Sources:
Federal Reserve Bulletin (March 1956), pp. 303–5, and BIS, *Twenty-Sixth Annual Report* (Basle, 1956), p. 150.

This raises a grave issue which is periodically brought before the world's attention by the South African delegation to the annual meetings of the Board of Governors of the International Monetary Fund. Needless to say, South Africa sees a ready-made solution in a general revaluation of gold in terms of the United States dollar and other currencies.[6] Such a revaluation, however, would have to be very drastic indeed to meet the dimensions of the problem suggested by the previous analysis, and would appear totally unpalatable to public opinion in the United States and many other countries. Most of all, the barrenness of this proposal

6. A secondary "equity" argument for gold revaluation is based on the comparison of the purchasing power of gold in the 1930's and today. This loses much of its force if the comparison is carried back instead to the 1920's. A third argument, aiming at solving the "dollar shortage" through a revaluation of gold, is open to even more objections in view of the disappearance of the dollar shortage and because of the preference of the United States for channeling its financial assistance to countries which may both need and deserve it more than the major gold-producing countries. See Miroslav A. Kriz, *The Price of Gold*, Essays in International Finance, Princeton, July 1952.

makes it most repugnant to those who think that the international need for liquidity can be put to better use than financing digging gold from the entrails of the earth and reburying it in the vaults of Fort Knox and other gold graves.

The rejection of the gold revaluation solution, however, does not dispose of the problem itself. An alternative answer lies in the further development of the gold *exchange* standard and in the continued growth of foreign exchange, alongside of gold, as a component of international monetary reserves. The only two currencies which have so far been used extensively in this fashion are the pound sterling and the United States dollar. Official balances in these two currencies at the end of 1955 amounted to about two thirds of the gross gold holdings of the United States and the United Kingdom, and exceeded by more than one third the total gold reserves of all other countries taken together. It was becoming apparent that further increases on the scale necessary to ward off monetary pressures toward deflation and trade restrictions would be bound, sooner or later, to overtax the strength not only of the United Kingdom but even of the United States, and to endanger the acceptability of the dollar itself as a safe reserve medium for other countries.

The solution of this dilemma should lead us to explore more fully than has been done up to now the possibility of broadening the basis of the gold exchange standard and of protecting the system against erratic and unnecessary shifts from one reserve currency into another and from reserve currencies into gold. This could be done by inducing or requiring all countries—or at least all major countries—to maintain an appropriate proportion of their international monetary reserves in the form of a deposit account with the International Monetary Fund. Such accounts would be fully usable in international payments, and would carry an exchange risk guarantee with respect either to gold or to an internationally defined unit of account. They could be drawn upon at any time to make payments in any currency whatsoever, or even converted into gold, as long as the proportion of the country's international deposits to its total reserves is maintained above the minimum agreed to.

These deposits would be reinvested by the Fund through stabilization loans or open market operations, carrying an exchange guarantee similar to that granted to the depositors. This guarantee, together with participation in the Fund's earnings, should make such deposits a particularly safe and attractive reserve medium for the central banks concerned. The countries in whose currencies they are invested would be protected against the sudden and unpredictable drains to which reserve center countries would otherwise be exposed under the traditional gold exchange standard. This would be particularly useful in connection with outstanding sterling balances and the restoration of sterling convertibility. Transitional arrangements could ensure that any excessive conversions of freed, convertible sterling balances into gold, other currencies, or Fund deposits should be offset, at least in part, by the Fund's investments on the London market. In the longer run, the investment of the Fund's assets should gradually aim, directly or indirectly,[7] at a broad distribution of its stabilization operations in support of international convertibility for all its members. The aggregate amount of such interventions should be governed by an appraisal of world-wide inflationary or deflationary pressures, and the Fund's intervention in a particular market should be related to individual countries' needs and to the soundness of the national policies pursued by them. This would make for a far more beneficial use of the countries' willingness to accumulate international reserves in the form of foreign exchange assets than the traditional channeling of monetary reserves exclusively toward the hardest currency markets.

Such a system would preserve the advantages of the gold exchange standard while eliminating the major sources of weakness unanimously denounced as having been the cause of its downfall in the early 1930's. Reserve holders would be guaranteed against unilateral devaluation or inconvertibility decisions on the part of the reserve center countries, and the latter would not be forced into such unilateral and undesirable action by sudden and unpredictable withdrawals of foreign funds from their market. These safeguards would also be of considerable help for the revival of international currency confidence and of "normal" rather than "hot money" capital movements from one market to another.

They would, by the same token, enhance the willingness of creditor countries to finance abnormal surpluses through the accumulation of convertible accounts on the Fund, and minimize

7. Directly through investments in local money markets, or indirectly through investments in the larger, international money centers of the world.

the recourse to trade and exchange discrimination as a last line of defense against the spread of deflation or restrictions.[8]

Transitional arrangements would obviously be an indispensable prerequisite for such a revolution in international currency practices. The major questions raised in this respect concern the status of existing official dollar balances (about $8.4 billion at the end of 1955) and of sterling balances held outside the sterling area (about $2.2 billion) or even outside the dependent territories of the United Kingdom (about $6.9 billion). An attractive solution of these problems would be to grant the United States and the United Kingdom overdraft facilities with the Fund, which could be drawn upon to cover all or part of any future declines in such balances. Any overdraft actually used might be made repayable by installments over a period of ten to twenty years. On the other hand, these same countries would grant to the Fund permanent overdraft facilities equivalent at all times to the amount of such balances still in existence.

One may shudder at the negotiating difficulties which the implementation of such proposals would raise. Here again perfectionism and universalism should not become roadblocks in the path of feasible progress. A European clearing house such as suggested above, or even ad hoc agreements among the major countries only, would go a long way toward providing a workable solution for the obvious deficiencies of either a pure gold standard or an unorganized gold exchange standard. In any case, the problem is likely to force itself upon us within a not too distant future, and deserves more attention from academic and government economists than it receives today.

V. SUMMARY AND CONCLUSIONS

The international trade and payments system of the nineteenth century rested on the happy coincidence of unilateral decisions by several scores of independent states, but particularly by the major trading powers of the Western world, in the exercise of their national sovereignty. The broadening of the horizons of economic policy objectives and the enlargement of the techniques of state intervention in economic life have all but destroyed the chances

8. See above, pp. 253–4.

of reviving a stable framework for international trade and payments on such a happy-go-lucky basis.

The catastrophic depression of the 1930's and the havoc visited upon the world by the Second World War at first reinforced the trend toward economic nationalism, and spelled an inevitable doom for the overambitious blueprints hammered out at Bretton Woods. The only really constructive international action of the early postwar years was the external financing, primarily by the United States, of accelerated reconstruction and development in the war-torn and economically retarded areas of the world.

The success of these policies in strengthening national economies suffered only a temporary setback as a result of the Korean conflict and the subsequent rearmament drive. The years 1953–56 marked an unprecedented era of high employment and rapid economic growth combined with external balance and internal stability. Western Europe, particularly, has far more than made up for its wartime losses. Large-scale investments, together with monetary readjustments, have brought to its economies a degree of strength and vitality contrasting sharply with the relative stagnation and recurrent monetary instability of the prewar era.

Great progress has also been achieved in the relaxation of restrictions on trade and payments. Regional cooperation, under the aegis of OEEC and EPU, has exhibited a realism and efficacy far above those of parallel world-wide institutions. Contrary to the widespread fears expressed at an earlier stage, it has not tended toward the artificial construction of a "little Europe," i.e. of a high cost area sheltered by restrictions and discrimination from the wider sweeps of international competition. On the contrary, regional liberalization has been accompanied or followed by a gradual relaxation of barriers against third countries and a progressive dismantlement of trade and exchange controls in general. Most European nations have reached a stage which may be described as "de facto convertibility" or "near-convertibility." The European Payments Union area together with the dollar area cover such a wide part of world trade as to relegate to comparative insignificance the possible role of bilateralism in residual trade and payments relationships.

Two opposite conclusions are currently being drawn from the experience summarized above.

A first group recognizes the role played by regional cooperation as a transitional device from the monetary chaos and narrow bilateralism of earlier years to the growing balance and liberalization of world trade and payments. This very success, however, is regarded as an indication that such forms of cooperation have now outlived their usefulness and should make room for a full-fledged return to world-wide convertibility, unhampered by regional crutches or blinders.

An opposite view has been taken in this study. The enormous expansion of the objectives and techniques of state intervention in economic life seems to me incompatible with the restoration and maintenance of convertibility on the basis of the uncoordinated national decisions and policies of several scores of independent sovereign states. The institutional framework of international convertibility needs to be greatly strengthened if it is to survive the inevitable shocks occasionally to be expected from unfavorable developments and policies in some of the major trading countries. A collective organization and effective internationalization of the present gold exchange standard are particularly essential in this respect, if we are to eschew the well-known pitfalls unanimously denounced by economists and sadly demonstrated by events in the early 1930's.

Closer cooperation and integration, on a regional scale, is equally indispensable to organize a "defense in depth"—rather than a mere "Maginot line"—against the spread of deflation, restrictions, and bilateralism. The fundamental dilemma of international economic relations in this twentieth century lies in the inadequacy of national sovereignty as a framework for policy decisions and their administrative implementation in an interdependent world. This dilemma cannot be resolved overnight through a sudden and radical transformation of our institutions and habits of thought. The days of a world government are not yet at hand. The mushrooming and overlapping of international and regional institutions since the Second World War are both bewildering and disappointing to the logical mind. This proliferation, however, merely reflects our persistent efforts to remedy the partial failure of previous, half-hearted gropings after new forms of political organization necessary to reach and implement collective decisions where their need is sufficiently felt to overcome old prejudices and inertia. The ambitious framework of universal cooperation, indispensable as it is in many cases, often limits feasible coordination to ad hoc—and often ex post—attempts to smooth out conflicts of views and interests on specific issues and proposals. Regional cooperation, on the other hand, is far more likely to succeed in developing habits of continuous consultation and negotiation over a broader range of governmental responsibilities; and it may, if successful, gradually evolve toward the actual merging of areas too small and too interdependent on one another to preserve national welfare and security on the basis of national sovereignty exercised within present political boundaries.

We have long been familiar with the first problem, but we still fail to see clearly the full implications of the second for the reorientation of international economic theory as well as international economic policy.

STATISTICAL APPENDIX

STATISTICAL APPENDIX

Most of the following data or estimates are derived from only a few standard statistical sources and publications, and particularly:

I. International Monetary Fund: *International Financial Statistics Balance of Payments Yearbooks.*

II. Organization for European Economic Cooperation:
Statistics of National Product and Expenditure, 1956 Edition (Paris, 1956)
General Statistics Bulletin
Foreign Trade Bulletin. Series I: *Foreign Trade by Areas*
Foreign Trade by Areas: 1928, 1937–1953
Annual Report of OEEC
Annual Report of the Managing Board for the European Payments Union

III. Bank for International Settlements: *Annual Report.*

IV. Board of Governors of the Federal Reserve System: *Federal Reserve Bulletin.*

V. U.S. Department of Commerce: *Balance of Payments of the United States, 1919–1953* and *Survey of Current Business.*

These sources should be consulted for additional details on the exact coverage and construction of the series used.

Usual symbols (such as — for zero or negligible amounts) are used throughout, except for the author's predilection to indicate by a *plus* (rather than a *minus*) sign increases in monetary assets and decreases in monetary liabilities, and by a *minus* (rather than a *plus*) sign decreases in monetary assets and increases in monetary liabilities.

Apparent errors in addition or subtraction are due to the rounding off of all data and estimates to the closest million, billion, decimal, or per cent.

General Note on Tables II–VII (Chap. 2) and
Appendix Tables 9–11 and 13–18

All the estimates used in the calculation of the tables listed above and of the corresponding charts are derived from the OEEC *Statistics of National Product and Expenditure, No. 2, 1938 and 1947 to 1955* (Paris, 1957) and from the OEEC *General Statistics Bulletin.*

These sources report as "official" all GNP estimates subsequent to 1948 for France and Germany and to 1947 for all other countries, except Switzerland, for which "official" estimates are reported only for 1954. "Official" estimates are also given for GNP at constant (1954) prices for Sweden and the United Kingdom in 1947 and for Denmark, Norway, and Italy in both 1938 and 1947. Finally, "official" estimates at current prices are reported for Austria and Germany in 1938 and for Denmark, Greece, Italy, the Netherlands, Norway, and the United Kingdom both in 1938 and in 1947.

The completion of the tables involved, therefore, the use of other estimates identified in the source either as "unofficial estimates" or "rough estimates by the OEEC Secretariat." This qualification applies to all Swiss estimates except for 1954, to all French estimates for the years 1938, 1947, and 1948, and to estimates at constant (1954) prices for Sweden and the United Kingdom in 1938, for Austria, Belgium, Greece, and the Netherlands in 1938 and 1947 and for Germany in 1938, 1947, and 1948. No estimates of GNP at current prices are published in the source for Austria in 1947, Belgium in 1938 and 1947 and Germany in 1938, 1947, and 1948. I had therefore to resort, for these years, to unpublished estimates used by OEEC only for the calculation of GNP totals for the OEEC area as a whole.

Table 1. BALANCE OF PAYMENTS OF THE UNITED STATES, 1850–1918

(yearly averages, in millions of U.S. dollars)

Fiscal Years	1850–73	1874–95	1896–1914	1914–18 [a]
I. *Current Account*	−100	−50	−55	+2240
A. Trade	−60	+115	+490	+2630
B. Invisibles [b]	−40	−165	−545	−390
II. *Capital Inflow* (+) *or Outflow* (−) [c]	+55	+45	+65	−300
III. TOTAL (I + II), offset by:	−45	−5	+10	+1940
A. U.S. Government Lending (+)	—	—	—	+1710
B. Gold Inflow (+) or Outflow (−)	−45	−5	+10	+230

Notes:
a. July 1, 1914–Dec. 31, 1918.
b. Including unilateral transfers (private remittances).
c. Including errors and omissions, but excluding U.S. Government lending.

Source:
Balance of Payments of the United States, 1919–1953, U.S. Department of Commerce, 1954.

Table 2. BALANCE OF PAYMENTS OF THE UNITED STATES, 1919-39

(yearly averages, in millions of U.S. dollars)

Calendar Years	1919-21	1922-29	1930-33	1934-39
I. Current Account	+2760	+717	+301	+390
A. Trade	+3336	+757	+437	+456
B. Invisibles a	−575	−40	−136	−66
II. Capital Inflow (+) or Outflow (−)	−2593	−639	−277	+1393
A. U.S. Capital b	−1261	−929	+199	+294
B. Foreign Capital	−166	+423	−612	+698
C. Errors and Omissions	−1166	−133	+136	+401
III. Gold Inflow (+) or Outflow (−)				
(I + II)	+167	+78	+25	+1783

Notes:
a. Including unilateral transfers, consisting almost exclusively of private remittances.
b. Primarily private capital. U.S. government loans were negligible during this period, except for long-term loans of $2,397 million in 1919 and $239 million in 1920.

Source:
Balance of Payments of the United States, 1919-1953, U.S. Department of Commerce, 1954.

Table 3. THE WORLD DOLLAR SUPPLY, 1919-39

(yearly averages, in millions of U.S. dollars)

Calendar Years	1919-21	1922-29	1930-33	1934-39
I. U.S. Expenditures on Current Account a	6075	5457	3190	3460
II. Private U.S. Capital	437	971	−168	−298
III. TOTAL	6512	6428	3022	3162

Note:
a. Imports of goods and services, private remittances, pensions, and other transfers.

Source:
Balance of Payments of the United States, 1919-1953, U.S. Department of Commerce, 1954.

Table 4. International Gold and Dollar Transactions, 1946–55 (Foreign Countries and International Institutions)

(in billions of U.S. dollars)

	Total			Years			
	1946–55	1946–49	1950–55	1947	1953	1954	1955
I. Balance on Current Account and Private U.S. Capital	−29.3	−27.9	−1.5	−10.3	+0.7	+0.8	−0.1
A. Transactions with the U.S.	−33.5	−29.5	−4.0	−10.8	+0.3	+0.2	−0.7
1. Current Account	−38.1	−29.3	−8.8	−10.8	+0.2	−1.2	−1.4
(a) U.S. Military Expenditures	(+14.1)	(+2.4)	(+11.7)	(+0.5)	(+2.5)	(+2.6)	(+2.8)
(b) Other	(−52.2)	(−31.7)	(−20.5)	(−11.3)	(−2.4)	(−3.8)	(−4.2)
2. Private U.S. Capital	+9.5	+2.9	+6.6	+1.0	+0.4	+1.6	+1.2
3. Errors and Omissions	−4.9	−3.0	−1.9	−0.9	−0.3	−0.2	−0.5
B. Gold Monetization	+4.2	+1.6	+2.6	+0.4	+0.4	+0.6	+0.6
II. U.S. Government Grants and Credits (Net)	+39.7	+24.7	+15.0	+8.9	+2.1	+1.6	+2.2
III. TOTAL (I + II), Reflected in Increase (+) or Decrease (−) in Gold and Dollar Assets	+10.4	−3.1	+13.5	−1.5	+2.7	+2.4	+2.1

Note:
This table is derived from the U.S. balance of payments estimates of the Survey of Current Business, supplemented by increases in foreign gold reserves resulting from the monetization of gold (item IB) acquired by central banks from new gold production, private hoards, or U.S.S.R. gold sales. Gold monetization (included also under item III) is arrived at by comparing U.S. gold sales or purchases with the over-all change in gold reserves outside the U.S., as reported in the Federal Reserve Bulletin and International Financial Statistics.
Private remittances, pensions, and other transfers are included under current account transactions.

310

Table 5. GOLD RESERVES AND DOLLAR HOLDINGS, 1938–55

	In Billions of U.S. Dollars, at the end of:			1955 in % of		In % of Annual Imports		
	1938	*1949*	*1955*	*1938*	*1949*	*1938*	*1949*	*1955*
I. *World* (Gold)	26.3	35.4	38.0	+44	+7	112	53	38
II. *United States* (Net = A − B)	12.4	16.3	6.5	−47	−60	504	217	53
A. Gold	*14.6*	*24.6*	*21.8*	+49	−11	*593*	*327*	*178*
B. Dollar Balances	*2.2*	*8.2*	*15.2*	+590	+86			
III. *Other* (Gold plus Dollar Holdings)	13.8	19.1	31.5	+127	+65			
A. International	—	3.3	4.0		+22			
B. Foreign Countries	13.8	15.8	27.5	+99	+74	65	30	36
1. Continental Western Europe and Dependencies	7.3	6.3	13.6	+85	+116	82	31	41
2. Sterling Area	3.9	2.8	4.0	+2	+46	50	15	17
3. Latin America	1.0	3.1	4.0	+320	+30	62	58	55
4. Canada	0.40	1.5	2.6	+560	+70	50	52	51
5. Asia	0.76	1.6	2.6	+250	+70	54	47	53
6. Eastern Europe	0.43	0.38	0.32	−26	−17			
7. Other Countries	0.10	0.14	0.32	+240	+130	41	13	27

Note:

Data on gold reserves—excluding the U.S.S.R.—and dollar holdings are derived from the *Federal Reserve Bulletin* and include, beginning in 1949, U.S. government bonds and notes with original maturities of more than one year. The totals for foreign countries and the world in the last three columns are calculated exclusive of Eastern Europe and mainland China, for which complete trade data are not available.

Table 6. The World Dollar Supply, 1938–55

Calendar Years	1938	1946	1947	1948	1949	1950	1951	1952	1953	1954	1955
I. *In Billions of U.S. Dollars* a	3.2	8.0	9.9	11.8	10.8	13.9	16.6	17.4	17.6	18.3	19.7
A. U.S. Expenditures on Current Account b	3.2	7.6	8.9	10.9	10.3	12.6	15.6	16.3	17.3	16.7	18.5
B. Private U.S. Capital	−0.1	0.4	1.0	0.9	0.6	1.3	1.1	1.2	0.4	1.6	1.2
II. *Index at Current Prices*											
A. 1928 = 100	43	108	134	160	146	188	225	236	238	248	267
B. 1935–39 = 100	95	239	295	352	324	415	495	520	525	547	588
III. *Index at Constant Prices* c											
A. 1928 = 100	53	86	87	96	92	115	124	134	137	142	153
B. 1935–39 = 100	98	159	160	177	172	211	227	246	252	262	282

Source:

Derived from the U.S. balance of payments estimates of the *Survey of Current Business.*

Notes:

a. Excluding gold monetization (see note to Table 4).

b. Imports of goods and services, private remittances, pensions, and other transfers.

c. Current values, deflated by the U.S. index of wholesale prices.

Table 7. ANALYSIS OF OEEC EUROPE'S GROSS DEFICIT IN 1947

(in billions of U.S. dollars)

	1938	1947	Total	Difference 1938–47 Impact of Volume Changes	Impact of Price Changes
I. *Goods and Services*	−0.4	−7.2	−6.7	−5.4	−1.3
A. Exports	*9.4*	*11.1*	*+1.7*	*−5.7*	*+7.4*
B. Imports	*9.9*	*18.3*	*+8.4*	*−0.3*	*+8.7*
II. *Capital Exports and Repayments*	−0.3	−2.0	−1.8		
III. TOTAL, financed by:	**−0.7**	**−9.2**	**−8.5**		
A. Private Donations	*−0.1*	*−0.4*	*−0.3*		
B. UNRRA	—	*−0.2*	*−0.2*		
C. International Bank	—	*−0.3*	*−0.3*		
D. International Fund	—	*−0.4*	*−0.4*		
E. U.S. and Canadian Aid	—	*−5.3*	*−5.3*		
F. Decline in Gold and Dollar Holdings	*−0.6*	*−2.5*	*−1.9*		

Note:
The impact of volume changes is calculated at the average of 1938 and 1947 prices, and the impact of price changes is calculated at the average of 1938 and 1947 volumes. Wide discrepancies in the estimated breakdown of the 1938–47 deterioration of the balance of payments between the impact of volume changes and the impact of price changes originate in the choice of different base years in these calculations. The −$6.7 billion deterioration in Europe's balance can thus be alternatively broken down into a −$3.6 billion volume impact (at 1938 prices) and a −$3.1 billion price impact (at 1947 volumes), or into a −$7.2 volume impact (at 1947 prices) and a +$0.5 billion price impact (at 1938 volumes).

Sources:
These are extremely rough estimates derived from heterogeneous sources:
1. OEEC, *Statistics of National Product and Expenditure* for goods and services exports and imports.
2. IMF, *Balance of Payments Yearbook, 1948 and Preliminary 1949* (Washington, D.C., 1950) for the resources used to finance the gross deficit.
3. Item II (Capital Exports and Repayments) is a residual estimate and includes, therefore, the net impact of errors and omissions in other estimates.

Table 8. OEEC EUROPE: BALANCE OF PAYMENTS, 1947–55 [a]

(in billions of U.S. dollars)

	1947	1948	1949	1950	1951	1952	1953	1954	1955
I. *Current Account*	−6.8	−4.1	−1.3	−0.4	−1.1	+1.0	+1.7	+2.0	+1.6
A. Goods and Services	−7.2	−4.4	−1.5	−0.6	−1.3	+0.8	+1.4	+1.8	+1.4
B. Private Remittances	+0.4	+0.3	+0.2	+0.2	+0.2	+0.2	+0.3	+0.2	+0.2
II. *Capital Account*	+4.8	+4.1	+2.4	+1.4	+0.2	+0.4	−0.2	−1.1	−0.8
A. Private	−0.7	−0.7	−1.9	−1.2	−1.3	−0.1	−0.2	−0.9	−0.5
B. Official	+5.5	+4.8	+4.3	+2.6	+1.5	+0.5	—	−0.2	−0.3
1. Economic Aid	+5.8	+5.2	+4.6	+2.9	+2.3	+1.5	+1.0	+0.8	+0.6
2. IMF Transactions	+0.4	+0.1	—	—	—	—	−0.2	−0.1	−0.1
3. Other	−0.7	−0.5	−0.3	−0.3	−0.8	−1.0	−0.8	−0.9	−0.8
III. *Monetary Movements* (I + II) [b]	−2.0	—	+1.1	+1.0	−0.9	+1.4	+1.5	+0.9	+0.8
A. Sterling Balances	+0.6	+0.1	+0.5	−0.9	−0.3	+0.8	−0.7	−0.5	+0.2
B. Other Nondollar Balances	−0.1	+0.1	+0.4	—	−0.1	—	−0.1	−0.5	−0.2
C. Gold and Dollar Reserves	−2.5	−0.2	+0.2	+1.9	−0.5	+0.6	+2.2	+1.9	+0.8

Notes:

a. There exists no systematic presentation, on a uniform basis, of OEEC Europe's balance of payments for the whole period 1947–55. The above estimates can only be regarded as a rough approximation, derived from the invaluable *Balance of Payments Yearbooks* of the International Monetary Fund, with the following exceptions:

  (a) The balance on goods and services is derived from the more recent and thoroughly checked estimates of Europe's national accounts, published in the OEEC *Statistics of National Product and Expenditure.*

  (b) Net movements of private capital (item IIA) are derived by difference, and include errors and omissions.

b. Increases in monetary assets and decreases in monetary liabilities, under item III, are indicated by a *plus* sign, and reverse movements by a *minus* sign. This is contrary to usual practice, but seems to me less misleading to the average reader.

Table 9. OEEC EUROPE: BALANCE OF PAYMENTS ON GOODS
AND SERVICES, 1938–55

(in billions of U.S. dollars)

Calendar Year	1938	1947	1948	1949	1950	1951	1952	1953	1954	1955
I. *At Current Prices*	−0.4	−7.2	−4.4	−1.5	−0.6	−1.3	+0.8	+1.4	+1.8	+1.4
A. *Receipts*	9.4	11.1	14.4	15.9	15.3	20.6	21.6	21.8	24.1	25.9
1. Merchandise	6.5	7.0	9.5	10.8	10.9	15.3	15.6	15.3	16.6	17.6
2. Services	2.9	4.1	4.9	5.2	4.4	5.3	6.0	6.5	7.6	8.3
B. *Payments*	9.9	18.3	18.8	17.4	15.9	21.9	20.8	20.4	22.3	24.5
1. Merchandise	8.4	13.5	14.8	13.8	12.8	17.8	16.5	15.9	17.5	19.2
2. Services	1.5	4.8	4.0	3.7	3.1	4.2	4.4	4.5	4.7	5.3
II. *At Constant (1954)* Prices	−2.7	−8.9	−4.4	−2.6	+0.3	+1.0	+1.0	+1.1	+1.9	+1.4
A. Receipts	16.4	9.7	12.6	14.6	17.3	19.5	19.5	21.2	24.1	25.5
B. Payments	19.0	18.6	17.0	17.1	17.0	18.5	18.5	20.1	22.3	24.0

Source:
OEEC, *Statistics of National Product and Expenditure.*

Table 10. OEEC EUROPE: EXPORTS AND IMPORTS OF GOODS
AND SERVICES, 1938–55

(value, volume, and average value indices, 1938 = 100)

Calendar Year	1947	1948	1949	1950	1951	1952	1953	1954	1955
I. *Value Indices*									
Exports	118	153	169	163	219	230	232	256	276
Imports	185	190	176	161	221	210	206	225	247
Ratio of Exports to Imports	64	81	96	101	99	110	113	114	112
II. *Volume Indices*									
Exports	59	77	89	105	119	119	129	147	156
Imports	98	89	90	89	97	97	106	117	127
Ratio of Exports to Imports	60	86	99	118	122	122	122	126	123
III. *Average Value Indices*									
Exports	200	199	190	154	184	193	180	174	177
Imports	189	212	196	180	227	215	194	192	194
Terms of Trade	106	94	97	86	81	90	93	91	91

Source:
Value and volume indices are derived from Table 9 estimates at current and at constant prices. Volume indices are weighted by base year prices. Average value indices are arrived at by dividing value indices by volume indices and are therefore weighted by current year volumes.

Table 11. OEEC Europe: Production and Expenditure, 1938–55

(in billions of U.S. dollars) a

1. AT CURRENT PRICES AND EXCHANGE RATES

Calendar Year	1938	1947	1948	1949	1950	1951	1952	1953	1954	1955
I. *Production*	93.2	141.2	151.9	156.6	138.8	163.3	180.6	190.0	201.7	219.1
II. *Expenditure*	93.6	148.4	156.2	158.1	139.4	164.6	179.9	188.7	199.9	217.7
A. Consumption	79.7	123.8	130.1	130.8	115.2	132.5	147.1	154.2	162.0	173.8
1. Private	(64.7)	(103.0)	(109.4)	(108.9)	(96.2)	(109.3)	(119.0)	(124.9)	(132.0)	(142.5)
2. Public	(15.0)	(20.8)	(20.7)	(21.9)	(19.0)	(23.2)	(28.1)	(29.3)	(30.0)	(31.3)
B. Investment	14.0	24.6	26.2	27.3	24.2	32.0	32.8	34.5	37.9	43.9
1. Fixed	(12.4)	(21.7)	(24.1)	(24.9)	(22.5)	(27.0)	(30.4)	(32.5)	(35.6)	(40.6)
2. Stocks b	[1.6]	[2.9]	[2.1]	[2.4]	(1.7)	(5.0)	(2.4)	(2.0)	(2.3)	(3.3)
III. *Balance* (I − II = IIIA − IIIB)	−0.4	−7.2	−4.4	−1.5	−0.6	−1.3	0.8	1.4	1.8	1.4
A. Exports c	9.4	11.1	14.4	15.9	15.3	20.6	21.6	21.8	24.1	25.9
B. Imports c	9.9	18.3	18.8	17.4	15.9	21.9	20.8	20.4	22.3	24.5
IV. *Saving* (I − IIA = IIB − III)	13.6	17.4	21.8	25.8	23.7	30.7	33.5	35.9	39.8	45.3

2. AT CONSTANT (1954) PRICES AND EXCHANGE RATES

Calendar Year	1938	1947	1948	1949	1950	1951	1952	1953	1954	1955
I. *Production*	148.9	136.0	146.3	156.9	168.9	179.4	182.9	192.2	201.7	213.9
II. *Expenditure*	151.6	144.9	150.6	159.5	168.7	178.4	181.9	191.2	199.9	212.4
A. Consumption	127.0	119.8	125.7	131.2	138.4	143.7	150.0	156.6	162.0	169.8
1. Private	(105.0)	(97.5)	(103.5)	(107.4)	(114.0)	(117.3)	(120.6)	(126.7)	(132.0)	(139.6)
2. Public	(22.0)	(22.3)	(22.2)	(23.8)	(24.4)	(26.4)	(29.4)	(29.9)	(30.0)	(30.2)
B. Investment	24.6	25.2	25.0	28.2	30.2	34.7	31.9	34.5	37.9	42.7
1. Fixed	(22.4)	(22.3)	(22.9)	(25.6)	(28.2)	(29.4)	(29.9)	(32.3)	(35.6)	(39.5)
2. Stocks b	[2.2]	[2.9]	[2.1]	(2.6)	(2.0)	(5.3)	(2.0)	(2.2)	(2.3)	(3.2)
III. *Balance* (I − II = IIIA − IIIB)	−2.7	−8.9	−4.4	−2.6	0.3	1.0	1.0	1.1	1.9	1.4
A. Exports c	16.4	9.7	12.6	14.6	17.3	19.5	19.5	21.2	24.1	25.5
B. Imports c	19.0	18.6	17.0	17.1	17.0	18.5	18.5	20.1	22.3	24.0
IV. *Saving* (I − IIA = IIB + III)	21.9	16.3	20.6	25.6	30.5	35.7	32.9	35.6	39.8	44.1

Notes and Source: see next page.

Table 12. AMERICAN AID TO WESTERN EUROPE, 1947–55

(in millions of U.S. dollars)

| Calendar Year | Military Grants | Other Aid | | | Total as % of Imports of Goods and Services |
		Grants	Long-Term Loans	Total	
1947	43	672	3,737	4,409	24
1948	254	2,866	1,213	4,079	22
1949	170	3,951	503	4,454	26
1950	463	2,775	180	2,955	19
1951	1,112	2,317	84	2,401	11
1952	2,151	1,453	453	1,906	9
1953	3,435	1,138	172	1,310	6
1954	2,313	1,018	105	1,123	5
1955	1,593	800	74	874	4
TOTAL	11,534	16,990	6,521	23,511	13

Source:
"Balance of Payments of the United States" as estimated by the U.S. Department of Commerce and published in the *Survey of Current Business,* July 1954 and later issues.

Notes to Table 11:
   a. The reader is cautioned against using these estimates to compare the real level of Europe's product and expenditure with that of the United States, since the exchange rates used to convert European currencies into dollars considerably understate the relative purchasing power of these currencies and hence the real level of goods and services shown by the dollar estimates.
   b. Figures for change in stocks include crude or even conjectural estimates for several countries. Those for 1937, 1947, and 1948 are particularly uncertain and should be regarded only as rough indications of the probable order of magnitude.
   c. Goods and services.

Source:
OEEC, *Statistics of National Product and Expenditure.*

Table 13. CURRENT MONETIZATION, FOREIGN BALANCE, CHANGES IN MONEY SUPPLY AND GNP PRICES, 1947–55

(in % of money supply at the beginning of each year)

	1947	1948	1949	1950	1951	1952	1953	1954	1955	Average 1949–55
I. Current Monetization										
Greece	+256	+212	+237	+167	+139	+71	+99	+67	+44	+92
Italy	+108	+49	+24	+13	+22	+29	+21	+12	+14	+18
France	+36	+45	+28	+14	+22	+18	+13	+10	+9	+15
Norway	+35	+16	+20	+12	+11	+8	+16	+16	+10	+13
Sweden	+25	+11	−3	+4	+8	+2	+1	+3	+3	+3
Denmark	−4	−2	−1	+10	+8	+2	+3	+5	−2	+4
Netherlands	+39	+22	+7	+9	+4	−15	−11	+3	−1	−1
United Kingdom	+9	—	−2	−6	+7	−5	−1	−2	−1	−1
Belgium	+16	+10	+3	+6	+2	−2	+1	+1	−1	+1
Switzerland	+11	+6	+1	—	+5	−2	−7	−5	−2	−2
Austria	+26	+39	+32	+28	+44	+18	+13	+17	+12	+20
Germany			+43	+25	+5	−6	−7	−5	−3	+3
II. Foreign Balance on Goods and Services										
Greece	−164	−184	−163	−151	−112	−63	−56	−50	−42	−72
Italy	−61	−14	−9	−3	−6	−13	−8	−4	−3	−6
France	−13	−14	−4	+1	−4	−5	−1	+4	+5	—
Norway	−22	−12	−18	−12	−3	−1	−12	−12	−8	−9
Sweden	−21	−6	+6	+2	+11	+2	+4	−1	−3	+3
Denmark	−5	−5	−4	−12	−4	+2	+2	−7	+3	−3
Netherlands	−27	−17	−4	−15	−1	+25	+18	+3	+9	+5
United Kingdom	−7	+2	+3	+8	−5	+5	+4	+5	+1	+3
Belgium	−13	−5	+1	−6	+6	+5	+3	+1	+7	+2
Switzerland	−5	−4	+6	+3	−1	+6	+12	+8	+5	+6
Austria	−22	−23	−24	−16	−24	−10	+11	+8	−11	−7
Germany			−23	−10	+13	+17	+20	+18	+13	+10
III. Changes in Money Supply (I + II)										
Greece	+92	+28	+74	+16	+27	+8	+44	+17	+3	+20
Italy	+47	+35	+15	+10	+16	+16	+13	+8	+11	+12
France	+22	+31	+25	+15	+18	+13	+11	+14	+13	+15
Norway	+13	+4	+2	—	+13	+7	+4	+4	+2	+4
Sweden	+4	+6	+4	+6	+19	+4	+4	+2	—	+5
Denmark	−9	−6	−4	−3	+4	+5	+4	−2	+1	+1
Netherlands	+12	+5	+3	−6	+3	+10	+7	+7	+8	+5
United Kingdom	+2	+2	+1	+2	+2	—	+3	+3	—	+2
Belgium	+3	+5	+4	—	+8	+3	+4	+2	+6	+3
Switzerland	+5	+2	+7	+3	+4	+3	+4	+3	+3	+4

	1947	1948	1949	1950	1951	1952	1953	1954	1955	Average 1949–55
Austria	+4	+16	+8	+13	+20	+8	+24	+25	+1	+14
Germany			+20	+14	+18	+11	+13	+13	+10	+14

IV. *Changes in GNP Price Level*

	1947	1948	1949	1950	1951	1952	1953	1954	1955	Average 1949–55
Greece		+42	+17	+15	+10	+2	+19	+12	+8	+11
Italy		+14	−1	+3	+7	+4	+2	+2	+2	+3
France		+50	+9	+6	+18	+17	—	+1	+2	+9
Norway		+1	+5	+5	+20	+6	−2	+4	+3	+6
Sweden		+6	—	+2	+23	+7	−1	—	+4	+5
Denmark		+4	+4	+6	+9	+5	+2	+2	+4	+4
Netherlands		+6	+3	+7	+10	+2	−3	+5	+2	+4
United Kingdom		+7	+3	+2	+7	+9	+2	+1	+3	+4
Belgium		+2	—	−2	+9	+3	−2	+1	+2	+1
Switzerland		+2	+1	—	+3	+4	—	—	+1	+1
Austria		−13	+15	+12	+20	+15	−11	+3	+3	+7
Germany			+25	−5	+8	+5	−1	—	+2	+5

Sources and notes:
Current monetization is measured by the annual excess of money supply increase over the balance of payments surplus on goods and services. All basic estimates are derived from the same data as those used in Table 14 and are uniformly presented in per cent of money supply at the beginning of each year, except for changes in the GNP price level, which are expressed in per cent of the GNP price level of the previous year. See Table 14 for other notes.

Table 14. MONEY SUPPLY, PRODUCTION, DOMESTIC INFLATION, PRICES, AND LIQUIDITY, 1938–55

(*indices, 1938 = 100*)

	1947	1948	1949	1950	1951	1952	1953	1954	1955
I. *Money Supply*									
Greece	5,995	8,995	13,853	19,011	23,184	26,937	34,026	44,537	53,368
Italy	3,258	4,563	5,629	6,329	7,161	8,282	9,463	10,463	11,474
France	811	1,029	1,310	1,566	1,827	2,106	2,362	2,660	3,020
Norway	437	473	486	490	521	572	601	624	643
Sweden	255	267	279	293	331	366	381	393	397
Denmark	302	294	278	269	271	282	294	298	296
Netherlands	263	286	298	294	289	308	333	358	382
United Kingdom	302	307	312	317	322	325	330	341	346
Belgium	332	346	363	368	382	389	418	429	445
Switzerland	211	219	232	241	249	259	269	278	287
Austria:									
1938 = 100	433	478	536	594	691	781	908	1,130	1,262
1949 = 100	81	89	100	111	129	146	169	211	235
Germany:									
1949 = 100			100	117	136	155	175	197	219
II. *GNP at Current Prices*									
Greece	13,106	21,211	28,526	33,485	40,076	41,995	56,466	65,300	75,218
Italy	3,810	4,501	4,741	5,245	6,092	6,472	7,070	7,553	8,234
France	941	1,533	1,906	2,179	2,682	3,205	3,296	3,490	3,799
Norway	222	239	255	282	353	387	391	425	453
Sweden	194	218	228	244	299	327	337	354	380
Denmark	216	235	254	291	314	332	357	374	388
Netherlands	225	264	295	327	364	384	406	445	488
United Kingdom	186	206	218	230	254	276	294	313	332
Belgium	396	429	436	446	513	537	539	557	590
Switzerland	194	203	201	211	226	235	242	255	267
Austria:									
1938 = 100	278	340	472	581	779	901	911	1,027	1,173
1949 = 100	59	72	100	123	165	191	193	218	249
Germany:									
1938 = 100	68	92	134	152	192	213	227	246	277
1949 = 100	51	69	100	113	143	159	169	183	207
III. *Production*									
Greece	68	66	76	77	84	86	97	101	107
Italy	89	92	98	105	114	116	124	130	139
France	91	99	113	121	126	128	132	138	148

	1947	1948	1949	1950	1951	1952	1953	1954	1955
Norway	120	128	131	138	143	148	152	159	164
Sweden	119	126	132	139	139	143	148	156	161
Denmark	113	118	122	132	131	132	139	143	143
Netherlands	103	114	123	128	129	132	144	151	162
United Kingdom	102	106	109	114	117	116	121	127	131
Belgium	109	115	117	123	129	132	136	140	144
Switzerland	115	118	116	122	126	127	131	137	142
Austria:									
1938 = 100	63	89	107	118	131	132	135	148	164
1949 = 100	59	83	100	110	123	123	126	138	153
Germany:									
1938 = 100	57	67	78	94	109	116	126	135	149
1949 = 100	72	86	100	119	139	148	159	172	191

IV. *Domestic Inflation* (I ÷ III)

	1947	1948	1949	1950	1951	1952	1953	1954	1955
Greece	8,764	13,691	18,275	24,571	27,541	31,209	35,035	44,056	49,765
Italy	3,649	4,943	5,764	6,037	6,296	7,130	7,608	8,023	8,236
France	892	1,044	1,164	1,296	1,453	1,646	1,792	1,922	2,036
Norway	363	369	372	356	364	385	395	393	393
Sweden	214	211	211	210	237	256	257	251	246
Denmark	266	249	228	203	206	214	211	208	207
Netherlands	256	251	243	230	225	232	231	237	235
United Kingdom	295	290	285	279	275	279	273	269	264
Belgium	306	301	309	299	295	295	308	307	309
Switzerland	183	185	200	198	198	205	205	203	202
Austria:									
1938 = 100	687	540	501	503	526	591	671	764	771
1949 = 100	137	108	100	100	105	118	134	152	154
Germany:									
1949 = 100			100	98	97	105	110	114	115

V. *Prices* (II ÷ III)

	1947	1948	1949	1950	1951	1952	1953	1954	1955
Greece	19,160	32,283	37,633	43,278	47,604	48,654	58,139	64,843	70,139
Italy	4,267	4,885	4,855	5,003	5,356	5,572	5,684	5,791	5,911
France	1,034	1,554	1,694	1,804	2,133	2,506	2,501	2,522	2,560
Norway	184	186	195	205	246	261	257	268	277
Sweden	163	172	172	175	214	229	227	226	235
Denmark	191	199	207	220	239	251	256	261	271
Netherlands	219	232	240	256	283	290	281	295	301
United Kingdom	182	194	199	203	217	237	243	246	254
Belgium	365	373	371	363	396	407	397	399	409
Switzerland	169	172	174	174	179	186	185	186	188

	1947	1948	1949	1950	1951	1952	1953	1954	1955
Austria:									
1938 = 100	440	384	441	493	593	683	673	694	717
1949 = 100	100	87	100	112	134	155	153	157	163
Germany:									
1938 = 100	120	137	171	162	176	184	182	182	185
1949 = 100	70	80	100	95	103	108	106	106	108

VI. *Liquidity* (I ÷ II = IV ÷ V)

	1947	1948	1949	1950	1951	1952	1953	1954	1955
Greece	46	42	49	57	58	64	60	68	71
Italy	85	101	120	121	118	128	134	139	140
France	86	67	69	72	68	66	72	76	80
Norway	197	198	191	173	148	148	154	147	142
Sweden	131	123	123	120	111	112	113	111	104
Denmark	140	125	110	92	86	85	82	80	76
Netherlands	117	108	101	90	79	80	82	80	78
United Kingdom	162	149	143	138	126	119	112	109	104
Belgium	84	75	77	77	69	67	72	71	70
Switzerland	108	108	115	114	111	110	111	109	107
Austria:									
1938 = 100	156	141	114	102	89	87	100	110	108
1949 = 100	137	123	100	90	78	76	87	97	95
Germany:									
1938 = 100			51	53	49	50	53	55	55
1949 = 100			100	103	95	98	103	108	106

Sources and notes:

The above indices are derived from the GNP estimates at current and at constant (1954) prices reported in the OEEC volume on *Statistics of National Product and Expenditure* and from the money supply series of the OEEC *General Statistics Bulletin*.

The money supply index is based on the average between money supply at the end of the current year and at the end of the preceding year. It is divided by the index of GNP at constant (1954) prices—production index under item III—to calculate the index of domestic inflation under item IV, and by the index of GNP at current prices to calculate the liquidity index under item VI.

The price index under item V is obtained by dividing the index of GNP at current prices by the index of GNP at constant prices.

The liquidity index for Germany is based on a 1938 liquidity ratio which refers to prewar Germany as a whole rather than to the present territory of the Federal Republic. It uses estimates of 30.9 billion reichsmarks for money supply and 100.2 billion reichsmarks for GNP in 1938, quoted in the 1956 *Annual Report* of the Bank for International Settlements, p. 197. More detailed, but probably incomplete, data from the League of Nations *Money and Banking, 1942–44* would yield a much lower estimate of money supply for Germany in 1938 and increase correspondingly the postwar liquidity index to about double the estimates in the above table.

Table 15. COST COMPETITIVENESS BEFORE EXCHANGE RATE
ADJUSTMENTS AND U.S. GNP PRICE INDEX, 1947-55

(*1938 = 100*)

	1947	1948	1949	1950	1951	1952	1953	1954	1955
Greece	11,080	17,643	20,475	23,251	23,915	23,931	28,111	31,176	33,373
Italy	2,468	2,670	2,641	2,688	2,691	2,740	2,748	2,784	2,812
France	598	849	922	969	1,072	1,232	1,212	1,212	1,218
Norway	107	102	106	110	124	128	124	129	132
Sweden	94	94	94	94	108	113	110	109	112
Denmark	110	109	113	118	120	124	124	126	129
Netherlands	126	127	130	138	142	143	136	142	143
United Kingdom	105	106	108	109	109	117	117	118	121
Belgium	211	204	202	195	199	200	193	192	195
Switzerland	98	94	94	93	90	91	90	89	90
Austria	255	210	240	265	298	336	326	334	340
Germany	69	75	93	87	88	91	88	87	88
U.S. GNP Price Index	173	183	184	186	199	203	207	208	210

Sources and notes:
See Table 14.
The cost competitiveness indices before exchange rate adjustments are calculated by dividing
the GNP price indices of Table 14, item V, by the GNP price index for the U.S. (last line of
the above table).

Table 16. EXCHANGE DEPRECIATION, 1947-55

(*average U.S. dollar price in national currencies, in % of 1938*)

	1947	1948	1949	1950	1951	1952	1953	1954	1955
Greece	4,952	8,730	10,049	13,369	13,369	13,369	23,396	26,738	26,738
Italy	2,523	3,026	3,093	3,288	3,289	3,289	3,289	3,289	3,289
France	340	713	827	999	999	1,000	1,000	1,000	1,000
Norway	121	121	135	175	175	175	175	175	175
Sweden	90	90	100	130	130	130	130	130	130
Denmark	104	105	116	151	151	151	151	151	151
Netherlands	146	146	162	209	209	209	209	208	210
United Kingdom	121	121	135	174	174	175	174	174	175
Belgium	148	148	153	170	170	170	169	169	170
Switzerland	98	98	98	99	99	99	98	98	98
Austria	186	186	204	397	397	397	455	483	483
Germany	134	134	143	169	169	169	169	169	169

Sources and notes:
OEEC *General Statistics Bulletin.* For Italy, however, the 1947 index is calculated on an
estimated average of 485 lire per dollar, derived from data and estimates presented in *International Financial Statistics* (Sept. 1950), pp. 94 and 173.

Table 17. COST COMPETITIVENESS AFTER EXCHANGE RATE
ADJUSTMENTS, 1947–55

(1938 = 100)

	1947	1948	1949	1950	1951	1952	1953	1954	1955
Greece	224	202	204	174	179	179	120	117	126
Italy	98	88	85	82	82	83	84	85	86
France	176	119	111	97	107	123	121	121	122
Norway	88	84	79	63	71	74	71	74	75
Sweden	104	104	94	72	83	87	84	84	86
Denmark	106	104	97	78	80	82	82	83	86
Netherlands	87	87	81	66	68	68	65	68	68
United Kingdom	87	88	81	62	63	67	68	68	69
Belgium	143	138	132	115	117	118	114	114	115
Switzerland	100	96	96	94	91	92	91	91	91
Austria	137	113	118	67	75	85	72	69	70
Germany	52	56	65	52	52	54	52	52	52
OEEC EUROPE	**96**	**91**	**87**	**71**	**73**	**78**	**76**	**77**	**78**

Sources and notes:
The above indices are uniformly derived by dividing the indices of Table 15 by those of Table 16.

Table 18. FOREIGN BALANCE, 1947–55

(ratio of goods and services imports to exports)

	1947	1948	1949	1950	1951	1952	1953	1954	1955
Greece	293	310	322	357	296	217	157	154	123
Italy	257	128	121	107	112	132	119	110	108
France	144	131	106	98	106	109	102	93	91
Norway	136	127	128	115	98	101	113	112	108
Sweden	138	109	90	97	91	98	95	101	103
Denmark	114	110	106	114	104	98	99	106	98
Netherlands	150	123	104	114	101	85	88	98	95
United Kingdom	120	96	93	88	107	93	95	93	99
Belgium	126	108	98	110	94	93	97	99	92
Switzerland	109	107	88	94	102	90	81	86	92
Austria	291	205	174	125	130	113	88	91	114
Germany	163	187	141	112	90	87	84	87	89
OEEC EUROPE	**165**	**131**	**109**	**104**	**106**	**96**	**94**	**93**	**95**

Source:
OEEC, *Statistics of National Product and Expenditure.*

Table 19. INITIAL QUOTAS IN THE EUROPEAN PAYMENTS UNION

(in millions of dollars) a

Member Countries	Quotas	Credit Lines b
United Kingdom	1,060	636
France	520	312
Belgium	360 c	216 c
Netherlands	330	198
Germany	320	192
Sweden	260	156
Switzerland	250	150
Italy	205	123
Norway	200	120
Denmark	195	117
Portugal	70	42
Austria	70	42
Turkey	50	30
Greece	45	27
Iceland	15	9
TOTAL	**3,950**	**2,370**

Notes:
a. The term "dollar" is used throughout for simplicity's sake, although all operations are carried out in units of account whose value might diverge from that of the U.S. dollar. See above, p. 170 n. 3.
b. Sixty per cent of quota.
c. Belgium's quota as a creditor is reduced to $330.6 million, and its credit line to the Union to $201.3 million, Belgium's "initial debit balance" of $29.4 million being considered as an integral part of its quota commitment.

Table 20. INITIAL SCHEDULE OF GOLD AND CREDIT SETTLEMENTS

(in % of surplus or deficit)

Quota Range	Deficits		Surpluses	
	Gold	Credit	Gold	Credit
From 0 to 20% of quota	0	100	0	100
From 20 to 40% of quota	20	80		
From 40 to 60% of quota	40	60		
From 60 to 80% of quota	60	40	50	50
From 80 to 100% of quota	80	20		
CUMULATIVE TOTAL	**40**	**60**	**40**	**60**

Note:
Starting on July 1, 1952, the proportion of gold in settlements was raised, for the debtors, from 0% to 20% for cumulative deficits in the quota range 10–20%, and from 20% to 30% in the quota range 20–40%, but lowered from 60% to 50% in the quota range 60–80% and from 80% to 70% in the quota range 80–100%. This left unchanged, at 40–60, the over-all gold-credit ratio for debtors making full use of their quota credits.

The gold-credit ratio was unified, both for creditors and debtors, at a flat 50% gold ratio from July 1, 1954, and at a 75% gold (25% credit) ratio from August 1, 1955, irrespective of the cumulative surpluses or deficits incurred.

Table 21. INITIAL BALANCES AND SPECIAL RESOURCES

(in millions of U.S. dollars)

	Initial Balances	Special Resources				Total
	1950–51	1951–52	1952–53	1953–54	Total	
I. Granted to						
Greece	115.0	107.4	25.9	19.4	152.7	267.7
Austria	80.0	45.0	—	—	45.0	125.0
Norway	60.0 a	—	—	—	—	60.0
Netherlands	30.0	—	—	—	—	30.0
Turkey	25.0 a	47.5	21.4	—	68.9	93.9
Iceland	4.0	6.9	4.3	—	11.2	15.2
France	—	—	89.0	—	89.0	89.0
II. TOTAL, financed by	**314.0**	**206.8**	**140.5**	**19.4**	**366.8**	**680.8**
A. *Conditional aid to:*	189.0	—	—	—	—	189.0
1. United Kingdom	*150.0*	—	—	—	—	*150.0*
2. Belgium	*29.4*	—	—	—	—	*29.4*
3. Sweden	*9.6* b	—	—	—	—	*9.6*
B. *U.S. Dollar Transfer to EPU*	11.6 b	206.8	140.5	19.4	366.8	378.4
C. *EPU Long-Term Loans* a	35.0	—	—	—	—	35.0
D. *EPU Capital*	78.4 c	—	—	—	—	78.4

Notes:

a. Of the initial balances, $35 million took the form of 15-year loans to Turkey ($25 million) and Norway ($10 million), the remainder being given as grants.

b. The initial balance granted by Sweden to EPU originally amounted to $21.2 million, but was later reduced to $9.6 million, the difference ($11.6 million) being transferred by the United States to the Union against the cancellation of an equivalent amount of conditional aid allotments to Sweden.

c. Excess of initial credit balances established in the form of grants ($279 million) over initial debit balances ($189 million) and the $11.6 million received from the United States in compensation for the reduction in the Swedish initial balance.

Table 22. INTEREST RATES ON EPU CREDITS

(in % per annum)

Financial Years (July 1–June 30)	1950–51	1951–52	1952–53	1953–54	1954–56
I. By Debtors to the Union a					
A. Up to One Year	2	2¼	2½	2½	2¾
B. One to Two Years	2¼	2½	2¾	3	3
C. Over Two Years	2½	2¾	3	3¼	3⅛
II. To Creditors by the Union					
A. Within Quota	2	2	2¼	2¾	2¾
B. Outside Quota b	2	2	2½	3	3

Notes:

a. Within quota and rallonge. Interest charges on special credits beyond normal credit lines are decided in each individual case.

b. The rate of interest on the special credit granted by Belgium to the Union in 1952 is 2¼%.

JULY 1950—JUNE 1956

(in millions of U.S. dollars) a

	Net Cumulative Surplus (+) b or Deficit (−)			Net Settlements 1950–56 c		EPU Credit		
	Over Two Years 1950–52	Over Four Years 1952–56	Total 1950–56	U.S. Aid	Gold	Total	1950–54	1954–56
I. Creditor Countries	+1,697	+2,199 / −172	+3,724	+39 / −30	+2,718	+996	+1,343	−346
Germany	+311	+1,707	+2,018		+1,419	+598	+604	−5
Belgium	+768	+238	+1,006	—	+784	+192	+247	−55
Netherlands	+205	+138	+343	+29	+248	+125	+207	−82
Switzerland	+171	+116	+287	−30	+209	+79	+181	−103
Sweden	+242	−172	+70	+10	+58	+2	+105	−102
II. Debtor Countries	−1,993 / +297	−2,299 / +275	−3,720	−616 / +150	−2,447 / +25	−832	−1,177 / +102	−158 / +400
Iceland	−13	−15	−28	−15	−8	−5	−6	—
Portugal	+88	−131	−43	—	−43	—	+30	−30
Austria	−142	+41	−101	−125	+25	−1	+73	−74
Denmark	−29	−208	−237	—	−136	−100	−98	−3
Greece	−222	−56	−278	−268	−10	—	—	—
Norway	−59	−226	−285	−50	−125	−111	−99	−12
Turkey	−163	−215	−378	−69	−254	−55	−55	—
Italy	+209	−791	−582	—	−420	−162	−122	−40
United Kingdom	−969	+234	−735	+150	−562	−324	−485	+162
France	−396	−657	−1,053	−89	−889	−75	−312	+237
III. Net Increase in:								
A. Surpluses	+1,994	+1,730	+3,724	+9	+2,718	+996	+1,446	−450
B. Deficits	−1,993	−1,727	−3,720	−466	−2,422	−832	−1,177	+345

Notes:

a. The quarterly data used in constructing Charts XVIII and XIX (pp. 184 and 185) will be found in the OEEC *General Statistics Bulletin*. They differ slightly from those summarized in the table above, which include under the net cumulative position, for simplicity's sake, receipts and payments of EPU interest and existing resources. Both are excluded from the legal definition of cumulative positions recorded in *General Statistics*, although the economic significance of existing resources is identical with other debt amortization receipts and payments affecting net surpluses and deficits.

b. A *plus* sign is used to reflect surpluses, decreases in deficits, extinction of initial debit positions financed by U.S. aid, receipts of gold, and extension of credit or repayment of debt to EPU. A *minus* sign indicates deficits, decreases in surpluses, the use of initial credit balances or special resources to cover deficits, payments of gold, and borrowings from EPU or amortization of former credit claims on EPU.

c. The dates refer to the EPU financial years (July–June) after end-of-year adjustments, except that the amortization payments made on July 1, 1954 are included under the last (1954–56) column of the table.

Table 24. EPU Amortization Agreements, 1954–56

(in millions of U.S. dollars)

| | Cash Repayments July 1, 1954—June 30, 1956 | | | Future | |
	July 1, 1954	August 1954— June 1955	Total	Installments	Total
I. *By Debtor Countries*	224	397 [a]	622 [a]	640	1,262 [a]
United Kingdom	99	102	201	254	455
France	58	179	237	125	362
Italy	39	60	99	120	219
Denmark	16	30	45	67	112
Norway	13	24	36	72	109
Iceland	—	3	3	3	5
II. *By EPU* [b]	130	—	130	—	130
III. *To Creditor Countries*					
(I + II)	354	397	752	640	1,392
Germany	147	177	323	210	533
Belgium	69	75	143	144	287
Netherlands	42	67	109	122	231
Switzerland	41	46	87	83	170
Sweden	32	23	54	46	101
Austria	15	8	24	19	42
Portugal	10	2	12	16	28

Notes:
a. Of which $142 million ($130 million by France and $12 million by Italy) of voluntary repayments to EPU—distributed by it among the creditors—and the remainder under bilateral amortization agreements.
b. From EPU's own gold and dollar funds.

Table 25. Reconstitution of EPU Credit Facilities, June 1954—June 1956

(in millions of U.S. dollars)

	Credit Available Within, or Used Beyond (−), Quota		Reconstitution, or Absorption (−), of Credit Facilities Under Quota July 1954—June 1956			Credit Rallonges, July 1, 1956 (f)	Total Credit Facilities Available, July 1, 1956 (g = b + f)
	June 1954 (a)	June 1956 (b = a + c)	Total (c = d + e)	Current Operations (d)	Amortization (e)		
I. For Settlement of Surpluses	−381.6 / 70.0	−298.4 / 416.3	429.5	−453.6 / 131.3	751.8	461.5	579.4
Germany	−303.8	−298.4	5.4	−318.0	323.4	374.0	75.6
Switzerland	−31.4	71.4	102.8	16.3	86.5	62.5	133.9
Austria a	−30.8	42.0	72.8	49.2	23.6	—	42.0
Belgium	−15.7	19.4	35.1	−107.9 b	143.0	25.0	44.4
Netherlands	6.3	87.8	81.5	−27.7	109.1	—	87.8
Portugal a	12.4	42.0	29.6	17.8	11.8	—	42.0
Sweden	51.3	153.6	102.3	48.0	54.4	—	153.6
II. For Settlement of Deficits	204.9	−39.0 / 589.5	−54.0 / 399.6	−276.1	621.8	210.8	761.3
Greece c	(27.0)	(27.0)	—	—	—	—	—
Turkey c	—	—	—	—	—	—	—
France c	—	237.4	237.4	—	237.4	22.8	260.1
Italy	0.7	−39.0	−39.7	−138.8	99.2	132.0 d	93.0
Iceland	3.4	3.8	0.4	−2.2	2.6	0.8	4.6
Denmark	19.4	16.6	−2.8	−48.1	45.3	9.1	25.7
Norway	30.8	19.3	−11.5	−47.8	36.4	7.4	26.7
United Kingdom	150.6	312.4	161.8	−39.2	201.0	38.8	351.2

Notes:

a. Austria and Portugal shifted during this period from a net cumulative surplus to a net cumulative deficit, but opted to settle all of the latter through gold payments rather than EPU credit.

b. Including EPU amortization installments of the special credit received from Belgium in 1952.

c. Greece, whose quota is blocked, and Turkey, which has exhausted its credit facilities, settle their net deficits 100% in gold. France also elected to settle its deficits 100% in gold during this period.

d. Including the special credit of $50 million, referred to above, p. 196.

26. EPU SETTLEMENTS, JULY 1950—JUNE 1956 (in millions of U.S. dollars)

	Totals, 1950–56			Yearly Totals					
	Surpluses (a)	Deficits (b)	Total (c = a + b = d + e + f + g + h + i)	1950–51 (d)	1951–52 (e)	1952–53 (f)	1953–54 (g)	1954–55 (h)	1955–56 (i)
I. *Bilateral Monthly Balances*	15,790	15,787	31,577	6,166	8,675	5,338	3,898	3,570	3,930
A. Before Existing Resources and Interest	15,835	15,835	31,669	6,345	8,680	5,342	3,870	3,542	3,891
B. Impact of Existing Resources	−95	−95	−189	−175	−14				
C. Impact of EPU Interest	+50	+47	+97	−4	+9	−4	+27	+29	+39
II. *Compensations*	11,851	11,851	23,702	4,063	6,431	4,890	2,740	3,061	2,517
A. Multilateral	7,179	7,179	14,357	2,997	3,460	2,910	1,884	1,667	1,438
B. Over Time	4,673	4,673	9,345	1,066 c	2,971 c	1,980	856	1,393	1,079
III. *Net Positions (I – II)* b settled in:	3,939	3,936	7,875	2,103	2,245	448	1,158	510	1,412
A. *Gold and Dollars (1 + 2 + 3)* b	2,754	2,458	5,212	449	1,141	207	1,277	615	1,524
1. Within quotas and rallonges	1,727	1,396	3,123	397	799	41	424	291	1,171
2. Full settlements beyond quotas	—	441	441	51	66	166	274	−42	−75
3. Amortization:	1,027	622	1,648	—	276	—	578	366	428
(a) by and to EPU	(548)	(142)	(690)	—	(276) d	—	(130)	(160)	(124)
(b) bilateral	(479)	(479)	(958)	—	—	—	(448)	(206)	(304)
B. *EPU Credits (1 – 2)*	996	832	1,829	1,195	888	100	−189	−105	−111
1. Current settlements:	2,024	1,454	3,478	1,195	1,164	100	439	261	318
(a) within quota	(1,716)	(1,380)	(3,096)	(1,160)	(1,061)	(74)	(359)	(151)	(290)
(b) under rallonges	(298)	(39)	(337)	(—)	(53)	(36)	(90)	(120)	(38)
(c) special loans	(10)	(35)	(45)	(35) e	(50) f	(−10) f	(−10) f	(−10) f	(−10) f
2. Amortization	1,028	622	1,650	—	276 d	—	578	366	429
C. *American Aid* b	189 g	646 h	835	458	217	141	19	—	—

Notes:

a. Financial years (July–June), including end-of-year adjustments.

b. Apparent discrepancies with corresponding totals in Table 23 are due to the netting in Table 23 of offsetting Table 24 entries for:
(1) $180 million of U.S. aid which increased, rather than decreased, the net cumulative imbalance of the Netherlands (by $30 million) and the United Kingdom (by $150 million);
(2) $25 million of gold payments to Austria for accounting surpluses arising also from previous U.S. aid receipts in excess of the over-all Austrian deficit over the period as a whole; and
(3) $11 million of gold payments to Portugal, under amortization agree- from a net cumulative surplus to a net cumulative deficit in EPU.

c. Including $28 million offsetting entries in accounting of initial balances of Sweden and Iceland.

d. Special July 1, 1952 settlements of Belgian and Portuguese credits beyond quotas.

e. Initial balance loans to Norway and Turkey.

f. July 1, 1952 Belgian loan to EPU ($50 million) and subsequent amortization installments ($10 million per year).

g. Initial debit balances, compensated by conditional aid to the creditors.

h. Initial credit balances as grants ($279 million) and special resources ($367

Table 27. FULL GOLD SETTLEMENT OF DEFICITS BEYOND QUOTAS,
JULY 1950—JUNE 1956

(in millions of U.S. dollars)

Net Yearly	Total 1950–55	1950–51	1951–52	1952–53	1953–54	1954–55	1955–56
France	196	—	—	211	158	−109	−64
Turkey	234	—	40	30	95	40	29
Greece	10	24	−24	2	21	27	−40
United Kingdom	—	—	59	−59	—	—	—
Austria	—	24	−7	−17	—	—	—
Iceland	—	3	−3	—	—	—	—
NET TOTAL	441	51	66	166	274	−42	−75
Payments	764	51	99	243	274	67	29
Reimbursements (—)	−323	—	−34	−77	—	−109	−104

Table 28. GEOGRAPHICAL PATTERN OF OEEC COUNTRIES'
TRADE, 1928–55

(in billions of U.S. dollars)

	Intra-OEEC Exports = Imports	Imports from Other Countries Total	United States	Exports to Other Countries Total	United States
1928	7.2	9.9	2.35	6.4	0.97
1938	4.7	7.7	1.38	4.6	0.48
1947	5.9	15.2	5.56	6.9	0.73
1948	7.6	17.0	4.5	9.3	0.94
1949	8.7	16.2	4.5	10.2	0.79
1950	9.8	14.4	3.1	10.0	1.22
1951	13.1	20.6	4.4	14.1	1.81
1952	13.1	19.1	4.0	14.1	1.88
1953	13.5	17.9	3.0	14.0	2.14
1954	15.0	18.8	3.3	14.8	1.87
1955	17.1	21.6	4.5	16.2	2.24

Source:
OEEC, *Foreign Trade Bulletins: Foreign Trade by Areas.*

Table 29. Regional Distribution of World Exports in 1954

1. IN BILLIONS OF U.S. DOLLARS

Exports to

Exports from:	World	EPU Area							Dollar Area			Rest of the World			
		Total	OEEC Countries			Other			Total	U.S. and Canada	Latin America	Total	Non-$ Latin America	Eastern Europe and China	Other
	Total		Total	Non-£	Sterling	Total	Non-£	Sterling							
I. EPU Area	43.8	32.1	22.9	16.3	6.6	9.3	2.2	7.1	4.9	4.0	0.9	6.7	1.3	1.2	4.2
A. OEEC Countries	29.9	21.9	15.0	12.4	2.6	6.9	1.9	4.9	3.2	2.4	0.8	4.8	1.1	0.9	2.8
1. Non-£	21.6	15.6	12.3	10.3	2.0	3.3	1.8	1.4	2.2	1.5	0.6	3.9	0.9	0.8	2.3
2. Sterling	8.3	6.4	2.7	2.1	0.6	3.7	0.1	3.5	1.0	0.9	0.2	0.9	0.2	0.1	0.6
B. Other	13.9	10.2	7.8	3.9	3.9	2.4	0.3	2.1	1.7	1.6	0.1	1.9	0.3	0.3	1.4
1. Non-£	3.0	2.2	1.9	1.7	0.2	0.3	0.2	0.1	0.5	0.4	0.1	0.3	0.2	—	0.1
2. Sterling	10.8	8.0	5.9	2.2	3.7	2.1	0.1	2.0	1.2	1.2	—	1.6	0.1	0.3	1.3
II. Dollar Area	20.3	6.9	4.7	3.1	1.6	2.2	1.0	1.2	10.2	7.6	2.6	3.3	1.0	—	2.3
A. U.S. and Canada	16.2	5.5	4.2	2.7	1.4	1.4	0.2	1.1	7.7	5.2	2.5	3.0	0.9	—	2.1
B. Latin America	4.1	1.4	0.6	0.4	0.2	0.8	0.8	0.1	2.5	2.4	0.1	0.3	0.1	—	0.1
III. Rest of the World	11.8	6.0	4.5	3.4	1.2	1.5	0.1	1.4	2.6	2.4	0.1	3.2	0.8	(0.5)	2.0
A. Non-$ Latin America	3.7	1.6	1.5	1.1	0.4	—	—	—	1.2	1.2	—	0.9	0.5	0.2	0.3
B. Eastern Europe and China	1.6	1.1	0.8	0.7	0.2	0.2	—	0.2	0.1	0.1	—	0.4	0.1	...	0.3
C. Other	6.6	3.4	2.1	1.6	0.5	1.3	0.1	1.2	1.3	1.2	0.1	1.9	0.2	0.3	1.4
IV. World	76.0	45.1	32.1	22.8	9.3	13.0	3.3	9.7	17.7	14.1	3.6	13.2	3.1	(1.6)	8.5

2. IN PER CENT

I. *EPU Area*	58	52	37	15	21	5	16	11	9	2	15	3	3	10
A. *OEEC Countries*	73	50	41	9	23	7	17	11	8	3	16	4	3	9
1. *Non-£*	72	57	48	9	15	9	7	10	7	3	18	4	3	10
2. *Sterling*	77	33	26	7	44	2	43	12	10	2	11	2	2	7
B. *Other*	73	56	28	28	17	2	15	13	12	1	14	2	2	10
1. *Non-£*	72	62	55	7	10	6	4	17	15	2	10	6	—	5
2. *Sterling*	74	55	20	34	19	1	18	11	11	—	15	1	2	12
II. *Dollar Area*	34	23	15	8	11	5	6	50	37	13	16	5	—	11
A. U.S. and Canada	34	26	17	9	8	2	7	47	32	16	19	5	—	13
B. Latin America	34	14	10	5	20	18	1	60	58	2	6	3	—	3
III. *Rest of the World*	51	38	28	10	13	1	12	22	21	1	27	7	(4)	17
A. Non-$ Latin America	43	42	30	11	1	—	1	32	31	1	25	13	4	8
B. Eastern Europe and China	72	57	42	14	15	1	14	3	3	—	25	5	...	20
C. Other	51	32	24	8	19	1	18	20	19	1	29	3	5	21
IV. *World*	60	42	30	12	17	4	13	23	19	5	17	4	(2)	11

Note:
This table is derived from GATT, *International Trade, 1955* (Geneva, 1956), pp. 222-3. Data for Eastern Europe and mainland China do not include intratrade, for which no reports are available.

Percentages for exports to (first column) and exports from (last row) the world are taken with relation to world totals. Other percentages are in terms of each area's total exports to the world.

POSTSCRIPT

While This Book Was in Press

POSTSCRIPT

While This Book Was in Press

Suez, Europe, and the Dollar Shortage in 1956

The optimistic conclusions of this book were put to an immediate and acid test by the developments arising from the Suez crisis. A sharp setback to European recovery and a quick relapse into another era of dollar shortages were freely predicted last summer as the manuscript left my hands for those of the publisher.

The pessimists may still prove right in the end. Only the most venturesome crystal-gazer would dare prophesy at this time the ultimate economic and political consequences of events which have deeply upset the international balance of power and brought the Middle East and indeed the whole world to the very brink of war.

All that can be said is that the short-run economic impact of the crisis has proved so far much milder than had been feared at first. The last quarter of 1956 witnessed, for the first time in many years, a reversal in the steady increase of the United States short-term indebtedness to foreign countries and international institutions. Foreign countries, however, still increased their gold and dollar holdings by about $250 million over these three months, and the OEEC area's losses are estimated at only $50 million. The difference was made up for the most part by a decline of $575 million in the gold and dollar holdings of international institutions, particularly the International Monetary Fund.

Aside from the Suez crisis, the broad trend of economic developments over the year 1956 as a whole did not differ greatly from that of the previous two or three years. The net gold and dollar position of the United States declined by a further $900 million to $5,600 million, while foreign countries' gold and dollar holdings rose again by $1,900 million to a record level of $29,300 million. Nearly all countries and monetary areas shared in this gain, the major exception being the sharp reversal in the French situation from a net accumulation of $650 million in 1955 to a decline of $600 million over the year 1956. Such a reversal had to be expected in view of the progressive drying up of United States reimbursements for

previous military expenditures in Indochina, the continued drain-
ing of French resources into the "pacification" of Algeria, and the
overvaluation of the French franc noted in Chapter 2 of this study.
The current rate of reserve losses is such that the long-smoldering
crisis may well have broken into the open by the time this book
reaches the reader.

These financial stresses coincided with new record levels of
production in France as well as in the rest of Europe. Developing
bottlenecks, however, slowed down the unprecedented rates of
growth of the previous three years. The excess of demand over
production capacity simultaneously tended to resurrect upward
pressures on wages and prices and to spill into sharp increases in
imports from other areas. Goods and services imports from the
United States into Western Europe and its dependencies rose by
nearly 20% during the year and by more than 40% over the two
years 1955–56. These dollar expenditures were more than financed,
however, by steady receipts from United States military expenditures—close to $1.8 billion—by other dollar earnings on current
account from the United States and third countries, and by record
levels of private American investments in the area. All in all, the
increase in gold reserves and dollar assets exceeded by nearly $700
million in 1956 as in 1955 Europe's net receipts of official grants
and capital from the United States. Most encouraging of all, however, is the sharp and sustained rise—by 16% in 1955 and 18%
in 1956—of metropolitan Europe's current earnings, net of military transactions, in the United States market.

These trends are not confined to Europe alone. They characterize as well the pattern of dollar transactions for the world
at large. United States expenditures abroad on current account
rose to a new high in 1956: $20.4 billion as against $18.5 billion
in 1955. Foreign expenditures in the United States increased even
faster, from $19.9 billion to $23.3 billion, and swelled the United
States surplus on current account from $1.4 billion to $2.9 billion.
This could be financed almost entirely, however, by foreign gold
production and by private United States capital exports which,
net of errors and omissions, tripled between 1955 and 1956. Grant
aid and net official lending abroad were thus reflected once more
in an almost equal increase—of about $2 billion—in foreign gold
reserves and dollar assets.

This brief summary of recent economic developments does not

call for any basic modification of the conclusions derived in this study from an examination of previous trends. On the contrary, the rapid increase in United States private expenditures abroad would seem to justify so far our optimistic expectations as to the possibility of a further liberalization and expansion of dollar imports by the rest of the world, and by Europe in particular. One should, however, anticipate a gradual tapering off of the enormous increases in foreign gold and dollar assets which have characterized the years 1950–56, and a parallel slowdown in the growth of dollar balances held by the rest of the world. This may alleviate the excessive fears entertained in some quarters about possible withdrawals of such balances and the impact of consequent gold losses by the United States upon our financial system. It leaves intact, however, the doubts raised in the last chapter of this study about the adequacy of current and prospective gold production to maintain, in the long run, appropriate levels of international liquidity in an expanding world economy.

The International Monetary Fund, Convertibility, and European Integration

While the Suez crisis has strained almost to the breaking point the fabric of political cooperation among the Western countries, one of its by-products has been a considerable and totally unexpected strengthening of financial cooperation and, in particular, a most active use of the long-neglected instrumentalities of the International Monetary Fund. When criticizing mercilessly in Chapter 3 of this study the policies "of the Fund," I have been guilty of using a short-cut, but misleading, terminology, and should have spoken instead of the policies—or lack of coherent policies— "of the members of the Fund." A gradual realization of these past failings combined with the Suez emergency to bring about a revolutionary upsurge in Fund lending in the last quarter of 1956. Under its new and dynamic Managing Director, Per Jacobsson, the Fund met squarely and with record speed the responsibilities thrust upon it by the Suez crisis. Close to $1,600 million of new loans and stand-by agreements—of which $1,300 million with the United Kingdom and $262.5 million with France—were concluded in the closing months of 1956. Further and substantial credits were negotiated in the early months of 1957 with Chile,

India, etc. The boldness of these interventions has already done much to dispel the pall of gloom and disaffection which had gradually descended upon the Fund during its long years of lethargy, and to revive the hopes placed upon it in the nearly forgotten days of Bretton Woods.

Opportunities and needs for constructive Fund leadership are certain to arise again in the forthcoming months and years. The revamping of the prewar gold exchange standard has already been mentioned as one of the major issues likely to confront the Fund in a not too distant future. New regional developments in the sterling area and Western European countries will also call for an early revision of the Fund's procedures and policies.

The recent weakening of sterling on the international exchange markets has distracted attention unduly from the remarkable improvement of the United Kingdom's balance on current account, from a $220 million deficit in 1955 to a $650 million surplus in 1956. It should not be forgotten, moreover, that the liquidation of sterling balances prompted by the Suez crisis reduces *pro tanto* the vulnerability of sterling to future speculative movements. Finally, the ability of Britain to withstand and fight such movements has been strengthened enormously by the stabilization credits negotiated in recent months. The $1,300 million obtained from the International Monetary Fund, further Fund credits and stand-by agreements to other sterling area countries, the $500 million line of credit opened by the Export-Import Bank, and the authorized postponement of up to seven yearly installments of the 1946 American and Canadian loans seem to fulfill amply, if belatedly, one of the major "prerequisites" of Britain's ill-fated convertibility plan of 1953. This should not, however, be taken to mean that the famous "dash to convertibility" envisaged at that time is now imminent. Upward pressures on wages and prices, combined with a marked slowdown in the previous rate of economic expansion, have a sobering effect on convertibility enthusiasts. Most of all, public attention has veered from world-wide convertibility plans to the "grand design" of European economic integration.

The Common Market and Euratom treaties were signed in Rome a few days ago, on March 25, 1957, and are expected to enter into force on January 1 of next year. The United Kingdom is spearheading the move for a close association of other OEEC countries with the six countries of the Common Market group—France, Italy, Germany, and Benelux—in a Free Trade Area, encompassing all of Western Europe. Various working parties were set up by the OEEC last February to study the major problems raised by such an association, and it is hoped that the OEEC Council will be able to define at its next meeting, in July, the general outline of the proposed Free Trade Area convention.

The momentous implications of these events for the future of Europe—and indeed of the whole free world—will be obvious to the readers of this study.

New Haven, April 5, 1957

INDEX

In an effort both to guide the reader and save his time, the following index concentrates particularly on interlocking references facilitating comparisons between related concepts or institutions, but spurns mechanical and time-wasting citations of terms merely mentioned in the text.

Subheadings are ranked logically or chronologically rather than alphabetically. References to charts and tables are to the pages where they appear.

Abs, Herman J., 274 n.1
Administration:
  International Monetary Fund, 137, 294–5
  Organization for European Economic Cooperation, 138, 162–3
  European Payments Union, 177–9
  European Monetary Agreement, 231
  European Monetary Authority, 290, 293
  regional and world-wide agreements, 257–60
Agreements for Intra-European Payments and Compensations (IEPA):
  negotiation, 150–2
  provisions, 152–3
  operation and appraisal, 153–60
  Second Agreement, 159–60
  tables, 149, 154, 156
Alexander, Sidney S., 25 n.1
Amortization:
  of IMF credits, 111, 113, 132, 134–5
  of pre-EPU bilateral balances, 167, 174–5, 202
  of EPU credits, 189–90, 193–7, 199 n.10, 219
  of European Fund credits, 221–2
  under EMA multilateral settlements system, 226–8
  chart, 129; tables, 133, 195, 328, 329
Anglo-American Financial Agreement:
  provisions, 138–40
  operation, 140–1
  appraisal, 142
Ansiaux, Hubert, 147 n.1
Arbitrage, 212–20, 226–8, 281–2; table, 214; *see also* Multilateralism
Argentina, 217
Austria:
  internal monetary adaptations, 57, 69, 70, and 53–70 *passim*

cost competitiveness, liquidity and exchange rates, 71–82 *passim*
  in IEPA, 153
  in EPU, 176 n.12, 183, 192, 194 n.1, 196 n.5, 197, 201
  charts, 59–61, 63, 67, 79, 184–5; tables, 56, 65, 72, 77, 87, 154, 208 n.b, 222, 318–29, 331
Automaticity of credits, *see* Borrowing rights, Lending commitments

Balance of payments:
  of OEEC Europe, 31–46, 271, Postscript
  of OEEC countries, 70–87, 277
  of the United States, *see* Dollar shortage
  and American aid, 44–5
  in Keynes plan, 94, 96–9, 104–7
  in IMF, 109–36
  in bilateral trade and payments agreements, 143–51
  in IEPA, 151–60
  in EPU, 170–1, 174–7, 179–98, 200–8
  in EMA, 220–31
  adjustment mechanism, 20–30, 48–53, 70–3, 82–7, 88–92, 241–5, 251–5, 289–91
  charts, 4, 7, 10, 13, 15, 34–5, 37, 60, 78–9, 184–5, 206, 272; tables, 39, 72, 77, 87, 133, 149, 154, 156, 195, 202, 267, 270, 273, 308–15, 317–18, 323–4, 326–7, 330–3
  see also International reserves
Bancor accounts and credits, 95–100, 102–7, 140, 219
Bank for International Settlements (BIS), 169, 177, 231
Bargaining power, 27 n.2, 89–92, 99, 255, 264 n.5; *see also* Bilateralism
Belgium:
  internal monetary adaptations, 57, 68, and 53–70 *passim*